DATE			

Other Books by Stanton Peele

Love and Addiction

How Much Is Too Much

The Science of Experience

The Meaning of Addiction

Visions of Addiction
(edited volume)

Diseasing of America

Other Books Co-authored by Archie Brodsky

Love and Addiction

Burnout: Stages of
Disillusionment in the
Helping Professions

Medical Choices, Medical Chances

Sexual Dilemmas for the
Helping Professional

Home Birth: A Practitioner's
Guide to Birth
Outside the Hospital

Diabetes: Caring for Your Emotions
As Well As Your Health

If This Is Love, Why Do
I Feel So Insecure?

THE TRUTH ABOUT ADDICTION AND RECOVERY

•

THE LIFE PROCESS PROGRAM FOR OUTGROWING DESTRUCTIVE HABITS

STANTON PEELE, PH.D.
ARCHIE BRODSKY

with MARY ARNOLD

SIMON & SCHUSTER
New York Toronto London Sydney
Tokyo Singapore

Simon & Schuster
Simon & Schuster Building
Rockefeller Center
1230 Avenue of the Americas
New York, New York 10020

Designed by Laurie Jewell
Manufactured in the United States of America

1 3 5 7 9 10 8 6 4 2

Library of Congress Cataloging-in-Publication Data
Peele, Stanton.
The truth about addiction and recovery : the life-process program
for outgrowing destructive habits / Stanton Peele, Archie Brodsky,
with Mary Arnold.
p. cm.
Includes index.
1. Compulsive behavior. 2. Habit breaking. 3. Rehabilitation.
I. Brodsky, Archie. II. Arnold, Mary, III. Title.
RC533.P33 1991 90-27678
CIP

ISBN 0-671-66901-X

To Marie Arnold and Sara Fromberg,
for the heritage of grit,
self-respect, and positive values
they passed on to Dana Spencer,
Haley Marie, and Anna Sara Peele.

To Robert Asahina, our editor,
for his prescience and
independence of purpose.

CONTENTS

A NOTE TO READERS

Readers of this book who wish to share their stories of addiction and recovery can write to Dr. Peele at the following address:

Dr. Stanton Peele, author of
The Truth About Addiction and Recovery
c/o Simon & Schuster
1230 Avenue of the Americas
New York, NY 10020

INTRODUCTION

THE GROWTH of addiction treatment in the United States, predicated on the idea that alcoholism and addictions of all kinds are diseases, is a public-relations triumph, and not a triumph of reason or science. The idea that modern addiction treatment—like that provided at private alcoholism hospitals—is eminently successful is a myth. More people quit alcoholism and addiction on their own than do so through treatment, and evidence is that in many cases people trying to quit an addiction (such as smoking) are better off attempting it without the help of typical treatment programs. There *are* therapies that work better than disease-oriented alcoholism clinics or nicotine-gum therapies for smokers, but you would be hard-pressed to find such treatment if you tried.

We believe that many people want an open-minded, realistic way to understand and deal with addictions—their own, their spouses', their children's, their friends' and employees'. This book is a response to that need. It begins by making clear what addiction is and what it is not. Addiction is an ingrained habit that undermines your health, your work, your relationships, your self-respect, but that you feel you cannot change. Addictions *are* difficult to change, because you have relied on them—in many cases for years or decades—as ways of getting through life, of gaining satisfaction, of spending time, and even of defining who you are. Whereas some addictions involve drugs (like smoking or problem drinking), some do not (like shopping, or eating, or sex). It is impossible, therefore, to relate addiction to one chemical or biological process or another.

Because of the distinctive approach we take, you will find guidance here that in most cases you cannot get elsewhere. That is, we do not regard addiction of any kind as a disease. Thus, we do not recommend that you see a doctor or join a twelve-step group organized for one disease or another as a way of dealing with addiction. These approaches, we believe, have already been shown to be less effective than others that are available. The same is true if you are concerned that your children and their friends are using alcohol and drugs—the common practice of putting them in a hospital will usually do more harm than good.

Our approach, called the "Life Process Program" for changing destructive habits, is instead rooted in common sense and people's actual experience. This approach is more empowering—and therefore more effective—than conventional treatment or self-help methods. Because our approach differs so drastically from the messages you get constantly in public-service announcements and advertisements for alcoholism centers, we review a great deal of evidence to show you that the conventional notion of addiction as an uncontrollable "disease" is baseless. It doesn't get at what causes people to be addicted and it is ineffective for most people as a method of treatment or self-help.

It is disturbing that an approach to addiction that is widely claimed to be scientific is actually false and is more often harmful than beneficial. The good news is that many people are beginning to question how accurate or helpful it is to think of addiction as a "disease." These may be people with substance-abuse problems whose needs are not met by twelve-step support groups. Or they may be people who don't buy the claim of the alcoholism movement that announcing you are powerless helps you change. They may be researchers who find that the evidence doesn't back up the personal testimony of addicts who tell us incessantly in the media that conventional treatment works. They may be individuals who have been exposed to the treatment system—because their children used drugs or because they were arrested for drunk driving—and who were appalled by its coerciveness and irrationality. They may be especially mystified that anyone wants to weigh adolescents down with the message: "Because you have been drinking or using drugs, or because your *father or mother* did, you have a disease you can never overcome."

Sometimes people with questions like these stumble upon the

best-kept secret in the addiction treatment industry—that many more people give up addictions *on their own* than through treatment, without taking on the stigma that they suffer from a disease. TV talk-show host Oprah Winfrey, for example, discussed her struggle to lose (and keep off) weight on a show she did on the disease theory of alcoholism. She remarked that she could accept the disease theory "intellectually," but that she just didn't see how believing she was forever "powerless" could possibly help her with her weight problem. What Oprah and others like her should know is that calling addiction a "disease" is just as wrong "intellectually" as it is unhelpful.

Indeed, what about all the people who are so uncomfortable with twelve-step groups that they can't bring themselves to attend one or don't stick with it if they do attend? Are these people all, like Oprah, really in "denial"? As a result of such "failures," many people mistakenly think they can never overcome their addictions. Wouldn't they benefit from knowing that the great majority of people with addictive habits—particularly young people—can outgrow them without entering a hospital program or following a twelve-step regimen? They *may* be able to do it on their own. Or they may benefit from the kind of treatment represented by the Life Process Program—treatment that builds on people's own strengths, values, and confidence in themselves and on their existing ties with friends and family, while improving how they deal with their lives.

In 1990, *American Health* magazine published a study that finally told the public just that.[1] According to a Gallup Poll of a cross-section of the American population, people are about ten times as likely to change on their own as with the help of doctors, therapists, or self-help groups. Among the survey's surprising findings were these:

> Professional help has surprisingly little to do with important life changes, even health-related ones. Doctors helped people change only 3% of the time—while psychologists and psychiatrists, self-help groups and religious counselors got the credit even less often. Support was much more likely to come from friends (14%), parents, children, or siblings (21%), or a spouse, boyfriend or girlfriend (29%). And 30% of the time, people simply did what they had to do on their own, often with striking success.[2]

In other words, the support that is most crucial comes not from specialized treatments and support groups, but from the people one already knows. And sometimes people simply change when they realize that the time has come. The survey found this to be true even for giving up such tough addictions as smoking or excessive drinking—a majority of respondents described quitting as something they did naturally, on their own.

Positive feelings and desires more often motivated people to change than negative ones. These positive feelings fed on themselves: healthy habits become more secure over time. "Fully 86% of the time," the survey found, people reported that "as time goes on, my new habits become easier to keep up—they make me feel good."[3] Not only were positive changes self-maintaining, but they sparked other beneficial changes as the person's self-image and self-confidence improved.

One part of the survey focused on eating and nutrition. Again, common sense and life-style evolution won out over Overeaters Anonymous, Weight Watchers, or other groups or therapies. The techniques people used to lose weight were very straightforward. These typical Americans revealed that *the methods they relied on most* to lose weight successfully were cutting out snacks and desserts (42 percent), eating less altogether (37 percent), exercising more (32 percent), and cutting down on fat (32 percent). The ones they *least* often used successfully were weight-loss groups (9 percent), special diet foods such as protein powders (3 percent), and diet books (1 percent).[4] The lesson seems to be: If you want to succeed, do what you know you have to do. You can't rely on any intermediary to do it for you.

You cannot reconcile the *American Health* survey findings with the doom-saying of the twelve-step movement and the addiction establishment that people are out of control of the inevitable progression of their addictions. Still, these uplifting survey findings about real people tell only part of the story. Even if more than half the people surveyed were able to accomplish significant changes, a sizable minority were not, and many of those may have wanted to.

If this has been your experience, a more concerted approach to habit change may be called for. The positive changes reported in the survey were made by people whose lives were basically intact, but who let a single habit such as overeating or smoking get out of hand. But destructive habits may reflect deeper problems in a person's emotional or family life or social environment. In these cases, change must involve the total context of a person's life. To give up a bad habit, you may need to transform the life situation that supports the habit into one that discourages it. The Life Process Program is designed to help you do just that.

During the past couple of decades, researchers have discovered effective, nontraditional ways of understanding and attacking addiction. Sociologists have discovered large numbers of individuals who have given up addictions without going into treatment or to support groups. Psychologists have studied the personal techniques people develop on their own for initiating and maintaining behavior change. Alcoholism experts such as Harold Mulford of the University of Iowa have begun to explain how the natural paths a person takes into and out of addiction are woven into the fabric of the person's life. But these perspectives are little known to the public in the United States, which is still fed the simple-minded ideology of the disease movement. As a result, the most enlightened guidance on addiction has not been available to the many people it could help.

The aim of this book, therefore, is to put together the components of a workable approach to addiction into a practical framework for your use. Many people think of behavior therapy as an artificial system of rewards and punishments that are more effective in the laboratory than in life. In many cases, they are right. They aren't aware, however, that the single treatment proven most successful with severely alcoholic individuals—called the Community Reinforcement Approach—applies behavioral techniques to help people reshape their entire environments. This approach is used in other countries and has been adopted by some therapeutic communities in the United States. What we have done in this book is to adapt the concepts involved in such research and therapy to enable you to apply them in your own everyday life.

We have seen the need for such an integrated approach ever since we wrote *Love and Addiction*. Because we emphasized quitting addiction as a part of an integrated life change, many addicted persons (alcoholics and addicted drug users, overeaters, smokers, gamblers, shoppers, as well as those addicted to love) have said that that book talks directly to their needs. Now, based on this growing understanding of what addiction is really about, we will show how you can develop a self-tailored path out of addiction.

The disease model of addiction does more harm than good because it does not give people enough credit for their resilience and capacity to change. It underestimates people's ability to figure out what is good for them and to adapt to challenging environments. At the same time, it disempowers people, because it fails to hold them accountable for acting irresponsibly while under the influence of alcohol or drugs, or for excessive behaviors ranging from shopping to gambling. The disease theory of addiction can even serve to perpetuate addiction and to excuse repeated relapses. Our approach, in contrast, respects every person's capacity to make positive choices, even in the case of the most compulsive behaviors. Instead of undermining your integrity, we give you credit for being a responsible adult capable of self-management.

The Life Process Program takes us far from the frightening assumption that a compulsive behavior is a disease that you will have to live with forever. It brings us into the practical human realm of individual self-assessment, planning, and action. As you will see, the myths of addiction and the realities with which we contrast them offer radically different ways of freeing yourself from addictions ranging from overeating and smoking to alcohol and drugs. They also have different implications for how you deal with heavy drinking or drug use in a spouse or lover, a child, a friend, or an employee. The Life Process Program and the disease model also give you different messages about what it means if you come from a family with a history of some addictive problem, like alcoholism.

Finally, the two different approaches point in different directions concerning the social problems and public-policy issues that we confront, such as drunk driving, drug testing, and widespread drug abuse and drug-related violence in the ghetto. Popular attitudes about addiction, instead of locking people into their addictive dependencies, can instead encourage individual and community strength and autonomy. For although this book is mainly about overcoming addiction as individuals, the crux of the struggle against addiction lies in the social and cultural environments we create. The widespread failure to realize this holds more danger for our civilization than does crack or alcohol or any international drug cartel.

This book is arranged in three parts. First, it shows that addiction is not what the conventional wisdom says it is. Second, it shows how a more realistic understanding of addiction presents you with methods that you can actually use to change your habits and your life for the better. Third, it suggests how the same nondisease viewpoint can help all of us change the world we and our children inhabit into one that supports personal growth and responsible conduct.

Part I presents the evidence that the "disease" model of addiction does not account for the actual experiences of people who are addicted. Chapter 1 explains what the disease model is, why it is wrong, and what this book offers in its place. The chapters that follow apply our view of addiction in turn to alcoholism, drug abuse, cigarette smoking, compulsive overeating, and nonchemical addictions (gambling, exercise, shopping, love, sex). We put to rest the concern that alcoholism and other addictions are biologically determined and the fear that children are driven to addiction by their genes. And we document the encouraging fact that most people leave these destructive habits behind as they mature.

If being addicted is not a biologically determined state, then you have some real hope of doing something about it—of learning new and better ways of coping. Part II helps you do that by distilling into a practical self-help guide—with many examples of actual growth experiences—the techniques of the best therapies along with those used by people who overcome addiction on their own. We do not claim to give you anything that you aren't able to do on your own. But by learning how people routinely surmount the obstacles you face, you can move more quickly to make the positive changes in your life that might well occur anyway sooner or later.

Some readers, on the other hand, will be too impatient or feel too much pain to ride out these natural life processes, with or without the guidance of this book. If so, seeking treatment is a legitimate alternative that may be helpful. *Even when seeking treatment, however, you need to direct your efforts toward the most sensible alternatives and to realize your essential role in the change process.*

The key to giving up addiction is to mobilize the necessary motivation, values, skills, and environmental supports. In most cases, you already have these things. Our emphasis, therefore, is on kindling your desire to stop harming yourself and others and your belief that you can do so. We *never* tell you that you are powerless. When you feel strongly enough the urge to change your life in a healthful direction, you can often develop the *means* for stopping unhealthy addictions quite naturally.

Thus, instead of a single, prepackaged program for recovery, we provide the highlights of successful self-cures and successful therapy for you to use as signposts for change. You must then see how they fit into the rhythms of your own life. The Life Process Program, while it makes the experiences of others accessible to you, remains something you create for yourself out of your own experience and personal values.

After an introduction to the Life Process Program and a case of real-life behavior change, part II features several chapters on assessment. This is not one of those quizzes about whether you are an alcoholic if you sometimes drink alone or have a drink at brunch. Instead, it is a reasoned guide to assessing not only your habit, but your values, your resources, and your goals. With this assessment, you can go about setting and carrying out realistic plans to attain your goals. Part II then introduces you to actual behavior-change practices. It guides you both in mastering the addictive habit itself and in developing the life skills you need to maintain your freedom from addiction.

Part III fills out the larger picture of a nonaddictive environment. People are influenced in turning toward or away from addiction by the social forces around them. Some of these environmental factors—namely, the people you associate with and the groups you belong to where you live and work—are within your power to change. Others—namely, the values, attitudes, and practices of society as a whole—are much harder to change. But even if you cannot completely control your children's environment, you still have a lot to say about the values your children learn and the choices they will make. Finally, you can also play a role as a citizen to make sure your community doesn't fall prey to the excesses of the modern witch-hunt that looks for addiction under every bed, and then sends off all accused addicts to be reprogrammed at treatment centers that coerce them into admitting they are addicts (or recovering addicts) for life.

Our approach has no gimmicks. It is grounded in the reality of the numerous studies we cite and the many personal accounts we relate. Whatever solution proves right for you, it is unlikely that you will succeed by working on the addiction in isolation from the rest of your life. Indeed, as the Life Process Program shows you, you cannot escape addiction without dealing with your entire world, including your family, your community, and society as a whole.

PART I

FROM ALCOHOLISM TO SHOPPING ADDICTION

•

ADDICTION IS *NOT* A DISEASE

CHAPTER I

WHY IT DOESN'T MAKE SENSE TO CALL ADDICTION A "DISEASE"

WE FREQUENTLY HEAR FROM PEOPLE WHO SAY: "I drink too much sometimes, but I don't think I'm an alcoholic. And I don't want to stand up and talk about myself in front of a group. Is there any other way I can change the way I drink?"

"I'm overweight, but I understand that people are born to be fat and there's not much you can do about it. I know I've tried to lose weight a million times and failed. Does this mean I'm doomed to be overweight?"

"I saw an ad saying the only way to lick your addiction to nicotine is by going to a doctor. Is that really true? Don't people ever quit smoking on their own?"

"My father was an alcoholic. Does that mean I'm likely to become an alcoholic myself? Should I play it safe and quit drinking altogether? A friend of mine joined a 'Children of Alcoholics' group, even though she's never even been drunk. Should I join such a group? And what about my kids?"

"My son was caught smoking marijuana. Now I'm told that, unless I place him in an expensive residential treatment program, he could escalate his drug use and die. I don't have the money for this but, of course, if I have to save his life I'll mortgage the house!"

People are much concerned about bad habits (which sometimes reach life-consuming proportions) that they'd like to do something about—drinking, smoking, overeating, taking drugs, gambling, overspending, or even compulsive romancing. We hear more and more that every one of these things is a disease, and that we must go to treatment centers or join twelve-step support groups like Alcoholics Anonymous in order to change any of these behaviors. Is there really no other way to change a powerful habit than to enter treatment for a disease? Do personal initiative, willpower, or just maturing and developing a more rewarding life have anything to do with people's ability to overcome addictive habits?

As children, as spouses, as parents, as employers, as consumers, and as citizens we must struggle to understand and master the destructive potential of drugs, alcohol, and related addictions. The kinds of questions so many people face today include: What do we do if we discover our children are smoking marijuana, or worse? Should we put them in a treatment center that will teach them they are chemically dependent for life? How can we tell if co-workers, employees, and friends are secretly addicts or alcoholics? What is the most appropriate way to react to people who drink too much or do anything that harms themselves and others?

Furthermore, as a society, how should we deal with these problems? Are our incessant wars on drugs really going to have the positive impact the generals in these wars always claim? Or is there some more sensible or direct way to reduce the damage people do to themselves through their uncontrollable habits? Rather than arrest drug users, can we treat addicts so that they stop using drugs? And if we expand the treatment for all the addictions we have seen—like shopping and smoking and overeating and sexual behavior—who will pay for all this treatment? Finally, does addiction diminish people's judgment so that they can't be held accountable for their behavior, or for crimes and financial excesses they commit while addicted?

This book is for those concerned with such questions. But what you will read here is not the same as what you see and hear in newspapers and magazines, on television, in addiction treatment centers, in twelve-step groups, and in most physicians' and therapists' offices—or what your children are learning in school. For in its desperate search for a way out of the convulsions caused by drug abuse and addiction, our society has seized upon a simple, seductive, but false answer that this book disputes. What we say is, indeed, so different from most things you hear that we have provided extensive documentation at the back of the book.

The simple but incorrect answer we constantly hear is expressed by the familiar statement, "Alcoholism is a disease." In other words, we can treat away these problems in a medical setting. This viewpoint has proved so appealing that it has been adopted by professional organizations and government agencies as well as by groups like Alcoholics Anonymous. And now the "disease" label is applied not only to alcoholism, drug addiction, cigarette smoking, and overeating, but also to gambling, compulsive shopping, desperate romantic attachments, and even committing rape or killing one's newborn child! A.A.'s image of "powerlessness over alcohol" is being extended to everything that people feel they are unable to resist or control.

But what lies behind the claim that alcoholism and other addictions are diseases? How accurate is it? What evidence supports it? Most important, what good does it do us to believe it? Will it really help you or someone you care about to overcome an addiction? This book will show that the answer is no—that, in fact, it may do more harm than good. What's wrong with calling a tenacious and destructive habit a disease? Three things:

- It isn't true.
- It doesn't help most people (and even those it does help might succeed just as well in some less costly, less limiting way).
- It prevents us from doing things that really would help.

In this chapter we will summarize what the disease model says, why it is wrong, and why it is harmful. In chapters 2–7 we will explore the specific addictive behaviors to which people are applying the disease model and offer different ways of thinking about each of these problems. By explaining how people really get addicted to drugs and other experiences, we will show why most people eventually overcome their addictions without treatment. As you will see, there is no good reason to label yourself or people you know as forever marked by an addictive "disease." Challenging this useless folklore is the first step toward understanding addiction and doing something about it.

Then, in part II of the book, we will present an alternative way of thinking about and dealing with addiction. We call this approach to dealing with addiction the Life Process Program. The accompanying

Ten Assumptions that Distinguish the Life Process Program from the Disease Model	
Disease Model	*Life Process Program*
1. Addiction is inbred and biological	1. Addiction is a way of coping with yourself and your world
2. The solution is medical treatment and membership in spiritual groups such as AA	2. The solution requires self-awareness, new coping skills, and changing your environment
3. Addiction is all-or-nothing; you are or you aren't an addict	3. Addiction is a continuum; your behavior is more or less addicted
4. Addiction is permanent and you can relapse at any moment	4. Addiction can be outgrown
5. Addicts are "in denial" and must be forced to acknowledge they have a disease	5. You should identify problems and solutions in ways that work for you
6. The recovering addict/alcoholic is the expert on addiction	6. Those without an addiction problem are the best models
7. Addiction is a "primary" disease	7. Addiction stems from other life problems you have
8. Your main associates must be other recovering addicts	8. You should associate with a normal range of people
9. You must accept the disease philosophy to recover	9. Getting better is not a matter of believing a dogma
10. Surrendering to a higher power is the key to recovery	10. You must develop your own power to get better

table previews the major differences between the Life Process Program and the disease model of addiction. Although we will describe how to use this method later, we present evidence in this chapter and elsewhere in part I that points to the effectiveness of the Life Process approach.

Myths Versus Realities

To highlight some of the surprising facts we will reveal, here are some common beliefs about various addictions:

- A person needs medical treatment or a program like Smokenders to quit smoking.

▸ Attending Alcoholics Anonymous meetings is the most effective way for alcoholics to stop drinking.

▸ Nearly all regular cocaine users become addicted.

▸ Very few people who have a drinking problem can ever drink in a normal, controlled manner.

▸ Drunk drivers who undergo treatment for alcoholism are less likely to repeat the offense than those who receive normal judicial penalties such as license suspension.

▸ Most people with an alcoholic parent become alcoholics themselves.

▸ Most people who are binge drinkers in their twenties go on to become alcoholics.

▸ Most of the American soldiers who were addicted to heroin in Vietnam remained addicted or became addicted again after they returned home.

▸ The fact that alcoholism runs in families means that it is an inherited disease.

▸ Fat children, because they have inherited their obesity, are more likely to be fat in later life than are people who become fat as adults.

Actually, as we will show in the chapters that follow, the best scientific evidence available today indicates that *none* of these statements is true. Such specific misconceptions grow out of a foundation of false assumptions about the nature of addiction generally.

What Is the Disease Model of Addiction?

At first, it seems hard to understand what is meant by saying that something a person regularly does (such as drinking alcohol) is a disease. Habitual, voluntary behavior of this sort does not resemble what we normally think of as a disease, like cancer or diabetes. What is more, A.A.—and even hospital programs for alcoholism—don't actually treat any biological causes of alcoholism. After all the claims we have heard in the past decade about biological discoveries concerning alcoholism, not one of these findings has been translated into a usable treatment. Instead, the same group discussions and exhortations that have been used for the last fifty years are employed in hospital programs. Nor is any biological method used to determine whether someone is an alcoholic other than by assessing how much that person drinks and the consequences of this drinking. And if we have no special biological information about treating or identifying alcoholism, we surely know nothing about the biological causes of "diseases" such as compulsive gambling, shopping, and loving, which have nothing to do with drugs or alcohol.

There is, however, a standard way those who claim addiction is a disease *describe* addictive diseases. This description has been developed by groups such as Alcoholics Anonymous, by the medical profession, and by various popularizers of the idea that alcoholism is a disease. What they say is in every regard wrong. When they tell you that you have the "disease" of alcoholism, "chemical dependency," obesity, compulsive shopping, or whatever, this is what they mean:

The basis of the disease is inbred and/or biological. There is no need to look for the causes of the disease in your personal problems, the people you spend time with, the situations you find yourself in, or your ethnic or cultural background. Addiction is bred into you from birth or early childhood. Your current experience of life has nothing to do with it; nothing you can do makes you either more or less likely to become addicted.

It involves complete loss of control over your behavior. Once involved in your addiction, you are utterly at its mercy. You cannot choose whether, or how much, to lose yourself in the involvement. No matter how costly it may be in a given situation, you will go all the way. You cannot make reasonable, responsible choices about something to which you are addicted.

Addictions are forever. An addictive disease is like diabetes—it stays with you as long as you live. The mysterious bodily or psychic deficiency that lies at the root of addiction can never be remedied, and you can never safely expose yourself to the substance to which you were addicted. Once an addict, always an addict.

It inevitably expands until it takes over and destroys your life. "Irreversible progression" is a hallmark of addictive diseases as they are conceived today. The addiction grows and grows until it devours you, like AIDS or cancer. No rewards, no punishments, not even the most momentous developments in your life can stay its course, unless you completely swear off the addictive substance or activity.

If you say you don't have it, that's when they really know you have it. According to this "Catch-22" of the disease theory, anyone suspected of having an addictive disease who insists that he or she *doesn't* have the disease is guilty of the added offense of "denial." In this way, the "disease" label is like a web that traps a person more firmly the harder the person fights to get out of it.

It requires medical and/or "spiritual" treatment. Thinking you can cure your addiction through willpower, changes in your life circumstances, or personal growth is a delusion (like denial), according to disease-theory proponents. Addiction is a disease of the body that can be controlled only by never-ending medical treatments. It is also a disease of the soul requiring lifetime membership in a support group like Alcoholics Anonymous. Why supposed medical treatment consists mainly of going to group meetings and why people can't develop their own spiritual approaches to life if they choose are questions disease-theory adherents ignore.

Your kids are going to get it, too. Since addiction is an inherited disease, the children of addicts are considered at high risk for developing the same disease—*no matter what you or they do or how careful you are.* Logical deductions from this viewpoint are that you should have your kids tested for their genetic predisposition to alcoholism or addiction before they start school, or that you should simply teach them never to touch a drop of alcohol or expose themselves to whatever your addiction is. Obviously, this approach presents special difficulties in dealing with addictions to eating, shopping, and making love.

Where did these notions come from—notions that, when examined in the clear light of day, often seem quite bizarre and contrary to common experience? The disease theory takes a set of precepts that were made up by and about a small group of severe, long-term alcoholics in the 1930s and applies them inappropriately to people with a wide range of drinking and other life problems. The original members of Alcoholics Anonymous, realizing they would soon die if they did not give up alcohol, adopted wholesale the dogma of the nineteenth-century temperance movement. The one major difference was that the A.A. members said drinking was a disease only for them, and not for everyone who drank—therefore not everyone needed to eschew "demon rum," as temperance advocates had insisted.

The A.A. model has struck a responsive chord among Americans. Obviously, with the rejection of Prohibition, the United States had decided against a national policy that everyone should abstain from drinking. Yet American society continues even today to show a deep unease about alcohol and about intoxication, which many people seek even while fearing its disturbing effects. Given this national ambivalence, we have been drawn to the "old-time religion" of temperance, as represented by A.A., now cloaked in the modern language of medicine and the neurosciences. But, as this book will make clear, the operative assumptions about addiction have *never* arisen directly from biological sciences. Rather, they have been superimposed on scientific research, much of which directly *contradicts* the assumptions of the disease theory.

Why the Disease Model Is Wrong

Every major tenet of the "disease" view of addiction is refuted both by scientific research and by everyday observation. This is true even for alcoholism and drug addiction, let alone the many other behaviors that plainly have little to do with biology and medicine.

No biological or genetic mechanisms have been identified that account for addictive behavior. Even for alcoholism, as chapter 2 will show, the evidence for genetic inheritance is unconvincing. By now, probably every well-informed reader has heard announcements that scientists have discovered a gene that causes alcoholism. In fact, as one of us wrote in *The Atlantic,* this is far from the case, and the study that prompted these claims has already been refuted by another study in the same journal (see appendix).[1] Moreover, if a gene *were* found to influence alcoholism, would the same gene cause drug addiction? Would it be related to smoking? Would it also cause compulsive gambling and overeating? If so, this would mean that everyone with *any* of these addictions has this genetic inheritance. Indeed, given the ubiquity of the problems described, the person *without* this inheritance would seem to be the notable exception.

How could an addiction like smoking be genetic? Why are some types of people more likely to smoke than others (about half of waitresses and car salesmen smoke, compared with about a tenth of lawyers and doctors)? And does believing that an addiction like smoking is genetic help the person quit (are all those smokers who quit not "genetically" addicted)? Returning to alcohol, are people really predestined biologically to become alcoholics and thus to become A.A. members? Think about the rock group Aerosmith: all five members of this group now belong to A.A., just as they once all drank and took drugs together. How unlikely a coincidence it is that five unrelated people with the alcoholic/addictive inheritance should run into one another and form a band!

The idea that genes *make* you become alcoholic cannot possibly help us understand how people develop drinking problems over years, why they choose on so many occasions to go out drinking, how they become members of heavy-drinking groups, and how drinkers are so influenced by the circumstances of their lives. Genes may make a person unusually sensitive to the physiological effects of alcohol; a person can find drinking extremely relaxing or enjoyable; but this says nothing about how the person drinks over the course of a lifetime. After all, some people say, "I never have more than one or two drinks at a time, because alcohol goes straight to my head."

As we document here and in chapter 2, we can actually predict the likelihood of people's becoming addicted *far more reliably* from their nationality and social class, from the social groups they join, and from their beliefs and expectations about alcohol or drugs (or other activities), than from their biological makeup.[2] Often, people who become addicted set themselves up by investing a substance or an experience with magical powers to transform their beings ("Getting drunk is great"; "When I drink I'm really at ease"; "Drinking makes me attractive to people of the opposite sex").[3] It is simply not within the chemical properties of alcohol or a drug, or the experience of an activity like shopping, to offer people what they want and seek from an addiction. People find this in an addiction when they believe they can't achieve the feelings they need in ordinary ways. Clearly, attitudes, values, and the opportunities available in a person's environment have much to do with whether the person has a significant risk for a particular addiction.

People do not necessarily lose control of themselves whenever they are exposed to the object of their addiction. On the contrary, many practice their addictions quite selectively. For example, military and religious personnel are often deprived of tobacco during training or on retreats, and business people realize they can't smoke in certain rooms. Orthodox Jews who smoke heavily abstain from smoking on the Sabbath, showing that their religious values mean more to them than nicotine does.[4] Alcoholics in experiments routinely control their drinking when it is in their interest to do so—say, when they must leave a cozy room with television and companionship in order to get more to drink.[5] These variations occur in real life just as they do in the laboratory—for example, when people avoid drugs or cigarettes when they are with people who won't tolerate those habits. When something they really care about is jeopardized if they continue to drink, smoke, or whatever, most people will stop or cut down accordingly.

Addiction usually does not last a lifetime. "Once an addict, always an addict" is a pessimistic notion that is both wrong and harmful. It leaves people two choices: either you stay constantly addicted and miserable until you die; or you abstain for life while attending group meetings and viewing yourself as the perpetually "recovering" person. Sadly, a small number of people do die of their addictions; and another group succeeds in quitting drinking, drug taking, or whatever by maintaining the role of the recovering addict. But *most* people are more resilient and resourceful than that. Most people who have addictive habits moderate or eliminate these habits over the course of their lives. And they do it without having to say "I am an alcoholic" or "I am an overeater" or "I am a sex addict" as long as they live. Remember that, today, a majority of the adult Americans who have ever smoked have quit—and nearly all did so without treatment.

Progression is not inevitable—it is the exception. If the majority of people give up addictive habits, then the idea of "inevitable progression" doesn't hold water. Calling addiction a "progressive disease" comes from looking at the few who *have* progressed to severe addiction and tracing the path by which they got there. The progression of addictive problems only *seems* inevitable after the fact. For example, the great majority of college overdrinkers, even those who black out at fraternity parties, become moderate drinkers in middle age.[6] When you consider that even most of the people who use narcotics and cocaine do not end up addicted, you can see that drug-and-alcohol use patterns are many and varied, even when a person uses a substance abusively for a time.

Treatment is no panacea. Contrary to all the advertising we hear, treatment for addictions is often no more effective than letting addiction and recovery take their natural course. The vast majority of people who have given up addictions (beginning with more than 90 percent of the forty-four million Americans who have quit smoking[7]) have done so on their own. This does not mean that treatment for addictions *cannot* work—research has shown that some forms of treatment *are* effective. But the ones that are more effective are not the ones that have become popular in the United States.[8] You can outgrow an addictive habit on your own or in therapy, but either way the principles are the same. Part II of this book—on the Life Process Program—describes these principles and techniques.

What about joining support groups such as Alcoholics Anonymous? Here, too, research reveals the opposite of what we have been led to believe. A.A. is a valuable community resource for those who find support in a certain type of religiously oriented group ritual. But the best we can say about A.A. is that it works for those for whom it works. Meanwhile, there are plenty for whom it doesn't work. There is no scientific evidence that A.A. works better than other approaches when randomly selected alcoholics are assigned to A.A. or other treatments. In fact, the evidence is that the people who are now often compelled to attend A.A.—after being arrested for drunk driving or being sent by a company Employee Assistance Program—do *worse* than those who are left on their own.[9]

How can we reconcile this finding with the glowing testimonials we hear about A.A.? The people we see in A.A. are the ones who like it, find it helpful, and stick it out. But there are many others who don't go to A.A. or who don't like it and drop out. And as we show below, those who seriously try to stop drinking on their own are more likely to maintain their abstinence than those who attend A.A. In addition, since many more people try to quit on their own than through therapy or joining a group, the *number* of self-curers is triple or more the number of successful treatment or A.A. cases.[10] But such self-curers are not very visible, because they are individuals without an organized group to publicize their success. This book tells the stories of some of these unaffiliated ex-alcoholics, ex-addicts, ex-smokers, ex-overeaters, and so forth, so that you can benefit from their examples.

These, then, are the key fallacies of the popularly held view of addiction. Even generally well-informed people may be astonished that we contradict such widely held beliefs. All of our refutations of conventional wisdom are carefully documented in the notes at the back of the book. But you don't need to read scholarly articles and scientific reports to test the accuracy of what we say. Just check it out against your own experience and observation. Don't you know anyone who used to drink excessively, at times uncontrollably, but who now drinks in a normal, appropriate manner? Obviously, most people who used to drink excessively but who have now cut back (or even quit) do not attend meetings where they must rise and declare, "I am an alcoholic." How many people of all ages do you know who quit smoking? How many of them did it by going through a medical program or joining a support group, and how many finally just decided to quit and made good on that resolve? What happened to all the people you knew who used illegal drugs in college, some quite heavily? How many of them are "chemically dependent" now? If we simply examine the cases of most of those we are close to personally, we will see how addictions usually do not follow the disease course.

Why the Disease Model Doesn't Work—Why It Even Does More Harm than Good

The assumption that calling addiction a "disease" actually helps people crumbles when subjected to critical scrutiny. Some people feel comfortable thinking of their addiction as a disease and are able to function better on this basis *for a time.* But whatever short-term benefits medical, disease-oriented treatment produces are double-edged even for the individuals who claim it has helped them. Many of the most "successful" recipients of disease treatment might achieve a real breakthrough by learning to think about addiction differently. Meanwhile, for the *majority* of people, the disadvantages of the disease approach clearly outweigh the advantages from the start. The disadvantages of that disease approach are that it:

- attacks people's feelings of personal control and can thus become a self-fulfilling prophecy;

- makes mountains out of molehills, since it fails to differentiate between the worst alcoholics and addicts and those with minor substance-use dependence;
- stigmatizes people—in their own minds—for life;
- interrupts normal maturation for the young, for whom this approach is completely inappropriate;
- holds up as models for drinking and drug use the people who have shown the least capacity to manage their lives;
- isolates alcoholism and addiction as problems from the rest of the alcoholic's or addict's life;
- limits people's human contacts primarily to other recovering alcoholics or addicts, who only reinforce their preoccupation with drinking and drug use;
- dispenses a rigid program of therapy that is founded—in the words of the director of the government's National Institute on Alcohol Abuse and Alcoholism (NIAAA)—"on hunch, not evidence, and not on science,"[11] while attacking more effective therapies.

How can therapy that so many people believe in and swear by actually do more harm than good? To illustrate this point, consider the case of a famous psychiatrist who evaluated his hospital's alcoholism program—one he felt was among the most outstanding in the world. This program first detoxified the alcoholic in the hospital, then mandated A.A. attendance, and finally actively followed patients' progress with an outreach counseling program. When the psychiatrist running the program, Dr. George Vaillant, evaluated how well his patients were doing two years and eight years after treatment, however, he found they had fared about as well as comparable alcoholics who received no treatment at all![12]

How could Vaillant have been so wrong as to think his patients were doing phenomenally well, when actually they were doing no better than if he had left them alone completely? Naturally, he *wanted* to think it worked. But his research prevented his rose-colored views from distorting the actual results of his treatment. When he counted *all* his patients, not just his successes, when he scrutinized and verified what they were telling him in order to see exactly how well they were doing, and when he compared them with alcoholics out on their own instead of just assuming that all these people died without the help of treatment like his, Vaillant found that his expensive hospital treatment was close to useless.

Very few people in the treatment industry or in A.A. are as scrupulous as is Vaillant. When we hear from A.A. boosters, they tell us only about those who have stuck with the program and are currently sober. The same is true of treatment programs. They parade their best stars up front. We don't hear about all their failures. Yet Vaillant, in a book that is cited as the *major source of support for the benefits of treating alcoholics according to the disease model,* concluded as follows: "If treatment as we currently understand it does not seem more effective than the natural healing processes, then we need to understand those healing processes better."[13] Indeed, Vaillant repeats another researcher's conclusion that "it may be easier for improper treatment to retard recovery than for proper treatment to hasten it."[14]

What are the dangers of this kind of disease treatment? Here are explanations of the disadvantages listed at the beginning of this section:

It sets people up for failure. All disease treatments emphasize how much out of control "patients" are, and what a delusion it is for them to feel they can exert any control over their addictions. Is it possible that such a message can do more harm than good? William Miller and Reid Hester, reviewing all the comparative studies on treatment for alcoholism, made a surprising finding: in the only two studies in which alcoholics were randomly assigned either to A.A., to other forms of treatment, or to no treatment, those assigned to A.A. did no better *or actually suffered more relapse* than those who received other treatment or who weren't treated at all![15] Intrigued by this outcome, one of us wrote George Vaillant and asked him whether subjects he studied who abstained without entering formal treatment did better if they joined A.A. Again, A.A. members were less likely to maintain their abstinence.[16]

Why would people be more likely to relapse if they entered A.A. than if they quit drinking on their own? There are several reasons. For one, people who enter A.A. are told they *cannot succeed on their own.* Therefore, if they should stop attending A.A., many are convinced that they will soon resume alcoholic drinking. A.A. and disease treatments are especially defeatist in dealing with relapse. That is, the disease theory labors to convince people that they can *never* drink in a controlled manner. Accepting the disease-oriented philosophy of inevitable loss of control thus makes it *more likely* that the alcoholic will binge if he or she *ever* has a drink. Yet, Vaillant found, nearly all alcoholics will drink again at some time.

It makes matters worse than they are. Can attending A.A. or going into addiction treatment really *cause* people to develop some of their alcoholism symptoms? In his book *Becoming Alcoholic,* sociologist David Rudy reports on the time he spent observing A.A. meetings. Rudy found that most people had to *learn* their role as alcoholics. An important "rite of passage" is the first time members tell their story for the group, beginning by acknowledging, "I am an alcoholic." In Rudy's words, the alcoholic's tale "is made up of two parts: a story about how bad it was before A.A. and a story about how good it is now."[17] This presentation is warmly greeted by the member's sponsor in A.A., and the entire membership responds with enthusiastic acceptance of the convert.

When alcoholics introduce their experiences and symptoms in A.A. or treatment, the group or therapist homogenizes them through interpretation and clarification. For example, most people who enter A.A. have not had blackouts, which are more typical of long-term alcoholics than of the younger drinkers now flooding into treatment and A.A. But blackouts are taken as the badge of alcoholism, and according to Rudy, "members learn the importance of blackouts as a behavior that verifies their alcoholism, and an indeterminable number of members who may not have had blackouts report them." Rudy continues:

> When newcomers to A.A. claim that they cannot remember if they had any blackouts or not, other members use this claim as evidence of the event in question. As one member put it to a newcomer: "The reason you can't remember is because alcohol fogs your brain. If it fogs your brain now after not drinking for a few days it must have fogged your brain before. See, you must have had blackouts then."[18]

A large part of alcoholism and drug treatment in America consists of group meetings where alcoholics or addicts "confront" one another and their problems. Newcomers who don't report the correct symptoms are treated with knowing condescension or are actively hazed—sometimes quite abusively—until they "get" and repeat the party line. When Dwight Gooden entered the alcoholism-and-cocaine program at the Smithers Alcoholism Center, he described being assailed by his fellow residents there during the constant group-therapy sessions. "My stories weren't as good [as theirs]. . . . They said, 'C'mon, man, you're lying.' They didn't believe me. . . . I cried a lot before I went to bed at night."[19] After he left the Betty Ford Center, Chevy Chase reported that he had often been angry at the counselors, who heckled the residents mercilessly, constantly denigrating them and claiming they had been living worthless lives.

Does all this sound like good therapy technique? It is simple common sense that belief in your personal value and your own strength is superior to having these things denigrated for getting your life under control.

It stigmatizes people for life. The disease model puts a label on you that you can never outgrow. Once diseased, always diseased. The effects of this defeatist view are especially tragic—and unjust—in the case of people to whom the "disease" label is most inappropriately applied in the first place: teenage binge drinkers, most drunk drivers, "adult children of alcoholics," recreational drug users discovered through drug tests, and—in areas not involving drugs or alcohol—overweight adolescents or "hyperactive" or "learning-disabled" children.

It brutalizes and brainwashes the young. The largest single age group of people undergoing hospital treatment today for chemical dependency, eating disorders, depression, and so forth is adolescents. A.A. members are also much younger today, on average, than when the fellowship was founded by a group of men with serious, lifelong drinking problems. Nonetheless, virtually *none* of these young people meet clinical standards of alcoholism or drug addiction. Indeed, numerous cases have been identified in which young people have been hospitalized for smoking marijuana or even for being *suspected* of using drugs. When one such case was revealed on national television, an unusually forthright consultant for the National Association for Alcoholism Treatment Programs confessed, "I'm afraid this happens far more than people in the field want to admit; it's something of a scandal."[20]

Meanwhile, A.A. and Alateen (for teenage children of alcoholics) groups now pervade high-school and college campuses. What is the impact of treatment that forces teenagers to take on the identity of addicts or alcoholics or children of alcoholics? Young people are warned that their substance abuse is a permanent trait, even though we have seen that a large majority will outgrow substance-abuse problems as they mature. Presenting this message to the young can only *prolong* or exacerbate their substance abuse, since it denies their own capacity for change and forces them to believe that *any substance use for the rest of their lives will lead them back to excess, addiction, and drunkenness.* Young treatment grads who constantly relapse and return to treatment are the norm, as in the cases of Carrie Hamilton, Erinn Cosby, Drew Barrymore, and other young "patients" whose stories are less well publicized. Of course, the relapses are then attributed to their "disease" and to their failure to heed the treatment's warning to abstain forever.

These programs fairly frequently involve emotional abuse. Such "treatments" for children include "refusing to allow them to wear street clothes, keeping them in isolation for prolonged periods, or forcing them to wear self-derogatory signs, engage in other humiliation rituals . . . , or submit to intense and prolonged group confrontation"—all of which, psychologists believe, "may destroy the youngsters' already fragile self-esteem."[21] When we describe these experiences, treatment specialists often argue in response, "Well, what if the kids would end up *dead* if we didn't do this to them?" In other words, to object to these programs is likened to promoting intoxication leading to death. Certainly, it is crucial to prevent children from harming themselves, and it can be worthwhile to remove children from a problem home, whether through a residential program or a visit to a sympathetic relative. But brainwashing, emotional blackmail, denigration, and psychological torture *never* work, except to make people so unsure of who they are or what they value that they will temporarily consent to the demands of those in charge.

Worst of all, therapies that were devised for the most incorrigible children—though they don't benefit even these unfortunate kids—have been spreading down the ladder to more and more children whose behavior represents typical adolescent exploration and insubordination. Parents are then confronted over whether they want to "save" their kids or allow them to die, as though the latter were the normal outcome of adolescence. The threat of their children's dying is then used as emotional blackmail to make parents accept the sacrifices necessary to place their children in expensive residential treatment programs.

It presents the alcoholic or addict as someone to emulate. Prominent graduates of treatment programs, like Drew Barrymore, Betty Ford, Kitty Dukakis, and a host of athletes now lecture to others about chemical dependency. If alcoholics and drug abusers suffer from a disease and are now recovering, then they can educate others about the disease and even about how young people should live and behave. If, on the other hand, we think of them as people who are tremendously poor at self-management, then it is indeed stupid for the rest of us, who have not been seriously addicted, to ask them for advice and information. Someone like former football star Bob Hayes explains that he took and sold drugs as a result of an inherited disease. One reviewer's reaction to Hayes's book, *Run, Bullet, Run,* could stand for any and all of these confessional tracts: "Aside from a brief closing statement on personal responsibility, he self-servingly portrays himself as a victim throughout the book."[22]

Alcoholics and addicts like Hayes now regularly come into schools to relay their tortured drinking experiences and to reiterate that alcohol is a dangerous drug. But nearly every child in these schools *will* drink. It is as though the schools wished to undermine children's sense of self-control and to attack their chances of becoming normal drinkers, which in most cases their "nonexpert" parents are. In treatment itself, "recovering" addicts and alcoholics counsel the drug or alcohol abuser—who usually has not drunk as destructively and hurt himself or herself as much as the counselors! In all types of twelve-step groups, the most severely debilitated person tends to become the leader and model for others, so that the most out-of-control shopping addict tells others about the nature of *their* problems. Who should be counseling whom? In the case of drug abuse, a number of reviews have found that informational and scare lectures by recovering addicts produce the worst results of all prevention programs. These programs have never yet been found to reduce drug use; on the contrary, several studies have found *increased* drug use in their aftermath.[23]

It ignores the rest of the person's problems in favor of blaming them all on the addiction. When someone like Carrie Hamilton lectures about her youthful drug abuse and delinquency (often alongside her mother, Carol Burnett), she makes drug abuse and family failures sound like mysterious, unavoidable illnesses that some people and their parents "have." Of course, this excuses her and her mother from dealing with painful problems they would prefer to avoid. But by adopting the disease identity as her protection through the rest of her life, the youthful convert guarantees that she cannot grow beyond the limitations of her adolescent family life. Can people hope for more than this?

When treatment views alcoholics as being victims of a different body chemistry that *forces* them to become alcoholics, the treatment process ignores the person's life problems and the functions drinking serves for the alcoholic. For example, in family therapy where the alcoholic's drinking is addressed as simply the result of a disease, the therapist and the family are not able to understand that some people use alcohol to air feelings they cannot express when sober. Ignoring dynamics like these leaves the drinker unable to cope with the things that led him or her to need to drink—such as doubts about self-worth, a difficult relationship with a spouse, roles (such as homosexuality) that create conflict for the person, and so on. *If the labeling of alcoholism as a disease provides welcome relief from the shame of overdrinking, it also prevents people from confronting the emotional tasks they need to accomplish to attain personal wholeness.*

It traps people in a world inhabited by fellow disease-sufferers. Many "recovering" people report that they feel comfortable only with others in exactly the same plight. They find they can't create intimacy outside of treatment and that they are driven constantly to talk about their alcoholism or addiction. This is a frequent hang-up for recovering alcoholics who attend A.A. meetings so religiously that they can't maintain a life outside of the group. The phenomenon of compulsive therapy attendance has made many people ask us, "Is there such a thing as addiction to treatment?" Indeed there is, when people rely on a twelve-step group or therapy to the point where it disables them from conducting outside relationships and activities.

One of us has treated a number of A.A. members or treatment graduates who now fear they can't deal with normal society. One man, who was regularly asked to head his local A.A. group, had dated a series of women he met at A.A. Unfortunately, all of these relationships had ended in bitterness and mutual recriminations. But when he tried to date outside the group, he discovered that nonalcoholic women found him overbearing and compulsive. "I don't want to be limited for the rest of my life to dealing with alkies—I'd like to think I can advance beyond that," he plaintively told us. This man felt that dealing exclusively with alcoholics was debilitating him, and yet he couldn't escape A.A.

It excludes other approaches, many of which are more successful. Even if one accepts that many A.A. members are happy and successful, it is simply absurd to discourage people from trying to recover without A.A. The National Council on Alcoholism and Drug Dependence (NCADD)[24] frequently announces statistics about the continually rising costs of alcoholism and the increasing number of alcoholics in our society. But, then, the NCADD is capable only of calling for more of the standard approach to treating alcoholism that has accompanied these increases, while discouraging all alternative approaches. Why should things improve all of a sudden if we simply do more of the same? The A.A. approach to America's drinking problems has shown conclusively that it cannot make a decisive difference for most active problem drinkers, since there are very few alcoholics who aren't already aware of—or who haven't already attended—A.A.

Meanwhile, greater numbers of Americans are being forced to enter private treatment centers and A.A. as a result of court orders, Employee Assistance Programs, or school counseling programs. *Despite the almost universal belief that compelling people to attend standard treatment programs is helpful, these programs regularly demonstrate they are no more effective than self-initiated programs for curing addictions.* Psychologists William Miller and Reid Hester, reviewing all the comparative studies on treatment for alcoholism, made a surprising finding: "virtually all of them [the standard treatments] lacked adequate scientific evidence of effectiveness." At the same time, they discovered, the "treatment approaches most clearly supported as effective . . . were very rarely used in American treatment programs."[25] What don't really work in the long run are the conversion-experience-type treatments; what do work (as we outline in part II) are therapies that teach people skills at self-management and coping.

Nonetheless, most American treatment personnel seem hell-bent on eliminating any other treatment for alcoholism besides twelve-step programs. In the United States, discredited disease-treatment programs—ones that NIAAA Director Enoch Gordis believes may be "frequently useless and wasteful and sometimes dangerous"[26]—proliferate and spread into whole new areas of behavior. This issue is important because the United States spends more money on health care than any other country—and the percentage of our gross national product that we spend on health care is growing *faster* than that in any other country. The fastest-growing component of the health-care system is substance abuse and related mental-health treatments. According to a hospital trade publication, "psychiatric, chemical dependency and rehabilitative hospital care—all largely unregulated by government payment mechanisms—are booming."[27]

This is one reason so many companies are being forced to cut insurance benefits or are asking employees to pay a greater share. What if your insurance rates were raised to pay for a fellow employee who was undergoing a repeat treatment for cocaine addiction, since he had relapsed one or more times? How would you feel about sharing the bill for a colleague who entered an expensive hospital eating-disorders clinic? Do you think that smokers who want to quit should enter treatment programs and be excused from work, with pay, while they concentrate on quitting? And, especially, how would you react if you had quit smoking on your own? It is morally and economically necessary for us to evaluate the effectiveness of alcoholism and other addiction treatments. For we are wasting limited health-care resources to place people in expensive treatments—treatments that have not shown they do more than inexpensive, straightforward skills counseling or than people accomplish on their own—often more reliably!

Dwight Gooden and Kitty Dukakis: "Chemical Dependency" Reduced to Absurdity

Two famous cases illustrate both the absurdity and the futility of our obsession with addictive "diseases." They show us two prominent people, one who denied his disease, another who accepted hers.

Dwight Gooden, the New York Mets' star pitcher, was sent to the Smithers Alcoholism Center for residential treatment after he tested positive for cocaine. His treatment costs and enormous salary while in treatment were paid by his team, partly through fans' ticket purchases. Gooden, who showed no symptoms of cocaine addiction, claimed that he never took the drug while pitching. When asked how he could control his drug use in this way, he replied, "I wasn't addicted, so I was able to lay off it during the baseball season."[28]

At Smithers, Gooden was also taught that, as a person at risk for chemical dependency, he must abstain for life from all other psychoactive substances, including alcohol. This although he had never shown any symptoms of alcoholism and had drunk beer calmly for years. As a result, Gooden ignored the warnings that he shouldn't drink beer after he left Smithers, leading to the following *New York Times* headline—"Gooden Is Focus of Concern: Drinks Beer Despite Advice":

> "I take a couple of beers," Gooden said, when asked about his personal habit. "Not every day. I know the people at Smithers tell you to stay away from everything—beer, whiskey, chewing tobacco, everything. But beer's not a problem with me."[29]

Here a man thought he had his life under control, and people on whom his livelihood depended spent thousands to convince him that he had two forms of chemical dependency. This fantasy comes down to us from the nineteenth-century temperance movement in America, which claimed that *anyone* who began to consume alcohol—the "fatal glass of beer"—would inevitably be led down the drunkard's path of destruction.[30] At Smithers, treatment professionals inculcated Dwight Gooden and others with the idea that beer would lead them down the garden path to strong booze, drugs, and destruction—all on the evidence that, like more than twenty million other Americans, they had used cocaine.

Kitty Dukakis has become the paradigm of the addicted person of the 1990s. Unlike Gooden, Kitty Dukakis has been eager all along to accept the "disease" and "chemically dependent" labels. Advertisements for her autobiography, *Now You Know,* trumpet the opening line of the book, "I'm Kitty Dukakis and I'm a drug addict and an alcoholic." Mrs. Dukakis seemingly has been either addicted or in treatment throughout her adult life. Shortly before she joined her husband in his 1988 presidential campaign, she revealed that she had been treated for a twenty-six-year reliance on diet pills, which she began before she married Michael Dukakis. Soon after her husband's defeat in the election, she began to drink herself unconscious and underwent a series of treatments for her alcoholism and for a variety of emotional problems.

That treatment has not succeeded. Mrs. Dukakis only began getting drunk after the election, for which she first entered the Edgehill Newport hospital. But soon after this treatment experience, she began having explosive relapses in which she drank rubbing alcohol, nail-polish remover, hair spray, and other commercial products containing alcohol. Moreover, she discovered during the course of writing her book that she suffers from another disease—manic-depressive disorder—and as a result she ends the book with the revelation that she is receiving lithium treatment. Previously, Mrs. Dukakis had been prescribed Prozac, a drug featured on the cover of *Newsweek* in 1990 as a new miracle in the treatment of depression, to no avail.

Mrs. Dukakis appears, in the book and on television, a forlorn being. Indeed, syndicated columnist Ellen Goodman, who had known Mrs. Dukakis, wrote a column entitled "Do Our Drug Treatment Programs Label Patients as Losers?" Ms. Goodman wondered aloud how labeling oneself as sick and without hope is helpful. "What happens when those who wrestle with problems of self-esteem are required to wear such a label? . . . Today, Kitty Dukakis describes herself by diagnosis. Drug addict. Alcoholic. Manic-depressive."[31] Ms. Goodman ended her column by wishing that Kitty Dukakis might see the brighter qualities that others have seen in her, and which seem entirely to have disappeared thanks to her various diagnoses and cures.

It seems clear that excessive drinking is only the tip of Mrs. Dukakis's problems, and that medical treatment will never get to the bottom of them. Labeling Kitty Dukakis as a "sick" person who needs medical treatment is a palliative for her uncomfortable marital and personal problems. Reviewers have commented about how insensitive and unaware of her problems Michael Dukakis appeared to be, yet Kitty never reflects on the limitations of her spouse or their relationship. Somehow, her never-ending disease-oriented treatment still fails to raise crucial issues for Mrs. Dukakis about a life and marriage she seems to find intolerable. Will Kitty Dukakis be writing another book in which she reveals she has discovered she is suffering from one more disease—that of codependence?

With Kitty Dukakis as our latest model of the addict/alcoholic, those who look to her life for answers are being fed yet another self-defeating solution. To call Kitty Dukakis's and her audiences' problems diseases is to evade reality, much as Mrs. Dukakis used diet pills and alcohol to do. Whether the pain Mrs. Dukakis and others feel is temporary or persistent, relatively mild or relatively severe, it does not need to rule the rest of their lives. Kitty Dukakis and the rest of us are more than our misery and problems. Moreover, what troubles her and those like her are life problems, not diseases. And when we have reduced them to life size, we can begin to deal with them reasonably and hopefully.

The Experience of Addiction

The question is: "If addiction isn't a disease, then what is it?" An addiction is a habitual response and a source of gratification or security. It is a way of coping with internal feelings and external pressures that provides the addict with predictable gratifications, but that has concomitant costs. Eventually these costs may outweigh the subjective benefits the addiction offers the individual. Nonetheless, people continue their addictions as long as they believe the addictions continue to do something for them. It is important to place addictive habits in their proper context, as part of people's lives, their personalities, their relationships, their environments, their perspectives. The effort to change an addiction will generally affect all these other facets of a person's life as well.

An addiction may involve *any* attachment or sensation that grows to such proportions that it damages a person's life. Addictions, no matter to what, follow certain common patterns. We first made clear in *Love and Addiction* that addiction—the single-minded grasping of a magic-seeming object or involvement; the loss of control, perspective, and priorities—is not limited to drug and alcohol addictions. When a person becomes addicted, it is not to a chemical but to an experience. Anything that a person finds sufficiently consuming and that seems to remedy deficiencies in the person's life can serve as an addiction. The addictive potential of a substance or other involvement lies primarily in the meaning it has for a person.

A person is vulnerable to addiction when that person feels a lack of satisfaction in life, an absence of intimacy or strong connections to other people, a lack of self-confidence or compelling interests, or a loss of hope. Periods such as adolescence, military service, and times of isolation or grief may for a time make people especially susceptible to an addiction. Under some circumstances, a harmful involvement can become so important to a person that addiction is very likely, as heroin addiction was for many in Vietnam. Situations in which people are deprived of family and the usual community supports; where they are denied rewarding or constructive activities; where they are afraid, uncomfortable, and under stress; and *where they are out of control of their lives*—these are situations especially likely to create addiction. The relationship between hopelessness, lack of opportunity, and persistent addiction is, of course, a template for lives in America's ghettos. Recognizing the connection between these situational factors and addiction will explain why our wars on drugs, including the latest, never succeed.

The "hook" of the addiction—the thing that keeps people coming back to it—is that it gives people feelings and gratifying sensations that they are not able to get in other ways. It may block out sensations of pain, uncertainty, or discomfort. It may create powerfully distracting sensations that focus and absorb attention. It may enable a person to forget, or feel "okay" about, insurmountable problems. It may provide artificial, temporary feelings of security or calm, of self-worth or accomplishment, of power or control, of intimacy or belonging. These benefits explain *why* a person keeps coming back to the addictive experience—an addiction accomplishes something for that person, or the person *anticipates* that it will do so, however illusory these benefits may actually be.

Addiction, drug abuse, alcoholism, obesity, and smoking all involve and are fueled by value choices. Think of people whose lives are "together"—who enjoy strong emotional bonds with others, productive work, satisfying feelings of competence and of fun, and a sense of responsibility toward others. Will they become addicted to drugs or alcohol because of some physiological susceptibility and allow the addiction to undo the fabric of their lives? For you personally, can you imagine getting so drunk that you would abuse your infant child? It just doesn't happen that way. If you have better things to do and value other things more than escape into intoxication, then you won't make intoxication the center of your life. And if you *are* addicted, you can best overcome it by creating or re-creating those personal strengths and values.

Whatever the subjective benefits of an addiction or the values that drive an addiction, the person pays a price for an addictive involvement. Addictions make people less aware of and less able to respond to other people, events, and activities. Thus, the addictive experience reinforces and exacerbates the problems the person wanted so badly to get away from in the first place. In the person's inner, subjective experience, the addiction may make things seem better. But in the real world, it only makes things worse. With the worst addictions, jobs and relationships fall away; health deteriorates; debts increase; opportunities disappear;

the business of life is neglected. The person is increasingly "out of touch" with nourishing contacts and essential responsibilities.

This growing disengagement from the realities of life sets the person up for the trauma of withdrawal. When the addictive experience is removed, the person is deprived of what has become his or her primary source of comfort and reassurance. Simultaneously, the person "crash-lands" back onto an inhospitable world, a world from which the person has been using the addiction to escape. Compared with these existential torments, the purely physical dislocations of withdrawal are, even for most heroin addicts, not particularly debilitating. After all, nearly everyone who receives powerful narcotics in the hospital gives them up after returning home or when the illness is over. Consider also that drug addicts and alcoholics indicate that the most unbearable drug withdrawal is from cigarettes. And if one puts all withdrawal on a scale, probably the worst of all occurs in the case of failed love relationships.

The experience of withdrawal, like that of addiction, is shaped by the way a person interprets it. In therapeutic communities like Daytop Village in New York, addicts are not excused from their normal duties when they undergo withdrawal; as a result, withdrawing addicts—even those who have had several withdrawal episodes previously—continue mopping floors and carrying out other duties. Cultural beliefs also play a crucial role in addiction—for example, beliefs that are widely propagated about the power of a drug to enslave a person and the difficulty of escaping it actually *contribute* to the difficulties of withdrawal. Equally important are the person's readiness to confront withdrawal and belief that he or she can manage it. If you are convinced that withdrawal will be intolerably painful and that you cannot withstand it, or if you don't have sufficiently powerful reasons to confront withdrawal experiences, you won't be prepared to withdraw from your addiction. The addict who feels incapable of existing without a drug can never successfully withdraw, and doesn't want to try.

Ironically, one of the beliefs that most contribute to the susceptibility to addiction is *the belief in the power of addiction itself.* Believing that drugs are stronger than you are means you will become addicted more easily and stay addicted longer. But if you recognize that drugs and alcohol *never* take away your own responsibilities and capacity to control your destiny—even if you have alcoholic relatives or have had addictive problems in the past—you always stand a better chance of avoiding addiction or dealing with it successfully.

A Commonsense Way of Thinking About Overcoming an Addiction

Although the schematic description above is useful for understanding what addiction is and how it comes about, we need not think of all our troublesome habits or fixations in such dire terms. In fact, when we overdramatize our addictions, we may do ourselves an injustice and make change more difficult. An addiction may be more or less severe—and a person may be more or less able to give it up—depending on the circumstances of the person's life. Addiction is more likely in stressful times, times when gratifications are slim, times when a person is less together or secure. Likewise, one type of excess may be more stubbornly entrenched in a person's routine, or more closely linked to a person's self-doubt and insecurity, than another.

Addiction occurs along a continuum—there is no easy test to tell you whether you have an addiction or just a bad habit. For example, by some estimates, half of all Americans are overweight. Are they all addicted overeaters? Many people encounter significant health risks because of the way they eat (recall that heart disease is America's major killer). Are these the addicts? Some people are preoccupied day and night with their eating; they are suffused with guilt over eating too much, yet they are unable to change their eating habits. Surely, these are the addicts, we think. A still more limited group of people encounter major health problems through their overweight, severely restricting their lives, but are unable to modify their eating habits.

At the furthest extreme of addiction are the minuscule number of people who become so fat they are completely immobile—people we sometimes see on television who may not even be able to fit through their doorways. If we call only these people—people who have given up all effort to control their eating—true addicts, we end up with a fraction of a percentage of addicted overeaters, and books wouldn't need to be written for millions of people who fear they have food addictions. Moreover, for this minuscule group, concepts such as "denial" hardly seem to have meaning—does the twelve-hundred-pound man who hasn't left his house in years really need to be told that he has an addictive eating problem?

For most people, the exercise of drawing the line that divides "addicted" from "normal" is not very helpful. We need to remember that nearly all people cut back and forth across these categories at different points in their lives and in different situations. Although letting your urges overcome you to gain total control of your life is a relatively rare phenomenon, everyone has addictive urges and sometimes gives in to them. Addiction characterizes some aspect of everyone's life—this is one reason why it is so ridiculous to think of it as a disease. Thin people whom we envy for their self-control will tell us there are some treats they can't keep in the house because otherwise they would eat them all at once. Remember that people whom we admire for having had the strength to quit smoking used to search ashtrays desperately looking for a butt when they ran out of cigarettes!

What we most need to know is not how bad off or how genuinely addicted we are but, rather, how people learn to resist successfully the addictive or unhealthy urges that come with being human. How do they construct full lives, develop alternatives to addiction, learn the strength to stop after having started or, when necessary, not to start at all? Let us start, then, with alcoholism, the addiction most commonly referred to as a disease. There must be—there *is*—a better way to understand and redirect the paths people take into and out of problem drinking.

CHAPTER 2

ARE PEOPLE BORN ALCOHOLICS?

A POPULAR YOUNG ENTERTAINER jeopardized a promising career with his out-of-control drinking. Sometimes he missed singing engagements while he went on binges lasting several days. One time when he did try to appear on stage when he was drunk, according to his biographers, "he stood pale and unsteady at the mike while the orchestra played the introduction to his song." When he opened his mouth to sing, "he vomited—on his suit front, his shoes, and on several members of his socialite audience, who had gathered close to the bandstand to hear him sing."[1]

If this singer were performing today, he would be rushed immediately to the Betty Ford Center for treatment, after which we would read in *People* magazine of his gratitude to the treatment center and its twelve-step A.A. program for showing him he was a lifelong alcoholic who could never drink again. We might read later about his various relapses, but these could be handled by A.A. and the treatment center, which would always be there for him.

Actually, the singer's name was Bing Crosby, nicknamed "Binge" Crosby early in his career. His hard-drinking days occurred more than half a century ago, when alcohol abuse was regarded as a problem in living rather than a lifelong disease. Life could still take its natural course; in this case, Crosby stopped drinking self-destructively when he began to socialize with the prominent people he previously had only entertained. As biographers Donald Shepherd and Robert Slatzer tell it, "It was during Bing's Gatsby period that he stopped drinking himself into unconsciousness. He quit drinking entirely for a while, and when he resumed, he would drink occasionally, but never let the bottle get the best of him again."[2] Crosby simply found that public drunkenness was not in keeping with his emerging image as a superstar.

No alcoholism treatment center in America today would turn down someone like Crosby. If they accepted Betty Ford, they would hardly turn down a man who went on three-day benders and appeared in public falling-down drunk! But what would Crosby have gained from deciding he was an alcoholic for the rest of his life instead of mastering his destructive drinking habits as he matured?

Although our current attitudes toward alcohol would actually make it *harder* for a Bing Crosby of today to come to terms with his drinking, somehow people still do it. Johnny Carson, for one, has said of himself on television, "I was never a good drinker." Carson's early abusive drinking was documented in a biography that described alcoholic rages and wife abuse.[3] Yet Carson, too, gradually cut back his drinking. Years later, following a mild relapse in which he was arrested for drunk driving after having too much wine at dinner, he said on the *Tonight* show, "That's never going to happen again," and it hasn't.

It was on *Tonight,* too, that Steve Martin told how he used to drink heavily during his early, difficult years as a comedian. Lacking confidence in his ability to win over an audience, he began emptying a bottle of gin as part of his act. Martin said that today he only drinks wine, at meals and special occasions. Instead of making speeches about alcoholism, Martin makes movies like *Roxanne,* a film in which people drank regularly but moderately in an atmosphere of warmth, communality, and celebration.

A recent biography of Robert Redford has described how, as a failing young artist in Paris, he drank himself into oblivion night after night in a lonely apartment.

> Rejection made Redford retreat further into himself until he was spending most of his time drinking in his room. Without food to dilute the effects, he would stare at a patch of ceiling for hours on end while his mind ran wild. Strange creatures formed in his brain and he started to hallucinate.[4]

Meanwhile, Mickey Mantle in his recent autobiography, *The Mick* (written with Herb Gluck), told how he played important games after drinking late into the morning. In this, of course, he simply imitated the great Babe Ruth and other sports stars.

Redford, Crosby, Carson, Martin, Mantle, and many other stars (such as Frank Sinatra, Rock Hudson, Nick Nolte, Casey Kasem, and Lee Marvin) drank more at one point in their lives, and to greater harm, than many who today call themselves alcoholics. Yet without resorting to that label they brought their drinking habits under control. When you look into it, you find that a large number of famous entertainers and sports figures—and a substantial proportion of the entire male population—have had periods when they could be diagnosed as alcoholics by today's loose standards. Most outgrow their drinking problems without ever thinking to enter treatment.

Who are the "silent majority" of alcoholics and alcohol abusers who recover without treatment? Why don't we hear them announcing on television that they overcame a drinking problem on their own and that others can do the same, while we *do* hear constantly from those who have joined Alcoholics Anonymous or gone to the Betty Ford Center? If we believe these public announcements—and the advertisements that treatment centers play regularly on television—we will accept disease-theory claims that people can never recover from a drinking problem if they don't seek treatment.

Experts in the treatment industry tell us that they have never met a single alcoholic who moderated his drinking or who quit on his own, and therefore that there aren't any. One of us once debated an official of the National Council on Alcoholism on a California radio call-in show. The first caller told us he was an alcoholic who had quit drinking on his own. The woman from the NCA claimed that this man was an exception and intoned that "over 99 percent of alcoholics, if they don't get help, will die from their drinking." How strange that the first call came from one of the 1 percent, the "exceptions"! Where did this woman come up with her figures? Actual data—even those compiled by researchers who swear by the disease theory—show that self-curers make up the large *majority* of former problem drinkers.[5]

We *do* hear about such drinkers and know many of them personally. Some of us may even have drunk ourselves when we were younger in a way that today would qualify us for A.A. or treatment for chemical dependency. Yet we are usually unwilling to let people know about our former drinking or substance-abuse problems. Nor do the stars who come to grips with their problems outside the Betty Ford Center want to publicize their triumphs over booze and drugs. Natural recovery from substance abuse is such a common, unremarkable process that studies find that alcoholics who enter hospitals are no more likely to become sober than those who do not.[6] In other words, even many of those who go the treatment-center route and tell us how it saved their lives would more than likely have done the same thing on their own!

Who Is Most Likely to Be an Alcoholic?

The National Institute on Alcohol Abuse and Alcoholism produced a famous poster with the banner "The Typical Alcoholic." The poster pictured representatives of every group—young and old; white, black, Asian, Native American; men and women. The point—one emphasized constantly in popular writings about alcoholism—is that everyone is equally susceptible to this disease. Alcoholism and addiction are, in the words of so many disease proponents, "equal-opportunity destroyers." This assertion is false. Furthermore, it is impossible to ignore its falsity.

Studies over the past quarter-century consistently show that alcoholics more often come from some ethnic and racial groups than others; they more often come from poorer socioeconomic backgrounds; they more often come from disturbed families, whether or not their parents were actually alcoholics themselves; they are far more often men than women; and young people—although not, strictly speaking, alcoholics—are far more likely to have drinking problems than old people.[7] You should be aware of many of these differences from your own life experiences, although the disease movement has labored mightily to convince you that what you know is wrong. Reaffirming the validity of your observations is, therefore, the first step toward a realistic understanding of drinking problems.

Groups with High Rates of Alcoholism

People in different ethnic groups vary tremendously in their likelihood of developing a drinking problem or becoming alcoholic. This statement can hardly be disputed; it is repeated in every piece of research, even by disease proponents themselves. For example, research *inevitably* finds that Irish and Native Americans (Indians and Eskimos) have very high alcoholism rates, and that Slavs, the English, and some other American Protestant drinkers are also at high risk for alcoholism. The Italians, Jews, and Greeks (and those from other Mediterranean cultures) and the Chinese have exceedingly low rates of alcoholism. In a book he wrote expounding that alcoholism is **a** disease, George Vaillant discovered that Irish Americans were *seven times as likely* to become alcoholics as Italians and other Mediterranean ethnic drinkers he studied in Boston.[8]

Vaillant also compared a group of college students with a large group of inner-city ethnics; both groups had been followed for approximately forty years. Those in the working-class population were more than three times as likely to become alcoholic as those in the college group.[9] Other research shows that blacks and Hispanics become alcoholics far more often than whites.[10] Of course, were it not for disease advocates' propaganda, it would hardly surprise most people to discover that deprived inner-city environments produce more serious drinking problems than affluent suburban ones. What is actually more surprising is that blacks and working-class Americans are more likely to *abstain* from alcohol as well as to be alcoholics. This is also true for other groups with a higher-than-average risk for alcoholism, such as conservative Protestants and Southerners.[11]

How Do Some Groups Produce More Teetotalers *and* Alcoholics?

Another way to put this startling finding is that better-off Americans and some ethnic groups are more likely both to *drink*, and yet to *drink without problems*, than those in other groups. Those in the higher-alcoholism groups are more wary of alcohol—they have a greater fear of drinking and more often avoid it altogether. When people in these groups do drink—including some of the same people who have striven to abstain—they are more likely to develop a drinking problem. For example, George Vaillant found not only that Irish Americans had more drinking problems than Italian Americans, but that Irish Americans believed that the only way to overcome a drinking problem was to quit drinking altogether, whereas Italian Americans who overcame a drinking problem were more likely to moderate their drinking. Vaillant summarized his findings about these ethnic differences in this way: "Irish culture see[s] the use of alcohol in terms of black or white, good or evil, drunkenness or complete abstinence, while in Italian culture it is the distinction between moderate drinking and drunkenness that is most important."[12]

Irish attitudes toward drinking and alcohol have often aroused comment. How does the Irish household inculcate the kind of drinking patterns that more frequently culminate in alcoholism? In the Irish home, the issue of drinking is often an emotionally charged one from the outset. The Irish American columnist Charles McCabe gave this version of how a young man's first drunk is simultaneously celebrated and bewailed by various family members:

> With the Irish, the treatment is tried—and untrue. All his life the kid has been hearing of the evils of the drink, and how his loving mother suffered at the hands of his rotten father because of it. And, at the end of the threnody, "Ah, but it's in the blood, I guess."
>
> [After the boy gets drunk] the wrath of God descends. The priest comes into the house. He makes it clear that what you have done is worse than the violation of a vestal virgin. The mother of the house sobs quietly. The old man, craven, orders another beer at the corner saloon. . . .
>
> If a system has been devised to produce a confirmed alcoholic to exceed this one in efficiency, I know it not.[13]

The Italians, Jews, Greeks, and other low-alcoholism cultures, on the other hand, teach youngsters to drink at meals and religious celebrations *within the family*. In these ethnic groups the whole outlook and atmosphere connected with drinking are different—it doesn't carry the emotional baggage that drinking does for groups with a greater susceptibility to alcoholism. In the homes of low-alcoholism ethnic groups, alcohol is usually served at home very early to children, who see drinking occur as an ordinary part of family celebrations. What they don't see occur when people drink is violence and drunkenness. According to a sociologist who studied the drinking of Chinese Americans in New York:

> They [Chinese Americans] drink and become intoxicated, yet for the most part drinking to intoxication is not habitual, dependence on alcohol is uncommon and alcoholism is a rarity. . . . The children drank, and they soon learned a set

> of attitudes that attended the practice. While drinking was socially sanctioned, becoming drunk was not. The individual who lost control of himself under the influence of liquor was ridiculed and, if he persisted in his defection, ostracized.[14]

This researcher examined the police blotters in the Chinatown police district between the years 1933 and 1949. Among 17,515 arrests, he found *not one* arrest due to disorderly conduct associated with public drunkenness.

The Jews are a fascinating case study. Every national survey of drinking problems has put the Jews at the bottom of the problem-drinking scale. At the same time, a new growth industry has developed around the enterprise of uncovering the "hidden" Jewish alcoholism problem, which is said to be suppressed because the Jewish community is so *guilty* about alcoholism. Two sociologists set out to demonstrate, by interviewing Jews in an upstate New York city, that alcoholism among Jews was much greater than previous surveys had suggested. Instead, the researchers found no sign that any of their Jewish subjects had ever abused alcohol. Turning to those who lectured about the alarming spread of alcoholism in the Jewish community, the researchers collected reports that there were five alcoholics in this city with about ten thousand Jews. In other words, the most dire, unsubstantiated claim was that Jews in the city had an alcoholism rate of one-tenth of one percent of the adult population.[15]

The two sociologists went further and asked Jews about their attitudes toward drinking and alcoholism. They found that Jews as a group are antagonistic to the disease view of alcoholism. Jews think alcoholics drink out of a psychological dependence, and they regard problem drinkers with distaste and avoid them.[16] In other words, groups with higher alcoholism rates, like the Irish and Baptists and Slavs and Scandinavians, *already* fear alcohol and readily accept that alcoholism is a disease, whereas the Chinese, Jews, and Italians—groups with the lowest alcoholism rates—think of alcoholism as a self-initiated problem that can be controlled. How, we might wonder, have the people with the worst drinking problems taken over in telling the rest of us about the nature of alcoholism and how we should drink?

Furthermore, these ethnic differences in drinking really don't surprise most people. Who, aside from people "educated" by the alcoholism movement, doesn't know there are more Irish than Jewish and Italian alcoholics? For it is the burden of the disease movement to tell us that such differences don't exist. The purpose of this message is to frighten us all equally about the dangers of alcohol. As the lesson of high-alcoholism cultural groups tells us, however, this fear doesn't translate into safer drinking practices. It seems that the healthiest drinkers are secure about the role of alcohol in their worlds and proceed to drink calmly, safely, happily, and without problems—and they are repelled by and avoid those who aren't able to do the same.

Recall the film *Moonstruck* (with Cher and Nicholas Cage), which was set in the New York Italian community. The movie depicted alcohol being served and consumed regularly around family, romance, eating, and socializing. These people didn't worry about alcoholism. Hadn't they learned the modern alcoholism movement's message that they were in imminent danger of going overboard and becoming alcoholic? Actually, this message is itself part of the problem, and its spread has led to more alcoholism. In 1962, Mark Keller—one of the founders of the alcoholism-as-a-disease movement in the United States—estimated that there were 4.5 million alcoholics in the United States.[17] By 1985, a best-seller entitled *The Courage to Change* reported that "twenty-two million Americans, one out of seven, are drinking alcoholically."[18] To say the least, discovering that alcoholism is a disease has not eliminated alcoholism the way the discovery of the Salk vaccine eradicated polio.

Hard-Drinking Groups

Not everyone functions as part of a definable ethnic group—in fact, most Americans must develop their own traditions in the absence of having clear social traditions handed down to them. And hard drinkers associate with other hard drinkers. This, too, may hardly sound like a stunning discovery. But, once again, searching for individual alcoholics who have medical conditions is not the best way to discover this truism. The author of a household-hints column, Mary Ellen Pinkham, wrote a book about her alcoholism, *How to Stop the One You Love from Drinking.* In it she proselytizes for getting everyone into treatment for alcoholism, treatment she claims produces a greater-than-90-percent recovery rate. At the same time she found out she was alcoholic, Mary Ellen discovered that her husband and many of those in her former drinking crowd were alcoholics and required treatment, too.

Since the disease of alcoholism is not contagious in the usual sense, it is strange how this inbred disease should show up in so many people in the same social network. Of course, what Mary Ellen Pinkham had really discovered was that hers was a hard-drinking social circle and that the group is more powerful than the individual. If you want to drink healthily, the best single thing you can do is to associate exclusively with people who drink moderately. A tougher strategy, but one that can make sense, is to organize members of the group to modify their habits together. The *least* sensible way to proceed is to convince the people in the group one at a time that they have a disease that requires treatment.

One group at elevated risk for alcoholism is men. Research of *every* type finds that men have more drinking problems than women. According to genetics researcher Theodore Reich, "Using systematic interview techniques and reliable diagnostic criteria, researchers found the six-month prevalence [of alcohol abuse] among men ranged between 8 and 10 percent, and among women, between 1 and 2 percent."[19] Very few women have alcoholic blackouts regularly, as the worst male drinkers do.[20] This obvious discrepancy in the prevalence of female alcoholism has fueled an all-out search by the alcoholism industry for hidden cadres of middle-class women who are busy disguising their alcoholism. It just doesn't happen that way. As one Harvard researcher who surveyed the literature discovered:

> The stereotype of the typical "hidden" female alcoholic as a middle-aged suburban housewife does not bear scrutiny. The highest rates of problem drinking are found among younger, lower-class women . . . who are single, divorced, or separated.[21]

There are more female alcoholics in the same groups—Irish, blacks, lower socioeconomic classes—that have more male alcoholics, but there are always *fewer* alcoholics among the women than the men in these groups.

Traditionally hard-drinking groups in the United States include those in the military, in fraternities, or working on oil pipelines—in fact, just about any exclusively male society. The Berkeley Alcohol Research Group has tracked Americans' drinking problems for two decades. In their surveys, this group has found that as many as 30 percent of American men have had some kind of a drinking problem during the previous three years. The Berkeley group found that the best predictor of whether you will have a drinking problem is how many drinking problems those in the groups you drink with have.[22]

Young men up to the age of thirty have the highest levels of drinking and drinking problems among all groups of Americans.[23] In an era when people are drinking less alcohol, when we warn young people more about the dangers of alcohol, and when we have raised the drinking age from eighteen to twenty-one, youthful drinking rose through the 1970s and has remained at *extremely* high levels.[24] Many of these young drinkers show the kind of extreme symptoms—like blackout drinking—that are associated with advanced alcoholism. Indeed, the young of America have provided a ready supply of recruits for the alcoholism treatment movement. The average age of Alcoholics Anonymous members has moved steadily downward. Today from a quarter to a third of A.A. members are under thirty. And where there is a market like this to cultivate, private treatment centers won't be far behind. The largest increase in hospitalizations has been among teens and young adults: hospitalization of teens has more than quadrupled throughout the 1980s.[25] Most are being treated for "chemical dependence," and they were either coaxed or coerced outright into entering the hospital.

"Maturing Out" of Drinking Problems

The Berkeley group found that, even for the large majority of problem drinkers who remain untreated, drinking problems drop precipitously by the age of thirty.[26] Most people, it turns out, simply curtail or eliminate their problem drinking with age. This phenomenon is a well-known one, after all, commemorated in the phrase "sowing one's wild oats." In the addiction field, the process of outgrowing substance abuse is called "maturing out."

Did you know people in a college fraternity or sorority who drank too much, or did you drink more than was good for you back then? As you may be aware, excessive college drinkers usually grow up to become moderate adult drinkers. The most thoroughgoing study of college drinkers first assessed the drinking of seventeen thousand college students in twenty-seven American colleges and universities from 1949 to 1952.[27] While in college, 42 percent of the men were classified as problem drinkers. When assessed for a second time in 1971–72, 17 percent of the men from a sample of the original group still had a drinking problem. Some problems, like binge drinking, were common in college but disappeared almost entirely after college age! In this study, problem drinking in men shows up as a normal hazard of the college years, one that infrequently persists into middle age.

Findings like these should be reassuring to those who are concerned about a teenager who may be drinking too much with friends. In their annual national survey conducted in 1988, University of Michigan researchers found 56 percent of male college students and 35 percent of female college students had consumed five or more drinks at one sitting within the previous two weeks.[28] This youthful binge drinking can be a serious problem; for example, we don't want to see young people hurting themselves and others by driving drunk. On the other hand, since no one would claim that 56 percent of the adult male population and 35 percent of the adult female population are alcoholic, we know that most of these young people will outgrow their excessive drinking.

But it isn't only college students or those with mild drinking problems who stop drinking excessively. Maturing out occurs at all stages of the life cycle, up to and including old age. This holds even for heavily alcohol-dependent individuals. The common occurrence of this maturation out of addiction is not questioned, even by medical experts who study the addictive process of alcohol dependence. One medical researcher who invented the "alcohol dependence" syndrome once marveled how most alcoholics "free themselves [from alcohol dependence]. The withdrawal process, and the associated desire and drive to drink, collide with the totality of the individual and the whole of life."[29] In other words, eventually people see more reasons to quit alcoholic drinking than to continue it.

The next large drop-off in drinking problems after the late twenties is the mid-forties. Geneticist Reich summarizes: "Rates [of alcohol abuse or dependence] dropped sharply after the age of 45."[30] A further drop in drinking and drinking problems occurs among the elderly. What about the horrible drinking problems faced by older Americans about which we so often hear? In *Alcohol and Old Age,* Brian Mishara and Robert Kastenbaum conclude, "Alcohol use appears to be more moderate among the elderly when compared with other age groups."[31] These investigators' conclusions run counter to conventional wisdom about the traumas of retirement and the "empty-nest syndrome." In fact, the data show, heavy drinking drops off sharply among men in their sixties and seventies, and among women in their fifties. Whereas a quarter of men aged fifty to fifty-nine reported heavy drinking in an Alcohol Research Group survey, only 10 percent of those aged sixty to sixty-nine and 4 percent of those above the age of seventy were heavy drinkers. For women, the most precipitous drop in heavy drinking occurred after age fifty—10 percent of women aged forty-five to forty-nine were heavy drinkers, but *only 1 percent* of those over fifty were.[32]

Most people seem to find retirement, as well as the departure of their children from their homes, relaxing rather than stressful. In addition, older people on a fixed income become less willing or able to pay for liquor. The effects of drinking are not so pleasurable in old age, and it requires extra caution to avoid getting sick or risking an accident. In the less stressful atmosphere of late-middle and old age, the payoffs from drinking go down as its costs go up. Notorious hell-raiser Lee Marvin told why he no longer drank much when he got older. "Booze doesn't act on me like it used to—a 15-minute glow, and the next three days are yuk," he confessed.[33] In a study of older drinkers, one researcher noted that three times as many men reduced their drinking with age as increased it. These are natural adjustments older people make to survive and continue to thrive, as well as a mark of a change in their values. This investigator related that "One man, a self-identified alcoholic, felt that he and his wife could not continue drinking and expect to be able to take care of themselves in old age. He wanted 'a future life, my health, money in the bank. So we got together and decided to quit.' "[34]

After hearing about all those who reform their drinking on their own, perhaps you might say, "It's easy to mellow out when you live in comfort as Robert Redford and Lee Marvin do. What do those examples have to do with *my* life?" But although they provide the most ready examples, the rich and famous are far from the only ones to get their lives sufficiently in order to stop drinking alcoholically. Here is the testimony of the manager of a state family-services administration, who dealt with society's least privileged cases:

> Over the years I've been involved in criminal cases and divorce cases, many involving people with long-lasting alcohol problems, some of them for twenty years. I'm talking about very active alcoholics, with all kinds of alcohol prob-

> lems, problems with the courts, family problems, arrests. The most typical problems were at work, in dealing with authority, or at home, in raising their children. In many cases, as people got older and the stresses in their lives were reduced, they stopped drinking—either because they couldn't take it any more physically or because they somehow grew out of it, and it ceased to be an important issue for them.[35]

Life Trajectories

Obviously, although the great majority of people temper their drinking with age, some do not. Some continue drinking at high levels, and a very small but extremely disturbing minority escalate their drinking and literally destroy themselves. Here are some typical phases of problem drinking and of maturing out:

Early maturing out. Here a person stops drinking excessively as an ordinary part of growing into adulthood, as soon as he or she develops a sufficient foothold in life. We described earlier how Robert Redford, as a young, unsuccessful art student in Paris, began drinking to the point of hallucinating. These hallucinations frightened Redford so much that he returned home, became involved with a woman, resumed his studies, and discovered acting as his primary career interest. Redford's intense drinking period had been precipitated by his sense of isolation and failure and disappeared with his maturing into a more successful role in life.

Mid-career maturing out. Here the drinker brings his or her drinking into line with a growing sense of security and responsibility that comes with career accomplishment and stable family life. Bing Crosby, who left his binge drinking behind as he came to live in a glow of public adulation, fits this pattern. Rod Stewart also described this process to a television interviewer when the interviewer reminded Stewart he had once said the most important things in life were "soccer, drinking, women—in that order." Stewart blushed and replied, "I said that a long time ago. Now children are the most important thing in my life."

Late-emerging addiction. Although most problem drinkers move in a positive direction, a few go the other way. This can occur when people's careers go off track and their early promise dissipates. Such reversal is not uncommon in the entertainment and sports worlds. Al Hodge, TV's Captain Video, died alone and destitute in a rundown hotel. His wife had left him years earlier when he became severely alcoholic after being unable to find work. Ringo Starr drifted into chronic and worsening alcoholism after his fame as a Beatle receded. Violinist Eugene Fodor found that winning a prestigious Moscow competition didn't guarantee a successful concert career, and fifteen years later his drug problems led to his arrest. We need always to remember that many more people become alcoholics because of failure than because of success.

Late maturing out. For a person who experiences crisis, decline, or escalating problems, two outcomes are possible: late maturation or persistent addiction. That is, while noting the worst and most intractable cases of addiction, we should realize that these are still a minority, even for those who go all the way to a full-blown state of alcoholism or addiction. The stories in Alcoholics Anonymous of people who hit bottom (or, more often, hit bottom repeatedly) and who then sober up are *not* examples of the power of A.A. as much as they are illustrations of the human being's natural recuperative power. George Vaillant found, for example, that throughout the course of people's lives, even among the most highly alcohol-dependent, more people quit drinking on their own than do so through A.A. or treatment.

Persistent addiction. What about the small minority who miss all these opportunities to mature out at various stages of the life cycle, but instead continue on the path of addiction, so as to fit the classical picture of incurable alcoholism? These individuals appear to fall into three groups.

First, there are those who are too socially isolated and economically and educationally disadvantaged to develop a productive orientation to life. These are Skid Row or other street alcoholics, whose alcoholism is marked by greater and greater separation from ordinary life satisfaction and success.

Second, there are those whose subjective experience is so painful that they require regular alcohol intoxication to make their lives tolerable. People like this (such as Richard Burton[36]) have deep-seated emotional problems for which they never find a solution and for which alcohol offers a costly palliation. They desperately seek artificial sensations of contentment and personal adequacy through alcohol, even when they experience the personal or professional successes that enable other people to outgrow alcoholism.

Third, and overlapping with the other two types of alcoholics, are those who fail to confront their worsening life situation because they are too insensitive to recognize they are escaping their responsibilities. This obliviousness is different from the disease model's notion of "denial." What marks *this* behavior is moral obtuseness, and not a blindness to a medical condition called alcoholism. Chronic alcoholics don't have the intellectual and moral wherewithal to confront their personal limitations and the damage their drinking causes—to themselves, those around them, and their communities (as when they drive drunk or throw up in public or abuse their families).

"But Isn't It Genetic?"

The straightforward, human view of alcoholism we have described—one that emphasizes social groups and personal responsibility—runs counter to the fashionable belief that alcoholism is an "inherited disease." For example, a front-page article in *The Wall Street Journal* in 1989 erroneously announced:

> Researchers have identified single genes as well as combinations of genes that are sometimes passed from alcoholics to their offspring that they believe create a predisposition toward alcoholism, much like blue eyes or nearsightedness.[37]

It is essential that we firmly refute this science fiction, which creates needless fears and concerns both about our own ability to overcome drinking problems and about our children's susceptibility to alcohol abuse.

Here, in highlight form, is what scientific research has shown about the inheritance of alcoholism (see appendix for further discussion):[38]

- It is true that children of alcoholics are perhaps two to three times more likely than others to become alcoholics themselves.

▸ How much of this inheritance is due to genetic factors is open to dispute, and important studies and reviews of the research suggest the genetic component is negligible.

▸ No genetic marker or set of genes for alcoholism has been identified.

▸ Even those researchers who believe they have shown alcoholism may be inherited largely restrict their claims to a small group of extreme male alcoholics.

▸ *No* research disputes that alcoholism takes a good deal of time to develop, and that all sorts of environmental and psychological factors—and personal choices—bring about the ultimate outcome. In other words, *no one* is guaranteed to become, or to remain, an alcoholic.

▸ A *majority* of the offspring of alcoholics do not become alcoholic, and many make sure to drink moderately *because of* their parents' negative examples.

Popular books that insist that alcoholism is purely a "genetic disease" appeal to an understandable desire we all may feel for simple answers about painful subjects, but they do not have a sound scientific foundation. Those who actually do research on the genetic inheritance of alcoholism speak far more cautiously, often downplaying the inheritance of alcoholism:

▸ Robert Cloninger, psychiatrist and genetic researcher, Washington University: "The demonstration of the critical importance of sociocultural influences in most alcoholics suggests that major changes in social attitudes about drinking styles can change dramatically the prevalence of alcohol abuse regardless of genetic predisposition."[39]

▸ George Vaillant, psychiatrist and alcoholism researcher (paraphrased in *Time*): "Vaillant thinks that finding a genetic marker for alcoholism would be as unlikely as finding one for basketball playing. . . . The high number of children of alcoholics who become addicted, Vaillant believes, is due less to biological factors than to poor role models."[40]

▸ David Lester, a leading biological researcher at the Rutgers Center of Alcohol Studies, after reviewing several surveys of genetic research on alcoholism, concluded "that genetic involvement in the etiology of alcoholism, however structured, is weak at best."[41]

Research on the inheritance of alcoholism has exploded since the 1970s. The first, and still the best-known, research of this kind was conducted by Donald Goodwin and his associates with Danish adoptees. They found that 18 percent of male adoptees with biological parents who were alcoholic became alcoholic themselves, compared with only 5 percent of male adoptees whose biological parents were not alcoholic.[42] Taken at face value, this is probably the strongest evidence of the genetic inheritance of alcoholism in all the research on the subject. Yet it shows that the great majority (82 percent) of men with alcoholic fathers do not become alcoholic solely by biological inheritance—that is, when they are not directly exposed to their fathers' influence.

This research shows that whatever genetic inheritance predisposes a man to alcoholism has only a weak link with the actual behavior that we call alcoholism. But the Goodwin research has an even more surprising message for daughters of alcoholics. Daughters who were raised away from alcoholic parents did *not* become alcoholic more often than female adoptees who did not have alcoholic parents.[43] To accept the Goodwin research, the research that established in many people's minds that there is a genetic source for alcoholism, is to *reject* the idea that women can inherit alcoholism! Other research confirms that alcoholism in women is hard to trace to genetic origins. But this raises an important question—if alcoholism is supposedly inherited, why is it only typed to one sex?

Quite a bit of additional evidence about genetic transmission of alcoholism has appeared since Goodwin's research was first published in the early 1970s. Yet, despite extravagant claims about our knowledge of the genetics of alcoholism, hardly any two researchers agree on what the inherited mechanism is that causes alcoholism. Rarely do two researchers report the same findings about the brain waves or cognitive impairments or alcohol metabolizing that each suggests is a major source for alcoholism. Other researchers have conducted large-scale studies that have not found *any* differences between offspring of alcoholics and those who did not have an alcoholic parent in terms of alcohol metabolism, sensitivity to alcohol, tolerance for alcohol, and mood.

Not only is there contradictory evidence about when, how, and by whom alcoholism is inherited, but other research casts doubt altogether on the increased risk for inheritance of alcoholism by biological relatives of alcoholics. Robin Murray, dean of the Institute of

Psychiatry at Maudsley Hospital in Britain, compared alcoholism rates for a group of identical and fraternal twins. Identical twins have the same genetic makeup, whereas fraternal twins are no more alike genetically than any brothers or sisters are. Therefore, if alcoholism were transmitted genetically, an identical twin of an alcoholic would more likely be alcoholic than would a fraternal twin of an alcoholic. Not so, Murray found. Nonidentical twins of alcoholics in his research were just as likely to be alcoholic as identical twins of alcoholics. We do not hear about Murray's research from popularizers of science in the United States. Murray has commented: "Students of alcoholism must continually beware lest they fall victim to the extravagant swings of intellectual fashion that so bedevil the field, and nowhere is such vigilance more necessary than in considering the possible etiological role of heredity."[44]

Research *does* generally find that alcoholics differ in having somewhat reduced cognitive capacity. But here is the problem. Alcoholics, as we have seen, are usually in worse socioeconomic circumstances and more often come from disturbed and abusive families. It is frequently very hard to separate these factors from any signs of impairment that offspring of alcoholics show. This may be why Marc Schuckit, a psychiatrist who has investigated college students and staff with alcoholic parents, did *not* find significant cognitive or neurological problems.[45] In other words, the few alcoholics who come from the middle- or upper-middle-class families that send people to college don't inherit the traits that supposedly characterize all alcoholics.

As a result of his research, Schuckit, though arguing that alcoholism is inherited, disputes the neurological mechanisms many researchers claim to be at the heart of the inheritance of alcoholism. Instead, Schuckit proposes that the susceptibility to alcoholism is inherited in the form of a *lessened sensitivity* to alcohol.[46] In other words, the children of alcoholics have an inbred tolerance for alcohol that means they feel fewer effects when they drink heavily (although this description sounds very different from the stories told by A.A. members, who typically describe getting drunk the first time they drank). The person may then drink excessively without realizing it for a long enough time to become fully dependent on alcohol. In this theory, even the alcoholically predisposed individual has to drink a great deal over a long period to become alcoholic.

Another of the best-known genetic researchers, psychiatrist Robert Cloninger, maintains that inherited alcoholism is present in a minority of male alcoholics, for whom it is transmitted through paternal genes via the same route as criminality.[47] The research Cloninger and his associates have conducted in Sweden suggests that what puts children at risk for alcoholism has little to do with biochemical reactions. These researchers identified personality as the main source of alcoholism for the high-risk group of men who either drink excessively or become criminals. Children's personalities were rated at age eleven and their alcohol use assessed at age twenty-seven. The children most likely to become alcohol abusers were relatively fearless, novelty-seeking, and indifferent to others' opinions of them. Indeed, 97 percent of the boys who ranked very high in novelty-seeking and very low in avoiding harm later abused alcohol, while only 1 percent of those very low in novelty-seeking and *average* in avoiding harm did so—a difference so enormous as to dwarf any supposed biological markers of alcoholism claimed by one or another researcher! At the other end of the scale, boys who were very harm-avoidant or very sensitive to others' opinions of them also ran a fairly high risk of alcohol abuse.[48]

Are these personality traits inherited or environmentally caused, or do they represent some combination? Whichever, they take us far away from alcohol metabolism as a prime risk factor for alcoholism. Instead, they describe *types of people* who become alcoholics. Few people accept that personalities, such as the "criminal personality," are wholly formed at birth. To do so, for example, would mean that we believe that the extremely high rate of crime among blacks is genetically caused, or that the visibility of Italians in organized crime is a biological phenomenon! Furthermore, to accept Cloninger's theory is to believe that offspring of alcoholics are as genetically predisposed to become criminals as they are to become alcoholics.

Personality and Values in Alcoholism

Cloninger is not the first researcher to note the heavy overlap between criminal traits and alcoholism. Researchers have consistently found that the personality profile most closely associated with alcoholism involves an antisocial disposition, aggressiveness, and lack of inhibition and impulse control. Several studies, indeed, have measured these traits in college and high-school men and then successfully predicted which young people were more likely to become alcoholics, without even examining how much they drank![49] One psychologist, Craig

MacAndrew, has established a scale that has regularly shown that alcoholics have "an assertive, aggressive, pleasure-seeking character" which closely resembles that found for criminals and delinquents. Women alcoholics as well as men often show this proclivity for excitement-seeking and criminality.[50]

There is a second, smaller group of alcoholics who express a great deal of emotional pain which they drink to relieve. A higher percentage of women alcoholics fall into this group. But whether a person is antisocial or not hardly seems like an inbred trait that is unaffected by environment and upbringing. Nor, on the other hand, is it likely that, just *because* a person has a painful sense of the world, he or she will become an alcoholic in response to these feelings. The role of personality in alcoholism suggests that a range of factors goes into producing alcoholism, even among those who find that drinking alleviates negative feelings. In addition to a predisposing personal orientation, a person must have *values* that set up and perpetuate the behavior we call alcoholism.

As we saw in the last section, psychiatrist Marc Schuckit finds that children of alcoholics inherit a lessened sensitivity to alcohol. Thus, they may drink more for longer periods without being fully aware of the effects. Why, however, don't such negative signs as hangovers, criticism from family and loved ones, legal and work problems, and so on discourage their continued heavy drinking? Psychiatrist George Vaillant's results from examining drinkers over forty years of their lives likewise demonstrated that alcoholism is the result of a long history of problem drinking. Vaillant found "no credence to the common belief that some individuals become alcoholics after the first drink. The progression from alcohol use to abuse takes years."[51] Whether or not you have some special sensitivity—or insensitivity—to alcohol, you must persist in problem drinking for years, oblivious to all the negative feedback your behavior elicits, before you develop a full-blown addiction. Whatever your biochemical reaction to alcohol, you have to have *reasons* to drink regularly and excessively over such a long period.

If, on the other hand, you have reasons *not* to continue destructive drinking—such as conflicting priorities, values, and social pressures—it wouldn't seem that you would continue on this path. You would heed the many warnings to change your behavior that you receive over a drinking career. The idea that many people avoid drinking too much because they don't like the consequences of overdrinking, regardless of how their genes prime them to react to alcohol, is straightforward and logical. We all know people who say things like, "After more than a drink or two I'm really out of it, so I rarely drink that much—maybe at a wedding." In fact, studies reveal that even young people develop strategies to control their drinking. Researchers sent nearly twenty-five hundred students at nine universities a questionnaire asking how important various reasons were in their decision to limit their drinking. The students' answers grouped themselves into four overall motivations (listed here with a few examples of each):

1. *Preference for self-control*
   "I've seen the negative effects of someone else's drinking."
   "Drinking heavily is a sign of personal weakness."
   "It's bad for my health."
   "I'm concerned about what people might think."

2. *Influence of upbringing and respect for authority*
   "I was brought up not to drink."
   "My religion discourages or is against drinking."
   "I'm part of a group that doesn't drink much."

3. *Attempts at self-reform*
   "I've become concerned with how much I've been drinking."
   "Someone suggested that I drink less."
   "I was embarrassed by something I said or did when drinking."

4. *Performance aspirations*
   "Drinking reduces my performance in sports."
   "Drinking interferes with my studies."
   "I wouldn't want to disappoint my parents."[52]

Here we see young people taking in feedback from the outside world, making value judgments, and adjusting their habits with a view toward health, responsibility, personal satisfaction, and social appropriateness. There's nothing medical or mystical about it.

Children Can and Do Reject Their Parents' Alcoholism

Even though an alcoholic is more likely to have alcoholic offspring than is the average person, nowhere near a majority of children of alcoholics become alcoholics themselves. That is, most people don't imitate their parents' problem drinking—at least they don't do so over the long haul. Often, they even learn to avoid problem drinking *because* of their parents' negative examples. Epidemiologists at the University of Michigan followed the drinking patterns of residents of Tecumseh, Michigan, for seventeen years, beginning in 1960. Their findings can only be called good news for those who worry that children of alcoholics, when they drink, are destined to progress to alcoholism. The researchers found that the children of moderate drinkers were much more likely to imitate their parents' drinking habits than were those whose parents were at the high or low extremes of alcohol consumption. "That is, whereas most offspring of moderate drinkers drink moderately, most children of heaviest drinkers also drink moderately and there are more abstainers' offspring who drink than who abstain."[53]

They conclude, based on their evidence and a review of the literature, that

> even alcoholic parental drinking only weakly invites imitation by offspring. Thus, despite the presence of familial alcoholism, the review of evidence indicates that parental heavy drinking (usually associated with interpersonal or social conflict) may not be followed closely by offspring and, in fact, that the majority of offspring seem to follow a less troublesome drinking style.[54]

Many children actually learn from seeing and feeling the consequences of a parent's alcoholism to avoid drinking destructively themselves. Children in the Tecumseh study who were of the opposite sex from the heavy-drinking parent were especially unlikely to imitate the parent's heavy drinking. Moreover, when a heavy-drinking parent had an evident drinking problem, this made offspring *less* likely to imitate them.[55] In such cases, it seems, it became easier for children to form an independent perspective on drinking and to reject their parents' model.

The more often the parent has drinking problems, the *less* likely the child is to follow the same path. This finding flies in the face of the notion of alcoholism as an inherited disease. But it is entirely understandable if we just think about what people really are like. A child may well be more likely to emulate a parent who is a quiet heavy drinker than one whose drinking has visibly unpleasant manifestations. The bigger fools the parents make of themselves, the less the child will want to imitate them. Consider, in this regard, Ronald Reagan's vivid recollections of how his mother picked his father up off the lawn after the father returned from a round of drinking, and how he himself resolved never to cause his mother this kind of unhappiness. That did not stop him, however, from drinking occasionally and moderately.

Not only are children of alcoholics *not* doomed to be alcoholics themselves, but several studies have shown that children of alcoholics who *have* developed a drinking problem do better at moderating their drinking (when that is the goal of treatment) than other problem drinkers.[56] It seems as if some childhood problems can strengthen a person's resilience and independence. Yet today we undermine such resilience by telling the person that those problems are permanently disabling. As one woman, a moderate drinker, remarked when she received some literature about children of alcoholics, "It would have been helpful for me as a child to know that my father's behavior when he was drinking wasn't normal. It *wouldn't* have helped me to hear that I was likely to become an alcoholic myself."

It is in families and groups with the greatest social dysfunction—where crime and open alcoholism are most rampant and positive social values most lacking—that alcoholism is likely to be passed on from parent to child. Alcoholism is most frequently transmitted in ghetto and economically disadvantaged households and those disrupted by divorce and child abuse, where children have the fewest opportunities to escape the social and economic pressures that dominate their parents' lives.[57] Most people who join Adult Children of Alcoholics (ACoA) groups, on the other hand, lead stable lives themselves and may have had a parent who was a "functioning" alcoholic.[58] This family structure less often produces alcoholic children. Indeed, the gigantic growth of the "Children of Alcoholics" movement—most of whose members are women with alcoholic or heavy-drinking fathers who are not alcoholics themselves—is testimony to just how many people refuse to become alcoholics merely because their parents were.

The Children of Alcoholics Movement

The term "children of alcoholics" has become a major therapeutic designation, sounding call for conferences, and means for labeling (and self-labeling) people. How do children of alcoholics differ from others who have emotional problems? According to pioneering genetics researcher Donald Goodwin, not at all.

> Goodwin said that "all the stuff" that has been written in recent years about adult children of alcoholics has been, in his judgment, something akin to a hoax. Adult children of alcoholics are about like adult children of everybody else with a problem, he said, and it's hard to build a reasonable case for giving them extraordinary attention.[59]

Children of alcoholics, like everyone else, have a range of life experiences and resulting psychological problems. Hitching these problems to your current interpretation of the previous generation's behavior does nothing to improve your chances for dealing with life. Rather, by making your parent's drinking problems the cornerstone of your identity, you make it *harder* to overcome the past and accept an adult role. The ACoA movement represents a tendency once popular among people undergoing psychoanalysis to dwell on their past to the *detriment* of their current relationships and activities.

If many people, even those without alcoholic parents, have the same disabilities as people whose parents drank too much, then perhaps many of us have grown up in "dysfunctional," debilitating families. This logic has produced a whole new spate of popular books, like *Toxic Parents,* which make it sound as though we all will bear for life the scars of our parents' ineptitude. A recent guide for ACoA labels up to *96 percent* of the population "children of trauma" who therefore would benefit from programs like ACoA. "Not knowing what hit them, and suffering a sourceless sense of pain in childhood," say the authors, nearly all Americans "perpetuate the denial and minimization which encase them in dysfunctional roles, rules and behaviors."[60] Here the fact that many people's problems are indistinguishable from those of children of alcoholics is generalized to mean that we all need the treatments that the alcoholism movement has decided children of alcoholics require as a birthright.

What will we gain from thinking about ourselves as deformed creatures ruined by our parents' misattempts at childrearing? Before we accept this viewpoint, let's first make sure we are doing a better job with our own children. After all, many children of alcoholics are hardworking, responsible people. In fact, the main claim about the nonalcoholic daughters of alcoholics who buy books and attend ACoA meetings is that they are too dutiful, controlled, and perfectionistic. In other words, they are overly well-adjusted people who take on "hero" and "caretaker" roles, often becoming—as described in such books as *Adult Children of Alcoholics*—"super responsible."[61] Yet the problems we are most concerned about in our children—particularly those who abuse drugs and alcohol—are the opposite ones, irresponsibility and an unwillingness to think of others.

Emmy Werner, who has studied a group of children of alcoholics over several decades, finds that they often show a heightened resilience. The additional responsibility they are given, she believes, can lead to greater competence and maturity.[62] It seems that many of our generation and previous generations had more such responsibilities than children today, and that social changes have reduced our and our children's sense that we are obligated to others. The Children of Alcoholics movement may express a shift in cultural attitudes about how willing we are to sacrifice our own interests for other people, including our family members. For example, children today are far less willing to look after an ill parent than their own parents would have been. But this may not be a very good thing for our society or even for the people the new consciousness is supposed to benefit.

Is it possible that identifying children of alcoholics and showing them how bad their lives are can do more harm than good? What exactly do children of alcoholics gain from deciding to adopt this label and to attend groups modeled after A.A.? Janet Woititz, author of the best-selling book *Adult Children of Alcoholics,* reported in her doctoral dissertation that children of alcoholics attending Alateen had *lower* self-esteem than children of alcoholics who went untreated. Undaunted by this evidence that focusing on the traumatic effects of parental alcoholism might actually undermine the self-esteem of teenagers, Woititz observed:

> Thoughtful analysis of the data and an understanding of the alcoholic family pattern can help explain this result. Denial is a part of the disease both for the alcoholic and his fam-

> ily. . . . This researcher suggests that the non-Alateen group scores significantly higher than the Alateen group scores because the non-Alateen children are still in the process of denial.[63]

In other words, if as the child of an alcoholic you are not sufficiently aware of your deprivation to suffer a loss of self-esteem, the movement will make clear to you just how bad your case is. Surely, Woititz's conclusion marks the *reductio ad absurdum* of the disease theory of alcoholism.

CHAPTER 3

WHICH IS THE MOST ADDICTIVE DRUG OF ALL?

•

Fill in the Blanks:

Maybe People Can Quit ___, But Nobody Can Quit ___
(Heroin, Cocaine, Crack, Crank, Ice)

WE'VE BEEN PRESENTED with one drug horror after another. The worst drug used to be heroin—we heard that, if you used it even once, you became permanently addicted. But then, in the eighties, we heard from pharmacologists like Sidney Cohen about cocaine: "If we were to design deliberately a chemical that would lock people into perpetual usage, it would probably resemble the neuropsychological properties of cocaine."[1] As if cocaine in its standard form wasn't bad enough, smokable cocaine and crack were developed. Even these weren't addictive enough for some, however, and soon we heard about new drugs like crank and ice that were said to be many times as addictive as crack.

We listened to one announcer saying that ice was *immediately* addictive, so that taking it once meant you were permanently hooked. But this was what was once said of heroin. Never mind that it *couldn't* be true, since many of us have received narcotics far more powerful than street heroin in the hospital without once considering using the drug after our hospitalization was over. But if cocaine is even more pharmacologically tailored to lock people into permanent usage than heroin, and crack is an even more addictive form of cocaine, and ice was synthesized to be many times as addictive as crack—then, surely, here is *really* a drug that everybody who takes it even once will be permanently addicted to!

But this is not how addiction works. No drug is inherently, permanently addictive. Not only that, but a majority of people who *are* addicted to *any* drug quit their addictions. No drug will ever be found that violates these precepts, unless we radically modify the human species through a never-ending propaganda campaign that convinces us we all must be addicts.

To see that this is so, consider a front-page article in *The New York Times* that surveyed America's leading drug figures on the crack epidemic. The article, subtitled, "In Shift, Importance of Users' Environment Is Stressed over Drug's Attributes," led off with the paragraph:

> Drug experts now believe that the extreme difficulties they face in treating crack addiction stem far more from the setting and circumstances of the users than the biochemical reaction the drug produces.[2]

A leading government researcher interviewed for the article, Jack Henningfield, indicated that only one-sixth of crack users become addicted, despite the fact that most crack users live in the worst inner-city environments! The article reported that addicts who were surveyed said cocaine, "either injected, sniffed or smoked," was easier to quit than alcohol, heroin, or *cigarettes.* For those who find such reports difficult to accept, think of New York newscaster Jim Jensen, who, when interviewed in *People* magazine about his drug treatment, said he found it far easier to give up cocaine than to give up Valium. In the single case of a crack addict described by the *New York Times* article, a crack dealer stopped using the drug while in prison even though he found the drug readily available there. This addict said that he

> had no trouble stopping because it lost its allure; that it was not so enjoyable to him when he was smoking alone in his cell; that when he was released from prison, he took up the habit again, mostly because crack addicts were the only friends he had. . . .[3]

Meanwhile, when President Bush delivered his 1989 speech to the nation announcing his war on drugs, he referred to a study conducted by the government's National Institute on Drug Abuse (NIDA) on how many Americans had ever used various drugs, were currently using these drugs (had used the drug in the last month), and were currently using these drugs daily or nearly daily (at least twenty of the prior thirty days). What percentage of all those who have ever used cocaine now use it daily, according to government figures? One percent. What percentage of those who currently use cocaine use it daily or almost daily? Ten percent.[4]

But we know all this is true. How do we know that cocaine users do not all become addicts who lose their jobs, give up their families, repeatedly enter treatment, and steal or perhaps murder to get drugs? Because over twenty million Americans have used cocaine, including many middle-class and college-educated users. If cocaine were as addictive as so many treatment "experts" claim (based on the highly selected sample of their patients), we would all know many addicts. Yet no mother in our neighborhood has been arrested for prostituting her daughter to get cocaine. If those around us, or we ourselves, have used cocaine, we didn't become addicted the way those we see on television become addicted. Why not? If we can find out how the large majority of middle-class users resist addiction, or why they make such good treatment patients compared with inner-city addicts, we will have a key to addiction, its treatment, and its reduction that is unmatched in its validity.

It is not *exclusively* (although it is largely) inner-city and other deprived groups who typically become addicted. Some middle-class users do become addicted—although their prospects for recovery are far better than they are for those in the ghettos. A Yale researcher quoted in the *Times* article on crack noted, "If crack were a drug of the middle or upper classes, we would not be saying it is so impossible to treat." But those from the middle class who become addicted are themselves far more likely to come from broken homes, not to be involved in positive social institutions and activities (like church or a satisfying career), to have serious psychological problems, and to have abused illicit and licit drugs (like cigarettes) before their cocaine use.[5]

We never learn these truths about cocaine, or else only discern them faintly amid the hyperbole about drugs in America, because major social forces—official, popular, scientific—are working to have us perceive the addictive horror that the *drug* creates. A TV news-magazine program showed researchers at Baltimore City Hospital (at the U.S. government's Addiction Research Center) recording people's reactions to cocaine on a computer. As a respectful reporter looked on, an addict described how great the cocaine he had just taken made him feel. The reporter questioned the addict about his ecstatic response, about how the intense pleasure the drug produced made it impossible not to want more.

If you accepted this program at face value, you would believe that anyone—yourself included—would become addicted after taking the drug a few times (or maybe once). Certainly, you have learned from hundreds of news reports and television specials that treatment centers are filled with white-collar professionals who thought they could control their cocaine use but then unwittingly became addicted. How different this is, you might think, from all those people you knew who took marijuana and hallucinogens in college in the 1960s and 1970s, nearly all of whom stopped taking drugs when they left school, got married, and entered the work world. Or, if you went to school in the late 1970s and early 1980s, when you knew many people who snorted cocaine without becoming addicted to it, you might think the cocaine derivative crack must be tremendously addictive because it is smokable.

In fact, two researchers who have surveyed all the studies of cocaine users found that "between 5% and 10% of those who ever try cocaine will eventually use it weekly or more often. Of this minority of users, probably one tenth to one quarter [that is, a range of from one-half to two and one-half percent of all users] become addicted at some point in their cocaine using careers."[6] Furthermore, in the largest North American study of cocaine users who had not entered clinics for treatment (the vast majority of cocaine users), the majority of those who had engaged in intensive cocaine use cut back on their own initiative, and, "in all, few participants experienced serious chronic reactions."[7] With cocaine, as with every illicit drug that has ever been used by large numbers of people, the majority of those who take it do not become regular users, the majority of regular users do not become addicted, and the majority of those who become addicted cease their addictions on their own, without treatment.

What, then, are we to make of the masses of addicts we hear about, of the youthful substance abusers (perhaps including our own children or those of our friends) who have to be sent off to chemical-dependency treatment centers and taught that they are lifelong addicts? Are our children really better off than were those of us who went to college between 1965 and 1980 and who experimented with and gave up drugs on our own? To keep youthful drug use in perspective, consider an example like basketball great Kareem Abdul-Jabbar. In his autobiography, *Giant Steps,*[8] Jabbar describes his drug use at UCLA in the late 1960s. Unlike a number of basketballers whose stories have dominated the 1980s (the Houston professional basketball team at one time boasted three recovering drug addicts on its squad), Jabbar gave up drug use because it was incongruent with his religion, his work, and his personal commitments. How perverse that we never hear from a former moderate user like Jabbar on the addiction lecture circuit, but we do hear from countless reformed sinners who cannot stay drug-free without being in treatment or, alternatively, feeling the "high" of the lecture circuit in which they talk endlessly about their addictions.

What we learn from ordinary drug users, from addicts who are able to recover, whether with treatment or without, and from perpetual addicts is that the drug alone is a small part of the equation. The person's values, outlook, and environment are by far the larger part. We *know* this to be true in the case of alcohol, since such a small percentage of drinkers become alcoholics. It is the same with drugs. Consider the cocaine addict hooked to electrodes at the Baltimore City Hospital who is presented as a television "case study" of the effects of cocaine. The fact that the man in the chair reacts ecstatically to cocaine does not explain why people prostitute themselves and steal to get drugs in the real world. Orgasms feel great, too, but that doesn't "prove" that everyone will compulsively masturbate or fornicate or become a rapist.

Will people give up their jobs for the drug? Will they sacrifice their family's well-being for it? Will they jeopardize their health for it? Will they risk going to jail for it? Actually, the man in the laboratory chair on TV was selected for study because he *had* sacrificed these things in order to become addicted to crack, which made him eligible for the study. Even outside the laboratory, this man had preferred cocaine to other satisfactions and involvements in his life. But the question is not: "How do the sensations from cocaine come to supersede all other feelings and outlets this person has?" The question is: "Why does he value cocaine-induced feelings over all the other things that people normally value and that keep the vast majority of people—even those who have experienced cocaine—from becoming, or remaining, enslaved to a drug?"

The Lessons of Narcotics

Traditionally, narcotics have been the primary object of the fear and hysteria now directed at cocaine. Like cocaine, narcotics were first labeled a public menace in the late nineteenth and early twentieth centuries. Before that, cocaine and narcotics were used commonly in patent medicines and other concoctions, and the word "addiction" meant more or less "bad habit."[9] At the turn of the century, heroin was marketed by the Bayer company as a nonaddictive substitute for morphine, and cocaine was originally the active ingredient in Coca-Cola![10]

Whereas cocaine largely disappeared from public consciousness between 1910 and 1970, narcotics have been a law-enforcement priority and a cultural bogey throughout this century. As a result, narcotics use has been observed much more extensively over a longer period of time, so that we know more about it. Although narcotics have never threatened the middle-class world the way cocaine is now said to do, we can learn a great deal about how people get hooked on—and unhooked from—cocaine by looking at how people and animals react to the better-known drugs heroin and morphine. Everything we know tells us that addiction to narcotics is far from automatic, inevitable, or permanently enslaving.

Maturing out in the ghetto. We first need to realize that most heroin addicts outgrow their addiction in their twenties or thirties, just as most young men outgrow problem drinking—and for mostly the same reasons. This is true even in the urban ghetto. In a national study of men aged twenty to twenty-nine, less than a third of those who had *ever* used heroin had used it in the year preceding their interview.[11] In the next section, we describe the ways in which many people accomplish this.

Soldiers addicted in Vietnam. In Vietnam, tens of thousands of U.S. military men used narcotics. Most of these users became addicted—they underwent withdrawal when they were unable to take a narcotic. Of these men who were addicted in Vietnam, Lee Robins and her colleagues at Washington University Medical School discovered, 50 percent used heroin in the United States. Yet only one in eight of those addicted in Vietnam—12.5 percent—became readdicted Stateside. The researchers were stunned that so many former addicts could control their narcotics use once they escaped the Vietnam War zone. They even found that heroin-using veterans were no more likely to use the substance daily than were marijuana and amphetamine users![12]

Hospital patients and morphine. One regrettable consequence of the antidrug hysteria of the late 1980s has been a growing unwillingness to use morphine to relieve pain caused by illness or surgery (heroin use for pain relief is totally outlawed). Doctors and nurses are afraid of addicting patients, and sometimes even patients reject appropriate analgesia out of a fear of addiction. This fear is completely misguided and unsubstantiated. Patients in hospitals receiving much stronger doses of opiates on a regular basis than heroin addicts on the street almost *never* become addicted. Dr. Mitchell Max of the National Institutes of Health reported on eleven thousand people treated with narcotics for cancer or after surgery: "Among these 11,000 people, there was one case of serious addiction [one-hundredth of one percent] and three other questionable cases that were noted [still much less than a tenth of a percent]."[13]

Max further observed, "If you're going to the hospital and you need a one- or two-week course of strong narcotic therapy for pain management . . . the risk of addiction from that is not even worth talking about."[14] The reason people who are given narcotics for medical reasons do not become addicted is that they do not take the drug for euphoria or for escape, do not think of themselves as drug addicts, and indignantly reject that label if it is suggested to them. Addiction is not their way of life; they use the drug only to neutralize the physical pain that interferes with their normal activities.

Addiction in animals. Unlike hospital patients, who are almost never addicted to narcotics, animals are addicted under certain laboratory conditions, convincing the public that narcotics are universally addicting by virtue of their chemical effects alone. This kind of research, however, is conducted under such artificial conditions that it doesn't tell us anything about how animals react to drugs in their natural habitat, let alone about human reactions to drugs. Animals in these experiments typically are kept in cages with an injection apparatus strapped to their backs, unable to experience the mobility and range of activities that are normal for their species. How they behave in a cramped, constraining environment proves nothing about the inherently addicting effects of opiates, since it does not tell us how interested the animals would be in opiates if they were free to live normally.

The inadequacy of such research has been demonstrated by a series of ingenious studies at Simon Fraser University in British Columbia.[15] The researchers designed a spacious, stimulating environment dubbed "Rat Park" in which male and female rats lived together; they then compared these animals with those housed in isolated cages. Unsurprisingly, the caged rats drank many times more of a sweetened morphine solution (in preference to water) than those living in Rat Park. Even after having been isolated and habituated to the drug, rats who then were given the opportunity to enjoy the space and companionship in Rat Park rejected the morphine solution almost completely in favor of water.

The Rat Park research indicated that rats and other animals actually *dislike* the effects of narcotics, particularly when they have available other animal activities, like sex. In his book *Intoxication,* Ronald Siegel found through systematic observations that animals consume vegetation with drug effects in the wild, but that they do not become addicted.[16] These observations replicate the Simon Fraser experimentation in showing that addiction is not a natural animal phenomenon, but a man-made invention. Indeed, Rat Park and other animal results show that under ordinary circumstances sex is a far more powerful reward—and should therefore be more addictive—than narcotics!

How Heroin Addicts Usually Overcome Addiction in Real Life

The common belief that no one can overcome heroin addiction except through treatment has been conclusively disproved by sociologists Dan Waldorf and Patrick Biernacki, who interviewed hundreds of untreated ex-addicts in California. In his 1986 book, *Pathways from Heroin Addiction: Recovery Without Treatment,* Biernacki lists the following among his findings, each of which attacks a key inaccuracy in our conceptions of narcotics use:

- Addicts can and do recover "naturally"—on their own without the aid of any therapeutic intervention.
- Naturally recovered former addicts are relatively easy to find and interview.

▸ Addicts are not alike in character or lifestyle.

▸ All addicts do not undergo the same social careers or become equally affected by their addiction.

▸ Some addicts lead basically "straight" lives, that is, they are not criminals.

▸ Some people drift in and out of their addiction without much conscious thought or consideration.

▸ Some addicts can and do overcome cravings to use opiates when they are abstinent and thereby avoid relapsing.

▸ Addict folklore and professional understandings do not adequately explain those addicts who have quit on their own.

▸ Some people who have stopped their addiction to opiates do not continue to think of themselves as addicted.[17]

The picture we get from the interviews is that of people giving up narcotic addiction with greater or less difficulty depending on their reasons for taking the drug in the first place and the changes that have occurred in their lives since then. Dan Waldorf describes how 40 percent of his subjects naturally outgrew heroin addiction as a normal part of their development, with almost no special efforts on their part. This group

> felt that their addiction had run its course and that it was time to do other things: time to assume marital or family responsibilities, time to travel, time to buy some things they wanted, time to grow up. There are in this response suggestions that opiate use and its accompanying life-style had been tried for a time and was found to be limited and lacking.
>
> One particular man illustrated this well. He used prodigious amounts of relatively pure opiates and methamphetamines daily in Nepal for nine months as an experiment in expanding his consciousness but cleaned up in order to travel to Sweden. A year later he spent four months in an opium den in Hong Kong and then decided to stop a second time to smuggle heroin to a South Pacific island. After these two episodes he used opiates on and off but he always

> felt that he could quit whenever he wanted to, and did so with little trouble when he returned to the United States.[18]

Those who protest censorship of unpopular political or artistic expression might consider that no television show will ever depict such a story about an addict.

Seemingly, most addicts come to realize what the addiction is doing to them and those they care for. One such realization is described by a woman Biernacki interviewed:

> I was real scared, real frightened, real terrified . . . of what would happen to me. I felt like I was at a point where either I had to clean up or become a dealer or prostitute, live on Main Street in downtown L.A.[19]

Personal pride was often crucial in the decision to give up narcotics:

> The one thing I did know was that I didn't want to be known as a tramp and I didn't want to feel like a nobody, a nothing. I was a very proud person, so I had to do something about those drugs. Either it was going to control me, or control my life, or I was going to stop using. My goals were the good old U.S. American dream that everybody has.[20]

Despite the obstacles that confronted them (including lectures many had heard to the effect that addicts can never escape addiction, at least on their own), these individuals made good on their resolve to quit by reshaping their identities. Some revived old relationships (as with their families) or created new relationships in the nonaddicted world. Some buried themselves in work or entered college. Specific thoughts, realizations, and techniques that helped them over these transitions will be presented in part II of this book.

These accounts contradict the fundamental treatment-industry axiom that people who are addicted must regard themselves as addicts for life. If you believe addiction is inbred and inherited, then you will always be addicted, no matter how your life changes. In his book *Junkie,* on the other hand, novelist and addict William Burroughs claimed that most narcotic users who stop for some length of time never resume regular use of the drug, even if they do try it again. This was certainly true of the Vietnam veterans who had used heroin. Many of Waldorf's and Biernacki's addicts likewise gave up their old addict identities. Waldorf compared addicts who cured themselves with those who entered treatment. Although people in the two groups often used similar methods to change, those who didn't enter treatment often tried the drug again without becoming readdicted:

> Unlike ex-addicts who come out of therapeutic communities (that follow the Synanon model) or alcoholics who attend Alcoholics Anonymous, the majority of untreated ex-addicts did not believe in total abstinence. Nor did they believe that a single injection of opiates would send them over the brink. Consequently, a sizeable number (26%) tested themselves by using heroin once—usually after they had been off for a year or two. This experiment was usually seen as a milestone of sorts, a benchmark that affirmed their ability to change and resist re-addiction. This was not the only such benchmark. One woman, a nurse, said her milestone occurred when the hospital in which she worked gave her the keys to the narcotics cabinet even when they knew she had once been addicted. This gesture assured her that they indeed trusted her and on her part she had no thoughts to use opiates or break that trust.[21]

Biernacki found that a few addicts who had quit on their own felt that they could never escape their addict selves: "A few notable exceptions to the tendency to speak of the addiction in the past tense were found in the study. Some of the respondents still feared that, under certain conditions, they might become readdicted. They still thought of themselves as addicts, although they had not been physically addicted for at least two years."[22] Many of these had been to A.A. and accepted the A.A. ideology that "once an addict, always an addict." This ideology seemed to prevent the total transformation many addicts achieve. In the book *High on Life,* Jerry, an ex-addict who had spent about half of his twenties and early thirties in jail, sums up the evolution that made drug use, in his case, "cease to be an option":

> When I was in the street, my friends were drug addicts, hustlers—people like myself. When I came to Blue Hills [a drug rehabilitation center], my friends were counselors, ex-addicts—people like myself. Now my friends are social workers, psychologists, professionals—people like myself.[23]

Jerry described how, after being drug-free for five years, he was severely burned in a fire in his home. Given morphine in the hospital, he was sent home with an unlimited prescription for the narcotic Percodan. A month later, when he no longer felt any pain from the burns, he stopped taking the drug. It occurred to him that at an earlier period in his life he might have said to himself, "Well, what the hell, I'll take another two and have myself a little high. It won't hurt anybody." As he saw it, though,

> I would have to work at relapsing by this point. I would have to begin not paying my bills, not showing up to teach my classes. I would have to let my personal life get slovenly. I would have to undermine the whole life structure.[24]

The Reality of Cocaine—and the People Who Use It

Researchers at the Addiction Research Foundation in Toronto conducted a community-based study of 111 cocaine users identified through personal referrals and advertising. Their findings were published in 1987 in a book with the misleading title *The Steel Drug.* The authors conclude that "the *actual* risks of infrequent cocaine use have been exaggerated in the media and consequently in the public's perception of the problem."[25] They explain that "the social-recreational users, the persons who use cocaine in an apparently 'controlled' way, also have been underrepresented in the media's sensational coverage of 'ruined lives.' "[26] Much of this media coverage comes from the United States. We learn far more about typical patterns of cocaine use in middle-class America from the Canadian study than from the relentless television coverage of crack wars in U.S. ghettos.

Most of the Canadians interviewed had used cocaine infrequently during the past year, although some had at one time been heavier users. For most, "snorting" cocaine was a social rather than an individual practice, limited to leisure hours in the company of others. Half of those surveyed had at some time felt an urge to continue taking the drug, but only 20 percent felt this craving regularly. When they recognized they were doing too much cocaine, most cut back or quit their use. American researchers have made similar discoveries. For example, Howard Shaffer and Stephanie Jones of the Harvard Medical School found that many cocaine addicts quit the drug on their own.[27] Even an American researcher such as Ronald Siegel, who frequently emphasizes cocaine's tenacity and virulence, noted that most cocaine users do not become addicts.[28] As the Canadian authors commented:

> . . . users did report recognizing the need to "detoxify" or limit their use of cocaine. Most seemed to be able to develop strategies to do this adequately without professional guidance. . . . In general, Siegel's study suggests that most social-recreational users can maintain a low to moderate use pattern without escalating to dependency and that many users can essentially "treat themselves."[29]

The Steel Drug includes case studies of controlled users such as this casual user, who earned a modest income:

> Since his introduction to cocaine several years ago, he had adopted a routine of buying a gram twice a year, for "special occasions." He emphasized that cocaine was "always combined with doing other things" over the course of an evening. There were many situations in which he would avoid it, and he cited examples of business meetings and sports. Suitable occasions for use might be a birthday, or "with cognac on Christmas Eve."

This sounds like the way a person might use marijuana (or the way Dwight Gooden used cocaine). The man had once used cocaine daily for a week when someone gave him a large quantity of the drug. Nonetheless, he had no desire to repeat this experience because "it wasn't worth it": the drug was expensive and "did not have a high priority in his life."[30]

A heavier user who regulated his use in keeping with a changing life-style was a successful professional with a $40,000 income and a stable family life. After periods of heavy cocaine use, including freebasing, his "drug use tapered off as the demands of his career expanded." As he explained it, "you get busy and use less." This man, who smoked marijuana almost daily "to relax after work," now used cocaine about twice a month, and never when he was working. The researchers concluded about this man that, "while his private life remained unconventional, his public persona was impeccable. Cocaine was a well-entrenched part of the private side, but had no role in the public one."[31]

Thus, if you see lurid stories about cocaine addicts and think, "That's not me," or "That's not my friend," your skepticism is well grounded. *The Steel Drug* realistically presents the range of problems people have as a result of using cocaine. Most common among these problems are nasal disorders (congestion, bleeding), rapid heartbeat, acute insomnia, irritability, and anxiety. Some of those interviewed experienced more serious reactions of paranoia (23 percent), violent or aggressive behavior (17 percent), or hallucinations (15 percent) at least once. In general, these problems occurred in direct proportion to frequency of use, and most users eventually cut back when they began suffering damaging symptoms.

One woman, for example, used cocaine daily for three months at a cost of $1,000 a month on a $25,000 annual income. During this period she saw the positive effects of cocaine—the added energy, the sharpening of the senses—turn into negative ones. "Cocaine made me miserable, depressed; my personality changed," she said. On her own, without treatment, she drastically reduced her consumption, giving up the habit without totally swearing off the drug:

> She reported that "it was easy to give up. I had taken myself to the limit, and spending all that money was incredibly foolish." She had continued to use occasionally, less often than once a month in the past year, but thought that she would use it even less, if at all, in the next year.[32]

The capacity of middle-class users to quit drugs more readily is evident in the National Institute on Drug Abuse survey President Bush reported. While overall drug use dropped, *daily* use of drugs—particularly cocaine—increased (although the number of daily cocaine users identified by the 1988 survey was still fewer than three hundred thousand).[33] The use of nearly all illicit drugs by high-school students continued to decline significantly in 1989. The proportion of seniors using any illicit drug during the preceding year dropped from 54 percent in 1979, the peak year, to 35 percent. The proportion using marijuana during the preceding year declined from one-half in 1978 to just under 30 percent in 1989, and those using marijuana *daily* dropped from 11 percent to 3 percent in the same period. Among college students, 8 percent had used cocaine in the year prior to the survey (down from 17 percent in 1985). These trends continued downward, as indicated by the 1990 NIDA drug-use survey. Crack use was negligible (1.5 percent) among college students in 1989, showing that the selected sample of the population that goes to college takes practically no interest in a drug with such a destructive reputation.[34]

The U.S. and Canadian data point to the same conclusions: Most middle-class people who are exposed to cocaine resist using it more than a few times. If they don't resist it, they control their use of it. If they can't control it, they give it up. That leaves only a small percentage of users with serious problems. How, exactly, do the others manage this?

A convincing answer is provided by a study in which students and former students at the University of Chicago were given amphetamines—powerful stimulants that many people experience as being similar to cocaine (the new scare drug "ice" is an amphetamine). These young people reported that they enjoyed the effects of the drug, yet they chose to use *less* of it each time they returned to the experimental situation. Why? According to psychopharmacologist John Falk, they turned down pleasurable, drug-induced mood changes

> probably because during the period of drug action these subjects were continuing their normal, daily activities. The drug state may have been incompatible either with the customary pursuit of these activities or the usual effects of engaging in these activities. The point is that in their natural habitats these subjects showed . . . that they were uninter-

> ested in continuing to savor the mood effects [of the drugs].[35]

The phrase "natural habitats" recalls the studies of opiate addiction in animals earlier in this chapter. What is true for animals is even more true for people: those who have more important things to do don't incapacitate their minds with drugs, any more than they would gorge themselves continuously on ice-cream sundaes. This is only common sense, but it needs to be emphasized at a time when it is so perversely denied, for in that common sense lies our best hope, as individuals and as a society, of doing something about our drug problems.

Sociologist Craig Reinarman and his colleagues found that, even when middle-class freebasers or crack users became addicted, they were unlikely to commit crimes. In fact, the possibility that they might have to steal was the reason most gave for quitting their drug use.[36] This same attitude is expressed by a man in the Canadian study who became disillusioned with cocaine "as he realized how self-centered and antisocial he was becoming."[37] To reach this conclusion he had, first, to know what it meant to be self-centered and antisocial. Second, he had to have a social life, a life among people, that he risked losing. Finally, he had to value his connections with people enough to want to hold on to them. In other words, he had to be tied in to some kind of civilized existence that he cared about maintaining. When people who have such resources and values find themselves losing control of their drug use, they are able to refocus on the things that really matter to them. This is true even for people who come out of the Betty Ford Center and testify to the world that treatment saved them.

The Middle-Class Addict

Middle-class people, some quite well known, do become addicted. Two of the best-known addicts/alcoholics are Betty Ford and Kitty Dukakis. Their cases give us an insight into the experience of middle-class addiction. Mrs. Ford and Mrs. Dukakis were not in the same position as the inner-city crack addict who steals or prostitutes herself or her children for crack. Unlike the street addict, they had guaranteed supplies of tranquilizers and diet pills so that they didn't have to resort to desperate measures to get their drugs (although, after Kitty Dukakis was treated for alcoholism at the Edgehill Newport hospital, she removed the alcohol from her house and ended up drinking rubbing alcohol). These women maintained their addictions through their secure ties to the medical establishment. Indeed, we might ask, should the physicians who prescribed those drugs for the women be liable for the same penalties, including death, that many propose for drug pushers? What if the lithium and antidepressants Kitty Dukakis's doctors have prescribed for her were subsequently labeled as addictive?

At the same time, Betty Ford's description of her drinking in *The Times of My Life*[38] is rather mild, especially when compared with that of someone like Marty Mann, founder of the National Council on Alcoholism, who was reduced to drinking on park benches from bottles in bags. Kitty Dukakis's revelation that she began drinking heavily at the age of fifty-three, after her husband lost the presidential election, likewise puts the diagnosis of alcoholism on a whole new plane from the early days of A.A. Nonetheless, even if their drinking problems were comparatively mild or late-developing ones, if Mrs. Ford and Mrs. Dukakis believed they were addict/alcoholics, then they were addicted.

Mrs. Ford's drug use first became public when she announced without regret, in an interview she gave to *Women's Wear Daily* when her husband, Gerald, became president, that she couldn't function without tranquilizers. Although this shocked some readers at the time (including us), Mrs. Ford—and apparently a number of physicians—didn't recognize her drug dependence until many years later. It would seem that Betty Ford and her doctors were insensitive to the value of sober consciousness and to the danger of relying on drugs to produce peace of mind. Many others would have seen a danger signal the moment they started using drugs daily, rather than nonchalantly describing such drug use to the press, as Betty Ford did.

Likewise, not everyone—certainly not the students in the University of Chicago experiment described above—would be ready to accept the steady diet of amphetamines that Kitty Dukakis took during the twenty-six years she tells us she was addicted to diet pills, or the maintenance doses of prescribed mind-altering drugs she has continued to take. Of course, many people would refuse to turn to diet pills in the first place as a way to keep thin. Why, then, were Kitty Dukakis and Betty Ford so oblivious to the meaning of drug dependence and so willing to turn their consciousness and bodies over to chemical assistance? Indeed, to understand this gives us the key to understanding drug dependence. Kitty Dukakis and Betty Ford appear to have shared the following traits:

- They lacked confidence in their ability to manage their lives and feelings independently.
- They didn't have the kind of self-reliance that would make them reject mind-altering prescription drugs from the start.
- They readily accepted medical expertise on how to regulate their lives.

We can see the same characteristics that resulted in Mrs. Dukakis's and Mrs. Ford's reliance on prescription drugs at work when the two women enthusiastically embraced medical treatment for their drug problems! Betty Ford's and Kitty Dukakis's allegiance to their treatments—including psychoactive medications—expresses the same kind of dependence on external agents and the wishful thinking that their problems can be medically isolated that got them in trouble with addiction in the first place.

Addiction appears among a small number of people who outwardly enjoy many advantages in life. Among this group, a still smaller percentage destroy themselves through their drug use. One was basketball star Len Bias, who took massive doses of cocaine as he cut all his classes during his last year at the University of Maryland. Another was John Belushi, who was grossly overweight, had a serious respiratory problem, and was a heavy cigarette smoker; who was alienated from his wife and from his work; and who in the last week of his life had taken large doses of heroin, cocaine, alcohol, Quaaludes, marijuana, and amphetamines.

Then there was David Kennedy, son of Robert Kennedy, who died with medically prescribed antidepressants and tranquilizers as well as cocaine in his system. The best medical care available couldn't save Kennedy from his inability to stay in one place and hold a job. Similarly, Jill Ireland's adopted son, Jason McCallum, died of the accumulated effects of drug use. Like the young Kennedy, Ireland's son had been in numerous treatment programs and was currently under the care of physicians (and was receiving several prescription drugs) when he died. These cases are horrible and tragic. But they don't make the case that addiction is a disease and that medical treatment is the cure. Once again, to be consistent, we might ask whether the doctors who prescribed the drugs that contributed to the deaths of these young men should be imprisoned or executed.

Drugs, however, are not the source of the problems displayed by the relatively few middle-class drug users who become addicted. We don't learn this obvious fact from watching the innumerable television specials that dwell exclusively on the alcohol and drug abuse of a few hard-core teenagers to the exclusion of any understanding of the children's family and psychological problems. The research on adolescent drug use produces results almost completely at odds with these media impressions. In the Michigan study of student drug use, the best predictors of high-school students' involvement with cocaine were, first, use of marijuana; second, truancy; third, cigarette smoking.[39] Another study found that adolescent drug users displayed more problem behaviors, placed less value on achievement, and were more alienated from school and organized recreational activities than non–drug users.[40] A third study identified the following key factors as predisposing adolescents to use drugs: "membership in social groups favorable to the use of drugs, participation in delinquent activities, and lack of attachment to conventional institutions."[41]

These traits in nearly all cases *precede* the young person's drug use and abuse. Two UCLA researchers summarized the research on drug abuse by the young: "These results [indicate] that . . . the abuse or problem use of drugs is generated by internal distress, limited life opportunities, and unhappiness."[42] A study by two Berkeley researchers took this point one step further, creating a furor when it was published in 1990. The researchers, Jonathan Shedler and Jack Block, were able to predict which *preschool* children were likely to abuse drugs when they were eighteen, based on their negative personality profiles as children. *Moreover, those youngsters with the best-integrated personalities were likely to use drugs in a controlled fashion, rather than abstaining altogether:* "the undercontrolled, alienated personality attributes of problem drinkers and the overcontrolled, diffident personality attributes of alcohol abstainers were quite similar to the personality attributes that characterize frequent drug users and drug abstainers in the present study."[43]

The authors provide a fuller picture of substance abusers:

> At age 18, the frequent [drug] users appear unable to invest in, or derive pleasure from, meaningful personal relationships. . . . Neither do they appear capable of investing in

> school and work, or of channeling their energies toward meaningful future goals. . . . The impulses are not adequately transformed or mediated by a broader system of values and goals. . . . [Frequent users are thus characterized] by the psychological triad of *alienation, impulsivity,* and *psychological distress.* The data indicate that the roots of this syndrome predate adolescence and *predate initiation of drug use.*[44]

Inner-City Addiction

The addictions of David Kennedy, Jason McCallum, and John Belushi are exceptions to the usual demographic pattern. We are constantly told that addiction is just as common for the middle class as for the underprivileged. Yet research and common sense consistently disagree. For example, the NIDA survey found that heavier drug use is more common among the underprivileged and ghettoized.[45] As we watch news stories of inner cities—like Washington, D.C.—almost completely disrupted by drug use, we are asked to believe that just as many people in the suburbs are completely absorbed by drug use, only they don't allow it to show. But if lack of control defines addiction, then to say that many middle-class people control their drug use is to say that they are not addicted.

These issues were sharpened in the United States in the late 1980s as more and more Americans turned away from drugs, yet addiction among inner-city Americans worsened, along with drug-related violence. In 1985, twenty-three million Americans reported that they had used an illicit drug during the previous month. By 1988, this figure had dropped to 14.5 million. Yet daily cocaine use, primarily among those worst-off economically, rose during the same period.[46] These trends continued in the 1990 NIDA national drug survey. These contrary trends—declining use, rising addiction—demonstrate that drug use and addiction are very different psychological and social realities, and that reducing the one will not necessarily reduce the other. They also document our society's worsening division into two cultures—a mainstream capable of controlling its drug use and an intractable core that does not find sufficient reasons to give up its addictions.

This phenomenon is summed up in the title of a *New York Times* article announcing the downturn in middle-class cocaine use in the latter part of the 1980s: "Rich vs. Poor: Drug Patterns Are Diverging—Drop in Drug Use Is Seen, Except Among the Poor."[47] The stabilizing factors that some of the middle class fail to achieve are often denied by birth to large numbers of ghetto youth. One cocaine researcher, psychiatrist David Musto, described the situation in this way:

> The question we must be asking now is not why people take drugs, but why do people stop. In the inner city, the factors that counterbalance drug use . . . often are not there. It is harder for people with nothing to say no to drugs.[48]

A sobering study conducted at UCLA, moreover, found that youths from drug-using environments do not significantly improve their lives even after they stop using drugs![49] So far are drugs from being a primary cause of social problems in the ghetto that even removing drugs as an immediate issue in a person's life counts for little in that overwhelmingly negative environment.

Black Americans, rural as well as urban, have for some time had a higher-than-average incidence of severe drug use. For example, Vietnam veterans from the inner city, even if they had not been involved with narcotics previously, more readily stayed addicted after their military service than other veterans.[50] The crisis of the urban ghetto grows out of dislocations (extending over half a century) in employment, housing, family life, education, and the whole economic, social, and political relationship between the ghetto and the larger society. Adding drugs to this volatile mix is like throwing a lighted match on oil-soaked rags, as the crack epidemic has shown.

Thus, we see, our futile drug war and treatment based on medical detoxification both make the same fundamental error—they focus on the drug rather than the user's life fabric. In the front-page *New York Times* article quoted early in this chapter, Herbert Kleber (deputy to former drug czar William Bennett) asserted that crack addiction can be treated, but "the addict must be given a place in family and social structures where they may never have been before"—a process he describes as "habilitation more than rehabilitation." The director of the National Institute on Drug Abuse, Charles Schuster, declared, based on research about drug treatments, that "the best predictor of success is whether the addict has a job."[51]

Even as we emphasize that the ghetto provides more fertile ground for addiction than the suburbs, we must also make clear that controlled drug use is not alien to the inner city. That is, most inner-city users also bring their substance abuse under control, and for the very same reasons—solidifying family and work lives—as youthful middle-class substance abusers. While the maturing out process is more subject to disruption in the ghetto, it is still a powerful force for positive change there. The growth of an inner-city underclass of youths who have no ties to ordinary socializing influences is the greatest threat to the reduction of drug abuse in this setting. Nonetheless, some informed observers report that more inner-city youths are rejecting heavy use of alcohol and marijuana, as well as crack, because they want to maintain control of their lives.[52]

It is encouraging that prominent drug experts have come to realize that crack addiction, like every other addiction (as we first argued fifteen years ago in *Love and Addiction*), is a product of the user's circumstances and expectations more than of the drug's chemical properties. Drug scares, like those spread about marijuana in the film *Reefer Madness*, appear regularly. Just as regularly, reputable research finds that these depictions are inaccurate and ignore the reality of the controlled or purposeful nature of most use, as well as of the previously disturbed lives of those who become addicted. In reality, no drug is addictive in and of itself. Rather, drugs have characteristics that make them addictive for some individuals and groups at particular places and times. Their addictiveness depends on how they are perceived and how and why they are used and by whom. As the researchers who investigated drug use by Vietnam veterans noted: "Heroin is 'worse' than amphetamines or barbiturates only because 'worse' people [that is, those more prone to social problems in the first place] use it."[53]

CHAPTER 4

SMOKING

THE TOUGHEST HABIT TO LICK?

IN CHAPTER 3, we reported that addicts themselves said crack cocaine was easier to quit than smoking cigarettes. This information was based on a number of surveys of addicts and alcoholics in treatment. In a study published in the *Journal of the American Medical Association,* for example, one thousand people who sought treatment for alcohol or drug dependence at the Addiction Research Foundation in Toronto were questioned. Although these patients usually rated cigarettes as being less pleasurable than alcohol or drugs, 57 percent said that cigarettes would be harder to give up than the substance for which they were seeking treatment.[1]

When we speak at addiction conferences, we ask the audiences—consisting largely of counselors and members of A.A. and similar programs—what drug they think is the hardest drug to quit. Nearly all shout out, "Cigarettes!" We then ask how many of them have quit smoking. Usually from one-third to one-half of those present have done so. Finally, we ask how many used a treatment program to quit. *At most,* a few hands go up. In audiences where more than a hundred people have quit smoking, we sometimes find no one who relied on a formal program to do it. Thus, an audience of people committed to the disease-treatment model have just told us that a very large number of them have given up an addiction tougher than drugs or alcohol without treatment.

The ex-smokers in these audiences are representative of smokers in the United States as a whole. The Office on Smoking and Health reports that 45 percent of all Americans (and 60 percent of college graduates) who have ever smoked no longer do so. By now, 30 percent of adult Americans—more than forty million—are former smokers. What's more, 90 percent of those who have stopped smoking have done it on their own.[2]

The 1987 surgeon general's report, *Nicotine Addiction,* announced that cigarette smoking is as addictive as heroin, cocaine, and alcohol. We have seen that this is true. Former Surgeon General C. Everett Koop had the admirable goal of informing the public that addiction is not associated only with illegal substances and that tobacco companies are purveying a highly addictive substance. Unfortunately, another message many derived from this report is that cigarettes must be awfully hard—perhaps impossible—for smokers to quit on their own.

This is certainly a point that various medical treatments and smoke-ending programs try to drive home in their advertisements. For example, Merrell Dow Pharmaceuticals has for a number of years taken out full-page ads proclaiming that *"physical dependence on nicotine"* is the major factor in people's smoking habits, and that because the unpleasant sensations of nicotine withdrawal "can defeat even a strong willpower, your chances of quitting successfully are greater with a program that provides an alternative source of nicotine. . . ." This ad is meant to encourage people to have their doctor put them on Nicorette, a nicotine gum marketed by Merrell Dow.

A research team that studied the effectiveness of Nicorette therapy published their results in the *Journal of the American Medical Association.* In this study, 10 percent of those receiving the nicotine gum and 7 percent of those receiving a gum that didn't contain nicotine were still not smoking after a year. The researchers concluded that the value of Nicorette in helping people quit smoking permanently is "either small or nonexistent."[3] This conclusion was criticized by a Dow spokesperson, who said that calling the gum ineffective because people were smoking a year after using it was "like blaming an antidepressant [drug] if a person gets depressed again a year after discontinuing the drug."[4] Must people continue taking Nicorette in order to stay off cigarettes? Is the purpose of the treatment not to free people from nicotine addiction, but simply to have them chew it rather than smoke it?

Many people have ignored the importunings of Merrell Dow's ads: "If you want to quit smoking for good, see your doctor." Stanley Schachter, a Columbia University psychologist, found that more than

60 percent of the people he polled in two communities who had tried to quit smoking had succeeded.[5] These people, on the average, had not smoked for more than seven years. Heavier smokers (three or more packs a day) were just as likely to have quit as lighter smokers—thus disproving Schachter's own previously stated view that heavy smokers are permanently "hooked" on nicotine.

The remission rate in this study was as high as it was because Schachter wasn't examining the results of a program at the end of a year, but the results of years or decades of efforts to quit. Schachter nonetheless found that those who never entered a treatment program to stop smoking were more likely to have quit than those who did! Research regularly shows that people do as well to quit smoking on their own as through a treatment program, but some question whether self-quitters actually do better.[6] However, the most comprehensive survey of American smoking, conducted by the Office on Smoking and Health at the Centers for Disease Control, strongly supported Schachter's results. Writing in the *Journal of the American Medical Association,* the researchers summarized their investigation of the methods used by the forty-four million Americans who have quit smoking:

> Daily cigarette consumption [that is, how heavily people smoked] did not predict whether persons would succeed or fail during their attempts to quit smoking. Rather, the cessation method used was the strongest predictor of success. Among smokers who attempted cessation within the previous 10 years, *47.5% of persons who tried to quit on their own were successful whereas only 23.6% of persons who used cessation programs succeeded.*[7]

This does *not* mean that those who quit on their own find it easy to do. It does mean, however, that the amount of assistance a formal program can give one on such a perilous journey is limited, *and even counterproductive.* For example, far from being helpful, Nicorette therapy produced results in the clinical trial in which 10 percent of smokers quit that are *worse* than those of other therapies, or of people's efforts to quit on their own. In the Centers for Disease Control study that found people are twice as likely to succeed when they quit on their own as when they seek treatment, nicotine-gum therapy was the *least* successful treatment of all.

The problem is that many people believe the ads for Nicorette programs that the *treatment* will get them off cigarettes without any effort on their part. Imagine the difference between two people who want to quit. The first says, "I *must* quit smoking now or I'm going to kill myself." The other person says, "I'm afraid I won't be able to stand the discomfort of quitting. I hear they have ways of making withdrawal painless." As a result, the second person signs up for a medical program that promises to minimize withdrawal discomfort. Who do you think is more likely to succeed? By holding out the prospect of some magical, medical way of getting off cigarettes, the treatment program actually undercuts the key to quitting: that is, the realization that you yourself must confront and overcome the discomfort of being without cigarettes.

How do smokers actually quit on their own? In Schachter's study:

> Roughly two-thirds reported that their only technique was deciding to stop. "I took the cigarettes out of my pocket," one said, "threw them away, and that was it." Another explained: "I said 'the hell with it,' and never smoked again."[8]

One study of people who quit on their own found that most quit abruptly ("cold-turkey") rather than gradually. Few used technical aids or smoking substitutes, although some did distract themselves at moments of craving with food, exercise, or chewing gum—nothing very complicated.[9] As columnist Russell Baker has put it, "To give up smoking, you quit smoking."[10]

We do not mean to make the task of quitting an addiction like smoking, the very toughest drug addiction, seem overly simple. After all, many of those who quit on their own also relapse. However, seriousness of intent and persistence of effort are what accomplishes the task, and eventually more than half of the smokers who try to quit succeed in doing so. Those who quit on their own may have tried to quit one or more times previously, but they try again until they succeed. In other words, quitting is part of a larger evolution in a person's life. For example, blue-collar workers in one study were finally able to stop smoking when they attained greater job security and thus had less anxiety at work.[11]

Based on a national survey in Britain, Alan Marsh concluded that people quit smoking when they "lose faith in what they used to think smoking did for them," while at the same time they create "a powerful new set of beliefs that non-smoking is, of itself, a desirable and rewarding state."[12] People succeed at quitting, in other words, when they get more from not smoking than from smoking. When the balance of forces in their lives—their concern (and their family's concern) for their health, the opinion of fellow workers, the image of self-control (rather than the image of masculinity, sophistication, or sexual attractiveness they previously associated with smoking)—tips decisively in favor of not smoking, they can make their resolve to quit stick. This may mean returning to the same method until it works or searching out methods that may work better for them than have previous, failed attempts to quit.

To someone who is still smoking, making the passage from being a smoker to being a former smoker, secure in other satisfactions and values, may seem a daunting challenge. We don't want to oversimplify any more than we want to overcomplicate the changes in a person's life that prepare the ground for him or her to stop smoking. Rather, we will describe and illustrate this process of change with examples of what smoking can mean, and what ceasing to smoke can mean, in the larger context of a person's life. No techniques can substitute for the inner personal reorientation that is the key to quitting; techniques can only express and reinforce that personal growth, as we describe in detail in part II of this book.

Learning to Depend on Cigarettes

Cigarette smoking is harder to quit than other addictions, like crack, because (a) it fits easily into an ordinary, productive life-style and (b) commercial cigarettes are an unparalleled delivery system for getting the drug into the blood and to the nervous system in the most efficacious way possible. Respectable people smoke cigarettes openly while going about their work and family lives—something far more difficult for illicit drug addicts or alcoholics. Despite its legality, as the surgeon general has indicated, smoking is an addiction like any other, be it to drugs, alcohol, or whatever. As we have seen with drugs and alcohol, however, this means that cigarette addiction is much more than a chemical process.

Smoking is another addiction to which lower-income, less-well-educated people are more vulnerable. According to 1989 figures, 18 percent of college graduates in the United States smoke, compared with 34 percent of those who never went to college.[13] College students are far less likely to smoke than others in the same age group.[14] Yet in 1964, when the first Surgeon General's Report on smoking appeared, virtually identical percentages of both groups smoked. Obviously, Americans who do not have a college education have hardly reduced their smoking, as is shown in the accompanying graph.[15]

Also, as we have seen with other addictions, people who are addicted to substances such as alcohol or narcotics are overwhelmingly likely to smoke cigarettes as well (just observe all the smoking that goes on at A.A. meetings). For example, most clinical studies of alcoholics find that 90 percent or more smoke.[16] The same is true for drug abusers. In addition, smokers are more likely to drink when they drive and have higher rates of traffic violations and auto accidents than nonsmokers (so that several auto-insurance companies now offer lower rates to nonsmokers).[17] Smoking cigarettes is also one of the leading

Percentage of Americans Smoking by Educational Level, 1980–1987

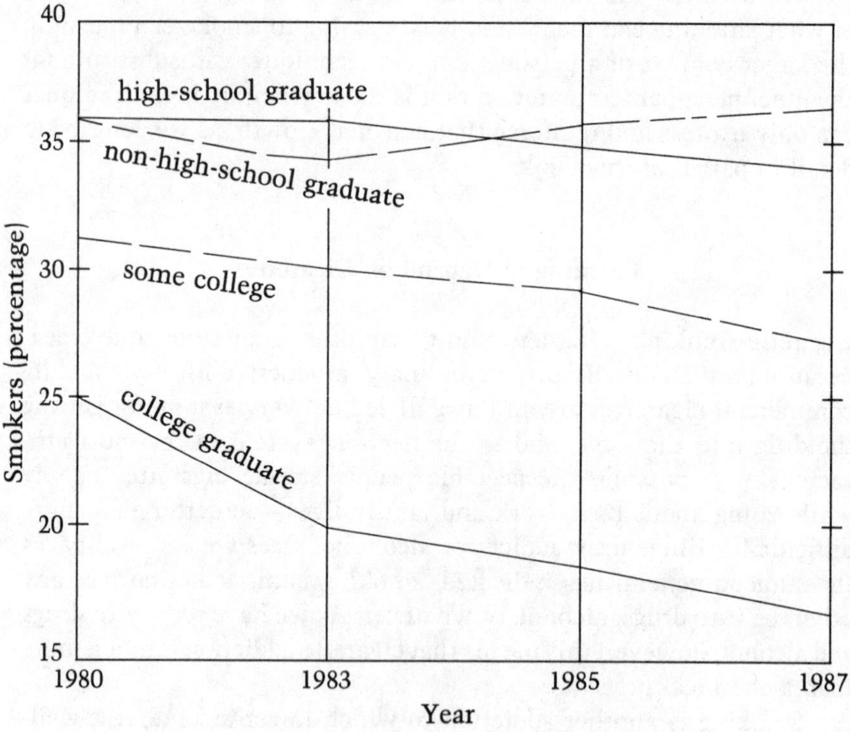

Adapted from 1989 U.S. Surgeon General's Report

risk factors for high-school students who abuse cocaine and other illicit drugs.[18] In other words, smoking is very often a sign of heedlessness toward health and safety. Cigarette addicts are more antisocial and less concerned for their physical well-being than nonsmokers.

Even so, smoking has until recently fit comfortably into mainstream American life. Most addicts and reckless drivers do smoke, but there has also been a large group of ordinary smokers who were unlikely to be addicted to other drugs or otherwise behave antisocially. As we shall see, the climate has changed significantly in the past several decades, and the epidemiology of smoking has likewise shifted considerably. This is reflected in the changing social-class structure of smoking addiction—in the 1950s, it would not have been possible, as it is today, to label smoking a largely working-class habit.

What is it that smoking does for people—for a good many who abuse other substances and for some otherwise nonaddicted individuals as well? In general, people smoke to maintain their emotional balance under varying degrees of stress. Psychologist Paul Nesbitt found that, whereas smokers are more anxious than nonsmokers, they feel more calm when they are smoking.[19] By using the nicotine high from a cigarette to maintain their internal stimulation, smokers seem to protect themselves from the ups and downs of external stimulation. In other words, smoking masks the tension the smoker would otherwise feel. One woman who no longer smoked remarked, "I used cigarettes for the same purpose others use alcohol—to deaden my emotions, to dampen my emotional force, so that I would just feel the black and white, not all the gradations in between."

As long as an addiction fits in with society's values, it will be accepted legally and socially. For most of this century, "normal" middle-class Americans, finding that cigarette smoking improved their concentration and increased their productivity, made smoking a regular—often hourly or even more frequent—routine. But the fact that smoking was accepted matter-of-factly by our society does not mean that ordinary middle-class addicts led lives of perfect harmony and balance and were only addicted as a matter of happenstance. All people experience fear, insecurity, discomfort, weariness. More is expected of us than we can fulfill, and our energy and attention levels are not always up to the demands of our jobs or families. We are not blessed with ideally fulfilling lives. For some, smoking has been a device for negotiating the gap between human frailty and a fast-paced, sometimes emotionally draining world. The more a person relies on artificial means of emotional regulation, however, the less practiced he or she becomes at regulating tension and anxiety naturally. Thus begins the cycle of dependence on nicotine, parallel to that which people experience with alcohol or drugs, in which the psychoactive effects of a substance become for a time an essential means of gaining a desired emotional state.

In a study of twenty-seven hundred smokers in Britain, Alan Marsh traced why smoking is taken up in adolescence and how the habit is reinforced in adulthood. He found that the belief in smoking as a way of controlling one's emotions—a crucial concern in adolescence—is a key factor in maintaining the habit:

> When adults say that adolescents are immature they mean that they have problems with their affect control. Their moods swing wildly from depression to euphoria, they are rash and gauche in conversation, alternately brash and embarrassed in company. Adolescents who take up smoking rapidly learn to attribute their growing ability to control their moods to their smoking. A cigarette covers embarrassment, lifts depression, restores youthful cool. What the smoking adolescent never has the chance to learn is that, like his non-smoking friends, he would have acquired that knack of affect control anyway. It is called growing up and nearly everyone does it, with or without the help of cigarettes. But he passes into adulthood firm in the belief that his ability to top and tail the range of his emotional responses depends on a daily intake of nicotine. Smoking is a *learned* experience.[20]

Smoking is also a way for adolescents to feel grown up. In particular, the most rebellious teens are the ones likely to pick up a smoking habit as a badge of their independence. When they get older, of course, many realize instead that smoking has become a badge of dependence.

Like all addictions, despite its undoubted pharmacological effects on the nervous system, smoking is a learned dependence that can be unlearned. Nothing about tobacco's reliably stimulating effects is *inherently* addictive; the reliance on these effects must be acquired over time. The beliefs that one can be physically enslaved by tobacco and that one cannot withstand withdrawal serve only to perpetuate the addiction. Consider the plight of Roger, a highly educated man who thinks his smoking addiction is a physiological imperative. Alone among his friends, he still smokes and believes that he can never really quit. Roger's training is in biomedical science; he is accustomed to thinking of human behavior in terms of endorphins or other brain chemicals rather than processes over which he exerts personal control. Only, unlike the many colleagues of his who have quit smoking, Roger takes his beliefs to the extreme of dictating (or rationalizing) his behavior. When supposed neurological mechanisms are used to excuse or explain bad habits that people need to oppose and change, that is not science, but its antithesis.

Unlearning the Dependence: An Existential Passage

According to the University of Michigan's annual surveys, while the use of other drugs by high-school students declined, cigarette smoking among the young remained relatively stable between 1984 and 1989.[21] The large numbers of young people who still begin smoking underscore the fact that fewer people are smoking not because fewer are taking up smoking, but because so many are giving it up. In Britain, noting that nearly half of the men aged fifty to fifty-nine who have ever smoked regularly no longer do so, Marsh concluded ironically, "It is not open to us to believe that the power of nicotine to produce dependence has mysteriously lessened."[22] Somehow, more and more people have been able to discard the false lesson they learned in their teens that they needed cigarettes to appear sophisticated, energize themselves, and regulate their feelings.

Obviously, the thoroughgoing campaign to inform smokers of the health hazards of smoking has had an impact. In addition to its direct influence, the growing awareness of the unhealthfulness of smoking has contributed to a new set of social pressures that work against smoking. Although society still values the productivity that smoking supposedly enhances, society is coming to value other things as well, and these are things that smoking threatens or undermines. More and more, we like to see people contribute to creating a clean, healthful, pleasant environment for others. We also want people to stay healthy themselves, because health is of value in itself and because illness is costly to families and society.

For some who have not been moved by the health message alone, these social pressures have made the difference. Teased and chastised by family and friends, hounded by nonsmokers and smoking regulations in airplanes, restaurants, and the workplace, smokers find themselves increasingly alienated from the best aspects of society—until they accept the new social consensus that smoking is "dirty" and swear off it themselves. This consensus, however, has been heavily concentrated in white-collar worlds, among people like business managers, physicians, and college teachers who find it more and more burdensome to maintain a smoking habit. Even those who do continue to smoke in these settings often do so privately (for example, only in their offices), a kind of personal choice that shows that even addicted smokers exert control over their habit.

But these influences are not felt equally strongly everywhere. For example, the pressures generated by our new health consciousness have little impact on people in the underclass and on many blue-collar workers. It is still possible to be a construction or factory worker or to carry out certain high-pressure sales jobs while smoking. In fact, in some of these groups, it is almost expected that people will smoke. The course of the antismoking movement bears out just how powerful are group social norms for affecting behavior, to the point of causing masses of people to quit severe addictions. At the same time, the recent epidemiological changes in smoking show us how unevenly the health messages we broadcast are received, and how key groups—like ghetto populations—we wish to reach are often unaffected by these messages.

Health considerations and social pressures can be key ingredients in the process of *unlearning* the dependence on cigarettes that was learned in adolescence. Attitudes that can lead a person to give up smoking are those concerned with:

- *health* (avoidance of heart and lung disease, decreasing tension through exercise, improved stamina);
- *acceptance by others* (family, friends, lovers, co-workers, strangers);
- *aesthetic values* (clean clothes and body, better complexion, ability to smell and taste);
- *self-esteem* (pride in having stopped smoking and in being a nonsmoker);
- *saving money.*

The change in attitudes has two overall components:

▸ Smoking goes from being *good* ("It keeps me on even keel," "It gets me through the workday," "I look 'cool' ") to *bad* ("It's filthy," "It will kill me," "People give me dirty looks," "I'll have to leave this important meeting to smoke," "I don't like being a slave to a habit").

▸ Not smoking goes from being *bad* ("I'm tense, irritable," "I don't know what to do with my hands") to *good* ("I can taste my food," "I'm in control of my life," "I'm setting an example for my children," "My throat doesn't hurt").

The more decisive this shift in attitudes, the stronger the person's desire to stop smoking (or commitment to stay stopped). A change in attitude toward smoking leads to an intention to stop smoking, which in turn leads to an attempt or series of attempts to stop.[23] The decision to continue to smoke or to stop is a choice, one that a person periodically reevaluates on the basis of shifting positive and negative attitudes toward smoking.

One's success in giving up smoking depends largely on two factors: the strength of one's *desire* to stop and the strength of one's *belief* that one can stop. In a study conducted at the University of Washington by psychologist Alan Marlatt and his colleagues, the smokers who had the most success both at quitting initially and at staying off cigarettes were the ones who were most insistent at the outset of the study that they wanted to quit.[24] Studies repeatedly show that the best predictor of successful abstinence is smokers' confidence that they can stay off cigarettes.[25] The person who begins an effort to quit by saying, "I don't really think I can do it," is giving a very good indication he or she will not succeed.

As smoking ceases to be rewarding, other incompatible rewards take its place. Not that this necessarily happens all at once, or even in a smooth, linear progression. It takes time, something that should not discourage people. Indeed, in Marsh's British study, those who had made several recent attempts to quit, far from being discouraged by their "failure," were emboldened to try again. Marsh explains how such relapses can contribute to positive change:

> As their faith in the benefits of smoking diminishes and as their beliefs in the benefits of not smoking grow stronger,

> so smokers are precipitated into experimental forays into non-smoking. As their new set of non-smoking attitudes becomes established it is then rewarded by first-hand experience of non-smoking. In this way they pass hesitatingly from being unquestioning habitual smokers eventually to become enduring ex-smokers.[26]

This description also can help us understand why upper- and middle-income people have an easier time giving up smoking than lower-income people. In part, it is a question of having more resources with which to create substitute rewards. A blue-collar worker weighed down by a demanding, unfulfilling job, by a tight household budget ready to rip open at the seams, and by unattainable material aspirations is less able to devise alternative gratifications ("I've had a tough day today, I think I'll play tennis or I'll take the family out to dinner") to replace the readily available smoke break.

People disengage from smoking at all stages of the life cycle. Those who do it right after college (or after only a few years of smoking) are those for whom smoking has been a response to temporary stresses brought on by the disempowerment of youth. They are people whose life-style, personal associations, and opportunity levels rule out smoking as a long-term habit. Others take ten, fifteen, or twenty years to "mature out," often quitting when life's stresses level off in middle age or when the physical effects of smoking can no longer be ignored. Then there are those, like Jerry Lewis and Governor John Y. Brown of Kentucky, who knock off four-pack-a-day habits after open-heart surgery. Whenever Jerry Lewis feels like smoking, he says, he looks down at the surgical incision running the length of his chest.

In 1979, Dr. Frank A. Oski wrote an article in *The New York Times* rationalizing, as a physician, that smoking was good for his health. Five years later, after having a heart attack at the age of fifty-one, he published another article announcing that he had stopped smoking. "Strange how the evidence that linked smoking to heart disease appeared equivocal to me last month," he commented ruefully, "and now the same data appear overwhelmingly convincing." Dr. Oski advises the reader:

> Was it easy to stop? Sure. Here is all you have to do. First, experience a severe crushing pain under your breastbone as

> you finish a cigarette. Next, have yourself admitted to a coronary-care unit and stripped of your clothing and other belongings. Finally, remain in the unit at absolute bed rest for four days while smoking is prohibited. This broke my habit. See if it works for you.[27]

A few of those who do not heed the increasingly insistent warnings over the years—from their hearts and lungs as well as from their social environments—spend their last months making television commercials imploring others not to smoke, or else suing tobacco companies for selling them an addictive poison. This is the classical case, unfortunately, of closing the barn door after the horse gets out. Though we might envy those who never started smoking or who quit after a couple of years, anyone is capable of responding to negative feedback about smoking at any point. People do it all the time, more and more of them with each decade of life. Here is an example of a man who did it as he entered middle age.

Uncle Ozzie

A man we know affectionately as Uncle Ozzie quit smoking in his early forties after maintaining a three-pack-a-day habit for a quarter-century, from the time he was a teenager. Ozzie worked at a bench, a proud and devoted union man—indeed, he was shop steward. One day, when the price of cigarettes had been raised, Ozzie prepared to put the additional coins in a machine to purchase a pack. A co-worker observing Ozzie joked, "Look at Oscar, the sucker! He'd pay any price for a smoke. The tobacco companies have him by the balls!"

Ozzie turned to the man, looked at him for a moment, and said, "You're right. I'm going to quit."

"Then can I have that pack of cigarettes?" his co-worker teased.

"What, and throw away the money I just spent?" Ozzie replied.

Ozzie smoked that pack, but he has never smoked again since that day over thirty years ago. In that moment of awakening, the contradiction between his smoking addiction and the value he placed on independence from management and corporate power loomed so large that he could no longer ignore it. From that point on, to continue smoking—to admit that the "bosses" controlled his life—would have been more painful than to quit.

Uncle Ozzie claims that he never thought about quitting until the day he actually quit. Still, the story a person tells years later may idealize the process, just hitting the high points rather than tracing the evolution of consciousness that went on both before and after the climactic moment. Well before he smoked his last pack, Ozzie may have had glimpses of how he was harming his family and his health by smoking.

Some people, like Ozzie, experience quitting in a matter-of-fact way. Others find it to be a personal liberation that opens up new possibilities and fulfillments. Making such a crucial choice for health can often inspire other changes, which eventually make the very idea of smoking unthinkable. Some question whether an ex-smoker must always bear the identity of smoker waiting (or potentially able) to relapse. Columnist and ex-smoker Russell Baker doesn't believe so: "Three or four years after going off tobacco, you forget you ever used the stuff and lose all interest in it except as an excuse for bullying pitiable smoke addicts and doing some strutting about your own smoke-free superiority."[28]

Baker's period of identity change is three or four years—he once described in his column how he returned to smoking after having a cigarette at a party soon after he quit for the first time. But, remembering that the belief in one's ability to stay off cigarettes is the key, we see that Baker restoked his resolve and quit again, this time for good. Others find the transition to permanent abstinence takes less or more time. But there is no doubt that for some, eventually many, the shift is permanent, like the woman who said, "After I had my first child, I was more likely to saw my arm off at the elbow than to ever start smoking again." This kind of firm refutation of addiction, to cigarettes or whatever, is possible, desirable, and common. Uncle Ozzie, for instance, is really not worried about returning to smoking.

CHAPTER 5

OBESITY

ARE PEOPLE BIOLOGICALLY PROGRAMMED TO BE FAT?

THE ADDICTION PROBLEM that affects the most Americans is eating and overweight. *Sixty percent of Americans* believe they are overweight.[1] If we decide that overweight is a disease and that obesity is biologically determined, then practically every American home is implicated in this disease. Moreover, since eating is legal, ubiquitous, and—for most people—pleasurable, overweight and overeating may be the *hardest* addiction to overcome. In addition, overweight/overeating—and not drug or alcohol abuse—is the fastest-growing substance-abuse problem among the young.

There are two ways in which biological theories tell us we can't control our weight or our eating. One type of theory is that weight level and fatness are inbred, and that we can't fight the body weight we are born to. The other seeks to explain excessive eating, binge eating, and eating disorders such as anorexia and bulimia as addictive diseases. Both natural body weight and addictive overeating are used to explain obesity. Meanwhile, anorexia (or pathological undereating) can be viewed either as an addiction or as an unhealthy effort to overcome one's natural body weight. Other addicted eaters, called bulimics, try to keep their weight down through vomiting or the use of diuretics.

Both biological and disease theories agree that eating habits or weight cannot be controlled consciously and are not affected by the state of our lives. Both types of theories regard overeating leading to obesity as a biological imperative. From the preset body-weight standpoint, if you're fat, your body wants you to be that way, and eating less for a time just builds up the pressure subsequently to overeat and to regain your lost weight. From the disease standpoint, some physical sensitivity to food dictates that you overeat: you must attend meetings and avoid certain foods, thus staving off the inevitable loss of control that comes if you eat these foods.

We present the contrary view that, like all addictions, excessive eating is a way of coping with life's stresses—one that provides predictable satisfactions for people. It makes one feel good for the moment, but it usually proves to have even greater costs. As with other compulsive habits, destructive eating is triggered by feelings and situations to which a person has learned to react by eating. Addiction to food differs from other substance addictions, however, in that it represents the overdoing of a habit that is necessary for survival and is a part of every healthy life. Unlike smoking, drugs, or drinking, there is no avoiding the need for moderation and self-regulation in eating. We have to come to terms with food and to learn to approach it sensibly and responsibly.

What is clearly wrong with biological theories about overweight, like those about other addictions, is that they shortchange the complexity of how people learn to eat and regulate their weight. Eating habits, obesity, and weight control express one's way of life, one's values, and one's self-conception. One's physical self-image is part of a sense of belonging to a certain community or culture, as moving up or down in the world, as being like or unlike the people around one. It goes with a feeling of being satisfied or dissatisfied, confident or fearful, assertive or passive. It is a statement about oneself, about who one wants to be or what one wants to be like. Just as alcoholics and drug addicts give up virulent addictions when they no longer see the addicted life-style as suitable to their self-images, obesity, overeating, and eating disorders like bulimia and anorexia often melt away when people enter new phases of their lives.

Can There Be a Twelve-Step Approach to Eating Diseases?

With food—precisely because it is a necessity of life—the idea of addictive eating as an uncontrollable, chemically based reaction to a foreign substance becomes very hard to maintain. The loosely reasoned views offered by the disease model vis-à-vis alcohol, narcotics, cocaine, or nicotine must be modified drastically—especially the prescription of total, lifelong abstinence. Telling people they are powerless over food or eating, after all, is a road map to nowhere. Indeed, the ways disease-theory advocates adapt A.A. and abstinence models to eating disorders actually discredit the whole conception of addiction to which they subscribe.

There is a twelve-step equivalent to A.A. for overeaters called Overeaters Anonymous (O.A.) that emphasizes the fat person's powerlessness over food and that relies on group meetings and sponsors. In this way, O.A. takes over the lifetime-addict-identity and the conversion-experience aspects of A.A. Some in O.A. inveigh against eating certain substances—usually refined sugar or refined/bleached flour—in the same way A.A. identifies alcohol as the root of all evil. But the very nature of eating problems—where real abstinence is impossible—has forced O.A. to be more flexible. Unlike A.A., where one "diet" (total abstinence) fits all, O.A. allows members to select their own diets to follow, with the help of the group.

Private treatment centers face similar difficulties in approaching eating problems as diseases. For example, some treatment programs for bulimia define abstinence as no longer indulging in binges or vomiting. A program teaching this kind of abstinence is actually making the cure into the treatment (this is called a tautology) by saying, "Don't do what you came to treatment to learn to stop doing." On the other hand, anorexia (compulsive undereating), like the "starvation" phase of the bulimia cycle, already represents a misguided attempt at abstinence. Curing an eating disorder clearly means getting beyond the "all-or-nothing" model of consumption which A.A. has made the centerpiece of its treatment program.

Despite the absurdity of abstinence-oriented treatment for eating problems, the imagery of food addiction as a lifelong disease is tenaciously promoted. According to the director of the eating-disorders treatment program at Saint Cabrini Hospital in Seattle, eating disorders are "a chronic, primary disease with an identifiable progression and predictable symptoms," characterized by "denial around food."[2] A physician promoting his eating program at Mount Sinai Hospital in Cleveland wrote in the hospital's *Caring* newsletter (Fall 1985):

> "Obesity is an incurable disease," stated Dr. Hazelton. "We don't know its complete etiology. We can, however, put a patient into remission for a lifetime through our weight-loss

> program. . . . We try to make our patients aware that their obesity is a disease, that it is incurable, and that they will need maintenance assistance for the rest of their lives."

Each addiction has its own fatalistic myth that explains why that particular addiction is overpowering and lifelong and demands perpetual treatment. We have heard about the universally addicting properties of narcotics, the mysterious genetic traits that make some people inevitably lose control of their drinking, the "nicotine dependence" that enslaves smokers. We have seen, however, that these word pictures do not describe the behavior of actual human beings exposed to the substances in question. The same is true when the substance is food, particularly when an eating program actually applies the alcoholism model literally to food. Such programs declare that certain foods or types of foods are addictive for some people in the same way alcohol is for the alcoholic. The addicted eater, they say, is "powerless" over these foods—typically refined sugar—and must therefore avoid eating them altogether. Two doctors wrote a book, *The Hidden Addiction,* claiming sugar as the source not only of food addiction, but of *all* addictions.[3] According to this interpretation, it is the alcoholic's conversion of alcohol into sugar that sets off drunken loss of control.

Because this prohibition is so unrealistic in today's world, some treatment programs speak of "sugar addiction" metaphorically, treating sugar as a symbol of uncontrolled eating. Others teach abstinence not from sugar in every possible form but only from sweet desserts. All of this proves just how relative abstinence can be, and how the individual eater has to decide what the word means. At the same time, all former compulsive eaters at some point have to allow themselves occasional slips and yet strive to continue with the sensible eating they have learned, or else they must limit their lives so drastically as to make it impossible to live in the real world.

For these reasons, nearly all weight-loss programs—including many that claim to follow the disease model—employ primarily a behavioral and not a disease model for changing eating habits. Programs may even employ disease terminology at the same time they teach clients the inappropriateness of approaching overeating as a disease! Rather than banning sugar, for example, some programs teach people to be aware of how much sugar they are eating and to recognize how sugar affects them. Programs may advise people to allow themselves one dessert a day, so that they don't build up their desire for a sweet to a point that sets them on a binge. If people slip and have one too many cookies, they are told to retrench and not to give in to their former binge-eating tendencies. Indeed, food counseling, with its need to get people to recognize what is healthful to eat and how to go about eating reasonable portions, along with exercising and other means of balancing calorie intake with calorie expenditure, gives us a positive model for approaching other addictions, such as alcoholism.

Is Overweight Biologically Programmed—Set-Point Theory

Americans have been concerned about their weight for far longer than A.A. has dominated the landscape. And people often have claimed excuses for overweight that were beyond their control—big bones, metabolism, a glandular condition—"It doesn't matter how little I eat, I can't lose weight." It certainly is true that different individuals add or drop weight differently, and that two people who eat the same amount can be at different weights. Nonetheless, eating more than usual causes every individual to gain weight, and people who cut their food intake will lose weight. Let us look at research cited to support the idea that heredity in large part determines people's weight and show how in fact it makes the same points we do about overweight.

In one widely cited study, twelve pairs of identical twins were fed an extra thousand calories a day for three months. Twins in each pair gained the same amount of weight, but each set of twins gained a different amount: the average weight gain was eighteen pounds, and the range was from nine and a half to twenty-nine pounds gained.[4] The most obvious finding in this study is that if you eat more you gain weight, no matter who you are. Every subject in this study put on weight. There were none of those individuals who supposedly can eat whatever they like without gaining weight. In an interview, the chief investigator in the study also revealed that most of the subjects lost the added weight within six months of the study. In other words, those who put on more *took off more* when they cut out the added calories.[5] Finally, this research said nothing about what determines people's weight levels initially—the study did not investigate how subjects' weight levels at the beginning of the study affected how easily they put on weight when they ate more food than usual.

The theory that a person's weight is genetically or biologically determined is different from the idea that overweight is a *disease.* If weight level is inherited, then overweight is *normal* for certain people. One version of inherited overweight, called set-point, insists that each person's body is set to maintain a particular weight level. If a person's weight drops below that level, the person feels a strong urge to eat more until his or her weight returns to its set-point. Likewise, if the person gains weight in excess of the set-point, the person will eat less until his or her weight drops back to its personal norm.

Set-point removes the issue of overweight from the realm of addiction. What is biologically programmed, according to this model, is not an addictive craving for a chemical substance like sugar or carbohydrates. Rather, it proposes, biological inheritance determines weight level itself. Some people are born to be fat; some are born to be thin; others are born to be in between. To tamper with one's natural weight by dieting is worse than futile, set-point advocates believe. It only creates anxiety and guilt and may lead to eating binges. This is because the dieter has in effect been starving his or her body. Desperate to regain a feeling of equilibrium, the dieter then goes overboard in the *opposite* direction by overeating and thus gaining more weight than the diet took off.

The set-point theory, first proposed in 1972,[6] was popularized in books such as *The Dieter's Dilemma*[7] and *Breaking the Diet Habit*[8] and was picked up in numerous articles in health sections of magazines and daily papers. The idea that individuals have their own natural weight levels has appealed to the "fat-is-beautiful" movement, to people who sought to remove the stigma from overweight, to women who wanted to free themselves from unrealistic goals of weight reduction and stereotyped images of svelte beauty. These are the people who would be most offended by the idea that "obesity is an incurable disease," since they wish to show that their overweight is unavoidable.

The set-point theory thus makes an important cultural statement, one whose value is independent of its scientific validity. It argues against a preoccupation with thinness, which is unattainable for many people for whatever reasons. To resist the culture's demands that people (especially women) conform to advertising images, and to encourage people to feel good about themselves regardless of their weight—these are laudable aims. It is not necessary, however, to burden ourselves with an inaccurate and unduly pessimistic biological determinism in order to accept and value human diversity and even human frailty.

Susan Wooley, coordinator of the Clinic for Eating Disorders at the University of Cincinnati Medical College, describes that clinic's approach to getting fat people to recognize their limitations:

> Our goal for treatment is different from other kinds of programs. If what they're interested in is solely a weight-loss program, they shouldn't come to us. The only thing that we can promise is to help them get off the seesaw dieting, off the misery of the way they feel about themselves. We'll help each person try to get a very accurate picture of exactly what's involved in losing weight and maintaining that lower weight, and then really examine the question of whether or not it's worth it to them.[9]

There is much to recommend in this procedure. The "seesaw of dieting" really is unproductive and anxiety-producing and carries with it additional health problems besides those of merely being overweight. Therapy that treats people with respect and that acknowledges the complexity of personal values and needs is sound and beneficial. Still, Wooley ("who has learned to be comfortable at 200 pounds herself"[10]) and her colleagues reinforce to their patients the message that overweight is largely biologically determined. But if, as we believe, the scientific evidence indicates that people can lose weight—and people *do* have good reasons to do so, such as their health and vitality—then they should and can do so.

Is it really the case that trying to lose weight or restrain one's eating is doomed, and will only end in the frustration of rebounding to one's original weight or above? The evidence against this pessimistic position is in our view formidable, and the options open to people to change their weight are correspondingly great. Consider that:

1. *Just about all people restrain their eating to some degree.* Otherwise we would all gorge ourselves constantly on our favorite goodies. Ask thin people—they have rules about what they will eat when. They won't eat cookies before having dinner, for instance.

2. *Many people do lose weight, sometimes intentionally, sometimes as a result of a life change.* They do so when they can arrange their lives so as to take in less food and/or expend more energy.

3. *This last option—expending more energy—is one that even some set-point theorists recognize.* Some claim that exercising speeds up one's metabolism and so resets the person's weight-regulating "gyroscope."[11]

Fattening Our Children at the Altar of TV

Besides these positive reasons to believe that people can control their own weight levels, let's look at the opposite side of the coin. Why are Americans getting fatter? If people's weight tends to stabilize at a biologically determined level, why are American children *gaining* weight overall? According to researchers at the Harvard School of Public Health and Tufts New England Medical Center:

> Data from four national surveys indicate pronounced increases in the prevalence of pediatric obesity in the United States . . . [including, since the mid-1960s] a 54% increase in the prevalence of obesity among children 6 to 11 years old and a 98% increase in the prevalence of superobesity.

Among adolescents twelve to seventeen years old, the study pointed out, there was a 39-percent increase in the prevalence of obesity and a 64-percent increase in superobesity. And overweight among the young is continuing to rise, unlike drug use and drinking. In other words, the substance problem that seems to be most out of control for Americans is food. The authors of the study conclude, "Such rapid increases in obesity indicate that environmental causes are likely responsible."[12]

What factors account for Americans' growing fatness? The researchers, William Dietz of the New England Medical Center and Steven Gortmaker of the Harvard School of Public Health, have pinpointed one such environmental cause: television. Dietz and Gortmaker found that obese children did not differ significantly from normal-weight children in terms of how many friends they had, how much time they spent with friends and how well they got along with them, or how much time they spent alone, listening to the radio, reading, or in leisure activities. But they did watch more television. Furthermore, watching television was found to *cause* obesity, rather than vice versa. Even when other possible causes such as prior obesity, race, income level, and family factors are taken into account, television viewing remains an independent cause of overweight in childhood.[13]

It is easy to see why, on the average, children who watch more television weigh more. Watching television is a passive, sedentary way of spending time that substitutes for physically active play. It is strongly associated with eating snacks—a habit reinforced by all the food advertising on children's television. Finally, spending a lot of time watching television can itself be an escapist response to life problems—that is, an addictive involvement. One of us, speaking on an afternoon call-in radio program about addictions, asked all the callers with their various addictions what they had done the previous evening. All dozen or so said they had watched television. Thus, one antidote we can offer to overeating or *any* addiction is: "Stop watching so much television and go out and find more active ways to spend time."

Television by itself, however, does not account for all of our obesity. With health clubs booming, parks and avenues filled with joggers, and magazines dispensing advice on nutrition and physical fitness, why are children—and not only children—becoming heavier? "As leanness has been increasingly prized, Americans have actually become fatter," say Bennett and Gurin. These proponents of biological set-point go on to explain that "Americans are gaining weight because their environment has changed irrevocably in ways that encourage fatness."[14] Reduced physical activity at home and at work; foods that are richer, sweeter, and easier to prepare (as indicated by the terms "fast food" and "junk food"); the fascination with electronic entertainments—these trends make it harder for people to balance their caloric intake with an equivalent expenditure of energy. The entire breakdown of community life, as people become less involved with their neighbors and young people rarely go outside to play on their own, is part of the trend toward inactivity and obesity.

Wild animals have to work to eat. This natural economy of nutrition has been lost in human society, where every street corner is a cafeteria of sweets and fats. It is not surprising that children exposed constantly to easily obtainable snack foods would, if left to their own devices, eat in an undisciplined way. We once observed a group of high-school students stopping at a convenience store on the way to school. One of them loaded up with two cans of soda, two candy bars, and a bag of potato chips. When we asked what that food was for, he replied,

"Lunch." Here was someone who had lost all sense of food value and of eating to ensure survival and well-being. Yet whole families and segments of society have lost touch with normal nutritional values and restraints.

Nonbiological Factors in Obesity

Discussing the roles of social and individual values and life-styles in obesity returns us to the issues of addiction and health that we have emphasized throughout this book. These differences among people and groups are present in eating just as they are in drinking, love relationships, smoking (or not smoking), and everything else we call addiction. And environment, values, and changes in circumstances and life options are crucial determinants of people's eating and weight levels. Consider, then, the following data about obesity:

Weight is greatly affected by income level and social status. "Why Kids Get Fat: A New Study Shows Obesity Is in the Genes," announced a headline in *Newsweek* in 1986.[15] The article told of a study of Danish adopted children by psychiatrist Albert Stunkard of the University of Pennsylvania. These adoptees were found to resemble their biological rather than their adoptive parents in their degree of fatness. Stunkard's research was well timed to draw headlines in a decade when people became accustomed to being told that anything and everything is "in the genes." Since then, in 1990, Stunkard and his group reaffirmed their Danish results with twins they studied in Sweden.[16]

Is this all there is to overweight?—that it's inbred? Despite finding indications that overweight was inherited, the *Newsweek* article assured readers, Stunkard was continuing with a weight-loss program in which he was involved. In an interview about his 1990 study, Stunkard added that "it was clear from other studies that people could overcome their genetic 'destiny.' For example, he said, 'very few people in the upper class are obese,' presumably because social pressures force those with a tendency to become fat to take stringent measures to prevent it."[17]

In the 1960s, Stunkard had been part of the team that examined the relationship between economic status and weight in the famous Midtown Manhattan Study.[18] This group found that obesity was six times more common among women of low socioeconomic status than among women of high status. Furthermore, upwardly mobile women were less likely to be obese. The longer an immigrant's family had been in this country (that is, the more time they had to climb the social ladder), the less likely the woman was to be fat. Numerous studies have now demonstrated people's capacity to change their physiques when they rise in social status.[19]

Likewise, numerous studies in various countries have confirmed that the poorest women (although not men) are the fattest.[20] Taking education as well as income into account, this is the picture that obesity researcher Stanley Garn paints of socioeconomic status (SES) and obesity in men and women:

> . . . males with the least education are leanest but their wives are fattest; men who have gone beyond high school are the fattest of the three SES groups but their own wives are the leanest of them all. However, adding a fourth category—college and beyond—we find that the most educated men and their wives are both lean. . . .[21]

No genetic theory can explain the impact on weight of people's gender or socioeconomic status. Low-income men may burn more calories than low-income women because of the kinds of physical work they typically do. Perhaps they stay thin to keep up a macho image, whereas it is considered acceptable and normal for their female counterparts to be overweight. Meanwhile, the most highly educated men *and* women are extremely well attuned to the value our society now places on thinness, and these people are the most consistently thin. In that social stratum, both men and women do whatever they must—eat less, exercise deliberately—to look "fashionably" thin, despite not having to perform physical labor. As Garn comments, if set-point theory is correct, it must be "a set-point that reads income-tax returns."[22]

On the average, children from higher socioeconomic groups are likely to be heavier than children from lower socioeconomic backgrounds.[23] But this pattern changes as the children—especially girls—grow to adulthood. In other words, people for the most part grow into the social roles and images they establish for themselves. Heavier rich girls have ample opportunity—and desire—to lose their childhood fat, whereas poorer women do not. Garn notes, "leaner, poorer girls emerge as fatter, poorer women, while fatter, richer girls mature as leaner, richer women."[24] At the same time, we must keep in mind that American youth is getting fatter overall and that, for all age groups, there is more inactivity, more eating of junk foods, and more exposure to propaganda that invites people to eat and to eat unhealthily.

Long-term weight loss is a common occurrence. A funny thing happened to William Bennett and Joel Gurin on their way to writing their book on set-point, *The Dieter's Dilemma.* They both ceased to be fat. Biographical information on the authors states they were fat as children. From the looks of his picture, today Bennett is quite thin. We *know* Joel Gurin, who is editor-in-chief of *American Health* magazine, and he is of average build. Obviously, these two men would fall into the category of better-educated, economically well-off people who are more often able to lose weight. But their experience of losing childhood fat is far from atypical.

Many—probably most—children who have some periods of overweight do not end up being obese adults. Physical anthropologist Stanley Garn studied twenty-five hundred people's weight levels over two decades. He found that fatness was far from a fixed trait, and that high percentages of people—40 percent of women and 60 percent of men—ceased being obese over the course of the study. Moreover, "the percent of obese who become less than obese increases in succession for adolescents, for children, and finally for preschool children."[25] In other words, the *younger* the obese person you observe, the *more* likely he or she is to outgrow it. There is one caveat to this finding—Garn's research was conducted in a white, middle-class community (Tecumseh, Michigan). Nonetheless, such fluctuation in fatness for any group argues strongly against the genetic programming of obesity.

In chapter 4 we reported Stanley Schachter's discovery that people in two upper-middle-class communities had commonly quit smoking on their own. In the same communities, Schachter found—again to his surprise—that 62 percent of those who had ever been obese and had tried to lose weight had succeeded. They had taken off an average of 34.7 pounds and had maintained that weight loss for an average of 11.2 years. Incidentally, Schachter found (exactly as he had with smokers) that those who had never gone into weight-loss programs showed better long-term weight loss than those who had![26]

Schachter's is not the only study to demonstrate that people routinely gain control of their weight problems without treatment. In a survey comparing the prevalence of obesity in one suburban population in 1973–74 and 1980–81, 55 percent of men and 79 percent of women were found to have achieved significant weight loss simply by limiting their calorie intake.[27] Another study revealed that women frequently gain more than 20 percent over their ideal body weight in one decade, only to lose it in the next.[28] And, supporting Schachter's finding that treatment made little difference for weight loss, a review of evaluations of weight-loss programs concluded that untreated control groups who were given a straightforward diet and a placebo injection showed greater weight loss than those actually treated with many of the most sophisticated weight-reduction therapies.[29] Finally, an analysis of a sample of twenty-eight thousand Americans revealed a significant decline in obesity among both men and women after the age of fifty-five.[30]

Proponents of set-point claim that findings such as these do not apply to those whose "excess" weight actually represents their natural, biologically fixed weight level. For instance, this is how Polivy and Herman explain away Schachter's data in their book, *Breaking the Diet Habit:*

> For adult onset obese people—*presumably the vast majority of the overweight population*—their excess weight represents "unnatural" accretions for whatever reasons (changes in eating patterns, emotionally induced overeating, and so on). This weight in excess of the body's natural weight is reasonably amenable to reduction, since the body is not disposed to maintain the extra weight. Thus, *for 60–70 percent of overweight people,* weight loss may not always be all that difficult, and maintenance of the lowered weight simply requires that one refrain from prolonged overeating. For the other 30 percent of the overweight population, however, weight loss involves eluding the body's defenses of its natural weight, which seems to demand chronic semistarvation.[31]

Here two researchers write a book that announces that dieting is futile because weight is biologically programmed, only to admit in a brief, hidden section that most overweight peole *can* shed their excess pounds comfortably. Why not instead title the book *Beating the Pessimism Trap* and encourage people to see if they are among the "vast majority" who can maintain a lower weight level by changing their eating habits?

In fact, there is even more reason for optimism than Polivy and Herman concede. Recall that Stanley Garn's research in Michigan (as well as several other large population studies) found that obese people have a better chance of losing weight the younger they are. In other words, being fat as a youngster does not prove that you were born fat; it shows you have more time to adjust your eating habits over your lifetime to achieve your desired body weight. All of this calls into question the very notion of "juvenile-onset" obesity. Overweight infants or adolescents may be more likely to be overweight in later years than those who are not initially overweight, but this outcome is far from inevitable.

Overall, there is no age at which an obese individual can definitely be predicted to remain obese. Garn concludes that "people taken in context, not in an obesity clinic, are more labile in fatness than had been supposed; they 'track,' but far from completely."[32] In other words, when we hear that overweight is incurable, we usually hear it from a group of people who have been in and out of weight clinics and have tried every diet. But they do not represent every overweight person. Many people prove able to lose weight over the course of their lives, and a majority can do so under favorable environmental circumstances.

People get fat when the people they live with are fat. Garn's and other epidemiologists' work strongly suggests that other factors—such as family environment, personal values, changes in life situation—have more influence on a person's weight than does biological inheritance. Garn, for example, has found that obesity does run in families, but that this is not because of genetic inheritance. For example, research shows that adopted children grow up to be fat if the parents they live with are fat, and to be thin if the parents they live with are thin. The earlier the age of adoption, the less a child's weight correlates with that of its biological parents. This illustrates a general rule Garn calls the "living-together effect"—family members living together, whether or not they are biologically related, tend to resemble one another in weight. This pattern of resemblance includes spouses, parents and children, grandparents and grandchildren, and brothers and sisters.[33]

The convergence in weight levels increases the longer family members live together and decreases the longer they live apart. For example, children more closely resemble their parents in fatness until they reach the age of eighteen. After they leave home, the degree of resemblance drops off. Garn and his colleagues summarize: "People living with fat people tend to become fat [the reverse is also true], and this generalization applies to dogs and cats and even birds as well."[34]

The influence between generations in a family runs in both directions: children tend to gain weight when their parents do, and parents tend to gain weight when their children do. Obviously, genes could hardly cause spouses or parents in their forties and teenage children to gain or lose weight simultaneously. Such coordinated variation, Garn concludes, "can have no explanation in genes shared in common; . . . it appears to be deliberate, reflecting altered attitudes toward energy intake and energy expenditure, and the entire family participates in the change."[35]

Incidentally, for those who are reading this material closely, Garn's data from a number of studies disagree starkly with Stunkard's findings, reported earlier, that adoptees resemble their biological rather than their adoptive parents' weight levels. Other researchers, such as Dietz, critique the conclusions of Stunkard et al. because (1) the Scandinavian settings of Stunkard's research are characterized by more uniform social customs and diet than are found in America, so that one would expect less difference due to individual family rearing, (2) Stunkard did not measure actual fatness but instead divided subjects' height by their weight (Garn and others use skinfold thickness), and (3) the Stunkard research didn't study obesity, but variations within normal weight ranges.

Parents transmit attitudes that shape a child's eating habits. Eating habits—and weight levels—associated with particular families, social classes, and ethnic groups are transmitted to children through parental socialization. That is, children *learn* to eat in a certain way, which leads them to maintain a certain weight level. When parents know little about nutrition, don't think much about the dangers of obesity, and have fewer resources to devote to changing an unhealthy life-style, their children will likely pick up these disadvantages. In our story earlier in this chapter, the teenager who called soda, candy bars, and potato chips "lunch" was more likely to have been from a family with less education. On the other hand, no matter what their social class, individual families differ in their awareness of food value and the kinds of foods they prefer or find acceptable.

Such differences in the *kinds* of food people prefer and their eating *habits* predict obesity. Psychologists Erik Woody and Philip Costanzo have found that obesity in boys is associated with different factors from those associated with obesity in girls. For boys, being overweight goes along with being less physically active, less excitable, and less involved with others, as well as with particular food preferences, such as one for meat. Overweight girls, on the other hand, experience greater emotionality, self-doubt, parental restriction, and rejection by their peers. Overweight girls typically eat more in response to both positive and negative moods, whereas overweight boys generally do not discriminate between foods that will enable them to control their weight and those that will not.[36]

These different descriptions of boys' and girls' experiences are related, in turn, to the different ways parents respond to obesity in boys and in girls. Parents tend to think of an overweight son as well adjusted and well behaved. They are inclined to meet his demands for food; if anything, they intervene too little to change his living habits. In contrast, parents see an overweight daughter as "difficult," emotionally high-strung, and lacking in self-control. Fearing for her future social adjustment and success (which they believe depends on her physical attractiveness), they intervene perhaps too much to restrict her eating. The internal tension about eating that parental behavior can create may underlie the adult pattern of indulgence-guilt-dieting-frustration-indulgence and the pattern of repetitive dieting-bingeing cycles.[37]

The Addictions of Bulimia and Anorexia in a Life Context

At the extreme, the internal tension between overeating and internalized parental strictures to be thin may express itself in bulimia or anexoria. Note that the parental patterns Woody and Costanzo observed concern middle-class parents. Although obesity in women is more common in lower social classes, the strange combinations of indulgence, despair, denial, and self-punishment that mark bulimia and anorexia are middle-class phenomena. Though these problems are real, we need to examine carefully—as we have with other addictions in this book—their actual incidence and severity in our society.

As with the public hysteria that attends other current behavioral "diseases," alarming accounts of the dangers of bulimia or anorexia are accompanied by extravagant claims about how common these conditions are. We can find estimates of the incidence of such eating disorders among adolescent girls and young women that range from 15 percent to 50 percent. However, research finds that very few women display the full array of symptoms said to characterize these problems. In one thorough study, 41 percent of the working women and 69 percent of the college women surveyed said that they sometimes engaged in binge eating. However, only 9 percent of the working women and 17 percent of the college students feared a loss of control of their eating during a binge. And only 1 percent of the working women and 5 percent of the college women reported purging (resorting to vomiting or laxatives), which is the defining symptom of bulimia.[38]

Why do a few people go to these extremes of overeating and then striving to attain thinness through such unhealthy counteractive measures? Instead of seeking weight reduction and physical well-being through a healthy balance between eating and exercise, some adolescent girls emerge into a world where women are "supposed" to be thinner than they are, and they take desperate measures to close the gap. The standard of thinness may be unrealistic, or their living habits may make it impossible for them to be as thin as they want. Rather than learn new habits, they may turn to emergency measures that offer a quick fix for the problem.

In one extreme form of this problem, some women who everyone would agree are thin become convinced that they are overweight and need to diet. For other women, however, these fluctuating extremes constitute a strategic approach to indulging while remaining thin, or having their cake and eating it, too. Jane Fonda reported that she used diuretics for a long time, although eventually she replaced this approach to weight control with aerobic exercise (and made a fortune doing so). Or consider this characterization of Gloria Steinem:

> There is a certain eccentricity to Gloria Steinem, an odd ambivalence between her private life and her cause. Behind the revolutionary who inspired so much change is a woman who seems overwhelmed by the very things she helped others to master. She still lives like the girl-just-making-the-rent that she once was, consuming entire Sara Lee cakes at a single sitting, then not eating anything else for several days.[39]

This reporter didn't seem to feel the need to blow the whistle on Steinem as a diseased bulimic. And though nutritionists would see Steinem's behavior in this regard as being far from ideal, it would also be incorrect to assume that she is completely out of control of her eating. Some people do use personal techniques that no nutritionist would recommend to compensate for overindulgence, but they may otherwise maintain basically healthy habits.

The pressures felt by women to make themselves thin contribute to bingeing and purging and to the extremes of bulimia and anorexia; so does middle-class parents' interference with their daughters' normal eating habits, as we described above. The contradictions that lead to extremely out-of-kilter eating patterns are intensified on college campuses, a highly suggestible atmosphere where many women are struggling to decide what kind of people they want to be and how they want to live. However, the study of college and working women shows that as women mature they usually leave behind the extreme manifestations of bulimia. They continue to be concerned with eating and weight, but the intense and sometimes bizarre behaviors the college-age group engages in rarely survive after college. Again, social environment and self-image (i.e., insecure student versus productive, responsible adult) have a large impact on the persistence of a so-called lifelong disease.

Can You Lose Weight?

Based on all the evidence we have presented, the genetic component of weight seems far from decisive for most people. Set-point is another biological theory put forward without biological evidence to support it. The more exceptions it allows—for example, set-point can be "reset" lower by exercise, higher by making ready-to-eat and nutritionally deficient food too available—the less it means. Bennett and Gurin note that "Upper-class women tend to be far thinner than lower-class women—in part because they are under greater pressure to diet, but also because slender women have greater opportunities in education, business, and marriage."[40] Think about how nearly all rock stars remain thin, as do those in other areas of the entertainment business and other public figures.

What this all means, of course, is that, if you have enough reasons to lose weight or remain thin, you are more likely to do so. It also helps to have more resources at your disposal to put into the effort—health clubs, healthy foods, time to plan and practice diet and exercise programs, and so on. What is crucial, from the standpoint of avoiding the dangerous excesses of addiction represented by bulimia, is to integrate your program for controlling your weight into the rest of your life, so that it is not a matter of constant self-restraint and an ordeal. When such life changes are made, one's "natural weight" changes along with them.

The set-point theorists are correct when they say that dieting usually doesn't work. This has become eminently clear in response to the liquid-formula diet craze, where people yo-yo between large losses and gains. Dr. Thomas Wadden (of Albert Stunkard's research team) found that 95 percent of those who undergo low-calorie diets regain their weight loss in five years.[41] If you go on living the same life, if you don't change the way you spend your time and get your rewards, if you don't move into a new social environment or life situation, if you don't come to value different things, you won't change your weight and make it stick. This is the message of the Life Process Program: that to focus on life context is as important as—or more important than—focusing on losing weight *per se.*

Although people do regularly regain lost weight, two researchers discovered that there were a considerable number of formerly obese people who had lost substantial weight (an average of forty pounds) and who no longer indulged in binge eating.[42] Thus, the researchers found, it is not the case that all those who shed a lot of weight are constantly hungering for more food and are ready to launch into an eating binge at the drop of a hat. We see that reliable and permanent weight loss is possible, and happens all the time. What such weight loss requires is that you build into your life structures the rewards for keeping weight off—so that your daily habits and attitudes militate against putting it back on. This then translates into a new self-image when you no longer see yourself as a fat person pretending to be thin, feeling that you only *look* thin outwardly but that this is not the real you. The real you is who you declare yourself to be, a matter wholly under your own control.

CHAPTER 6

ADDICTIONS TO GAMBLING, SHOPPING, AND EXERCISE

HOW WE EVADE MORAL RESPONSIBILITY

THE TITLE OF AN ARTICLE in a 1989 issue of the magazine *Mademoiselle* read: "Addiction Chic: Are We Hooked on Being Hooked?" The article described the explosion of self-help groups like "Overeaters Anonymous, Debtors Anonymous, Pill Addicts Anonymous, Smokers Anonymous, Gamblers Anonymous, Depressives Anonymous, Impotence Anonymous, and WWL2M (Women Who Love Too Much)." It estimated that twelve to fifteen million people—up from five to eight million in 1976—are involved in half a million such individual groups. "Perhaps the most prevalent addiction of all," the author commented, "is this country's obsession with reading and hearing about addiction."[1]

TV talk shows such as *The Oprah Winfrey Show, Geraldo, Donahue,* and *Sally Jessy Raphael* have featured a stream of confessed workaholics, compulsive shoppers, "adult children," "codependents," love-addicted women and sex-addicted men, victims and perpetrators of abusive relationships. We see the same thing in bookstores, where books on "addiction and recovery," many applying the twelve-step model to a whole range of disparate behaviors, have leapt off the psychology shelves to commandeer sections of their own. "It speaks to something desperate in our society that there is such a demand," remarked the president of a major publishing house.[2] Publishers are starting whole new imprints exclusively devoted to addiction/recovery books.

Can one be addicted to gambling, shopping, exercise, sex, or love in the same sense that one is addicted to alcohol or drugs? Is overspending every bit as much an addiction as overeating? Fifteen years before the *Mademoiselle* piece, in *Love and Addiction,*[3] we wrote that any activity, involvement, or sensation that a person finds sufficiently consuming can become an addiction. Oddly, at that time, we had to face tremendous criticism for (a) claiming that such wholesome activities as loving could evolve into addiction, and (b) denying the chemical reality of alcoholism and drug addiction. We argued instead that addiction can be understood only in terms of the overall experience it produces for a person (from its chemical, cognitive, and emotional effects) and how these fit in with the person's life situation and needs.

Today, however, the tendency to label all kinds of compulsive behaviors "addictive diseases" points in the opposite direction from what we argued in *Love and Addiction*. Today's fashion is to insist that other behavioral excesses are caused by mysterious chemical or other uncontrollable forces, the way alcoholism and drug addiction are presumed to be caused. Thus, we have begun to hear about the "chemical high" of shopping or gambling. The chemicals most often implicated are endorphins, as in the "endorphin high" of running. Endorphins are opiatelike chemicals (also called "endogenous opioids") that occur naturally in the body.

The faddish invocation of endorphins is an example of how people believe something you say is scientific if you can translate it into neuroscientific terms, irrespective of the evidence. What kind of evidence? Well, if running or eating or anything else produced endorphins in the body to which people then became addicted, we would expect that more of such substances would be found in addicts of all kinds. Yet no such reliable differences have ever been measured. According to two prominent neuroscientists who have studied the endorphin-addiction link, "At this time there is not sufficient evidence to conclude that endogenous opioids mediate the addictive processes of even one substance of abuse," let alone all the addictions in which endorphins are said to play a role.[4]

Today, not one reputable scientist insists that endorphins underlie narcotic addiction or alcoholism. Where, then, is the enthusiasm for endorphins that was rampant in the magazines and television programs of the 1970s and early 1980s, when endorphins were thought to hold out the cure for all sorts of problems? According to Richard Restak, who wrote the first popular article on endorphins in *Saturday Review* in 1977,

> It's hard to leave out the exclamation points when you are talking about a veritable philosopher's stone—a group of substances that hold out the promise of alleviating, or even eliminating, such age-old bugaboos as pain, drug addiction, and, among other mental illnesses, schizophrenia.[5]

Over a decade later, do you hear much about endorphins eliminating drug addiction or schizophrenia? But endorphin enthusiasts, having failed to explain and cure narcotic addiction, seem to have moved on to greener pastures.

Endorphins don't make people run until their feet bleed or eat until they puke. The idea that people do these things to themselves because of some naturally occuring chemical in their bodies is ludicrous, and harmful. Anne Wilson Schaef, one popularizer of the idea that everything about the American way of life is addictive, asserts that an addiction "takes control of us, causing us to do and think things that are inconsistent with our personal values. . . ."[6] On the contrary, an addiction is not isolated from but an *expression* of our personal and cultural values. Whether, to what, and how severely we become addicted is based on who we are and what we value, just as recovery is a matter of who we want to be and how we want to change our lives.

The addictions discussed in this chapter, with the exception of gambling, differ from substance addictions in that they are excesses of the middle class. More important, they differ from substance addictions in that the implausibility of the claim that they are biologically caused is so self-evident. With habits that do not involve eating, drinking, smoking, or injecting anything, it is easy to see why the disease model of addiction is wrong and why it doesn't work. Undaunted, promoters of the disease model apply it to compulsively making love or running up debts just as they do to alcoholism, drug addiction, and smoking. We, too, believe that there is no essential difference between substance abuse and other addictive activities. Only we draw exactly the opposite conclusion from this fact—that none of these compulsive syndromes is a disease.

Gambling

Gambling has been recognized as an addiction since well before the current addiction craze. (Gamblers Anonymous was founded in 1957.) The intense concentration, the excitement of risk, the swirl of emotions as exhilaration alternates with despair, the feeling of being drawn in beyond one's control—all mark gambling as an activity with tremendous addictive potential. The familiar saga of the gambler who goes deeper and deeper in debt to cover prior losses, finally embezzling money or impoverishing his family, parallels that of the drinker or drug addict who consumes ever more in a desperate attempt to stave off withdrawal and recapture past "highs." Indeed, heavy gamblers frequently *are* heavy drinkers and smokers,[7] and gambling takes place in settings—from the casino to the pool room—where liquor flows freely and the air is heavy with tobacco smoke.

It is this similarity—and overlap—with alcoholism that convinces leading figures in the alcoholism field that gambling is exactly the same kind of disease as alcoholism. Sheila Blume, former scientific director of the National Council on Alcoholism, is one such figure. "Because compulsive gambling has so much in common with alcoholism and other drug addictions and because these symptoms so often occur in the same people and families," says Dr. Blume, director of the Alcoholism and Compulsive Gambling Program at South Oaks Hospital in Amityville, New York, "compulsive or pathological gambling has been conceptualized as an addictive disease. Compulsive gamblers are often treated in programs modeled on those for addicts or in the same programs with alcohol and drug abusers."[8]

But, then, Dr. Blume's definition of a "disease" clearly does not fit gambling—she says a disease is "a condition in which bodily health is seriously attacked, deranged, or impaired; sickness; illness." Blume's main argument for calling compulsive gambling a disease is actually that this labeling makes funds available for treatment. Riley Regan, director of the New Jersey State Division of Alcoholism, complains that, although both private and Veterans Administration hospitals have set up inpatient programs for compulsive gamblers, "most of the insurance companies still have their heads in the sand when it comes to the treatment of the illness of compulsive gambling."[9] But is there any wonder why those who pay the freight for medical treatment—including all of us who pay premiums as well as insurance companies—

question exactly why a person who gambles too much requires hospital care? Moreover, the evidence is that viewing and treating gambling as a disease doesn't reach most gamblers and doesn't help most of those who do enter treatment.[10]

Blume repeats with gamblers the bromide (invented for alcoholics) that the disease label absolves the addict of guilt. "Involuntariness is part of the general idea of disease; it 'happens to' one," she says.[11] In other words, one is a victim of compulsive gambling and not the perpetrator. One person who declined to grant such absolution was the late baseball commissioner A. Bartlett Giamatti, who banned Pete Rose from baseball for gambling on baseball. The Pete Rose case has been presented as a dramatic example of gambling as a disease. The executive director of New Jersey's Council on Compulsive Gambling predicted to the press that Rose "will do for compulsive gambling what Betty Ford did for alcoholism."[12]

Giamatti instead affirmed that Rose's violation of one of baseball's ironclad rules would not be tolerated or excused. Giamatti encouraged Rose to seek whatever treatment he thought might help him get back on track, but this had nothing to do with the disposition of his case. (Incidentally, Rose was later sentenced to jail for failing to declare income he made signing products at baseball conventions.) Some people were willing to excuse Rose because they felt he had to be in the grip of an illness to risk his career in this way. But what if Rose enjoyed the excitement of gambling more than family life or other activities, now that he had stopped playing baseball? Rose may well have believed that he could always cover his losses by relying on his personal prestige if he couldn't pull out the big win he sought. Many people employ such logic when they take unhealthy risks or behave antisocially. But if this is a disease, what misbehavior or rule-breaking isn't?

Previously, Rose was one of a group of Philadelphia Phillies who were prescribed massive amounts of amphetamines. Rose denied taking the drugs under oath at a 1980 hearing for the prescribing physician (who had been wrongly accused of writing false prescriptions to get drugs to sell on the black market), but the confession of one Phillies pitcher and a subsequent newspaper investigation showed that Rose was lying.[13] Does this prove Rose was addicted to drugs and practicing denial then, as he originally did about his gambling? Oddly, Rose did not display denial in an earlier *Playboy* interview in which he admitted taking the amphetamines. What about the other players who used the drug and denied it—like Tim McCarver—and Phillies and state officials who also apparently lied, while the one player who confessed his usage was quickly traded? It seems denial can affect a whole organization. If Rose were asked today whether he ever took amphetamines and if he denied it again, would this prove he was still in denial despite his treatment for and acknowledgment of his gambling addiction?

Many of us have had gambling experiences so intensely gratifying or frustrating that we can imagine how we might have become addicted had we kept at it. Perhaps it happened the first time we went to an Atlantic City or Las Vegas casino, before we realized how futile and stupid it was to waste our money there. Perhaps it was earlier, back in childhood, when we lost a few dollars at a local fair. Maybe we went so far as to go home and take money from our parents' cash box to continue playing. But we didn't grow up to be embezzlers. As our priorities in life solidified, gambling took a minor place in our lives: the office football pool, small-stakes pinochle or poker with friends, an occasional weekend in Atlantic City, a birthday gift of a strip of tickets to a high-payoff lottery game.

According to one estimate, only 3 to 4 percent of those who gamble are compulsive gamblers, while an additional 10 to 15 percent sometimes bet more than they can afford.[14] These figures parallel closely the very small percentage of drinkers who are alcoholic and the somewhat larger minority who have intermittent drinking problems; or the very small percentage of people who are seriously obese and the larger minority who are moderately overweight (the ones who could stand to lose ten to thirty pounds). Again, addiction is not an all-or-none thing, but a continuum from moderate excess to severe compulsion. Somehow, no single addiction is sufficiently compelling to divert more than a small percentage of the population from the duties and pleasures of life.

What we actually learn when treatment professionals report that compulsive gambling is just as much an illness as alcoholism, and when alcoholic gamblers tell us that their compulsion to gamble is as powerful as their compulsion to drink, is that biology doesn't drive addiction, even alcohol or drug addiction. Who, for example, are the 3 or 4 percent of people who gamble compulsively? The typical gambling addict is not someone with extra money to spend, but a black or Hispanic man under thirty years of age who earns less than $25,000 a year.[15] This is the same group that produces the most alcohol and drug abusers.

Here we see that substance and gambling addictions are created by the same social conditions, just as the same psychological motivations drive many of the same people to gamble and drink excessively. Psychologically, gambling and drinking both provide people—primarily men—with illusions of power, prestige, and glamour. When lost in these activities, they tell us, they feel that nothing can touch them, that they are on top of the world, their fantasy images of themselves fulfilled. Of course, after a gambling or drinking binge, they are likely to feel even more material and psychological deprivation than before.

The social conditions that foster addictive gambling flourish among low-income groups. Deprivation, a lack of meaningful alternatives, and hopelessness about the future leave people vulnerable to fantasies of making up for it all with one big payoff. This mentality has begun moving into mainstream America as well—indeed, it is actively being "pushed" there—through mechanisms like the lottery. Nonetheless, like other forms of gambling, the state lottery (which pays out in winnings only about half of what it takes in, as against the 75–85 percent that racetracks and casinos pay out[16]) is patronized disproportionately by the poor.[17] People who earn less than $10,000 a year buy more tickets than any other income group, and the proportion of family income spent on the lottery goes up as family income goes down.[18]

At the same time, with gambling now made available by legitimate institutions rather than the underworld, and with the spread of high-tech video gambling at casinos and "sports centers" and even in the home, the middle class is becoming less inhibited about gambling.[19] What is most crucial in the modern spread of gambling is that state governments are *promoting* gambling through extensive and deceptive advertising. Lotteries offer bigger and bigger jackpots at longer and longer odds because their market research shows that people respond mainly to the size of the payoff, not the probability of winning. If all of the 102 people who came over on the *Mayflower* had purchased a lottery ticket once a week, and if all their descendants had continued to do so for three hundred years, the chances are four out of five that none of them would have won by now.

Here we see American society engaged in a deliberate campaign to spread a debilitating addiction. The promoter of an interactive home betting program on live TV game shows and sports events claimed: "This would allow the customer to play and win on impulse with immediate gratification."[20] Incredibly, society is teaching its citizens the magical thinking that they can miraculously improve their lives without making any real effort or sacrifice. Fantasies that obfuscate the real probabilities in gambling encourage citizens to forgo critical thinking and to do *the opposite of what people really need to achieve their goals and improve their lives.* For all but a very few randomly fortunate individuals (and perhaps even for them), this is a path to failure and self-contempt.

Imagine if our children learn from all this that they should search for an easy route to wealth and personal satisfaction—exactly the antisocial values that addicts and criminals espouse. In southern California the number of high-school students participating in any form of gambling increased by 40 percent after the state lottery was introduced.[21] A 1987 study of New Jersey high-school students found that 86 percent had gambled in the past year, and 32 percent gambled at least once a week.[22] (The irony is that gambling was sold in these states as a way to provide funding for education.) Meanwhile, Mario Ferretti, a "recovering gambler" and president of the Massachusetts Council on Compulsive Gambling, predicts that the "hidden illness" of compulsive gambling will be the epidemic of the nineties. With his Alcoholics Anonymous approach, Ferretti teaches about the plight of gamblers' families ("The problem gambler affects seven to eight other people").[23] However, what will cause the ranks of Gamblers Anonymous to swell is not some mysterious family disease, but continued inner-city poverty and a society-wide attack on the values of genuine achievement.

Shopping and Indebtedness

In a world that encourages fantasies of winning large sums of money to fulfill your dreams, it isn't much of a step to purchasing the stuff of one's dreams without having the money to pay for it. Both are good ways to end up deeply in debt. According to a 1986 estimate, one out of twelve Americans is overwhelmed by debt. "Twenty million Americans are only one paycheck ahead of catastrophe," says the president of the Budget and Credit Counseling Service in New York.[24] For these troubled overspenders, Debtors Anonymous was formed in 1976 by a member of A.A. Ten years later, it was growing at the rate of five new chapters a month. Debtors Anonymous uses A.A. techniques such as confronting members thought to be in denial, as well as offering members practical help such as keeping track of and planning their spending. There is little possibility here to claim an inbred biological deficiency;

members instead address psychologial issues such as fear of success, fear of responsibility, "use of money as a mood-changer," and "a desire to be taken care of."[25]

"It's an addiction, just as serious as cocaine, pills or alcohol," says a typical group leader and therapist.[26] In response, self-help groups have sprung up with names like SpenderMender and Shopaholics Limited. But what does it mean to call compulsive purchasing a disease? Psychotherapists explain that millions of Americans "shop excessively out of boredom, anxiety, anger, joy or fear of being hurt"[27]—in other words, nearly every human feeling. Calling compulsive spending and shopping "diseases" shows mainly that we have lost all other ways of talking about compulsive behavior and addiction, and so we discuss them as diseases no matter how implausible the connection becomes.

This confused mixture of common sense and disease and A.A. ideology was illustrated by the discussion of "spendaholics" on a *Sally Jessy Raphael* show devoted to the topic. Three "recovering shopaholics" and one "recovering spendaholic" appeared with Janet Damon, psychotherapist and author of *Shopaholics: Serious Help for Addicted Spenders.*[28] Damon explained why this form of compulsive behavior really is an addiction:

> . . . when people perform a behavior over which they have absolutely no control, and they behave this way consistently, repetitively, as a way of escaping from profound feelings of worthlessness, profound feelings of helplessness and powerlessness and anxiety, and this is the way to avoid and escape from what's going on inside and what's going on outside in their lives, you better believe it's an addiction.[29]

This is a realistic description of addiction that could help people gain insight into what they are doing and why—except for the phrase "over which they have absolutely no control." Loss of control is *subjective;* the addict *feels* he or she has no control. To accept this as an objective description is actually to impede recovery.

The program's participants had an idea of why they got hooked in the first place. One gave these reasons:

> No self-esteem, basically, is what it was. . . . You feel a big void and an emptiness and nothing will fill it, and you just

> go ravenously to buy something. . . . Loneliness, and a need for like something that would enhance myself.[30]

They also cited cultural influences—the credit cards teenagers get in the mail, the incessant displays of the "good life" on television, a federal budget deficit that sets an example for personal extravagance, liberal bankruptcy laws that allow a person to "bail out" and start again. This combination of individual and environmental factors underlies the addiction.

But in order to justify her claim that this is an addictive disease, author Damon relied on biochemical language:

> No, it's more than whoopee, it's a neurological change, Sally. People get a real high and a wiry high. I've had coke addicts who said it's the same kind of high, and then they crash.[31]

A panelist added, "Yeah, it's like the endorphins when you work out, it's just like it."

Meanwhile, another panelist, when asked whether she felt guilty and ashamed after shopping, replied, "Always. There's the crash." To which Damon added, "And that just plummets you into worse self-esteem." This is the addiction cycle: each indulgence leads to worsened anxiety and guilt, which in turn lead one to want to escape further into oblivion. Biological terminology is a cover-up for the understanding necessary to recognize this cycle of self-entrapment. You can use biological words to describe feelings, but what does this accomplish, besides making for sexy television programming?

An exchange then occurred in which someone in the audience showed how the very assumptions made about addictive "diseases" conflict with common sense and mislead people from helpful and healthy thinking. This audience member commented: "I think, after listening to them, they're self-centered. They should find something to do, volunteer or help somebody else," to which author Damon replied: "Would you call an alcoholic self-centered? Would you call a cocaine addict self-centered?"

MS. DAMON: These people are addicts.
AUDIENCE MEMBER: They could put their time to better use.
MS. DAMON: They're addicts.[32]

In answer to Ms. Damon's question: Yes, you might very well call an alcoholic or a cocaine addict self-centered. Giving complete primacy to immediate sensory experience and gratification (as does an infant), to the exclusion of other obligations and responsibilities, *is the essence of addiction of all kinds.* The "uninformed" audience member who brought up this point was exactly right—having meaningful activities, relationships, and social concerns works against the inclination or need to indulge in the behavior described by the panelists. But this insight was too threatening for the show to consider seriously, so Damon repeatedly intoned the word "addicts" to stop any attempts to put the panelists' actions in a social and moral context.

Damon concluded that "there are people who can handle liquor, there are people who can handle credit cards. These addictive people cannot, and credit cards are to these people what alcohol is to alcoholics. . . ."[33] Here Damon struggles to preserve the disease-based abstinence model in a situation where it is even more inapplicable than it is with alcohol. Will these people really never be able to shop again? One panelist described how she stopped shopping compulsively:

> It's interesting, I went to buy some spring clothes recently, because I really didn't have anything for the season. You know, I have a job where I need to dress halfway decently. And I went and I bought and that was it, and then I stopped. And I think I did overbuy. I think I bought one outfit too many, but all right, you know, in this case I had the money to do it, I said all right, I'm going to do it, and that's it.[34]

If we take this ex-addict's solution seriously, we learn that addicts can control their lives so that they don't need to go on a binge every time they are exposed to a sale, a cookie, or even a drink!

We will never come to terms with overspending as the result of "chemical euphoria." We must consider instead the way society incites people to live beyond their means and to aspire to frivolous possessions that they don't earn enough to purchase in the first place. The best way to attack addiction to superfluous shopping is to get people more committed to solid accomplishments, values, relationships, and activities. What the Debtors Anonymous program deserves credit for is its insistence that group members pay back their debts in full. Such a commitment acknowledges that the real issues in spending addiction are values like fairness, accountability, and responsibility. If you want someone to take you seriously as a person, recovering or otherwise, you had better be able to meet the expected standards of normal social conduct.

Exercise

Exercise addiction is a case of too much of a good thing. A subject of much public attention after the running boom of the 1970s, compulsive exercise (like most of today's addictions) has only recently been discovered, because it is a product of the experiences of contemporary Americans.

The model of addiction we have outlined is as applicable to the excess of exercise as it is to all the compulsive activities discussed thus far. As mentioned earlier, the fashionable explanation of the "runner's high" is that it results from the release of endorphins, the body's natural, opiatelike painkillers. This account has an up-to-date, "scientific" ring, but no empirical support. Researchers at the University of North Carolina found no relationship between endorphins and the runner's high: "It is more likely," the chief investigator concludes, "that this feeling of well-being comes from adrenaline or the release of built-up stress." The addictive appeal of prolonged exertion, he speculates, "is probably psychological. It is so good at relieving stress that some people who are particularly susceptible to stress may begin feeling like they can't do without it."[35]

Suppose somebody finally did find that the release of endorphins *does* produce the runner's high. What exactly *would* this prove about people who run until they get divorced or fracture bones in their legs? People get addicted to feelings and sensations, however these are triggered. The question that remains is why some people require particular sensations that they don't otherwise get and become dependent on an addictive involvement to provide them. Even then we must still ask why they pursue these sensations beyond all reasonable benefit, and are unable to quit when all signs in their life say "Stop!"

What makes some runners seek out with compulsive regularity the sensations that running produces even in the presence of disabling, excruciatingly painful injuries? Why do some runners put it ahead of their jobs and families? One study found similarities between the personalities of addicted runners and anorexics. Those who ran compulsively were "generally self-effacing, hard-working, high achievers from affluent families who were uncomfortable with anger and who characteristically inhibited the direct expression of" emotion. Furthermore, these excessive runners were found to be "characterized by grim asceticism and an assiduous avoidance of passive, receptive pleasures."[36] The researchers went on to suggest that those who feel driven to run do not have a stable sense of themselves. They feel they must go on running, as the anorexic must go on dieting, to keep proving themselves. "They are satisfied by moving toward a goal, not by achieving it."[37]

Running and exercise addiction is thus different from other addictions—to drugs, alcohol, and gambling—we have reviewed in that it enlists higher achievers, albeit ones with low self-esteem and other problems. However, the susceptibility to this addiction, like all others, is very much a matter of the situations in which people find themselves at a particular time. As the researchers noted about their running-addict subjects:

> Their singular commitment to running occurred at a time of heightened anxiety, depression, and identity diffusion. Assuming an identity as a runner served an adaptive function, providing a sense of self, a feeling of control over internal and external circumstances, and a difficult but attainable goal.[38]

Once again, in order to make sense of addiction, we see the need to go beyond *pro forma* biological mechanisms and into the realm of experience. Suppose you are someone who "got into running" with a vengeance after being divorced, separated, or bereaved; moving to a new locale; going through a business failure or a career change; or giving up another addiction such as smoking. These are times of heightened susceptibility to whatever addictions one finds accessible and acceptable. During such unpleasant transitions, you might find running can provide an ego boost, a feeling of doing something for yourself, an outlet for feelings of frustration or dissatisfaction, and a way of organizing a disoriented world. Typically, such intense involvements in running are temporary, coinciding with the period of readjustment. If your days then fill up with new people, activities, and responsibilities, you will put running back in the wholesome place it deserves within a balanced life.

Even a heavy running schedule can be part of a healthy adjustment to life. Since exercise really can reduce anxiety and depression and increase self-esteem, your personal and working relationships may improve as a result of running. A study of marathoners found that, despite the problems that a serious commitment to running created for the runners' families, these families experienced *less* conflict than comparable families without a serious runner.[39] The danger of addiction comes when chronic self-doubt or persistent discontent with job or family gives the exhilarating sensations of prolonged vigorous exercise a larger-than-life air. One man who started jogging after fifteen years of inactivity exclaimed, "I feel like I'm alive now—I was dead for the last 15 years."[40] That sentiment could mark the start of either a positive transformation—with some of the new energy transferred from running to other involvements—or an unbalanced pursuit of a constant "high" the person feels nowhere else. You are pretty far gone into addictive unreality if you experience what this runner did:

> At five miles or so into my daily run I developed a sense of invincibility—I was truly indestructible in that transcendent state. The cares of the day would quickly pass at about 5 miles, and nothing bothered me. I guess you could say I was omnipotent at that point.[41]

This man ran through a year of intense pain until he could no longer walk down steps. Reconstructive surgery on his foot left him with a permanent limp. Like an alcoholic or a drug addict, he found the subjective experience of his addiction so rewarding compared with his ordinary state of consciousness that he made himself oblivious to the consequences.

Fortunately, as with all addictions, only a small percentage of runners—perhaps even smaller than with other potentially addictive involvements—reach this self-destructive extreme. In the words of the researchers who likened compulsive runners to anorexics:

> Their behavior becomes pathological as a result of an extreme degree of constriction, inflexibility, repetitive thought, adherence to rituals, and need to control themselves and their environment. . . . The pathology resides in the intensity and exclusiveness with which the adaptation is maintained.[42]

People give up overexercising in different ways. A man in his forties who had been running regularly since high school settled into a routine of running every day at noon. One day in 1970 (before running became a fad and the "runner's high" a household term), he found himself in conflict about attending an important staff meeting he had scheduled. Although he planned to attend, he felt increasingly perturbed about missing his daily run. As sports psychologist William Morgan tells it:

> When the final hour arrived, he proceeded to the dressing room, changed, departed on his run, and said, "The hell with that stupid staff meeting!" While his absence apparently did not result in any reprisals, he spent the evening trying to understand his behavior and concluded that he was addicted to running. He prided himself on his complete control of his behavior and was not willing to let anything control him. Therefore, he stopped running the next day. I have seen him from time to time during the past eight years, and while he plays an occasional game of tennis or golf, he has not resumed running.[43]

This man showed the ability to take stock of his behavior and to stop doing something that violated his self-image. On the other hand, had he been less rigid in the first place, he might have learned to exercise moderately rather than quit cold turkey.

Some people give up running only when pain and disability make it physically impossible to go on (like the alcoholic who can no longer stomach liquor). Many more make less dramatic accommodations after a few indications that their knees or ankles won't take it. Often, they switch to a more tolerable form of aerobic exercise such as swimming, walking, bicycling, or perhaps controlled running—like light jogging. But what about all those endorphins they used to get from running? Apparently, the power of these chemicals pales in comparison with most people's concerns about their health and overall well-being.

CHAPTER 7

LOVE, SEX, AND CODEPENDENCE

•

OVERCOMING TRAUMA

WHEN WE WROTE *Love and Addiction* in 1975, we intended it to be a radical critique of the conventional notion of addiction as a physical dependence on a drug. If love can be an addiction, we argued, then addiction is not what people think it is. Initially, our ideas met a lot of resistance. One talk-show host said that Zsa Zsa Gabor knew more about love than we did because she had been divorced so many times. Others accused us of being too judgmental. Scientifically minded readers scoffed that love could not be a "real" addiction because it didn't involve use of a chemical. Yet, in the decade and a half since then, the public has gone from incredulity to acceptance—indeed, love and sex addiction and "codependence" have become the most popular topics for self-help books, therapists, and television talk shows.

Lost in this hoopla, however, has been the underlying purpose and meaning of our work. Instead of giving up the discredited notion that addiction is some kind of physical disease, therapists and the media have simply labeled love and other nonsubstance addictions as new variations of the disease. Instead of looking critically at how our whole way of relating to one another distorts our intimate relationships, the self-appointed experts think they can treat love addiction as an individual sickness. The fate of the ideas we presented in *Love and Addiction* is a disturbing demonstration of the power of a culture's myths to co-opt a challenging new way of thinking about a problem like addiction.

What Are Love Addiction and Codependence?

Before we continue with the current history of the love-addiction idea, we need to lay out the varieties of this idea:

Love addiction. In *Love and Addiction* we described love and addiction as opposites. You couldn't be addicted to love—love is a good thing. We said instead that people had addictive, unhealthy relationships. In other words, what some people experience as "love" is actually an addiction.

Too much love. For us, there couldn't be too much love. But author Robin Norwood described women's problems in relationships as being that they often "love too much." Really, Norwood was describing *unhealthy* ways of relating, not love. In most cases, these involved women who are too dependent on men.

Codependence. Many of the worst examples of addictive, unhealthy relationships are found among spouses (usually wives) of alcoholics and drug addicts, who may accept terrible consequences in order to stay with a mate. As the idea was accepted that relationships themselves could be addictive, the label "codependent" was attached to the spouse of the chemically dependent man or woman. Such people supposedly seek intimacy by taking care of others, often because their parents were alcoholics or otherwise "dysfunctional."

But this evolution had one further step to go. As we had indicated in *Love and Addiction,* you didn't need to be involved with an addict to be addicted to a person. Thus, books like Melody Beattie's *Codependent No More* took the word "codependent" back from its association with spouses of alcoholics and drug addicts and applied it to all women in dependent and destructive relationships. In these relationships, the man is usually overdependent on the woman as a caretaker.

Sex addiction. In *Love and Addiction,* we labeled one variety of interpersonal addiction often found in men as sex addiction. This has now become a whole separate concept, as though people become addicted to sex in isolation from their relationships to their sex partners. True, sex addicts often (but not always) shift partners rapidly. But we regarded this as one variation of the expediency, superficiality, and mutual exploitation that we believe characterize all addictive relationships.

How seriously do people take the idea that addiction to love or sex, or having a relationship with an alcoholic or addict, is a disease "just like alcoholism or drug addiction"? If the idea of gambling as a disease peaked with Pete Rose, sex addiction received the most public scrutiny when another baseball star, Wade Boggs, claimed he maintained an extramarital affair for years because he was addicted to sex (a condition he learned about from watching *Geraldo*). Columnists lampooned Boggs (and the concept of sex addiction) mercilessly. Two psychologists point out the underlying reason people had a hard time swallowing Boggs's excuse: "The more familiar the public is with a particular behavior, the less likely it is to be mystifying and to receive public sympathy."[1]

Nonetheless, hundreds of thousands of readers are turning to such books as Patrick Carnes's *Out of the Shadows: Understanding Sexual Addiction* and *Contrary to Love: Helping the Sexual Addict*, where "Carnes courageously continues his ambitious task: to describe and define this illness in order to help others get well." In these books, the publisher's advertising assures us, "The importance of the use of the adapted Twelve Steps of Alcoholics Anonymous is emphasized." Conferences on addiction as well as publishers' catalogues feature row upon row of books on sex and love addiction, women too much in love, and codependence. Self-help groups such as Al-Anon (for codependent spouses), Women Who Love Too Much, and Sexaholics Anonymous (predominantly made up of men) abound.

For some time now, Al-Anon groups have been growing more rapidly than A.A. itself. Enormous sales of *Women Who Love Too Much* and *Codependent No More* (far greater than the sales of any books about alcoholism or drugs) would indicate that many women suspect they suffer from these problems. At the same time, the executive director of the National Association on Sexual Addiction Problems estimates that "10 percent of the adult population has a sexual addiction that requires treatment"—a number that, he says, the "extreme figures in the field" would raise to 25 percent.[2] Clearly, love and sex addiction is a far more pervasive social problem than alcoholism or gambling addiction.

What problems do these books, groups, and ideas address? In *Codependent No More*, Beattie confesses: "Up to this point, I have been using the words *codependent* and *codependency* as lucid terms. However, the definitions of these words remain vague."[3] Beattie assures readers that the vagueness is justified. "Codependency has a fuzzy definition because it is a gray, fuzzy condition." Finally, she offers this definition: "A codependent person is one who has let another person's behavior affect him or her, and who is obsessed with controlling that person's behavior."[4]

"An estimated 80 million people are chemically dependent or in a relationship with someone who is. They are probably codependent," Beattie indicates. On top of that, "People who love, care about, or work with troubled people" as well as "many people with eating disorders" and "people who care about people with eating disorders" are probably codependent. In fact, she warns, "you may be reading this book to help someone else; if so, you probably are codependent."[5] Is it any wonder that one professional publication now claims that 96 percent of the population is codependent? A woman who attended Al-Anon asked the group how they could tell who was codependent and who was not. She was told that the group never made such a decision. After attending several meetings, she saw that no one who came to the group was ever told she didn't have the disease, and that anyone who decided not to return was accused of denial.

To get a handle on codependence, let's turn to this characterization:

> . . . our low self-worth or self-hatred is tied into all aspects of our codependency: martyrdom, refusal to enjoy life; workaholism, staying so busy we can't enjoy life; perfectionism, not allowing ourselves to enjoy or feel good about the things we do; procrastination, heaping piles of guilt and uncertainty on ourselves; and preventing intimacy with people such as running from relationships, avoiding commitment, staying in destructive relationships; initiating relationships with people who are not good for us, and avoiding people who are good for us.[6]

Is this a disease? Beattie hedges here. Though not taking a position herself, she explains that one

> reason codependency is called a disease is because it is progressive. As the people around us become sicker, we may begin to react more intensely. . . . Codependency may not be

> an illness, but it can make you sick. And, it can help the people around you stay sick.
>
> Another reason codependency is called a disease is because codependent behaviors—like many self-destructive behaviors—become habitual. We repeat habits without thinking. Habits take on a life of their own.[7]

Nonetheless, the tremendous response to Beattie's work is closely tied to the growth of Al-Anon, Adult Children of Alcoholics, and similar disease groups and concepts.

The disease model of codependence is promoted by prominent lecturers on the addiction and alcoholism circuit such as Sharon Wegscheider-Cruse and Claudia Black. But if codependence is a disease, is it inbred, biological, and permanent? One book, *Painful Affairs: Looking for Love Through Addiction and Codependency*,[8] is divided into sections on chemical dependence and codependence. Its author, Joseph Cruse (who is Wegscheider's husband), split his references between genetic and neurological research on alcoholism and popular works on codependence. Cruse created a chart to convey his view that alcoholism and codependence are equivalent disease states. The first panel in the chart shows a brain, the second shows a valentine-type heart, and the third panel has the brain within the valentine and an arrow through both!

Of course, when Cruse, who was both alcoholic and codependent, says these experiences are equivalent in their power, he unwittingly tells us something important about addiction—namely, that addiction is not a chemical reaction or a reaction to a chemical. But, in taking the disease model to such an absurd extreme, Cruse and others try to make sense of these disparate compulsions by relating them all—however figuratively—to their brains or their "chemical selves." Several books have claimed that women who form overly dependent relationships inherit this problem (one author calls it "limerence") or that women seek out such unhealthy relationships because of the impaired action of neuroregulators in their brains.[9]

The highly pessimistic message for women is that they are doomed to react to men and sexual relationships in compulsive, self-destructive ways, unless perhaps they take antidepressants and remain under a psychiatrist's care. Many codependence groups, even though they don't take the disease theory to these lengths, nonetheless reinforce passivity and griping in place of taking action to change one's life. As a result, several feminist critics of codependence have remarked on the self-absorption that goes with thinking of your personal problems as a "disease."[10] According to these critics, the assertion of powerlessness can be self-fulfilling.

Psychologist Carol Tavris described how the codependence movement averts its gaze from the inequities women experience in their family and social systems: "It is safer, certainly, to feel guilty rather than angry," she concluded. "When women begin to look outward, instead of always inward to their own faults and failings, their self-esteem is bound to rise."[11] In Al-Anon and Women Who Love Too Much groups, observers note a great deal of complaining and self-pity. Journalist Elissa Schappell attended a series of such meetings:

> The more I think about my group, the sadder and angrier the "therapy" it offers makes me. I see a lot of women here who have real problems they need to conquer. But the group seems to suppress any kind of emotion; instead, it offers up propaganda and a hollow spirit. The women seem to no longer think of themselves as Jane, a pianist, or Tess, a student, but as Jane, a Woman Who Loves Too Much, and Tess, a Woman Who Loves Too Much. They wear the term "love addict" like a tag. And that is sad.
>
> I don't know whether or not these women are truly love addicts. But I know that it's unlikely any of them could ever be remotely changed—not to mention cured—by the experience of being here. And yet they are addicted to this group, or to the idea of needing it; that much seems painfully clear. And that, I feel, is really Too Much.[12]

Where Does Love Addiction Really Come From?

If so many people are codependent, then codependence is more of a social than a personal problem. This is the point of Schaef's book *When Society Becomes an Addict*. But Schaef then leaps to the idea that addiction is a disease from which we all suffer, and as a result of which we need a massive, society-wide twelve-step program.

What are the real issues that both the obfuscations of psychiatrists and the bromides of twelve-step groups evade? We discuss the cultural backdrop of love addiction in *Love and Addiction.*[13] First, there is the breakdown of communities and of mutual responsibility that leaves people vulnerable to addictions of all sorts. In addition, modern Americans have come to see love relationships as being magically potent, as though love could remedy all our emotional deficiencies, like our impersonal work and barren community lives. As a result, our personal relationships always seem to fall far short of what we need. Yearning for more, we attach larger-than-life emotional reactions to love relationships, even with completely inappropriate people. It is paradoxical that we seem so insecure about our intimate relationships while political figures and the media constantly emphasize and reinforce the value of the nuclear family. In the post–World War II world, extended families with relatives living in the same house, neighborhood, or even city or state have become uncommon. Children do not have intimate contact with others, like grandparents, uncles and aunts, cousins. With fewer people to turn to for warmth and help, they also get less practice at intimacy with anyone aside from their parents, siblings, or—later—their lovers and spouses. Parents, meanwhile, have the sole responsibility for childrearing, and they seem constantly to feel inadequate to the task and guilty about their shortcomings. Books like *Toxic Parents* drive these shortcomings home.

Meanwhile, because people cannot turn for support to their extended families and communities, the world outside the home looks more and more frightening. Children's time is increasingly structured around protected, organized activities, with little room to interact freely with neighbors and friends or to explore their surroundings on their own. The family begins to seem like an emotional bastion to which people turn for all their personal needs. Children have few meaningful friendships outside the family to prepare them for creating adult intimacy, or for dealing with later inevitable disappointments in love. Children who never have the freedom to play on their own, as most children throughout history have done, lose the opportunity to exercise their own initiative and independence and thus to learn self-management skills.

Addiction specialists now talk and write about the dysfunctional family as an almost universal experience. As noted in chapter 2, one book claims that 96 percent of families produce "children of trauma." But the dysfunctional families in these works look less like drunken child-abusers than overburdened couples who cannot possibly meet all of their children's needs for nurturance—on top of all the demands the outside world makes on a two-income family.[14] In some cases, these frustrations lead to actual child abuse; in many more they take the form of a persistent sense by family members of being emotionally "shortchanged." In adulthood, this lack of love and emotional support looks much like what "women who love too much" are complaining about, and what their spouses (or ex-spouses) probably feel equally.

In a world that neither fully satisfies children's dependency needs nor teaches the skills and confidence that confer independence, many people approach relationships from a position of weakness. They are unlikely to have their emotional needs met, because the partners available to them usually have similar problems. Too often, then, a relationship becomes a battle of competing dependencies. The very idea that people's problems come about because they "love too much" expresses this aggrieved outlook, this feeling that one is getting shortchanged in a struggle for scarce emotional resources. These relationships sound more like mutual exploitation than love as giving freely in the knowledge that you will be loved and nurtured in return.

In love addiction, you expect your partner and the relationship to fulfill impossibly demanding needs. In the case of codependence, you may look to a debilitated lover to be more controllable, and less able to walk out of the relationship. These twisted efforts to gain and hold on to love, though understandable (and certainly not the results of brain chemistry), lead to repeated disappointment, pain, and abuse, and they must be changed.

Like any other addiction, love addiction is not an all-or-none thing. There are degrees of dependency ranging from the normal to the self-destructive. People go up and down this range according to the stresses of their lives, the opportunities available to them, and their personal development.[15] Another indeterminacy in love addiction is that it is often hard to declare that a particular person is purely good or bad for you. The choices are to deal with imperfection or to decide you're better off without this person as a lover. Then giving up the person becomes like giving up alcohol or drugs—the involvement fulfills emotional needs, but overall it isn't worth it. What to do when the ex-lover comes around again? As one woman said, "He might be somebody you'd want to have as a friend, if that were possible—and you want to believe it's possible."

People regularly find themselves having to evaluate the costs and benefits of relationships, to decide whether or not to continue a relationship that may be pleasant but may not have enough potential to justify deeper involvement. These decisions are stressful. If you can't make them, however, you won't be able to seek out and approach desirable partners. Love addicts are the people most willing to settle for a relationship that is simply available for the taking. As a result, they end up in the most treacherous, self-defeating liaisons. In contrast, those who have the best chance of fulfillment in love are those who take control of their lives and who are selective about their partners. To find someone worth loving means getting to know a wide range of people and deciding how much of ourselves to give to each. It's complicated, but the alternatives are to give in to any coupling that presents itself, or else to avoid emotional commitments altogether.

One case study of the most extreme form of destructive and neurotic "love" is that of Dr. Elizabeth Morgan, who spent two years in jail for contempt of court after sending her five-year-old daughter into hiding because she believed the child was being abused by her former husband (the child's father), Dr. Eric Foretich. A child traumatized, separated from her parents, forced to live as a fugitive; a mother in prison; a father denying the abuse and seeking the return of his daughter. How did all this come about? Here is an account of the couple's brief marriage:

> *Morgan v. Foretich* all began with Morgan plus Foretich, and that began when they met in 1981 at Fairfax Hospital in Virginia, where they were both on staff. After a whirlwind courtship—and with Morgan pregnant—they flew to Haiti to marry, since Foretich was separated but not divorced from his second wife.
>
> "My initial feeling, which I should have listened to, was that he was a jerk," Morgan says. "I remember thinking he was a bit of a come-on." But she agreed to a date, and she fell in love. "He's clever, he's attractive, he has lots of energy. He is an intelligent, educated, dangerous psychopath."
>
> Foretich will not even acknowledge that "Morgan," as he often refers to her, and he ever were legally married. "We had a ceremony in Haiti, and as soon as I came back I found out it was never a legal ceremony." Foretich's second wife, Sharon, found out about her Haitian divorce and his subsequent remarriage from a *Washington Post* gossip column.

Eric Foretich's reaction to Elizabeth Morgan mirrors hers to him: "She's very articulate, very smart, but she's also a very sick person," he says, adding that he married her because she was pregnant. "It was the noble thing to do, but it was the wrong thing to do. I wanted to give my baby a name."

The marriage lasted five months. Morgan left Foretich a week before Hilary was born, she says, after he knocked her down and kicked her—which he denies. She obtained a divorce in Haiti three months later.[16]

Here were two accomplished professional people at sea in the complexities of intimate human relationships. Unwilling to take time to get to know each other before conceiving a child and committing themselves to marriage, unable to make reasonable judgments about each other's character and suitability, oblivious to the process of sorting and testing that goes into forming an enduring relationship, they have devastated their own and their child's lives. Foretich may be a child abuser, which is one tragedy; the other tragedy is that he might not be one. Just as you would not go into a business deal with someone you couldn't trust, you need to ask some elementary questions about a prospective lover or spouse: "Will this person be good for me?" "Will this person enhance my life?" "Is this person worthy of my love and trust?" And it takes more than a few dates to decide these things.

Overcoming Trauma in Your Family and Love Relationships

Phrases like "children of trauma" make us all sound like the walking wounded. But aren't people capable of overcoming problems with parents or lovers, even if they have been abused? Surely, if there is one thing people who have been unhappy or abused do not need, it is to think that their plight is somehow a permanent condition from which they can never escape. Rather, they need to take their lives in hand and to assert their right to decent treatment. Likewise, it does not help to be told that one who suffers violence is likely to become a perpetrator of violence. Two psychologists found that, without this indoctrination, most children overcome the legacy of parental violence:

> . . . acceptance of the intergeneration hypothesis [of child abuse] has had many negative consequences. Adults who were maltreated have been told so many times that they will abuse their children that for some it has become a self-fulfilling prophecy.[17]

Now the traumas people experience in life are enshrined in the psychiatric manual DSM-III-R as Post-traumatic Stress Disorder. Here psychiatry almost demands that people must suffer for a lifetime from the bad things that happen to them. Yet not everyone experiences trauma and loss as permanently threatening experiences. Nonetheless, if you survive traumatic events or losses—such as an abortion or death in the family (or even an earthquake or a war)—without visible emotional scars, you must surely be guilty of denial! Denial is often given as the reason many people aren't interested in the help of the cadres of therapists and counselors who descend on them after a tragedy, demanding that they give vent to their hidden distress.

On the contrary, psychologist Camille Wortman's research proved to her that "we need to expand our notions of what is a normal reaction to loss." She added, "People don't realize how common it is for grief to be borne lightly." The absence of extreme distress "can be a sign of resilience," she explained, "but that possibility has never been considered." Furthermore, her data showed

> that if people are not greatly distressed at first after a loss, they probably never will be.
>
> And those who are most upset immediately after a loss tend to be among the most upset a year or two later. The findings call into question the widespread assumption that a period of severe distress leads to a more balanced adjustment.
>
> The new data lead Dr. Wortman to conclude that people who are the most upset by a loss are at greatest risk for emotional difficulties in the long run. And contrary to clinical lore that lack of distress just after the loss leads to "delayed grief," those who have a relatively mild initial reaction seem to stay less distressed.[18]

What distinguishes people who experience intense grief from those who do not? Psychologist Jack Mearns studied people's reactions to breakups of romantic relationships. Those who got over the hurt more readily were those who coped actively—for example, by finding a new hobby or making new friends. Those who did not take such active steps experienced more severe grief and depression. Mearns concluded that the "people who didn't think they could bring themselves out of their depression generally didn't."[19] In other words, some people learn that they can deal with their trauma. For others, the expectation that a breakup will be followed by traumatic grief becomes a self-fulfilling prophecy. Like all addictions, love addiction thrives on the belief in its own potency. To challenge that myth successfully requires a belief in oneself and in one's own efficacy; it also requires active coping skills, other concerns, and other things to do.

We have already dealt, in chapter 2, with children of alcoholics: how most do not inherit alcoholism, and how burdening yourself with a sense of permanent inheritance—either of the alcoholic gene or of the ACoA personality—does you no good. We return to children of alcoholics to end part I because they highlight two crucial points: First, are adult children of alcoholics so different from the rest of us, since we are now being told that hardly any of us are free from a dysfunctional family? On the other hand, how hard is it for people to outgrow childhood traumas? We do not want to leave readers with the impression that, since addiction is fostered by larger social forces we all confront, we are all doomed to having addictive relationships.

One book by an ACoA highlights these issues in an unusually frank way. Phyllis Hobe, author of *Lovebound: Recovering from an Alcoholic Family*, reveals:

> In fact, some recovery program administrators like to mention that many people don't even realize they are ACoAs until someone describes the symptoms to them. "Then most everybody sort of gasps and says, 'Hey, that sounds like me!' " one administrator told me. And when you look at the laundry list of so-called ACoA characteristics, you can understand why almost anyone would identify with many of them. . . . The person who learns he is an ACoA is likely to think that everything about him is a symptom of a terrible, all-consuming ailment.[20]

Now that we are all being told we are children of trauma, walking wounded, and part of a society that is an addict, will we all be better off to acknowledge our diseases and to join a twelve-step group? Hobe thinks not. She was dismayed by the things she heard at the ACoA and Al-Anon meetings she began attending, one of which was that she could not avoid forming codependent, unhealthy relationships because of her background:

> Perhaps I was fortunate in having to wrestle with the problems of being an ACoA before I ever heard of the term. Or before I read the literature or attended any of the programs. In therapy, and in my sometimes awkward attempts to put my life in order, I began to see myself as an individual who could change, instead of a type imprisoned by a rigid pattern of behavior. That may be why I was surprised by the sense of helplessness I found among some of the groups I attended. . . . I didn't feel the way I was being told most ACoAs feel. I was not living in fear of becoming an alcoholic or embracing some other form of addiction. I enjoyed close relationships, but I didn't feel trapped in them. . . . I had uncovered plenty of emotional handicaps, but I had already dealt with many of them and knew I didn't have to live with them forever. Unfortunately I was not finding that kind of a hopeful attitude—even among many ACoAs who had been in and out of one program or another over several years.[21]

Hobe describes what she felt such programs offered in place of what she and others like her needed:

> ACoAs aren't getting the kind of help they really need because most forms of treatment tend to reinforce their problems.
>
> When we finally get up enough courage to go into a recovery program, we already feel worthless [and] guilty. . . . We certainly don't experience relief after being told how many things are wrong with us—and that there isn't any cure. . . . We have always felt powerless to do anything about the condition of our lives; in recovery we are told

that this is true—and it's not going to change. Instead of teaching us the skills of self-sufficiency, which we desperately need, we are urged to expect a "Higher Power" to look after us.[22]

A Final Word to Part I

How can we—as children of alcoholics, of abusive parents, of dysfunctional parents, and of just plain, ordinary parents—overcome our own problems, in love and elsewhere? If there is any addiction that people routinely outgrow on their own, it is love addiction. Obviously it is not done through abstinence, since love and intimacy are parts of a complete life. We all have known teenagers who lived and "died" for immature love relationships. It is a normal part of adolescence. Lacking self-assurance and experience, not knowing what it is like to bounce back from a breakup, young lovers rotate through relationships (often ill-chosen ones) at a high emotional pitch. But as people mature, they become more aware, choose better partners, and develop more confidence. With maturity, unrealistic emotional demands and jealousies recede. This natural developmental process is a model for how people outgrow all addictions, and for the Life Process Program of treatment and self-help presented in part II.

PART II

THE LIFE PROCESS PROGRAM

•

SKILLS FOR TAKING CONTROL OF YOUR LIFE

CHAPTER 8

THE LIFE PROCESS PROGRAM

YOU MIGHT ASK, "If my problem habits aren't diseases, how do I do something about them?" or "If sending my child into treatment isn't the answer, what is?" The recommendations in this part of the book flow directly out of what was revealed in part I. Our recommendations are based on the methods used (deliberately or not) by most people who overcome habits that threaten their well-being. We call this "natural" way of licking addictions the Life Process Program.[1] We don't even like to call it a "therapy," and we certainly don't regard readers of this book as "patients." Therapy claims to impart special techniques and wisdom to suffering addicts. We, instead, seek to help you mobilize the considerable assets we expect readers of this book already have.

Of course, some people are at the end of their rope and feel they have few resources to call on. We don't want to minimize the misery people often feel when they are trying to escape addiction. Even in these cases, however, the disease model's strategy of convincing the person of his or her powerlessness is unhelpful. Though disease-oriented programs like A.A. are often the only ones available to offer a helping hand, we find that even the most down-and-out addicts would benefit from a different outlook. Instead of focusing on the person's failures and weaknesses, the Life Process Program draws on those strengths and personal resources the addict retains. Throughout part II, we will draw connections between the normal maturing process and what the most severely addicted people require in order to regain their balance.

As we have seen, people give up their addictions when they hear unmistakable signals that something they have considered crucial to their lives is hurting them badly. As most people mature and assume responsible, satisfying roles, life-disturbing habits become less appealing to them. These natural developments in people's lives can be encouraged by therapies that focus on real skills in coping and self-management. They also point us to strategies that you can use yourself or to help someone you care about. The techniques we outline will guide you as you

- assess where you stand in life and what a particular habit means to you, what it does *for* as well as *to* you;
- set realistic goals for change, based on your personal resources and positive values;
- strengthen your life at the same time as you strive to change your habit;
- create environments for yourself and others that make addiction both unnecessary and undesirable.

This kind of personal growth may sound difficult, and sometimes it is. Sometimes it involves hard-won self-awareness and sustained, long-term effort. In other cases, it happens with remarkable ease as the building blocks of a better life fall into place. Just remember that, *for most people, these life ingredients evolve sooner or later.* Most likely you are already undergoing a trial-and-error learning process by which you eventually will find your way out of addiction. By highlighting these positive aspects of your experiences, our suggestions can speed up the timetable of your emancipation, halt the damage to your health and well-being, and help you get on with your life.

Part I highlighted some encouraging facets of human nature:

- More often than not, people rise to the occasion when they are given positive options.
- People typically strive to set their lives straight and, given time, usually succeed.
- Age tends to ameliorate or eliminate bad habits while bringing greater self-contentment and improved coping.

▶ Nearly all people have values that are incompatible with their addictions—the most remarkable cases of "instantaneous" cure occur when these values crystallize so that people reject the addiction.

Once you take off the blinders of the "disease" mythology, you can examine with optimism the ordinary changes people make to set their lives straight. You can build upon your own capacities and discover within yourself the strengths for positive change. Feelings of independence, self-reliance, confidence, accomplishment, pride—together with the crucial *desire* to change—are the basic ingredients for recovery. This book can help you to gather together the resources that already exist in your life. With them, you can develop the skills in dealing with yourself and your environment that you need to make the changes you want.

Can Learning to Take Care of Teeth Tell Us Anything About Curing Alcoholism?

When you deal with addiction in the context of everyday life, you may be surprised to find that addiction is not so different from many other personal problems you have successfully mastered. Let's visualize the range of addictive problems as a pyramid, with the worst dependencies at the top (the street inebriate, the person so fat he or she can't leave home) and the mildest excesses at the bottom:

Pyramid of Alcohol Abuse

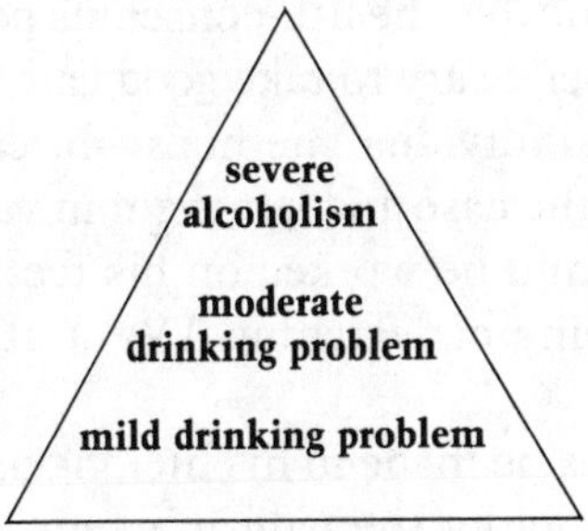

Pyramid of Overeating

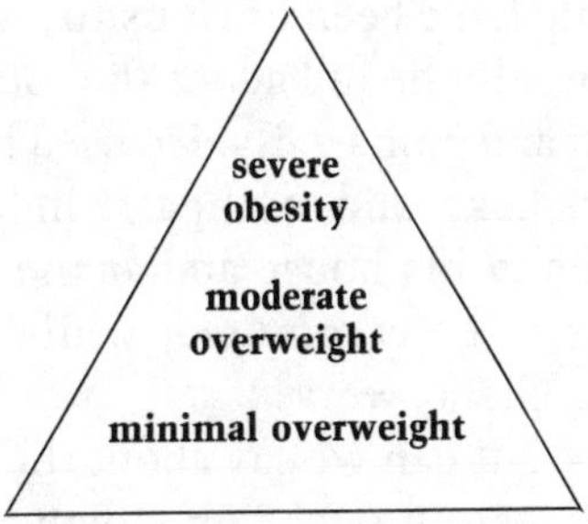

You might find yourself at any point on the pyramid, but you are more likely to be near the bottom than the top. People's addictions fluctuate in severity in response to stress and other changing circumstances, so you may move up and down on the pyramid. Clearly, anything that brings you down to a lower point and keeps you there is a positive development.

It makes no sense to prescribe the most drastic remedies for *everyone* on the basis of the experiences of the few people at the top of the pyramid. Instead, let's start at the base of the pyramid, where most people are. Let's think about ordinary kinds of behavior—lifelong habits that people get deeply involved in and attached to—and how people change them. We will find this everyday model more applicable even to full-blown addictions than we might expect.

Here is an example from one of the authors' experiences of basic behavior change. He came from a long line of people who had good teeth without spending much time on dental care. The patriarch of his family—his grandfather—didn't brush his teeth his whole life, but kept his own teeth until he died in his eighties. As a result, our author didn't think he had to pay much attention to his teeth. Even though he didn't brush his teeth regularly, he got through adolescence and early adulthood with few cavities and often was complimented for having good teeth. In his thirties, though, he developed abscesses in his gums. Having successfully ignored his teeth all his life, he had difficulty recognizing that he would not be able to ignore his gums.

Thus began a process over five years or more of slowly learning better dental care. At first only sporadically, he began to follow some of his dentist's recommendations (brushing more often, flossing, picking, etc.), but he would also backslide. The dentist would always tell him, "It's better than last time," but then perform procedures that became more painful with each visit. He was forced to consult a periodontist and to have his gums scraped. Despite his slowness to do what should have been obvious to a well-educated, health-conscious person, eventually he did adopt the routines necessary to take good care of his teeth and gums daily. He used his own individual methods—he carried floss, picks, and toothpaste in his attaché case and left them in various rooms in his house and at the office, and he worked on his teeth and gums as he commuted, while exercising or watching TV, or at slow moments at work.

What can we say about the changes he made in his lifelong habits? They were brought on slowly but surely by the pain inherent in *not* changing these habits. Change required some planning and adjustment in his environment. The change was supported by the concern of his family and by the good results from making the changes—fewer painful and expensive medical procedures and better-feeling gums. After a time, caring for his teeth became such second nature to him and so ingrained in his daily life that it would have taken another conscious effort to return to his old habits! But, even though these habits were now second nature to him, we can't lose sight of the fact that for thirty or more years his dental care had been abysmal, and predicted ultimate disaster—dentures—for him in later life.

This example is typical of all kinds of adjustments that people make in their lives, based on their growing awareness of the changing impact of their behavior on their health and well-being. Sometimes these changes happen more slowly than they should. Old habits and satisfactions tend to feel more comfortable and rewarding than new ones do, because you are *sure* of what the old habits accomplish for you, however little that may turn out to be. What is remarkable is that—despite all the inertia of the human animal—people *do* change. They change because they get enough information over a long enough time to see that what they are doing is harmful, and because they learn that there are better ways of doing things.

It takes time for the balance to shift, but eventually it often does, and your image of yourself changes. In the case above, the person stopped admiring himself because he didn't take care of his teeth and began to think more of himself because he did. When *this* change occurs, the possibility of your returning to your old habits becomes very remote.

This same process occurred with the authors concerning driving with seat belts. When we were twenty-five, we couldn't be bothered to buckle up. It was too much trouble; it didn't look good or feel good to be constrained that way; and we were in a hurry to get places. Subsequently, these considerations mattered less than the accumulating evidence about the safety benefits of seat belts. We began to use our seat belts—first only for highway driving, then only when going out of the neighborhood, and eventually at all times. Of course, family life and setting examples for children came to be perhaps the major reason for changing personal habits. These changes took place almost imperceptibly, but they represented a significant evolution in what it meant to us to be "smart" or to "feel good" or to be who we felt we were. When we went from feeling funny about being strapped in to feeling funny when we *weren't* strapped in, we could tell that the change was real and permanent.

Quitting "Real" Addictions

Teeth, gums, and seat belts—what does all this have to do with alcoholism, drug abuse, or chain-smoking? What can those suffering the agonies of addiction learn from such innocuous anecdotes? These matter-of-fact tales of personal development and maturation contain the kernel of every story in this book about people overcoming addictions—serious addictions. When we learn that most heroin addicts "mature out" in their twenties or thirties, it should not surprise us that the process of giving up addiction is essentially one of growing up—at whatever age.

As we mature, we typically curb impulses, assume responsibilities, and satisfy needs in ways that get us in less trouble and are less annoying to others. We are able to learn to do these things because, as we age, we tend to resolve adolescent emotional conflicts, we gain more control of our lives, and we become more focused on the things we want to accomplish. As part of this process, we may give up smoking, moderate our eating habits, and cut down or cut out drinking or drug-taking. Most of our excessive habits occur near the base of the pyramid of addiction. We should be able to temper most of these excesses as we proceed through life, as long as we remain alert to signs from our bodies and our surroundings.

The idea that quitting an addiction is a cataclysmic event utterly unlike ordinary habits only gets in the way of recovery. Severe addictions that fit this melodramatic stereotype are relatively rare, and it doesn't help most of us to model our experience after this stereotype. Indeed, becoming an addict is a matter of interpreting our behavior as being the result of our addiction and acting accordingly. For example, if you are convinced you are addicted to alcohol because you have drunk too much in the past, the next time you feel like having a drink you may believe you cannot help getting drunk. As a result, you are more likely to act like and become an alcoholic.

People interpret their feelings and behavior in line with the images they are sold. If they see and believe media images of addicts in a frenzied, all-consuming pursuit of drugs or alcohol, they are likely to imitate such models if they consume these substances. The same is true for other potentially addictive experiences, such as shopping. Let's say you have frequently spent beyond your means. If you saw the TV show on this subject described in chapter 6, you might call yourself an out-of-control "shopaholic," forever destined to chase the "endorphin high" or "chemical euphoria" you'd get from a binge in the department store.

However, if you didn't know what a shopaholic was, you could more easily interpret and deal with the disparity between your shopping behavior and your other goals in life. You might think, "I always seem to be going over budget these days. Why do I spend more than I have? My sister doesn't have this problem." You could ask yourself whether doing this much shopping is consistent with your values—do you want people to think shopping is the most important activity in your life? You could begin to figure out why you overshopped. You could limit your shopping outings or put other restraints on your spending. You could find better things to do with your time. In some form or another, you *need* to go through this kind of process to solve the problem.

The disease and the Life Process Program views of addictions present two very different versions of the same behavior. The Life Process Program presents a recipe for change through toning down overblown and frightening rhetoric about addictions and by instead appealing to the strength, intelligence, and instinct for self-preservation in every person. Addiction *is* a problem, and for some people a very severe problem. But you can best address that problem by reminding yourself of everything about you that is normal and healthy and by applying those strengths to your weakest areas of functioning.

Similarly, if your child is abusing drugs, you rightly worry about the potentially serious consequences of that behavior. But these immediate concerns do not obviate the need to address the values, relationships, and activities that constitute the young person's life. Whether it is you or a loved one who must cope with an addiction, don't discount your own resourcefulness. At the very least, the chapters that follow should help put you back in touch with sound, traditional ideas that aren't currently in fashion, but that you can discover by applying your own common sense.

The Life Process Program for Change

The Life Process Program we recommend is outlined in the accompanying table. It does not focus exclusively or even primarily on the addiction itself. You will certainly need to work on your addiction specifically, but the most crucial work you need to do is on the direction of your overall life, of which an addiction is just one expression.

The Life Process Program Summarized

Nondisease Approach

—addiction to an experience

—failure of disease treatment

—emphasis on natural processes

- builds on individual strength
- focuses on social environment

—treatment is finite

Different Assumptions from Disease Approach

—person as evolving being

—individualized treatment

—client-centered

—coping prevents addiction

—goal: personal efficacy

Elements

—motivation

—values

—skills

—life involvements: family, work

—community

Although insight can be a useful tool, the Life Process Program differs from psychoanalytic therapy in that it concentrates on current rewards, satisfactions, and obstacles rather than what went wrong in your past. It also differs from behavioral techniques that shape behavior through contrived rewards and punishments in that it seeks rewards and punishments to encourage new behaviors *in the natural structure of your life.* Also, our Life Process Program is very much a *values-based* approach. We believe your values are the most crucial ingredient in orienting—or in reorienting—your life. Developing and living by a set of values, expanding your connections to the world, and aiming for and accomplishing worthwhile goals are key factors in the Life Process Program.

Why should you have confidence in these "natural" methods? Have they been proved to work? The proof is in the previous chapters, and in the research about which therapies are most effective. The change process is not a mysterious or arcane one: What works best for self-help is the same as what has been shown to work best as therapy. Studies of the effectiveness of therapy for addiction consistently demonstrate the decisive importance of the client's motivation and active involvement in the change process. It isn't the characteristics of the therapy that matter most, but the characteristics and intentions of the person who goes into therapy. Even when you enter therapy for an addiction, you *must* realize that your fate remains in your own hands.

Treatments That Work

Some therapies *are* more effective than others. Effective therapies have the following characteristics:

- They are pragmatic rather than ideological.
- They are geared toward concrete results rather than labeling you and reinterpreting your experience for you.
- They examine your life in its totality rather than focusing exclusively on your addiction.
- They work by strengthening the foundations of your life rather than quarantining you in groups of fellow sufferers.

When psychologists William Miller and Reid Hester (as noted in chapter 1) reviewed all available comparative studies on treatment for alcoholism, they found that the treatments most commonly used in the United States—Alcoholics Anonymous, alcoholism education, drug therapy (Antabuse), individual or group counseling, and confrontation—showed little or no evidence of effectiveness. On the other hand, they found that a number of treatments *had* demonstrated their effectiveness. Effective therapies for alcoholism include aversion therapy, which associates drinking with punishments or unpleasant images, and behavioral self-control training, which teaches problem drinkers moderation techniques.

Most successful therapies for alcoholism and addiction, however, go beyond the drinking behavior itself to strengthen the "life skills" a person needs to replace an addiction with deeper satisfactions and better ways of coping. These include marital and family therapy, social-skills training, job skills, and stress management. The most effective and comprehensive therapies for alcoholism—the Community Reinforcement Approach—and for drug addiction—therapeutic communities—address people's whole lives as well as their addictions. These therapies set up a home and work environment that discourages drug and alcohol intoxication while fostering the development of problem-solving skills. This "environmental management" comes closest to the approach we advocate.

Our Life Process Program outlines self-help procedures adapted from these successful therapeutic models as well as from the experience of natural recovery. In the following chapters, we discuss specific addictive behaviors and ways to modify them. But we always place primary emphasis on strengthening your life structure and skills. Family relations, social and vocational skills, and stress management are featured here, as they are in the most effective therapies. Our strategy throughout this book is to link behavior change with the real issues in your life, the ones that matter most to you.

Making Therapy Work

The changes that need to happen if you are to put an addiction behind you can happen in or out of therapy. If you make these changes on your own, you are in good—and plentiful—company. If you go about it in therapy, you must be clear that the necessary changes are actually occurring. Be sure your therapy measures up in terms of the improvements you need in your life, and not just in terms of fulfilling the demands of the therapy. Otherwise, you may find you do better at being a "good" therapy client or group member than at helping yourself. In other words, six months or two years down the road, are you dealing better with your problems, or are you just attending the same groups and saying the same things over and over again?

The approach to giving up addictions that the Life Process Program presents is so obviously sensible and effective that it is amazing that people turn instead to groups that sell a particular ideology, like so many twelve-step–based groups. Why aren't really effective therapies more widely practiced in the United States? Why are people so readily satisfied with the shortcuts and simplifications of the disease model? The disease model seductively plays on our wish for a cure that doesn't require us to struggle with life issues—as if changing our lives were as simple as abstaining from a drug or alcohol. For patient and therapy provider alike, this shallow version of treatment is itself an addictive experience.

Abstinence can be a small step toward larger goals. Quitting drinking or strictly limiting one's calorie intake may be vital for some people at a key moment in their lives. But if the slogan "one day at a time" actually works, it must be more than a daily preoccupation with avoiding the addictive habit. It must refer to a larger, positive transformation from an alcoholic or an addict to a person with a nonaddicted orientation to life, or from a habitual overeater to a person who eats normally. This shift in life-style and perspective takes time and may not furnish immediate gratification every step of the way, but its beneficial effects ultimately far exceed those of the twelve-step formula.

Stages of Change: How People Really Do It

For many who evolve out of their addictions naturally, an inner reorientation has usually taken place *prior* to giving up the destructive habit, so that quitting has the appearance of a miracle cure. Other people must make a deliberate effort to change, in which the early steps toward change are hard and sometimes painful.

In order to sustain your change effort, you must envision your long-term goals at the same time that you create intermediate rewards for yourself. The Life Process Program—which grows out of the particular circumstances of individual lives—cannot be reduced to a universal prescription. Nonetheless, we can identify the major stages of self-liberation that people go through. Don't rely on these stages as a step-by-step formula; instead, use them as categories for developing your own change strategies. These are the stages you will pass through, like the many people who recover from addiction in the cases in this book (and hundreds more that we have read or heard):

You become convinced that the activity or involvement violates more important values. This realization may take months or years to sink in. Yet it sometimes seems as if it occurs in a flash, as when an alcoholic, after years of bar-hopping, looks at himself and says, "Why am I here with these people and not home with my family?"

You develop alternative rewards that are more meaningful than those of the addiction. Effective therapy for addiction encourages people to engage in two types of alternative activities: those that give immediate pleasure and those that lead to long-range goals. In natural recovery, these components of a satisfying life fall into place for people as they mature. But if these developments do not occur of their own momentum, people who are determined to give up addiction may move, make new friends, get involved in a career, or take up new interests. You may do any or all of these things in order to create *enough work, play, and love so that you have better things to do than be addicted.*

You rely on friends, family, and groups to help support the change in behavior. Although some people do find groups of "fellow sufferers" supportive, becoming completely immersed in such a group (and remaining totally preoccupied with the addiction) can seriously limit a person's development. There are significant advantages to relying on the support of friends, family, co-workers, fellow church members, or people who appreciate healthy behavior but who are not ex-addicts. These contacts are part of the network of normal life that you must develop as part of giving up an addiction.

You arrange your life so that you get better rewards from not being addicted than you used to get from being addicted. People want something in return for giving up the gratifications previously provided by the addiction. Their new rewards come in the form of a new self-image and a sense of righteousness (or power, or triumph) in having licked the habit, in approval from old and new associates, and in the enjoyment and accomplishment that flow from the new activities that replace the addiction. For example, exercising during and after losing weight makes you aware of your newfound physical capacities; feeling energetic and clearheaded makes up for the "lift" you once got from smoking and coffee drinking; enjoying time with your children replaces the sensations that drugs or alcohol used to provide.

You avoid situations and ways of thinking that provoke relapse. Avoiding relapse doesn't just mean staying away from bars or old drinking buddies. You must also manage predictable stresses that formerly triggered your addictive behavior. Finally, you must avoid fatalistic, self-fulfilling ways of thinking about relapse, such as: "If I have this one piece of cake, then I'm off my diet and I might as well go whole hog."

You will sometimes slip or be less than perfect, but you must keep these bad moments in perspective. Occasionally we hear about a person who returns to smoking after ten years of abstinence. Yet you should be able to balance a day or week of smoking against the decade of not smoking and regain your balance.

You eventually develop a new self-image, a view of yourself as a *former* addict. As time passes and you experience years of a new life, you should develop a new identity based on these life experiences. You no longer see yourself as weak, vulnerable, or at a disadvantage compared with "normal" people. No longer must you be preoccupied with re-straining food intake, fighting off images of cigarettes, liquor, or co-caine, and maintaining constant vigilance in order to avoid relapse. Instead, you become a genuine normal eater, nonsmoker, moderate drinker, or drug avoider who laughs—or groans—at the thought of going back to your old life.

The ultimate goal of the Life Process Program is a full personal transformation—which disease-oriented treatment says is impossible. There is no reason why you cannot shed the addict identity altogether and put yourself permanently on a new plane of existence. It is within reach, if you believe it and act on that belief. The accompanying table summarizes how the Life Process Program differs in its assumptions and recommendations from the disease approach to addiction:

The Differences Between the Disease and Life Process Approaches to Addiction	
Disease Model	*Life Process Program*
Your addiction is inbred (genetic, biological)	Your addiction is a way of coping with life experience
You get the same therapy as everyone else	You design a treatment that fits you
You must accept your identity as an addict/alcoholic	You focus on problems and not labels
Your therapy and cure are dictated to you	You arrive at your own goals and therapy plan
Either you are addicted or you aren't	Your addiction will vary depending on your situation
Your addictive symptoms are drummed into you	You identify the negative consequences of the addiction
Any claims you have to being okay are attacked as denial	Positive aspects of your self-image are accepted and amplified
You are taught you have no control or ability to choose	You accept the need for self-control and to make choices
Therapy focuses on addiction	Therapy focuses on life environment
Total abstinence is the only successful resolution	Improved control and relapse reduction are sought
You must avoid challenging situations	You must be more aware of and deal better with difficult situations
Your primary social supports are fellow addicts	Your primary social supports are work, family, friends
You need the same treatment and group support forever	Your treatment or group support evolves over life
You are always an addict	You can lose your addiction and no longer need to think of yourself as an addict

CHAPTER 9

QUITTING AS LIFE PROCESS

THE CASE OF PAULA

SINCE MOST PEOPLE find that smoking is the most difficult addiction to quit, a twenty-year smoking habit might seem almost insurmountable. Yet Paula, a person not that different from many people we know, quit just such a habit. After she quit, she had two sessions with a therapist to bolster her choice. Looking back at Paula's years of smoking and the way they ended, we find that her sudden liberation was actually the culmination of a long life process. Paula stopped smoking as a result of a gradual, almost imperceptible realignment of forces in her life. By understanding how those forces worked and how she changed, we can more clearly identify the essential steps that a person trying to break out of addiction needs to take.[1]

Paula, a college-educated member of the "sixties generation," does not look like someone who would smoke for twenty years. A combination of circumstantial and emotional problems, however, kept her from expressing the positive values she espoused. Her smoking went hand in hand with these unresolved issues, and she licked the habit only when she could take control of all areas of her life.

When Paula entered a small liberal-arts college in the mid-1960s, the first surgeon general's report linking smoking with lung cancer had already come out. But Paula was not about to heed an "establishment report," especially when it sounded like the nagging headmistress who preached against smoking at the strict girls' school Paula had attended. She wasn't about to listen to such nay-sayers—her father smoked, and he was an artist whom Paula admired and imitated. At college, where "everyone" smoked in the dorms and in classes and no one seemed to mind, Paula felt liberated from the confines of the girls' high school she had just left. In a short time, Paula was smoking a pack a day. She thought it helped her focus on her schoolwork, and she thought it helped her stay thin, too. But the main reason she smoked had to do with her self-image. "I thought, 'I'm an adult now, and I can smoke if I want to.' " As for the health hazards, "When you're that young you feel you're immortal and your body doesn't matter. You don't believe *anything* can hurt your body."

Paula began hearing a different message after she graduated from college as a music major. "Maybe now you should think about quitting smoking," a friend suggested. Many people she knew did stop smoking when they graduated. But to Paula, "it was as though a Martian had landed and proposed an odd idea. It still wasn't real to me. It seemed silly to worry about those things." Still, Paula was now getting her first antismoking messages from people she took seriously: "The first Earth Day was held in 1970, and people were beginning to eat healthy food, not eat meat, and care about the environment." But there were not yet enough of those people to sway Paula. Instead, she entered on a period of informal, transient living arrangements typical of the 1960s and early 1970s, where smoking cigarettes and marijuana were just two things people like her often did.

A few years later, Paula spent the summer working on a farm where a friend of hers was beginning to raise a family. Her friend, who had recently stopped smoking, asked Paula not to smoke so that she herself would not be tempted. Paula quit for two months. She had not planned to stop, but she did it with little difficulty. She was not preoccupied with cigarette withdrawal and did not think of smoking as addictive. She assumed that she could stop and start at will, and she did start again as soon as she left the farm. She remembers how she felt at the time:

> I was on the road, and all of a sudden I felt very free. I bought a pack of cigarettes at a rest stop. "I want to smoke, and now I can do what I want," I thought. I felt somehow that in that farmhouse I had been losing my identity. Two months of very hard labor, child care and all—it wasn't the life that I wanted; it wasn't *my* life. Now I could get back to whatever my life was going to be.

Paula had been smoking regularly for about seven years. "By then," she says, "I may have begun to realize that it was hard to stop, but I still didn't *want* to stop. I didn't believe my life would be any better without cigarettes."

As the chaotic intensity of counterculture life died down in the 1970s, people picked up the pieces and got down to work. For Paula this meant establishing herself as an orchestral violinist. Many of the musicians she worked with continued to smoke—it seemed to make the hard daily practice grind a lot easier. Paula could hardly imagine getting through a five-hour session without the relief of a few smokes. During this period, Paula was living with a couple, both accomplished musicians and both smokers. "By then we would talk about how it was a nasty habit, how awful it was, and how we should stop, but it was so much chatter." It became more real when the woman in this couple was found to have cancer.

Meanwhile, the leader of the string quartet Paula played with, a man who had smoked until he recently quit, also developed lung cancer. Paula was shaken when this man died in his mid-forties. She realized it could happen to her, too. By then, however, smoking had become the glue that held together Paula's otherwise fragmented life. Striving for auditions with better orchestras, living in different places, doing commercial studio sessions to meet expenses, and practicing alone day after day constituted a routine that did not allow Paula to create stable personal relationships, and she usually lived with married friends or groups of women. Smoking seemed to make it all bearable:

> Building my career was a mission; it was more important than my health. I didn't want to do anything that would upset my life. Smoking was part of the foundation I was operating on, and I didn't want to shake it, because I had bigger things to do.

By the early 1980s, Paula's smoking, once a badge of belonging, was increasingly a social barrier. Paula no longer felt comfortable smoking around her close personal friends and would not dream of smoking around her godchild, for whom she did not want to set a bad example. She smoked only when she was working and when she socialized with those musicians who still smoked. "By that time, all the people I knew believed that smoking was bad, but there were still some who felt they were hooked on it, and I could smoke with them." The only social context left for Paula to smoke in was a self-denigrating one: hanging around with fellow addicts.

Paula had been smoking between a pack and a half and two a day, but only on her routine days of long practices alone alternating with frenetic practical and professional activity. By now she could not smoke with most of her friends, nor did she feel the need to. A day hike meant a day away from cigarettes; a weekend staying with friends meant two days away. And she was surprised at how good it made her feel! When she wasn't smoking, she felt like a healthier person. If only she weren't so dependent on cigarettes to work!

Tired of touring and hiring herself out in different places, Paula finally found a regular job in a small city orchestra. This gave her the opportunity to settle down in one place; the trouble was, it was in a rural state where she didn't know anybody. Long hours, no friends or recreation, on top of which her father died and she was breaking up with a boyfriend she had left behind in the city where she formerly lived. Yet, despite all this stress, Paula found she could go without smoking for a few days whenever she got away from home. Smoking had become an anachronism, but she felt she couldn't deal with quitting while she was struggling to find a way out of her current situation and still earn a living.

Finally, Paula found a job in the string section of one of the better orchestras in the country, one located in a city where she could enjoy a reasonable life. Now, at social gatherings, Paula identified people who had stopped smoking and asked them, "How did you stop? What was it like, before and after?" She got better answers to the second question than the first. And what she heard was not about the agonies of withdrawal. Instead, people told her that she would feel more in control of her life and that she'd see how much better it was. But she couldn't get detailed instructions about how to make the leap from "before" to "after." She realized that she had never made a serious attempt to stop smoking. But she still worried that she was under too much stress to try to do without cigarettes.

Paula began looking into smoking-cessation programs; maybe, if she checked into a treatment center and committed money, time, and effort, it might work. But she didn't actually go into a program, because she felt she couldn't take time out from her busy life. Increasingly, however, she resented what smoking was doing to her. After chain-smoking her way through hours of rehearsing and performing under pressure, she would feel drained, her head aching and her chest singed with pain. People she played with would remark, "Paula, you look so skinny, you look so green." It was the cigarettes, along with her working conditions.

Then Paula came down with a severe chest cold that turned into bronchitis. Running a high fever for three days, she was too ill to work—or smoke. At that point, she decided to let go and let herself be sick. "I've been pushing myself for so many years," she thought, "I've done enough." As for smoking, she said to herself, "Maybe I'll just stop." For three weeks, as she recuperated, she cut herself off from music and all other obligations and stayed in bed with a stack of books she had wanted to read. For a time she had a bad cough, but even when she wasn't coughing she didn't have the desire to smoke.

As the three weeks went by, Paula sensed that she didn't need to smoke when she wasn't under pressure. If she was violating herself by smoking, it was because she allowed herself to be violated by excessive, invasive work demands. It was not just cigarettes, she realized; "I'm going to have to pull away from this whole crazy life-style." Thus, the meaning of smoking had come full circle for Paula. What once had symbolized freedom from control by others (the headmistress, her friend on the farm) now signified enslavement, a violation of self, a loss of identity. Years ago she had asserted herself by smoking; now she asserted herself against the conditions that drove her to smoke.

Once she got out of bed and back into circulation, Paula began to see that she had used cigarettes to mask other stresses besides work:

> When I was smoking, if someone would upset me on the phone, I could always hang up and comfort myself with a cigarette. There was always that solace for me after a difficult meeting. When I didn't have that anymore, I found myself getting sharp with people. I realized that I would have to respond more quickly and be more assertive, since I didn't have that consolation to fall back on.

After an argument with the man she was seeing, Paula recognized how she had smoked to bypass conflicts with people, substituting "consolation" for self-assertion:

> He went out on the porch to smoke, and I just got so angry because I didn't have that weapon anymore. I said, "I have

> to leave." I was so wound up I had to take a walk around the block, which made me feel infinitely better.

"For the first time in my life, I knew I definitely wanted to stop smoking," Paula recalls. In fact, she had stopped. But she knew that staying stopped would not be a sure thing, not when she had used smoking as her main interpersonal "weapon." So she contacted a therapist who ran behavior-modification programs for smokers. She explained that she "didn't want to go through a whole program with a bunch of people who were withdrawing," and the therapist wisely agreed. Paula came in for two sessions with the therapist, who told her that, based on his experience, "People know when they're ready to stop." That one remark made a deep impression on her. "I must have been ready because I had already stopped," she reflected. "I had quit in my own good time. I should have done it earlier, but when it came it was an internal decision. I had to have my own reasons."

The therapist recommended a book on assertiveness, to enable her to refuse work demands as well as to make demands on friends and co-workers when she needed to. He encouraged Paula to develop her interest in running. He taught her exercises in which she visualized herself in the midst of a pleasant scene and then visualized herself practicing the violin without smoking. He also prepared her for the possibility of relapse. "Don't judge yourself if you do smoke again," he told her. "People slip. I don't think you will. But if it happens, the world hasn't ended. I *know* you are at a point where you would quit again as soon as possible."

Relapse wasn't very likely for Paula, because she had been searching her soul, preparing internally to quit for years. The act of stopping had been almost anticlimactic, something long overdue. And relapse has since been made less and less likely by the continuing evolution of her life. "It's good to have a clear head, to feel free to make changes, and not to be obsessed—as I was in my last years of smoking—with the thought that I'm killing myself," Paula reflected. "When you make one internal decision, you find you're able to make others as well." Newly energized and self-confident, she has built up her stamina so that running has become a high point of her day. Paula has not felt any strong cravings for cigarettes, but she has been careful in situations that previously would have driven her to smoke. She copes with work stress by "being kind to myself." As she describes it:

> I'm no longer going to take on all kinds of jobs and crank out the music as a form of self-flagellation. I'll do my work, and then I'll do something for myself, whether it's to meditate, to run, or just to play some music as in "play," where it has nothing to do with money. I'll take my share of responsibility, but I'll also take some time to refresh and renew myself. It's important to me to get out in the sun for an hour and smell the lilacs. It's important to my health and to the quality of my life, which I won't sacrifice for work as I did for years.

Paula currently is reassessing her approach to music so that, "whatever directions it takes, it will be incorporated into a healthy life." As she makes these readjustments, smoking recedes further into her past. "If I have any advice for others," she concludes, "it's that you reach a point where to smoke any longer is to give up on the possibility that you'll ever really take care of yourself. Stopping smoking is an act of self-assertion and an act of kindness toward yourself, and you know when you need to do it."

Anyone who despairs of quitting an addiction should think of Paula. Quitting can be a long, arduous journey, as it was for her, but people who are "ready" can put aside the most long-entrenched habit once and for all. Though they may have failed at any attempts to quit along the way, eventually they find they are able to make the decisive move. Nor does it have to take twenty years. The guidelines in the following chapters translate the natural evolution Paula experienced into a planned, deliberate process that you can undertake. This is the Life Process Program for addiction cessation. If you consider each of these chapters seriously and make the appropriate applications to your life, you can progress more quickly than Paula did. Nonetheless, Paula's case can give us all confidence and courage.

CHAPTER 10

ARE YOU AN ADDICT?

ASSESSING ADDICTION IN THE LIFE PROCESS PROGRAM

WE DO NOT PROPOSE to tell you whether you are an addict or not. First of all, this is a question you must answer yourself. Second, the answer generally is not cut and dried. To say that for a time you may be, or may have been, losing control over a habit or an area of your life is not to say that you are forever out of control. Rather than seek a simple answer, you may need to ask yourself a series of questions, such as: Where am I with regard to this habit? How did I get to this point? How serious is it? How do I feel about it? Since assessment by a therapist or a group consists of asking the "patient" similar questions, the same issues are involved in clinical assessment as in self-assessment. However, for better or worse, in clinical assessment this information is filtered through the biases of those asking the questions.

In the "disease" routine as practiced in twelve-step groups and treatment centers, assessment really means showing people just how badly off they are. The therapist or group confronts individuals with all possible evidence of their disease so as to beat down their defenses until they acknowledge the diagnosis. *No available assessment tool asks, for example, about positive experiences associated with drinking, drug use, or other behaviors that may be addictive.* In addition, disease therapy strives to devalue all aspects of the suspected addict's life in order to prove how badly the addiction has affected the person. In no other area of therapy is it considered good practice to focus exclusively on the negative. For example, when interviewing a depressed or a neurotic person, no therapist would try to point out how really bad the individual's existence is! The purpose of browbeating patients when treating addictive "diseases" is to orchestrate a conversion experience, in which people reject their previous existence in favor of the new "nonaddicted" way of life promoted by the treatment.

In place of this grim indoctrination, we will show you a way of assessing addiction that we believe is more helpful as well as more humane. In the Life Process Program, the purpose of assessment is to make sense out of problem behaviors in the context of your life. Rather than reject and override your understanding of yourself, this approach elicits *your* perspective on your experience as the real starting point for change.

In the area of problem drinking, for example, psychologist William Miller of the University of New Mexico has developed a procedure he calls "motivational interviewing."[1] The comparison in the table below of the disease and Life Process approaches to assessment of addiction follows from Miller's work and from our table in chapter 8 outlining the differences between the disease and Life Process models.

Disease specialists in the field of alcoholism often ask questions—such as "Do you ever drink alone?" or "Do you sometimes drink more

Two Approaches to Assessing Addiction

Disease Approach to Assessment	*Life Process Approach to Assessment*
Forces you to admit you are an addict	You may conclude that your problem is more or less severe
The therapist or group is the expert on your disease	You must reach your own decision about the habit/problem
You must be confronted with evidence of your addiction	You review the impact of the habit/problem on your life
Only negative information about your life is admissible	You consider the strengths and positives in your life
You must admit that you are powerless and have no control	You have the power to consider a range of choices
You receive the same diagnosis and treatment as everyone else	You select a plan consistent with your situation and values
This diagnosis and prescription apply for the rest of your life	You monitor and re-evaluate the habit as your life evolves
You must assume the addict label forever	You want (and believe it is possible) to leave the addiction behind

than you planned?"—that are weighted to produce positive answers. George Vaillant, a psychiatrist, favors a "series of questions that circumvent denial . . . that can identify most people with alcoholism." The first question on this list is, "Do you occasionally drink heavily after a disappointment or a quarrel, or when the boss gives you a hard time?" The last (or twenty-second) question is, "Have you recently noticed that you cannot drink as much as you once did?" Just in case the last question doesn't apply to you, question 3 is, "Have you noticed that you are able to handle more liquor than you did when you were first drinking?"[2]

A remarkably high percentage of people show up on these lists as having some sort of drinking problem. A group of researchers used an alcoholism scale called the Short Michigan Alcoholism Screening Test with a random sample of drinkers in a white, largely middle-class community.[3] Over a fifth of the men (21 percent) and almost a fifth of women (19 percent) gave a "no" answer when asked if they felt they were normal drinkers (that is, they felt they drank too much); a fifth of men said a close relative had complained about their drinking; and almost a fifth (19 percent) said they had at some point felt guilty about their drinking. So a large percentage worried that they had some kind of drinking problem.

Yet very few had severe problems. Only 2 percent of the men and less than 1 percent of the women said they had ever gotten into trouble at work due to drinking; 2 percent of men and three-tenths of one percent of women said they had neglected their work or their families for two days straight as a result of drinking. At the point when these questions were asked in 1977 (just when the private hospital treatment of alcoholism was exploding), only 3 percent of men (and *none of 646 women*) had ever sought help for a drinking problem, and 1 percent of men (and two of 646 women) had been hospitalized for drinking. Clearly, if one could tap the guilt or worry of these middle-class respondents as a way to get them to seek treatment, the hospital and treatment rolls would expand dramatically. And, indeed, this happened. By 1984, 5.5 percent of men and 1.5 percent of women surveyed nationwide had been treated for an alcohol problem. At the same time, 27 percent of men (and nearly *one-third* of those under forty) and 12 percent of women (including more than one-sixth of those under forty) had been told by someone that they had a drinking problem.[4]

The diagnosticians have a conflict of interest, of course, since they are selling the solution for the problem they have just diagnosed. The person is told how he or she can't solve the problem alone, and how the prescription must be followed for the rest of his or her life, since the disease is incurable. The diagnosis is also, in Vaillant's words, meant to "circumvent denial" of drinking problems. But, really, it is most often people's guilt or anxiety (or their spouses') about their drinking, rather than any objective events, that shows up as a problem. This is why the phrase "If you *think* you have a drinking problem, then you do" (which is then translated into a diagnosis of and treatment for alcoholism) is such an effective marketing tool.

In contrast to a disease approach that emphasizes to people that their deepest fears that they may be alcoholics are true, the Life Process Program arms you with a self-developed awareness with which to analyze and understand your behavior. With this awareness, you can evaluate your behavior through the various stages and circumstances you encounter over your lifetime. This ongoing self-monitoring is the necessary alternative to turning yourself over to professional helpers or rigid group-think approaches every time you face a difficult life event or suspect that your ways of coping with life are flawed.

The Criteria for Addiction

According to the Life Process Program, addiction is not a clearcut ailment that you have or don't have. Actually, addictive problems occur along a continuum. Hardly anyone reading this book will fit the most extreme criteria for addiction. Moreover, extreme cases of addiction rarely require subtle analysis—a person who is having regular blackouts due to drinking or who is a hundred pounds overweight does not generally need to be told he or she has a problem. Nonetheless, to show how the Life Process Program applies to severe addictions as well as to the normal range of self-help situations, we will include among our illustrative examples extreme cases of addiction along with the more typical, milder problems you are likely to confront.

The main point of this chapter, then, is not to convince you that you are as addicted as (or more so than) you feared. Rather, it is to help you recognize the addictive elements and patterns in your daily habits and behavior so that you can correct habits that are hurting you. For this purpose, we have boiled down the essential features of addiction, as described throughout this book, into a checklist of questions. Our self-assessment questionnaire is more generally applicable than the typical alcoholism scale, since it applies to *any* addictive behavior or involvement. More important, it focuses not on *symptoms* but on the *meaning* a habit has for you and its role (positive as well as negative) in your life.

It is best to read this chapter with a pad and pencil, to jot down your responses and any other thoughts these questions suggest to you. Even if you've already thought a great deal about your habit, committing your answers to paper can crystallize the issues.

In order to assess a habit or area of behavior, ask yourself these four general types of questions:

▶ *What are the signs* that my habit or behavior is a problem; how is it hurting my life?

▶ *What experience does it provide;* why do I persist in the habit despite its drawbacks?

▶ *When* is it a problem; under what conditions is the problem most severe?

▶ *What are the major problem areas in my life,* aside from the habit with which I am concerned?

Signs of Addiction—
Addictive Feelings and Behaviors

These are the things *you can point to* that you know mean trouble. They include problems with feelings, behaviors, reactions by others, or health, legal, or job-related problems.

Feelings

Are you unhappy about something you're doing? Do you feel bad about yourself when you are doing it, or afterward? Does doing it always carry with it some kind of internal negative reaction, such as guilt? Are the bad feelings increasing, and are they crowding out any good feelings that the activity or habit used to create? Is your primary remedy for the bad feelings produced by the activity to *return* to it?

EXAMPLES

1. You spend time with a group of people who are very critical, and whom you are anxious to please. Nonetheless, after leaving the group, you are always overcome by anxiety and shame. You usually spend hours asking yourself if you acted properly and if those people are finally accepting you—and your answer is usually negative. But all this does is make you more anxious to return to the group and, *this time,* to please them.

2. You watch television alone a lot. When you finally turn off the TV, you always feel bad—you recognize that you wasted your time, and you're ashamed of your inertia. Pained by this realization, you quickly turn on the TV to forget about it.

Behaviors

Can you vary the behavior, stop or cut back when necessary? Or are your actions compulsive and inflexible? Do you continue them no matter how inappropriate or harmful, and are they interfering with and crowding out other activities and relationships? Are you getting increasingly negative reactions from people close to you; have you had legal problems due specifically to this activity; are you doing less well at your work because of it; does your body feel worse as a result of the activity—is it hurting your health and well-being?

EXAMPLES

1. You are exercising so much that your wife resents the activity.

2. Your children dislike your smoking and are more and more anxious about it—or, worse, *they* have developed health problems as a result of your ambient smoke.

3. Your mind is less clear at work as a result of drinking or drug use in the evenings or on weekends.

4. You took money you set aside for a gift and bought a large number of lottery tickets.

5. Instead of exercising, you go to the shopping mall whenever you have free time.

6. You believe that you didn't get a promotion because you're too heavy and don't look good.

7. You find you are tired as a result of worry, bad diet, lack of exercise, and other excesses, like smoking and drinking.

8. Your lover offends your friends and family, so that you are becoming more isolated, which then makes you more dependent on this one person.

Stepping back from specific examples, we see the danger signs of addiction are as follows:

- *Pain:* you feel worse overall as a result of doing something habitually, and the negative feelings are growing.
- *Deterioration of other activities and relationships:* you can point out the ways the addictive activity interferes with family, friends, work, health, and other hobbies and free time.
- *Inflexibility and calcification:* you can't change the pattern in order to cease, cut short, reduce, or delay the activity when it is completely inappropriate, when you receive negative feedback, or when you need to do something else.
- *Self-exacerbation:* your behavior has negative consequences, including bad feelings, that cause you to *repeat* the behavior.

The concept of denial that figures prominently in the disease model is very much overrated. People will react defensively when they are attacked for their addictions: they'll say "no" if you ask them, "Don't you know smoking will kill you?" or "Can't you see you're out of control of your eating?" Nonetheless, most people recognize their addictions for what they are and understand that they are harmful. Most people are acutely aware of their excess weight and of the unnecessary desserts or snacks they eat, often with little real enjoyment. No one but an adolescent boasts of smoking two or three packs of cigarettes a day. And even adolescents, including antisocial adolescents, feel lousy about getting stoned daily and will say they want to quit. They don't *have* to go to drug centers to be made to feel ashamed or to realize that there should be more to their lives.

Denial is most likely for the activities, like coffee drinking, that everyone (including many preoccupied with alcoholism, drug addiction, and codependence) accepts as normal. Indeed, it is hyping one addiction or another that blinds most people to the unexpected negative consequences of other activities. For example, alcoholics can be so worried about their drinking that they ignore addictions like smoking or coffee, or even *welcome* other addictions, like those to A.A. or a lover. It is many women's preoccupation with fat that inures them to their bulimia/diet-pill addictions; people who have become convinced that they are depressed or obsessive-compulsive readily accept addictions to tranquilizers and antidepressant drugs.

With socially approved addictions like love relationships, addicts often cite the very signs of addiction as positives. Bottomless love and concern for another cannot be a bad thing, most of us feel. The idea that a perfect mate is one who meets our needs flawlessly is hard to question. Exercise is another behavior that can be compulsive and harmful while people claim and believe they are enhancing their lives. It is with activities currently on society's "good" list that addictive signs must be more carefully examined. When you find you are harming the rest of your life, suffering increasingly negative consequences, and becoming more and more inflexible, the involvement is an addiction, whether it is interacting with your mother, golfing, or drinking and driving.

Addictive Motives

These are the experiences you seek from the addiction and the benefits you derive from it. Addiction is based on the fulfillment of needs that you are not getting fulfilled in other ways.

Experiences

How do you feel when you are involved in the addiction? Can you get these sensations or feelings in any other way? What will you miss most if you stop the addiction? Will your life be empty, boring, devoid of pleasure? Will you lack the energy or motivation to do your job, to get through the day, to meet your family obligations? Will you be too anxious or depressed? Will you be lonely?

EXAMPLES

1. A woman smokes because she fears she can't turn out the work she needs to otherwise.

2. A man fears that, without drinking, he can't fill his evenings at home alone.

3. A teenager feels confident around others when she is stoned.

4. A man feels powerful only when he is drunk.

5. A woman speaks out against her husband's abuse only when she has been drinking.

6. A man goes to the snack machine after every task he completes at work.

Benefits

Even if the habit has drawbacks, do you feel that these are outweighed by the habit's benefits? Why is this? Do you anticipate more pleasure or other benefits from the habit than you actually get?

EXAMPLES

1. A man looks forward to smoking, but, aside from a first cigarette in the morning and a few puffs from other smokes during the day, he finds the taste bitter and worthless.

2. A man imagines he will feel buoyant after a few drinks, but instead quickly becomes depressed.

3. A woman fantasizes all week about a date, which then turns out to be disappointing and demoralizing.

4. A middle-aged man says he feels good only if he runs six miles a day, even though he has constant pain in his knees.

In summary, an addiction fulfills the following primary experiences:

▸ *Organizes, structures, and fills time:* without the activity, your day is formless and barren.

▸ *Provides regular rewards:* the activity is the major reward you have in your day.

▸ *Makes you feel accepted, worthwhile:* your sense of yourself depends on the activity or habit.

▸ *Erases negative moods such as anxiety, depression, boredom:* it "makes you forget," "gets you through the night," creates a soothing oblivion.

▸ *Seems better in the anticipation than in actuality:* you consistently believe you will feel better as a result of the activity than you actually do.

It is the combination of these experiences and imagined benefits from the behaviors, sensations, and feelings described above that maintains the addiction. That is, having a job and a family gives most people a structure in life and a sense of value. Addictions result when your life is structured and made to seem worthwhile by activities that harm you or those close to you, detract from your environment and relationships, and deepen your feelings of self-doubt.

Addiction is part of a search for essential human experiences, like calm and contentment. But the addictive activity both subverts and substitutes for genuine satisfactions. The *addictive cycle* is the self-feeding reliance on an involvement for feelings that the addiction makes harder to get in any other way. For example, if you smoke or take tranquilizers to calm yourself, you mask your anxieties and don't deal with them constructively. But if you don't address your underlying anxieties, you will depend more on the drugs for peace of mind even as they begin to undermine your health.

Addictive Situations

When do you feel you can *least* do without the activity? What experience or mood drives you to engage in the addiction? With whom do you act in the most addicted way? In what setting do you give in most to your addiction? When in your life have you had the worst bouts of addiction? Can you predict when you are most likely to behave in an addicted way?

EXAMPLES

1. A teenager always drinks too much with one group of friends.

2. A man has resumed smoking every time he goes to talk about his son with his ex-wife.

3. A woman goes out for an excessive meal, including dessert, whenever she must work late.

4. A woman always calls her old, unsatisfactory boyfriend around Christmas, when she is alone.

5. Looking back on his life, a man realizes that every time he has been promoted he has gotten drunk and cheated on his wife.

Addiction thrives most in barren, frightening environments, some of which seem uncontrollable (like war zones) and even permanent (like urban ghettos), and some of which are actually life stages that are ordinarily left behind. All individuals are most susceptible to addiction when their lives place them in such valleys. The conditions that foster addiction are:

- stress and anxiety;
- the absence of opportunities for other rewards;
- settings similar to those of previous relapses or addictive bouts;
- life disturbances like divorce or unemployment;
- challenging life stages—including sometimes positive-seeming changes—that overwhelm the person or for which the person feels inadequate.

If you can recognize the environmental sources of your addiction, you can avoid these situations, or—if they are unavoidable or situations you *want* or *need* to confront—you can prepare yourself better to deal with them. When you have *lapsed* in an addictive setting, you can minimize your losses by quickly extricating yourself.

The Life Context of Addiction

Do you live with your family? Is your family life satisfactory? Do you have friends you can turn to? Do you feel confident you can form satisfying relationships?

Do you have a job? Is your career worthwhile? Do you like your work, co-workers, and boss? Do you feel you have skills others appreciate? Can you make a living doing what you are good at and what you like?

Are you happy? Do you know how to have a good time? Do you enjoy your free time? Do you have hobbies and activities that give you pleasure?

Do you think you are a good person? Should people like you? Do you think your life is worthwhile? Do you improve the quality of existence on earth? Do you have a purpose in life?

Do you consider yourself part of a community? Do you devote any of your work, effort, or thought to people who are not related to you? Do you believe that most people are good and that the world is a good place?

Clearly, you are susceptible to addiction if you lack the staples of existence, the sustenance that life offers people under normal conditions. You are most readily addicted when you lack the social supports of friends and family, inner security and peace of mind, and options for fun and constructive work. That is, you are most at risk for addiction when you do not have the following elements of a satisfying life:

- family and friends;
- satisfying work;
- enjoyable pastimes;
- a positive environment;
- a belief in your personal value;

- involvement in a community;
- a purpose in life.

Adaptation to Life

Addiction isn't an accident or an unfathomable mystery. It is a consequence of the confluence of forces in your life, of your needs and available ways of satisfying them. This understanding of the sources of addiction, far from forcing you to accept your addictions passively, gives you a way to combat them—namely, by alerting, inspiring, and empowering you to attempt significant adjustments in your living conditions.

When people are faced with situations like fighting in Vietnam or living in Beirut that are genuinely beyond their control, we can see why they are susceptible to an addiction. Even when a situation only *appears* to be irresolvable for a time, addictions can be a normal response. Although it may be harmful for a recently divorced man to come home and regularly masturbate or have four or five shots of bourbon, such a routine may be a reasonable compromise at this point in his life. In the same way, we cannot dismiss the anxieties of people facing situations like life in Beirut, where normal existence has ceased and the most casual activities can become life-threatening for oneself or one's family. In a country like Lebanon, where those who have money consume massive quantities of tranquilizers sold over the counter, we can only empathize with people's pain.

If you had an opportunity to practice an addiction in Auschwitz, would you reject it? Similarly, it is not our prerogative to lecture lonely old people who drink, or those with terminal pain who depend on painkillers. Realistically, some situations offer few or no options. Nonetheless, this book aims to nurture the kernel of hope that nearly everyone—and certainly anyone reading these words—has the opportunity to change.

The Far and Near Boundaries of Love

Assessing addictions seems pretty easy in the case of a habit like smoking—most smokers admit they are addicted, and few defend smoking as healthy or good. Most regular substance users are already wary of their habits—it is rare now for a person who smokes marijuana daily *not* to have heard that this is a potential health hazard or a drug dependence. It is a more interesting exercise in addiction assessment to examine love relationships in terms of the criteria and motivations for addiction we have listed. Not all such addictions are obvious, even to observers. However, the following case is obvious.

The extremes of addiction—murder and dying. A love relationship is most obviously addictive when a woman is being abused but nonetheless refuses to leave the relationship. There have been well-documented atrocities in which men have killed women, and vice versa, after the victim has left or tried to leave a relationship. Still, the large majority of abusive relationships are ones that women choose to continue, even though they suffer a variety of severe hardships.

An extreme case is that of Hedda Nussbaum. Nussbaum, who was Joel Steinberg's lover, sat by while he beat Lisa Steinberg and the little girl died after lying unconscious for twelve hours on their bathroom floor. In addition, Nussbaum herself suffered beatings and other "punishments" from Steinberg (like being forced to write out her transgressions against him). Over the course of their relationship together, Nussbaum had given up all outside relationships, her work, and any sense of normality or decency in order to continue her addiction to Steinberg. When police raided the Steinberg-Nussbaum apartment, they discovered that the children lived in filth, without real beds or decent food. When Nussbaum was taken into custody, her face and body were a welter of bruises and broken bones.

Hedda Nussbaum's relationship with Joel Steinberg obviously fits the criteria for addiction listed in this chapter: (1) the relationship was painful; (2) it destroyed Nussbaum's capacity to conduct other relationships and activities; (3) the relationship became more inflexible and Nussbaum's own behavior more rigid; and (4) the negative consequences of the relationship—the isolation, pain, and strict adherence to Steinberg's rules—made Nussbaum less able to go outside the relationship and more dependent on Steinberg for personal satisfaction.

Harder to grasp are Nussbaum's motives for maintaining this relationship. Addictive lovers, no matter how much they are hurt, are nonetheless seeking specific benefits and rewards from their relationships. Addictive lovers' motives exemplify the general motivations for addiction listed earlier in this chapter:

- *Organizing, structuring, and filling the addict's life.*
- *Providing regular rewards for which the addict has no superior alternative:* for Nussbaum, Steinberg was an exciting figure whose approval and companionship she welcomed, despite his periodic assaults.
- *Creating feelings of self-worth:* Nussbaum accepted and identified with Steinberg's grandiose claims about himself and felt her relationship with him gave her own life value.
- *Deadening awareness of pain and depression:* Nussbaum seemed deeply depressed even before she met Steinberg; she was unhappy with her relationship with her parents, who were her primary personal connections, since she had little to do with her co-workers.
- *Extracting, as a cost of the rewards it provides, penalties that make the person even more dependent on the rewards:* by losing her job and severing her relationships with others, Nussbaum was forced to become even *more* dependent on her relationship with Steinberg for her moorings and satisfaction in life.

The relationship could be rewarding only given the problems and deprivations with which Nussbaum began. She was already isolated and withdrawn. Her self-esteem was already severely degraded in order for her to put up with Steinberg's dominance and badgering from the start, and to assume she deserved the punishments he meted out. Her life was so barren that Steinberg's version of love seemed reasonable. With little else to sustain her, she continued to accept the increasingly bizarre conditions of her addictive life-style with Steinberg.

Is it love? When a woman is routinely beaten and a young girl is killed, we know we are dealing with a pathology. This is the extreme end of the continuum of addiction. Other cases are less clear. There are couples for whom the conditions of a relationship are mutually acceptable, no one is beaten or coerced, and both partners profess satisfaction and even love. Yet many such relationships display strong addictive elements. Chuck and Alice, for example, had both been married before they married each other. Together now for more than a decade, they do everything together. They are proud that neither ever goes anywhere without the other whenever they are both available, and people view theirs as a long-standing, successful marriage.

They had tried separate outings a few times earlier in their marriage—and these had been disasters! On an overnight sailing excursion, Chuck had had an affair. When Alice attended a workshop by herself, she fixated on a guru and wanted to move to India. As a result, they have found it safer to involve themselves in every aspect of each other's lives. Alice took up sailing, and Chuck, however reluctantly, went along to Alice's consciousness-expansion groups. In this way, they each curtailed the extremes the other tended toward, and they have managed to keep their lives in balance. When one of them has to do something out of the ordinary, such as an occasional favor for a friend, the other will call several times to keep track of the wayward spouse.

This relationship, too, fulfills the criteria for addiction. Primarily, it serves to shield the couple against the challenges of life that they feel inadequate to meet on their own. But by relying on the relationship for protection from their individual insecurities, they come to depend more on the relationship and are less capable of functioning independently. Relationships like this are often mistaken for love. Yet they are more reassuring than pleasurable. It is predictability rather than mutual appreciation that maintains them.

Of course, every intimate relationship has some characteristics that can be classified as addictive. Since addiction involves gradations and judgments, variations and phases, you must navigate through life by assessing your own habits. The guidelines for addiction in this chapter provide insights into the entire range of your habits and involvements. Even if you don't have an obvious pathology, your drinking, eating, or exercising may meet some of the criteria for addiction. Maintaining an awareness of the potential addictiveness of any habit permits you to make mid-course adjustments, so that you don't allow the activity to grow to the dimensions of a full-blown addiction.

Summary and Look Forward

The comprehensive assessment we have outlined gives the lie to the cliché that alcoholism and other addictions are "primary" diseases and that any associated problems in living are merely side effects of the "disease" state. On the contrary, addiction itself grows out of the interplay of people, experiences, and situations, as summarized in the accompanying table. Only by addressing all three of these components can you make the kinds of underlying changes that will bring addictive habits under control.

The Person, Experience, and Situation in Addiction		
The Person	*The Addictive Experience*	*The Situation*
Unable to fulfill essential needs Absence of values that contravene addiction: achievement motivation, self-value, consciousness, healthfulness Lack of self-efficacy, sense of powerlessness vis-à-vis the addiction	Creates predictable, reliable sensations Becomes primary focus and absorbs attention Temporarily eradicates pain and other negative sensations Provides artificial sense of self-worth, power, control, security, intimacy, accomplishment Exacerbates the problems and feelings it is sought to remedy Worsening functioning, loss of relationships	Barren and deprived, absence of positive options: disadvantaged social groups, war zones Absence of supportive social groups; disturbed family structure Peer groups that tolerate or encourage addiction Life situations: adolescence, divorce, bereavement; temporary isolation, deprivation, or stress

Adapted from S. Peele, *Diseasing of America: Addiction Treatment Out of Control* (Lexington, Mass.: Lexington Books, 1989), p. 147.

If you have personal needs that are impossible to fulfill in a given situation or environment, you may turn to an addictive experience to satisfy those needs. However, even in the most deprived situations, and with strong and unfulfilled needs, some people don't become addicts. Some people place such a high value on moderation, on consciousness, and on health that they are almost completely resistant to addiction, or more so than average. Thus, as the table shows, personal *values* have an essential place in the addictive equation. Having assessed your addiction, the next step is to reassert those values you have that are opposed to addiction.

CHAPTER 11

ASSESSING YOUR VALUES

KNOWING WHAT IS IMPORTANT TO YOU

CONTRARY TO THE CLAIMS of treatment centers, just realizing or admitting that you are addicted does little in itself. You have to *want* to change if you are to modify your behavior and situation. More than anything else, it is crucial that you have values in place that *oppose* the addiction and thus create the pressure to change.

Of course, these values sometimes lie dormant. After all, if the addictive activity were so antithetical to your value system, you wouldn't have gotten into it in the first place. In the fever pitch of an addiction, as when embarking on a love affair, people forget what's most important to them. To change, you must reconceive your most deeply held values, those most essential to your sense of yourself. Having assessed the damage the addiction is doing to important parts of your life, you must decide that those things are too important to sacrifice. If you really make that value judgment, the later steps in your self-emancipation will fall into place more easily.

Without that value judgment, on the other hand, the later steps probably won't do you much good. Attacking an addiction without addressing values is a precarious business. For example, if a man has used alcohol or drugs for years as an outlet for macho attitudes and behaviors, simply quitting alcohol or drugs won't address the basis of his addiction. He'll very likely find other ways to express his hypermasculine aggressiveness, ways that may be quite reminiscent of his drinking behavior—for example, browbeating people who disagree with his opinions. The rock group Guns and Roses swore off illicit substances because of complaints about their drug-marred performances. Soon afterward, however, they appeared drunk on the nationally televised 1990 American Music Awards, and one band member used the word "fuck" while accepting their award. The group's explanation was that "they were giving out free drinks." Apparently, the group hadn't learned that self-control and appropriate public behavior were more than a matter of swearing off drugs.

Bedrock Values Against Addiction

Here are some values you can discover within yourself that run counter to addiction. These values are a kind of unrealized strength that you can summon up: to the extent that you possess them, you are less likely to become addicted in the first place and are better able to surmount addictions that do develop. Consider how much you value:

- self-control and moderation;
- accomplishment and competence;
- self-consciousness and awareness of one's environment;
- health;
- self-esteem;
- relationships with others, community, and society.

1. *Self-control and moderation.* Some people simply will not permit their lives to get out of control. They cannot imagine themselves reacting automatically to some external stimulus. Instead, they regulate their behavior according to their own values, principles, and purposes. These people may be repulsed, amused, or sympathetic when they observe someone else who drinks too much, or who cannot refuse an extra helping of food. But if you value moderation, you don't tolerate this for yourself and are reluctant to accept it in the people close to you.

2. *Accomplishment and competence.* Addiction is much less likely to sidetrack those who value achievement and who revel in their mastery and exercise of life skills. College students become addicted to

cocaine and alcohol only rarely compared with deprived, inner-city people, because they have other plans for themselves with which addictions interfere. Even with the stresses and minimal rewards of student life, they are exercising skills and looking forward to greater accomplishments. If you do not value achievement and do not see accomplishment in your future, establishing the desire and the hope that you can achieve substantial goals is pre-eminent in eliminating addiction.

3. *Self-consciousness and awareness of one's environment.* Some people place more value than others on being alert and aware. For many drug addicts, such self-consciousness is actually painful, and drugs are the best remedy for this pain. Addiction will readily follow if a person strives to eradicate the pain of consciousness. The alternative is to value awareness and to believe that such awareness pays off—that if you are awake to your environment you will get more from it. You are also less likely to be addicted if you have faith that thinking about a problem will lead to a solution, and that blinding yourself to reality will get you in a deeper hole.

4. *Health.* What keeps most people from persisting in damaging addictions is the basic human instinct not to hurt themselves. Some individuals, on the other hand, don't care much that they are harming themselves: that they are battered, or destroying their lungs, or reducing their mental capacity. To tell a hard-drinking, hard-smoking sailor with tattoos (or, in many cases, a young drug and alcohol abuser) that his behavior is harmful often doesn't make much of an impression. This is because he doesn't see health as a value to pursue and maintain. If, however, your physical well-being is a personal priority for you, you will be likely to give up or moderate your addictive habits.

5. *Self-esteem.* Self-esteem protects against addiction in two ways: first, by reducing your need for habitual escape or consolation; second, by stopping you from destroying yourself. Addictions and drug and alcohol abuse are like mini-suicide—killing yourself a little each day. An adult who tolerates being put down or beaten (like Hedda Nussbaum) may feel she doesn't have the right to reject these assaults. Many who fall short of this degree of self-hate still don't value themselves. And self-destructive behavior is a natural outgrowth of this negative self-image. You can resist addiction, on the other hand, if you under-

stand that it is wrong to be beaten and put down and that you deserve to be treated well. The more you value yourself, the less you *want* to be addicted, and the less likely you are to *let* yourself be addicted.

6. *Relationships with others, community, and society.* Most addictions are antisocial. For starters, they involve an overconcentration on oneself and one's feelings. Addictions are a kind of dark, inverted version of self-esteem—though not caring about their own health and well-being, addicts are still so self-preoccupied that they hurt others as much as or more than they hurt themselves.

Addictions often require ignoring societal values. When you hear of a mother who locks her children in the house while she goes out to score drugs, or who locks herself in her bedroom to get drunk, or who prostitutes her children; or of a father who wastes all his money gambling, or who regularly falls down drunk in front of his children, or who beats them as well—you are talking about people whose values support the most destructive addictions.

By the same token, valuing your family and thinking it important to treat people well are strong antidotes to addiction. Being concerned for the community—not wanting to detract from the environment or to disturb others (unlike young beer drinkers who throw beer cans and harass people in parks)—means you will not give in to destructive self-gratifications. Wanting to contribute to society is perhaps the strongest guarantee of all that you can resist addictive self-absorption. Similarly, good manners and respect for normal social obligations can help you keep your romantic involvements in perspective, so that they do not become addictive.

Keeping these general categories of life-sustaining values in mind, you need to establish your own value profile. It goes without saying that different values are crucial to different people. For example, people in public and highly visible social positions can maintain many addictions secretly, but overweight isn't one of them. Political figures frequently lose weight to campaign for office; entertainers do so to take on new roles that put them before the public. The Rolling Stones are thinner than nearly all of us. We may muse about how several of the Stones don't have the self-control to quit smoking (and actually smoke onstage), and about why Keith Richard had to go to the wall in his battle with drugs, yet these men are able to maintain adolescent physiques that most of us forlornly waved goodbye to *decades* ago. Apparently, thinness is more valuable than sobriety and kicking cigarettes to many rock-and-rollers.

Clarifying Your Values

Your first, most important value assessment concerns how much your addiction bothers you and how much you want to change it. For example, in one study of smokers who quit on their own, different factors predicted which smokers succeeded at quitting initially and which ones maintained their abstinence. The exception—the one factor that predicted both immediate and long-term success at quitting—was how motivated people were to stop.[1] This information was gathered in a very straightforward manner—people were simply asked how much they wanted to quit.

Your first question, then, is this:

How much do you want to quit smoking (drugs, overdrinking, overeating, a bad relationship)?

very much   a good deal   somewhat   a little   not at all   I don't know

This is the most important question you can ask yourself. The answer is the best predictor of how well you will succeed (although many other elements still enter into the equation). Another way of asking this question is:

Are you ready to quit (or change) now?

ready to quit or change   not ready to quit or change

Obviously, if you haven't resolved that you want to quit, you are not very likely to succeed. Not unless you are forced into a boot camp, and not always then, because it is when you quit under duress that you are most likely to relapse once the pressure is off. On the other hand, if you are sincerely trying to stop, relapse will not be such a grave problem, because you will always be ready to launch a new effort at change.

This does not mean, however, that you have to give up hope if you are not ready to change right now. Your answer to this question can shift both in the near future and as you progress through life. And as the next section will explain, you may be able to hasten the shift by lighting the right kind of fire under yourself.

How much you want to quit overall is really the sum of a number of other questions you might ask yourself. For example, you can create the following two lists:

All the reasons you have for not changing:	***All the reasons you have for changing:***

Here, in the case of smoking, are reasons people list for quitting or persisting in the habit:

Reasons to continue	*Reasons to quit*
——— I'll gain weight	——— Health
——— I won't be able to concentrate	——— Self-control, freedom
——— I won't have my little moments of pleasure or consolation	——— For my family
	——— Money
	——— It's filthy
	——— Business reasons
	——— My friends don't like it
	——— Self-image

Every addiction lends itself to the creation of two lists like these. It doesn't really matter which list is longer—the one on the right just has to be better.

One last issue to keep in mind is that quitting or changing habitual behavior is difficult. To do so, you will need to overcome your personal resistance and the pressures and benefits that have maintained the behavior. In other words, you will have to endure the pain of change. Are you prepared for that? This translates into the following question:

If quitting or changing your addiction is uncomfortable or painful, how prepared are you to endure this discomfort in order to make the change?

very somewhat slightly

Shifting the Balance Toward Change

If you are at present unsure whether you want to change badly enough to make the necessary sacrifices and adjustments, you don't have to accept that uncertainty as a condition of your existence. Instead, you can take active steps to clarify your values. The task in changing is to weight the reasons to quit so decisively as to tilt the balance clearly and permanently in that direction. Simply thinking over both your reasons for quitting and your reasons for continuing can shift the scales. That is, reviewing the two lists you have made—for example, focusing on how much money smoking costs you, or reminding yourself how much it hurts your children to see you smoke (or to breathe your second-hand smoke)—can create the motivation for quitting.

On the other hand, focusing on your fear of gaining weight can lead you to find other ways to allay this concern, so that it does not continue to be a reason to smoke. Here what you are doing is lowering the value of the items that argue for continuing the addiction. Another way to do this is by what psychologist Albert Ellis calls *cognitive restructuring,* which is to challenge the benefits you believe you are getting from the addiction to show they are illusory.[2] For example, you believe that drinking makes you more personable at parties, yet people find your drunkenness off-putting and offensive. Or you think that drinking coffee nonstop enhances your productivity, whereas it cuts into your sleep and makes you groggy throughout the next day.

In order to maintain your motivation to change, you must keep your positive reasons for changing at the forefront of your consciousness. These considerations may not always be prominent in your thinking. Rather, they may wax and wane, and other values, like the comfort or reassurance of the addiction, may temporarily become more important to you. Concentrate on your reasons for changing. It is helpful, prior to and early into quitting, before these reasons become fundamental to your new life-style, to visualize concrete images of why you want to change. For example, some people motivate themselves to lose weight by hanging on the refrigerator a photo that makes them look especially fat.

Is "Hitting Bottom" Necessary?

A.A. emphasizes the experience of hitting bottom—getting to a place where you feel you can't go any lower, so that you must turn your life around. At A.A. meetings, people will describe some horrible event that occurred which almost dictated that they had to stop drinking. Interviews with addicts who rejected addictions on their own or in a twelve-step group often point to a major traumatic occurrence that caused them finally to stop. For example, one man realized that he had defecated into a heating duct in front of his daughter when he had been drunk.[3] A compulsive eater who was in an eating-disorder clinic sneaked out and bought a pizza. He dropped the pizza on the floor of an elevator, then scraped it off the filthy rug and rushed back to his room to eat it. One woman was humiliated by showing up at a friend's wedding, covered with bruises, without her boyfriend.

But other people with stories just like these continue in their addictions for years. And, far more often, when the change does take place, it occurs after an event that is completely innocuous to any outside observer, but that for some reason turns the person around. A nightclub musician had been drunk every night for years. Once, after drinking all night, he awoke on the median strip of an interstate highway. But he didn't quit drinking then. Instead, one night he arrived home drunk as usual and proceeded directly to the bathroom. His mother (with whom he had lived since his divorce) found him there the next morning, staring in the mirror. He turned to her and said, "I'm giving up drinking and, while I'm at it, smoking." Then he placed a bottle of beer and a pack of cigarettes on the mantelpiece. "What's that for?" his mother asked. "That's so I'll know where to find a smoke or a drink if I want one. And then I can kill myself." He hadn't touched alcohol or cigarettes for more than twelve years when we spoke with him.[4]

This story—and all hitting-bottom stories—describe something more than the specific occasion when the person quit, whether or not some extraordinary event occurred. They describe a moment when people see themselves starkly in terms of an inner view they have of themselves—one pegged to a set of values they hold strongly but have subjugated to the addiction. This moment may come at the end of a cycle of turmoil and pain, but more often it comes before a person reaches such a nadir. And it is just as genuine without following the dramatic bottoming-out scenario.

Drawing Value Connections—Epiphanies

Sometimes it isn't clear how particular values that are important to you contravene the addiction. That is, you haven't seen any reason why your concern for health should dictate that you lose weight, or why respect for society should make you stop buying drugs, or why obligations to other people require you to control your interpersonal addictions. Here, sometimes, the possibility for self-confrontation and sudden realizations comes into play—as when Uncle Ozzie (in chapter 4) saw that his smoking violated his commitment to the independence and power of labor and his antagonism toward capitalistic oligarchies.

Connections such as these may remain submerged until you are compelled to reflect on the internal contradictions in your life. As an exercise, first list the things that are most important to you personally. Items you might list include:

- my family;
- my career;
- my image and the opinion of others;
- my responsibility to society (or the universe);
- my relationship to God;
- freedom from outside control.

How do such basic values clash with addiction? Some people do change when they discover, for example, that others disrespect the addiction. Realizing that an addiction is not an *expression* of freedom, but an *inability* to be free, helped Paula (in chapter 9) to stop smoking.

You should now list the ways the things you have identified as most valuable to you are hurt by your addiction—for example, how deteriorating physical health due to an addiction will prevent you from enjoying the fruits of your successful career later in life (or seeing your children grow to maturity). Drawing these connections will help you find the motivation you need to change. Sometimes the values a person holds that break the addiction are idiosyncratic—like Ozzie's militant unionism. One political figure in New Jersey, after being indicted on corruption charges, promptly lost sixty pounds to get back to the weight he had maintained as a college athlete. When asked why he did so, he answered that the need to defend himself made him want to return to his fighting weight.

Such a realization can strike like a bolt of lightning. It can happen at an unlikely moment, before which you hadn't been prepared to see the connection. You may have reached a point where you are better able to handle—or more ready to act on—the insight. Traumatic events can push people either toward or away from addictions. The difference between feeling overwhelmed and feeling challenged by the situation is a question of *framing;* how you *think* about a problem can inspire different reactions to it. Conceiving the problem is the first stage in the coping process that we will tackle in the next chapter.

People sometimes do realize in a flash that their values dictate a change. It is unlikely, however, that they had never previously had similar thoughts; rather, they simply were not prepared to acknowledge and act on those insights. Of course, people often vow to change after a "moment of truth" and then don't stick to their vows. But even in these cases, such "epiphanies" tell us that something is building up in a person's mind that sooner or later may dislodge him or her from the addiction. These experiences represent fundamental values that are being sacrificed to the addiction and that persist as continuing sore points and potential prods to action.

One man we interviewed illustrates how the conflicts a person feels between his present behavior and the person he wants to be can reach a crisis at the right moment. This man had continued to drink even while he was attending A.A. meetings. As he began drinking in a bar one day after a business meeting, he saw an older man he respected. He believed that the man was staring at him disapprovingly:

> I just knew he despised me and what I was doing. I tried to get his attention, but either he didn't—or he wouldn't—acknowledge me. I became so upset that I turned around and left the bar, the hotel, and never drank again.

This man looked in the mirror—his own image reflected by the older man—and didn't like what he saw. He stopped drinking because he could not accept the way he appeared in the eyes of a person whose opinion he valued. That is to say, he decided that he disrespected himself in a way that he could no longer tolerate.

Valuing Health

Health is a particularly important value for combating addictions. Making the health consequences of a behavior concrete can be a powerful inducement for you to quit. Many people stop smoking or drinking after a radical shock to their bodies; for example, as noted in chapter 4, former Kentucky Governor John Y. Brown and comedian Jerry Lewis quit smoking after undergoing heart bypass surgery. Many people also finally succeed at losing weight and cutting their cholesterol levels after a heart attack. Obviously, however, severe heart disease is a dangerous incentive to count on—particularly since not everyone gets a second chance to do something about it. Likewise, getting lung cancer may finally cure you of smoking, but it is a Pyrrhic victory.

The idea is to quit far short of this point. You might quit smoking when you notice you are short of breath, or you are coming down with bronchitis regularly, or your voice is raspy. What helps people recognize they need to change is tangible—but not overwhelming—signs of the physical damage that results from their habits. A British study found that just as many alcoholics who had a single advisory session with a physician quit or cut back drinking as did those who underwent intensive hospital treatment.[5] A successful Scandinavian alcoholism treatment program made a virtue of the fact that people respond as much to concrete feedback about their health as to intensive therapy. In this program, a physician showed laboratory test results to patients with precirrhosis conditions and discused their drinking habits with them; five years later, this group had reduced its drinking-related problems significantly more than a comparison group.[6]

A physician in a network we participated in told this story:

> I have had patients who came in suffering from liver failure, GI bleeding, and problems due to drinking who simply liked to drink. One man honestly had no idea that he was drinking himself to death. When we explained his problem to him, he was surprised that just drinking a couple of six-packs every night was bad for one's health. Once he understood his predicament, he simply stopped drinking, with minimal withdrawal symptoms, and his health radically improved over the ensuing months.

The physician expressed amazement at this case. Yet it is more typical than not. His patient was never really under the misimpression that his drinking was good for him, but definitive proof that his body was failing him finally moved him to acknowledge and do something about it.

Your Changing Values in Life

It is wrong to think that you can acquire bedrock values only if they are built into your life from birth (a kind of disease theory of values). Values become more or less salient during a person's life. One tremendous shift in values often occurs when you commit yourself to supporting a family and raising childen. The evolution of values throughout your life—with some values coming into focus as others recede—is so crucial to combating addiction that we want to explicate exactly how this happens.

The values of teenagers are focused on establishing an identity and on being accepted. Teens rarely think about such long-term questions as where they will be in fifteen years or how their health will hold up. As an illustration of the adolescent outlook, think of unrequited puppy love. When an adolescent falls in love, and the object of this desire doesn't return the feeling, the teenager is likely to think, "What's wrong with me?" He or she doesn't have a secure enough self-image to think, "I'm a good person and they're missing out on something," and then simply to move along. Likewise, in order to be liked, teens are more likely to sacrifice other values.

Many people in their twenties and early thirties, particularly in an American culture that prolongs the irresponsibility of adolescence, continue to pursue personal gratification and excitement. Their lives may be filled with evenings out and abuse of substances—from food, to coffee, to alcohol and illicit drugs. Love affairs are other ways of seeking excitement and physical and ego gratification. But, often at the same time as they are pursuing such activities, many people in their twenties and early thirties become more realistic about what adult life is about and what they need to achieve stability and contentment. For most, these issues focus on love and family, work and career.

When people make serious commitments to their jobs and families, values that have been shifting gradually may now take a full about-face. A man who may have drunk heavily at fraternity parties or at happy hour after work thinks differently about this kind of behavior when he has a family at home. One man, after a business meeting where the liquor flowed freely, came home late and slightly intoxicated. His mind was flooded with the images of drinking and fun that he had experienced in college. As he tiptoed to his bedroom, he looked in at his little girl sleeping, and he immediately sobered up. Thinking the next day about his reaction, he reflected on how much more valuable were his feelings for his family than the trivialities of drunken weekends and casual sex he had known in his twenties.

Pregnancy is commonly a time for quitting substance abuse of all kinds, including the most severe heroin, alcohol, and cigarette addictions. Barry Tuchfeld describes one pregnant alcoholic:

> I was drinking [with a hangover from the previous night's drinking]. . . . I felt the baby quiver and I poured the rest of the beer out and I said, "God forgive me, I'll never drink another drop," and from that day to this I haven't.[7]

It is not the purpose of this book to argue that everyone should settle down to a steady job and a spouse and children. But these milestones in people's lives carry with them tremendous implications that sober most people up. When, on the other hand, Hollywood stars or athletes or just ordinary people act like heedless teenagers, flitting through unstable relationships that they glibly call love but just as quickly discard, or abuse drugs and alcohol, they are really undergoing prolonged adolescence. They don't have a mature enough self-image or sufficiently secure feelings about themselves to invest in substantial life and family goals.

In an interview for the National Public Radio special *Thinking About Drinking,* prominent radio personality Casey Kasem described a severe drinking problem he had developed a quarter-century earlier.[8]

> Going back to the sixties, when I first came to Los Angeles . . . on a nightly basis I was out visiting with people in different restaurants and drinking heavily. At the time I drank Scotch and could down about ten of them an evening, in between having something to eat. That was going on on a regular basis.

When he started drawing blanks the next morning on what he had done the night before, he cut back. But then,

> a few years later, I was managing a band off and on for about eight years, and I would go to a nightclub almost on a nightly basis, and started drinking heavily then, and back to the Scotch and water or Scotch and soda, and was drinking nearly as heavily as I had [before]. . . . What stopped me from doing that to myself any further was, one day—and by this time I was doing, oh, maybe hundreds and hundreds of commercials—I went in and did a spot for the Bank of America, and I couldn't clear my throat. . . . So, in that one day and in that one instant, I realized, "I can't clear my throat; it has to be the liquor that I'm drinking." So that's when I stopped, and that was the last time that I had anything that was heavier than wine.

The NPR producer of *Thinking About Drinking* told us that he received an avalanche of phone calls about the Kasem interview informing him that, as A.A. teaches, cutting back drinking in this way is impossible and represents a major delusion on the part of the alcoholic. But many people do cut back—just as others stop altogether—when something more important to them is threatened. For Casey Kasem, it was his career as a nationally prominent broadcaster that was on the line.

Many young drug users (as well as quite a few older ones) look at where their lives are going and at what they want to accomplish—sometimes in newly emerging careers, sometimes in long-established ones—and decide drugs won't get them what they want. The following is a fairly typical quote from the "heavy-duty" heroin addicts Patrick Biernacki interviewed who decided to quit drugs. This young man was a writer who had been addicted for four years:

> I was needing to put drugs and the Beat Generation behind me; I could understand the things that were not so hot about the Beat Generation at that point. My writing was changing and I no longer needed it for its sake to be part of the drug world. I was getting more used to my feelings and thoughts as I had made contact with people outside the

drug world. . . . I had a glimmer that there was somewhere else that I wanted to go.[9]

A Family Cures Its Eating Addiction

Michael and his brother—who was less than two years older than Michael—grew up in a tight-knit family as third-generation immigrants. Their grandparents, who had come from Eastern Europe, had all been very heavy and had had many of the problems of old age that overweight led to. Michael's parents, too, were heavy, as were Michael and his brother. Family meals were long, drawn-out affairs, and included many starches and fried foods and few vegetables and fruits.

Michael went through school as a chubby kid, but not an unpopular one. He got along with others and was part of a group at school. His brother was a very successful—if somewhat introverted—student. Michael decided to enter the world of finance. He found the summer job he took at a brokerage house the most exhilarating experience he had ever had. Meanwhile, his brother had decided to become a doctor. At this time, the two boys and their parents were all still heavy, and their social lives continued to revolve around fattening foods. For example, Michael generally enjoyed eating breakfast at a small, bustling restaurant in the financial district before entering work—even though he had already eaten another breakfast at home with his family!

But as Michael prepared to take a full-time job with the company for which he had worked during the summer, he recognized that the people he most respected—and who advanced most rapidly in the company—were all "lean and hungry." He saw that being heavy would clearly hold him back in this company. At almost the same time, his brother was entering his third year of medical school. As the brother told it, "Every single cardiologist I know has quit smoking and started running." So he began running, and soon Michael joined his brother in running several days a week.

But it wasn't just Michael and his brother who were hearing the message that thin was good. His parents also couldn't ignore the numerous articles they read that told them to lose weight, along with the problems they had observed in their own parents (one grandparent had died of a heart attack at sixty; another could walk only with extreme difficulty). Indeed, Michael's parents found it far easier to eat lighter meals after their children left home, sometimes having only scrambled eggs and a salad for dinner, or cottage cheese and fruit at lunch. Now that the father had retired, they also took a walk after every meal.

As Michael examined a portrait the family took together on the occasion of his brother's graduation from medical school, he couldn't help noticing how similar were the poses they had all taken to those in the picture of the brother's college graduation. But when Michael put the pictures side by side, he started laughing. The two groups of four people didn't resemble each other at all—but it was the later picture, when all the family were older, in which everybody looked healthier and more "with it"! In fact, he later told his brother, he didn't think people would believe it was the same four people in the two pictures, separated by only four years.

For Michael and his family, the changes of age, career, and new information and values served as a family cure for overeating and overweight. Their lives had led them all independently to this conclusion, although they then each reinforced their new behavior in one another. They had passed as a group from an immigrant sensibility that valued big physiques and heavy meals to a modern sensibility of eating and living light. And the fact that the entire family adopted this outlook guaranteed that it would become a family heritage.

Summary

Aging, maturity, and competing values and goals—such as family, work, and responsibilities toward others—have always been and will remain the best and most common antidotes to drug and alcohol addiction. Similar value shifts over the course of your lifetime, due both to life stage and to the environments you become a part of, offer you the best prospect of quitting other addictions as well. If we could simply package these value shifts—which enable most people to outgrow addiction—we would have the most tried-and-true treatment in the world. But it is more than a treatment; it is a "passage," part of the natural unfolding of your life. And if you don't have in place the interests and satisfactions, the meanings and investments in life that can compete with your addictive motivations, then you must develop these personal resources.

CHAPTER 12

ASSESSING YOUR RESOURCES

WHAT DO YOU HAVE THAT YOU CAN COUNT ON?

IN THE LAST CHAPTER, we discussed what you need to *want* or to *care about* in order to reject addiction. This chapter is about what you must *have* in order not to be addicted—that is, your personal resources and skills. These assets are just as crucial for overcoming addiction as your values. Addiction substitutes for more solid gratifications. When these real connections to life are established, the addictive involvement dwindles in importance.

The resources of which we speak are the foundations of a satisfying, well-filled-out life. In this chapter, we approach these resources from two directions: (1) the strengths you have going for you and can rely upon in preventing or overcoming addiction; (2) the weak areas of your life that you need to work on. Our emphasis here is on *assessing* these resources; later chapters will offer guidance in *developing* or *strengthening* them.

To inventory your personal or life resources is to take a good look at yourself—but a sympathetic, positive look, the way an admiring friend would see you. What is good, praiseworthy, commendable about you? You can start by making a list in response to these questions:

- What are your greatest accomplishments in life?
- What are you best at?
- Of what are you proudest?

- What gives you the greatest enjoyment?
- What do people like or respect most about you?

Here are some specific accomplishments, skills, and assets people report:

- "I am very proud of my relationships with my children."
- "I have made major life changes (such as quitting an addiction) before."
- "I am very good at making other people feel relaxed."
- "I have contributed a lot to my church groups."
- "I do my job very well."
- "I have a lot of friends."
- "I am a good athlete."
- "I'm an artist; I create beautiful and unique objects."
- "I love going to the beach; I feel at peace there."
- "I was president of my college fraternity."
- "I solved a financial crunch that saved our company."
- "I believe God loves me."
- "I can fix almost anything."
- "I organize our household better than anyone else could."
- "I'm smart."
- "I can figure out solutions to most problems."
- "I handle stress very well."
- "I do things that are making the world a better place."
- "I can spend time by myself, like a lot of people can't."

As the last statement illustrates, this list leaves you open to the sin of "pride." Indeed, some twelve-step programs actually ask people to record their violations of the "seven deadly sins" and to cite how pride is a sin that has gotten them into trouble.

In the Life Process Program, on the other hand, you are encouraged to congratulate yourself on what you do well and what distinguishes you from others. The things that make you stand above the crowd, together with the things that connect you with others in relationships of mutual caring and responsibility, are your anchors to life. The more of them you have, the better off you are and the better able to combat addiction. Every item in the list above gives you something with which to fight addictions.

An Audit of Your Assets

Following is a list of the *areas* of personal assets on which you can rely:

- *Intimacy and supportive relationships:*
  Family relationships
  Friendships, community and group involvements
  Enjoying the esteem of others

- *Work resources:*
  Work skills and accomplishments
  Career involvement and success

- *Activities and interests:*
  Active pursuits and hobbies
  Ways you have to relax and enjoy yourself
  Special areas of knowledge and appreciation (e.g., art, music, sports)
  Physical activities you participate in

- *Larger goals:*
  Spiritual, religious involvements
  Political, ecological, community, peace efforts
  Helping others

- *Coping with your world:*
  Practical, technical skills
  Social and group skills
  Problem-solving skills

- *Coping with yourself:*
  Emotional resilience and ability to withstand stress

Ability to occupy your time
Previous behavior change or success at overcoming addiction
Contentment, self-esteem

This list is an outline of what you need to sustain yourself and to overcome addiction. Let's detail each of these areas further:

Intimacy and supportive relationships. To paraphrase Barbra Streisand, people who love people (and whose love is returned) are the luckiest people in the world. Close relationships mean that you have people you can turn to when you feel bad or need help or advice. They mean that you are appreciated and that others care for you. They buoy your self-esteem with the admiration of others. They provide you with intimacy and the opportunity to share concerns and feelings. They give you people to spend time with pleasurably. They give you the satisfaction of supporting and contributing to the well-being of others, of making a difference in others' lives. They provide honest and caring feedback, so that you can know when you are doing something wrong.

Family—immediate and extended—is the starting point in this network of relationships. Your social network outside the home extends to neighbors, work colleagues, nearby and distant friends. Other ways in which you may relate to people include outings and excursions; group, religious, athletic, and community activities; and collaborative enterprises at work and elsewhere. Not everyone can have well-developed relationships in all of these areas, but every opportunity you have to be with people gives you essential human contact and the chance to form sustaining relationships. These relationships are substantial bastions in life.

Work resources. Involvement in work that you find meaningful, that you are good at, and that is appreciated is one of the most sustaining aspects of life. It fills your time constructively, supports your self-esteem, earns money with which to fulfill your needs, and provides you with an overall direction in life. One outgrowth of positive work involvements is that you develop a career plan and goals to shoot for in life.

Achieving career goals requires good work habits; these habits stand you in good stead on their own. One study found that the most important ingredient in enabling people to attain satisfaction throughout life—even in nonwork areas, like family life—is work habits. For most people, these habits appeared in childhood. It seems that being able to organize and carry through on work projects enables people to accomplish much of what they need to in life.

Activities and interests. Having activities and hobbies you enjoy, from collecting stamps to ballroom dancing to hiking, will give you pleasure in noncompulsive ways that can reduce the edge on the other areas of your life. Being able to relax and be with yourself in ways that don't even fit the label "activities"—such as just walking or sitting in your back yard or barbecuing—can be equally valuable. Spectator activities, like reading, following dance, drama and art, and sports (consumed in moderation), also fall in this category. What you should find after you pursue these interests for a while is that you have developed a new area of competence and expertise. That is, you know more than the average person about the activity and you can take pleasure in your mastery of the area.

Addiction is largely a matter of misplaced energy, in both a physical and a moral sense. Think of the addict hustling for drugs on the street, squandering real skills on antisocial pursuits. In the television program about shopping addiction described in chapter 6, someone in the audience remarked that the "shopaholics" on the panel appeared rather self-centered and "should find something to do." In other words, they were so busy trying to get their needs met through a futile compulsion that they missed obvious opportunities to redirect their energy more constructively. This observation, however uncongenial to the television panelists, was very revealing about addictions of all kinds—and how they can be overcome.

At the simplest level, physical activity constitutes a self-enhancing way to rechannel misspent energy. So many health benefits derive from physical exertion that this in itself constitutes an essential category of therapeutic activity. It includes anything you do to work up a sweat or that tires your muscles, including dancing, gardening, walking, and strenuous exercise. By enhancing your self-discipline and self-esteem, physical discipline can be a vital first step away from addictive dependency and paralysis. But the activities that most decisively reduce addictive diversions to irrelevancy are those that express a true engagement with others and a higher moral purpose.

Larger goals. A.A. is right that a higher vision provides a direction and an energy for living and a major bulwark against addiction. Only passively buying the A.A. doctrine does not provide as energizing a vision as does voluntarily committing yourself to some larger goal in life. Such goals include politics, religion, intellectual or artistic pursuits, social activism, or helping people in any way. For example, taking a day a week to work with the homeless, or battered women or children, or acting as a big brother, or tutoring people will put your own problems in perspective and give you greater strength for your own life. Collective action to improve the community, the environment, or the world can offer you a matchless sense of purpose and value. But please resist the temptation to lecture people on the addictions you just recently overcame!

Coping with your world. Any abilities you have translate into life competencies—such as cooking, driving, fixing things, dealing with people, filling out your tax forms. In fact, our world is quite a demanding place, and only a few coping flaws—like not knowing how to deal with members of the opposite sex or children, or how to communicate in general, or how to use everyday technology—can cause people severe problems in coping and leave them vulnerable to addiction. Thus, practical mastery of your environment has a tremendous impact on the accomplishment of your goals and on your contentment with life. At the same time, knowing you can deal with the demands of a complex world provides a great sense of satisfaction. And for those who are satisfied with themselves and their lives, severe addictions are unnecessary and unwelcome.

Dealing with people is, all by itself, a crucial life skill. From childhood on, your life is a series of negotiations. You may achieve fair success in life even though you don't deal well with others—but this is certainly not the easy road. In other words, you—along with everybody else—will benefit greatly from social skills such as communication, working within groups and organizations, leadership, collaboration, and caring and helping. Having these skills opens a lot of doors and spares you many frustrations that might otherwise lead you to seek out an addiction.

While mastering individual areas of competence is worthwhile in itself, each such example of mastery is part of a larger category of problem-solving skills. To solve problems, you must remain calm enough in the face of new or difficult situations to assess what the problem requires and to take the steps necessary to solve or overcome it. These general problem-solving skills are very important for you in handling the demands of life without resorting to addictions, which are spurious, self-deceptive ways of solving problems.

Coping with yourself. Problem-solving begins with a calm assessment of your situation; you need to approach a problem realistically and maintain emotional balance. If each new problem or crisis threatens your emotional equilibrium, then you are unlikely to approach it sensibly. Rather, effective coping requires that you put problems in perspective, break them into life-sized dimensions (this is called "framing"), and take whatever steps are necessary to improve the situation or turn it around.

Other personal-management resources you need to combat addiction include the ability to occupy your time constructively, both with other people and by yourself. If you enjoy your own company, then you are less likely to fill spare time with drugs, drink, overeating, addictive television viewing, futile sexual liaisons, and so on. Using time to relax or have fun or work or improve your body or mind will mean you have less room for addiction in your life.

In the introduction, we reviewed an *American Health* magazine survey of self-initiated behavior change. It reported that once people changed their behavior in one area, they were better able to do so in another. This finding has now been confirmed specifically in the case of addictions. Researchers at the Addiction Research Foundation of Toronto advertised for people with a drinking problem who had quit or cut back drinking without relying on treatment. More than half of those who also smoked who then quit (or drastically reduced) drinking also quit smoking.[1] The researchers noted this was "an unheard of kind of finding, to have stopped two very addictive behaviors on their own."[2] But it is not in the least remarkable—when you make a substantial life change, obviously, you develop confidence that you can make needed changes in your life.

Self-esteem and self-contentment are basic to your capacities to solve problems and use time constructively. Self-esteem enables you to see a problem as something to be solved rather than as an assault on your very being. And self-contentment allows you to spend time alone, devise positive activities for yourself, and keep your life on track without guidance from gurus, counselors, and twelve-step groups.

"I Don't Have Anything in Life"

Some people claim that they have nothing to live for. Taking this claim at face value, we see just how extreme a statement it is. Literally having nothing going for you would mean having no family—no children, siblings, parents, or spouse—or friends who count on or enjoy you, no skills you can exercise, no hobbies or personal activities you enjoy, no political or spiritual beliefs to which you adhere. If you have reached this degree of isolation and disillusionment, this book may not be helpful. But if your inventory of personal resources turns up anything positive in any of these areas, you have some basis for further growth. The film *It's a Wonderful Life* has been so remarkably popular over the years because it shows that every life has so much impact on so many others, and how valuable these ties are when the chips are down.

Even people who are habitually depressed usually have a range of personal strengths. In any case, depression is less linked to what people have going for them than it is to how well they can acknowledge their assets. It is not so much that depressed people *are* worse off than others as that they *feel* worse off. As a result, cognitive therapy for depression teaches people to focus on their list of resources rather than on their list of problems. In clinical trials conducted for the National Institute of Mental Health, people trained to concentrate on their strengths and pluses in life as a part of a cognitive-therapy program fared as well at combating clinical depressions as those given antidepressant drugs.[3] Those with milder depressions gained little more from either therapy than they did from the simple passage of time.[4]

Rather than dwell on discouraging thoughts, practice remembering

- what you have going for you,
- how many problems and crises you have dealt with successfully in the past,
- that, relatively speaking, your problems are no worse—and probably considerably milder—than those of many other people.

You can most likely fight off depression in this way as well as you can through relying on medication. In addition, positive thinking is less likely to lead to addiction than are drugs—even those prescribed by a physician. Here are some specific examples of "positive self-talk":

▸ "I'm a good person, as good as anyone else."

▸ "I will solve this problem, because I have come through much worse problems before."

▸ "They think I'm a really valuable contributor to this effort."

▸ "Life offers you a lot of chances; I'm really going to jump on the next one."

▸ "I have a lot of positives in my life—my family, my job, my health. I wish everyone were as well off as I am."

So Norman Vincent Peale had it right after all in *The Power of Positive Thinking!* Positive thinking, however, must be a part of an overall program of change. The next step after thinking positively is to rely on the energy of changed thinking in order to take action.

Chet: Assessing an Addict's Skills

The point of assembling a list of your resources and sharpening your awareness of what you've got going for you is more than to congratulate yourself for being you. It is these strengths on which you must peg your efforts to overcome your addictive tendencies. Every success story of a beaten addiction is really a story of a marshaling of personal resources.

Chet was a black man who had been alcoholic for more than a decade; for most of this time he had lived on the street. He had been in and out of any number of social agencies and had been to hundreds of A.A. meetings. He was generally docile and well mannered, but he never stopped drinking for any appreciable length of time. Whatever these organizations were offering, he hadn't bought. Something changed, however, during one of his stays at a homeless shelter that had been set up in a converted school. The school had a gym, and one day Chet picked up a basketball and began shooting.

Strange as it seems, Chet had almost forgotten that he had been an all-city basketball player in high school. He had been offered a college scholarship, which he hadn't taken, but after graduating from high school he had played with an industrial team on and off for almost ten years. As he hefted the ball and started rolling jump shots off his palm, an administrator of the shelter was watching. This woman quickly rounded up a number of bored children, brought them into the gym, and asked Chet to organize them into teams and show them some of the fundamentals of basketball.

For the next hour, Chet obliged. The administrator marveled—she had never seen Chet do *anything* so concertedly for an hour. Chet seemed really to concentrate on the job of teaching the children. The woman was particularly struck when Chet told one of the kids, who wouldn't pay attention and insisted on taking long shots he had no chance of making, "You'll find that it pays in life to learn the basics before you try to show off." After the game, one of the quietest kids in the group, who had made a shot and then slapped hands with all his teammates, went up to Chet and said, "Thank you, mister." Chet smiled deeply.

The woman who had been watching immediately contacted the director of a local boys' club. She described Chet and asked whether he might help out with some of the teams. The director, nervous, began by asking Chet to referee a single game. Chet was punctual and effective. During halftime, he again began taking shots. After Chet served as a referee for several games, the boys'-club director asked if Chet would mind helping out during practices with one of the teams, taking some of the boys off and working on their basketball skills. "But," the director said self-consciously, "you can't be drinking while you're doing this."

Chet agreed but, as the director feared, showed up drunk at the next practice. The director took Chet aside before any of the boys saw him and told him he couldn't help out in that condition. He told Chet to come back in two days, when there was another practice. Chet did, sober this time, and quietly did his job. From then on, he was sober at every practice. Complimenting Chet at the end of the season, the director said he had worried that Chet could never stay sober that long. Chet replied, "I never had any reason to before."

Previously, when Chet had entered treatment centers, the staff had always asked him about his drinking problems. Chet would nonchalantly list his arrests, lost jobs, failed marriages, health problems, and numerous prior treatment episodes. Not one of those centers had ever asked Chet what he did well or what his biggest success in life had been. It had never occurred to Chet to tell people he had once been an exceptional athlete, that he knew basketball, and that he thought he could teach kids.

But listing Chet's failures served no purpose—just seeing him shivering drunk on the street was evidence to everybody, himself included, that he was an alcoholic. What understanding Chet's strengths and resources offered was a path out of alcoholism—a chance to work and to gain self-respect and appreciation from other people. These were the building blocks with which he could begin to reverse the downward spiral of addiction that had described the last decade of his life.

Peter: Offsetting Weaknesses with Strengths

Chet's case is an extreme one, in which the addictive focus was clear and his sports and teaching skills were one point of promise in a bleak existence. Consider Peter, a more typical or average case: a married, employed professional who has gained weight for several decades and now finds himself obese with little chance for radical life changes.

An assessment of the addiction reveals a sedentary life, many opportunities for snacks, and a stable existence that accepts and permits overeating and encroaching obesity. Like many overweight people, Peter leads a stable, productive life but has developed a good deal of inertia. Thus, he has rewards in place that maintain his life-style and that overwhelm pressures to lose weight. He does his job well and succeeds in the "important" areas of his life, so that his family and workmates accept him as a valuable person and likewise accept his overweight.

This individual has a range of resources, many of which may be turned toward combating the addiction. These include:

- a stable existence that allows for meal planning and provides opportunities during the day for exercise;
- a thin family whose eating habits would support a healthful life-style for him;
- friends and acquaintances who exercise and encourage exercise;
- a strong career involvement and high expectations for future success;
- good problem-solving and planning abilities.

Obviously, other aspects of his life have not supported weight loss. These include:

- flurries of work activity and stress that are upsetting and that encourage self-rewarding snacking;
- periodic career challenges in which new efforts are not immediately rewarded;
- a personal style of impulsive reaction, of quickly addressing problems and moving on, of spontaneous immersion in situations.

Peter needs to structure his time better, to build in regular exercise periods with friends, to avoid unplanned snacks as a concomitant to intense work periods, and to find rewards in daily life that would replace food as a placeholder for the long-term rewards he seeks from his work. In the next chapter, we will show how life changes such as these can be programmed into daily plans and long-range goals.

What Works at One Time May Not at Another

People have emotional and coping strengths that work better at some points in their lives than at others. The good news is that having a traumatic stretch or a particularly unsuccessful life phase does not mean that you will fail forever. Though people's personalities remain remarkably consistent over their life spans, their addictions and emotional difficulties don't necessarily persist. Predicting how people will turn out based on their problems early in life turns out to be very hard. Moreover, the general trend over time is toward greater personal contentment and better control of one's life.

Researchers George and Caroline Vaillant analyzed data they and others gathered over a nearly fifty-year span in the lives of a group of men, most of whom were now around sixty-five. They found that being poor or orphaned in childhood, having parents who divorced, and having emotional problems in childhood or college had little to do with the well-being of these men in later life. "In the long run, people are extraordinarily adaptable," Dr. Vaillant said. "Given enough time, people recover and change; a half-century perspective shows that time heals."[5]

By age sixty-five the men who succeeded best at work, play, love, and personal contentment were most often characterized by pragmatism and the ability to organize themselves. Another important trait that led to well-being at sixty-five was the ability to handle an emotional crisis without allowing anger to simmer, becoming bitter, or covering up one's feelings. "The best way to handle emotional crisis, the study found, is to control the first impulse and give a more measured response."[6] This corresponds to the framing and problem-solving skills we have described. Another important predictor of well-being for these senior citizens was their having had strong relationships with their sisters or brothers.

If you are able to maintain a satisfying existence, including strong family relationships and social supports, and if you have good work and coping skills in place, you are likely to overcome the problems that you confront over your lifetime. You can be temporarily thrown off balance or suffer life reverses, but these should not overwhelm your coping resources.

The bad news is that success at a previous life stage does not guarantee a placid and successful life. In the Vaillants' study, there was little correlation between the abilities and strengths that predicted mid-life success and those that worked best later in life. Think of the people you knew who were most promising and gifted in high school and college; not all have realized their full promise in the years that followed.

What this means is that flexibility and adaptability will always play a role in your life, and that the ability to overcome addiction may need to be summoned at any point in the life cycle. You may react less well to growing up, or to raising a family, or to the free time of retirement than do most people. For the life stages you find difficult, you will need to plan carefully and to devise life strategies other than those on which most people ordinarily rely.

Where You Fall Short

The next chapter is about pursuing goals at which you have fallen short and overcoming the obstacles that have proved most difficult in your life, the ones that may have precipitated an addictive pattern. That is, there will always be some discrepancy between what you value and what you achieve, between what you want to be and what you are. Such discrepancies are inevitable, but they must be addressed. How to set and pursue realistic goals is the topic we turn to next.

In doing so, however, first remind yourself of your list of personal resources.[7] People often note how buoying they find it to write out a résumé. Simply by outlining their accomplishments in an upbeat way, they focus on their strengths and are reminded of their own worth. If you don't feel good about yourself and who you are, then you won't have the emotional wherewithal to withstand the tensions and work involved in change. On the other hand, even if you are not all the way to attaining your goals, you should commend yourself for what successes you have achieved. Being the first to recognize your own successes will help provide you with the strength to do better.

CHAPTER 13

I'M NOT THE PERSON I WANT TO BE

HOW PEOPLE CARRY OUT PLANS TO CHANGE

IN THE PREVIOUS CHAPTERS, you have assessed (1) your problems with your addictive activity (chapter 10); (2) what is important to you in life, and the person you would like to be (chapter 11); (3) what you've already accomplished, what you have to build on, and where you fall short and need more work (chapter 12).

This chapter is about narrowing the gap between your ideal self and where you are now—it describes methods for getting from *here* to *there,* whether "there" means giving up the addiction or building a stronger, more satisfying life structure (the two are, of course, inseparable). These methods come from a number of sources. Behavior therapists have been developing them for years. Such methods are also used in business, where they are known as "management by objectives." They involve these basic elements:

▸ *Setting goals.* You'll do better if you have something to shoot for. Your goals must be realistic (something you can actually attain), and they must be meaningful to you (something you can really get behind).

▸ *Tracking your progress.* You need a way to see how well you are doing, to remind you of your goals and how much progress you have made toward them.

▸ *Maintaining your progress.* You need to keep your motivation at a steady level and to continue to advance more than you fall back.

▸ *Getting beyond the addiction.* Your motivations and actions must eventually focus on positive goals, things in life that have nothing to do with your addiction.

The Life Process Program for goal achievement is defined by the following special features:

▸ developing rewards for the changed behavior from your everyday life routines;

▸ minimizing the unnecessary costs of quitting, such as deciding that you can never drink again or that you must attend A.A. meetings forever to conquer a drinking problem;

▸ combining the goal of quitting an addiction with the other goals you are trying to achieve in life;

▸ seeking an end point to recovery, when you are no longer a recovering person but a recovered one.

Setting Goals

You have already laid out the basis for the goals you seek in the previous chapter. These are the values you have—the ways you would like to be, but have not yet become. There are really two sets of these goals, one embedded within the other. You may be reading this book because you are concerned about specific behaviors, or addictions. You want to change these. But this change must take place within the larger context of attaining basic life goals. It is the synergy between these two types of goals that typifies the Life Process Program. Your desire for sobriety is enhanced if you believe sobriety will help you feel better, work better, love better, raise children better, and accomplish other things that are important to you.

Clearcut Goals

People work better when they have something to shoot for—this is the point of goal-setting. You know what you need to do and whether you have done it. Goals should be specific—you need to know what is expected and whether you have met your objectives. This is why people are often most productive under a deadline, when they know they must have something completed by a certain date. Numbers are the best example of concrete goals: you will eat this quantity of calories, lose this much weight, or shoot for this weight. You must commit yourself to these goals and to assessing how well you have done in reaching them. Goals aren't useful if you can't be sure whether or not you have achieved them.

Goals for combating addictions are often negative. For example, you will limit yourself to X number of drinks a day, or never drink before a certain hour or eat after 7:00 P.M. But goals and numbers can be made positive—not only goals directly connected to the addiction (such as "I will sit down and eat three leisurely and well-designed meals a day"), but goals in all areas: "I will exercise three days a week." "I will send out ten job applications a week." "I will write five pages of my novel a day." "I will have sex three times a week with my spouse."

CASE

Are we kidding about setting goals for sexual intercourse with your spouse? In sexual addictions, people are overcome with desire for a new partner. But, just as urgent as sex is initially, intense passion disappears when the relationship undergoes the normal duress of daily living. Under these circumstances, many people decide they no longer love one another and search for new partners with whom to rekindle their passion. As well as creating dissatisfaction, this view of love taken to its extreme becomes a sexual addiction.

One woman received as a fortieth birthday present a book about sex in old age. Although the gift was something of a gag, it started the woman to thinking. One sentence in the introduction particularly struck her: "Sex can be as important a goal in your life as you want it to be." The woman reflected that she had many goals in her life—she exercised every other day, turned out a certain number of pages of work per week, saved money for her children's college tuition—but that she had no goals whatever in her sex life with her husband.

Yet she had viewed sex as a crucial area of married life ever since a divorced friend told her, "I knew our marriage was gone when we had intercourse once a week, then once a month, than almost never."

So this woman resolved that she would aim for three sexual episodes a week. This required her to plan ahead, to rent sexually explicit videos, to get ready for bed earlier, and to discuss with her husband her goals for their sex life. When they began having sex on a more regular basis, the quality of the sex improved, too, and the woman was orgasmic more of the time and found nearly all their sexual interactions highly enjoyable.

Results Versus Process

Goals don't have to focus on the result, such as how much weight you will lose. They can focus on the process instead—you will eat only three meals and two small snacks a day; you will eat only at the kitchen table or in the lunchroom at work; you will eliminate or reduce eating binges; you will take a walk after lunch. Here the goals are behavior-oriented, and you assume that the result—like your weight—will take care of itself.

Controlled Use Versus Abstinence

One of the worst ways in which the disease theory of alcoholism has polluted the entire addiction field is by turning the religious absolute of abstinence into a therapeutic and medical absolute. One area in which there are no grounds to suppose abstaining makes more sense than cutting back is compulsive gambling. Gamblers Anonymous, of course, tells its members they have lost all ability to moderate their gambling. This is an almost exclusively American preoccupation. One researcher noted:

> The single goal of abstinence has definite limitations, and in some cases is counterproductive. . . . For many gamblers . . . abstinence is unrealistic.
>
> While conducting research with several nativistic [Native American] gambling groups I have, on many occasions, observed seriously troubled gamblers develop coping skills that helped them maintain participation in an acceptable manner. In so doing, the troubled gamblers learned how to become controlled gamblers. Additionally, English and Aus-

tralian researchers have successfully implemented controlled-gambling programs.[1]

When you cannot abstain from an activity (or choose not to), you must decide what a healthy level of behavior is. Abstinence is not a desirable goal for intimate relationships, eating, shopping, and other essential behaviors. Moreover, it may not be the wisest goal even in cases where it *is* possible entirely to abstain. Abstinence and controlled use are both viable alternatives for coffee drinking, along with other drug use. However, even though it might be possible—and beneficial—for people to moderate their drug use, it is highly unlikely that you can find a therapist to help you moderate your use of illicit drugs.

The addiction for which nearly everyone agrees abstinence is the best solution is smoking. Here, too, however, there are cases of people who successfully cut back. Sid Caesar experienced a number of addictions, including drinking, smoking, and overeating. In his autobiography, *Where Have I Been?*, Caesar revealed that he stopped smoking cigars compulsively around the clock and instead smoked one only after a good meal—a time when he appreciated the cigar and enjoyed it throughout.

Controlled Drinking

One of the hottest issues behaviorists and other therapists face is whether problem drinkers can manage to reduce their drinking. The answer is clearly yes for some people; the question is under what circumstances this is the best goal to shoot for and when abstinence is the preferable aim. Some of the indicators for a controlled-drinking versus an abstinence goal are milder drinking problems, repeated failures at abstinence, and a strong preference for some continued drinking.

One controlled-drinking therapist relies on such target drinking goals as:

- no more than four drinks in a day
- no more than 20 drinks a week
- at least one day of abstinence a week

- no drinking problems (sleep disturbances, missed meals, quarrels)
- avoiding drinking as a way of coping with difficult situations or negative emotions[2]

This researcher, Martha Sanchez-Craig, works at the Addiction Research Foundation in Toronto. In addition to utilizing controlled-drinking therapy in her research, she has trained Canadian physicians and others to carry out this therapy with suitable patients. No such organized program exists in the United States, where treatment centers usually prescribe abstinence and browbeat those who want to continue drinking. Consideration of both goals is clearly a better way to proceed. Ideally, a therapist should consider all possible nonaddictive options with the individual and allow him or her to select the one that seems most workable. Sometimes a therapist may prefer abstinence because an alcoholic has medical problems. But even when this is so, if the person won't accept the goal it is of little use.

CASE

Therapists who teach controlled drinking generally refuse chronic alcoholics. A Canadian physician trained by Sanchez-Craig in controlled-drinking therapy encountered an extremely alcoholic hospital patient who simply refused to abstain (he had already "failed" the hospital's alcoholism program). This alcoholic had hypertension and as a result had cut his drinking in half—down to a dozen drinks a day!

The doctor advised the patient to cut back further, to which the patient agreed. Physician and patient met at sessions where they agreed on drinking quotas. At each session, the patient was required to provide a record of his drinking. At these sessions, the doctor also reported to the patient his reduced blood pressure and other health improvements.

After five meetings over three months, the man had reduced his drinking substantially, to a dozen drinks a week, and his blood pressure had returned to normal. Six months later, he returned to the physician to discuss a bout of heavy drinking—which, it was good to see, now bothered the man himself. Once again the physician had the man monitor and record his daily drinking.

The doctor kept up this relationship for two years. Over this time, the man became a more and more conservative drinker, usually drinking no more than one or two drinks once or twice a week.[3]

The physician could easily have rejected this patient based on the man's refusal to abstain. But nothing would have been gained. Even though people frequently have a goal of abstinence, they may nonetheless drink themselves to death. The goal is simply unrealistic for them. In one famous study, single male alcoholics under the age of forty were shown to relapse more when they tried to abstain than when they reduced their drinking to nonproblem levels.[4] Apparently, younger, single men have a more difficult time staying away entirely from drinking situations than trying to control these situations.

Although we emphasize nonabstinence goals for problem drinking, abstinence can be a viable or even preferable alternative for some. Our techniques can be used with either abstinence or moderation goals. Offering abstinence as a choice rather than a requirement can benefit even abstainers, since forced deprivation often leads them to alternate periods of abstinence with explosive binges.

Self-selection

The goals should be yours; you should own them. This doesn't mean that a therapist, or a nutritionist, can't advise you about what you should shoot for. But you must buy into the goals, and they must make sense in terms of what you want and what you believe you can achieve. If you take on a goal *externally,* because someone else says it is right for you, you are far more likely to drop the goal when it becomes difficult to attain. In the case of the alcoholic above, the physician decided to work within the patient's own value system, and the man achieved a healthy outcome and moderate drinking levels.

Of course, alcoholism is far from the only area where questions of external versus internal goals arise. To take another example, you might strive for the ideal weight level on the insurance company's charts, or you might set up a more moderate weight-loss goal that would nonetheless mark an important improvement for you. You decide on a proper goal by examining your values—that is, what fits in with your life and who you are. If you can't come up with goals because your values are unclear, then your first job is to develop a solid set of values. It is possible simply to accept someone else's values wholecloth, as by joining an ashram or finding a guru. Such an expedient, however, can create problems of its own, for you are then wedded to the group or guru for direction and emotional security. This is a recipe for becoming addicted to them.

Flexibility and Evolution of Goals

The alcoholic man in the case above ended up drinking fewer than five drinks a week after two years. But if the physician had told the man to drink that little initially, the man would have rejected the suggestion. Although firm goals must be set, because otherwise people can't tell when they've met them, goals should also be flexible enough to reflect the reality of the person's experience. If a set of goals proves to be unachievable, then it should be modified. On the other hand, success at achieving a more moderate goal allows the person to shoot for a higher goal that earlier would have been unimaginable. Thus, the man revised his ideal drinking level downward on his own. Similarly, a person who doubts he or she can lose any weight will be buoyed by early weight-loss success and then strive to lose more weight.

The evolution to more ambitious goals occurs not only because of the encouraging effect of moderate self-control, but also because of what we call *the Life Process feedback loop.* This is the opposite process from the *addiction cycle* we described in chapter 1. You drink (eat, smoke) less; your life improves; you feel better about yourself; and so you drink (eat, smoke) even less. As your improved behavior and self-presentation gain you admission to more fulfilling social and work environments, anything resembling your past excesses becomes more and more inconsistent with your new image and your new self.

When it comes to abstinence versus controlled drinking, a person can shift goals in either direction. Someone like Bing Crosby (in chapter 2) may first abstain, then feel comfortable enough to take an occasional drink. (Acknowledged or not, this is par for the course, and even most "abstinent" alcoholics will drink at some point.) On the other hand, someone may cut back drinking enough to decide it would be better—and now possible—not to drink at all. People more often commit themselves to goals *they* select in therapy, but they also often shift to a different goal from the one they initially selected.

What is important, of course, is that people sort out their goals through their own experience. Martha Sanchez-Craig, the psychologist who developed the list of moderate-drinking goals above, reports: "Finding a drinking pattern that fits well with the client's lifestyle may take time. . . . As treatment progresses it may be necessary to make adjustments to the goal until a suitable pattern is established."[5] Any goal can be re-evaluated. Failure at abstinence or controlled use should not rule out these goals. But the failures should become less frequent and severe. Otherwise, you might want to switch to the alternative goal—either moderation or abstinence—and see if you do better with *it*. Finally, success at a goal does not mean that you can never succeed at a different goal.

CASE

What does a person do who feels she does not fit the alcoholism mold that available therapies want to put her into? Cindy was a woman of thirty who became disoriented for a time after leaving a small Midwestern liberal-arts college and moving to Boston. Somewhat overweight to begin with, she overate more in reaction to being socially isolated. As a result, she came to feel more unattractive and isolated herself more from others. Simultaneously, she began drinking heavily and developed symptoms of alcoholism. Reaching a point of near-despair about her life, she began attending A.A. meetings.

At the same time that Cindy turned to A.A. for help, she brought her compulsive eating under control without therapy or group support. Within a year, her weight was down to normal, and people began responding more positively to her. After a year of abstinence through A.A., Cindy felt sufficiently in control to see if she could drink again. She knew that she was eating differently without a twelve-step program for food, and by now she rarely even felt much of an urge to eat excessively. Why couldn't she drink differently, too? Yet controlled drinking was something with which A.A. could be of no help.

Cindy luckily discovered a therapist who didn't seem surprised by Cindy's plight and who agreed to help her achieve moderation. For Cindy, just finding a sensitive and smart person who supported her in the belief that she could resume social drinking was therapeutic. Cindy and the therapist planned strategies for Cindy to limit herself to a drink or two in social situations with men, where she experienced the greatest anxiety and temptation to drink to reassure herself about her attractiveness.

If you believe that the goal of moderating rather than eliminating drinking may be an appropriate one for you, you may or may not be as fortunate as Cindy was in finding a therapist who supports that goal. There are, however, detailed manuals you can turn to for guidance.[6]

Realism

Everyone has goals. But some people don't stick to them. The reason many don't is that their goals are too grandiose. When people fail at these unrealistic goals, they usually just give up. For example, one overweight teenager prayed that she could take a pill and wake up thin the next morning! This *is* goal-setting, but of a totally unrealistic sort. Adults, too, sometimes try to control their weight strictly with drugs—as Kitty Dukakis did for years. Here, too, the person seeks a magical, easy, or quick solution for a life problem.

The tendency to alternate between easy, predictable goals (like eating, drug use, and other quick gratifications) and grandiose, impossible ones (like immediate and total abstinence or rapid, permanent weight loss) is a mark of addiction. Getting goals into the middle range—useful, modest goals—is often the answer to addiction. Middle-range, achievable goals are important for attacking the addiction. They are also important for achieving any goal—like love, or exercise, or career goals. The important thing is maintaining the motivation to persist at each modest step up the ladder toward your ultimate goals.

In summary, the goals you need to conquer addiction should be:

- clearcut, specific, concrete;
- consistent with your values and other life goals;
- flexible, able to be modified by experience;
- realistic, moderate, continually upward.

CASE

A man who had been thin as a child and an adolescent had gained weight throughout his adult life. Although he had periodically tried to control his weight, he entered later middle age fat. But he resisted therapy as well as weight plans designed for fat persons, among whom he refused to count himself.

Still, the evidence that he was overweight was undeniable, so he designed a series of goals for himself that weren't specifically about weight. Rather, they were about ways of eating and living. His goals were the following:

▶ Eat at least one ascetic meal a day, a dietetic meal of cottage cheese, fruit, and plain bread.

▶ Cut down eating out to two or three times a week (from as many as five or ten).

▶ Do at least some mild exercise every day—biking, walking, swimming.

▶ Connect exercise with breaks in the workday and with rewards such as sitting down for a cup of coffee and playing a favorite record.

▶ Limit snacks to fruit—eliminate potato chips, etc., and desserts—two days out of three.

At least initially, the man didn't try any radical exclusions from his diet, like sweets or butter. But after pursuing the milder goals he set for himself, he found that it naturally made sense to go further in some areas, where his habits jeopardized his larger aims. He largely cut out fried foods, for example. Because his diet wasn't a radical one, weight loss was slow. But almost immediately he noticed his health improved from the exercise. After several months, his somewhat elevated blood pressure fell back within normal range. Then people began to remark that he had lost weight and looked fit.

Goals and Ideals: Love and Addiction

One area aside from eating where abstinence is generally more painful than addiction is in love relationships. Even here, though, the pain of addiction can still be overwhelming. If you have had troubling and destructive relationships in the past, how do you decide on goals for forming healthy relationships? For one thing, you can recognize and rule out the addictive behaviors you have displayed in the past, such as giving up your interests and friends to pursue the relationship or being afraid to stand up for yourself for fear of alienating your lover.

Another way to establish goals is to use an ideal image of the person you choose to be. In *Love and Addiction,* for example, we created an image of an ideal love relationship as a way to guide people's behavior. People don't accomplish their ideals in a day or, necessarily, ever. But in love, probably more than any other potential addiction, people are confused about what is right and what they *should* try to do. Based on our thinking on the topic, you are on the right track in a love relationship *if:*

▸ You are not preoccupied with jealousies over your lover's activities and friends.

▸ You are a self-motivated person pursuing your own career and life goals.

▸ You want a strong and helpful person who will fit in with your life and improve it.

▸ You want a lover you can admire, a positive person for others as well as yourself.

▸ You can spend time alone, you can have other friends, and your lover is comfortable doing these things, too.

Keeping Track of Your Progress

Lists and Record-Keeping

How are you doing at meeting your goals? If you set concrete, measurable ones, you should be able to tell pretty easily. However, the mind is a tricky mechanism. It can make assessing progress toward a goal difficult if you (1) forget or change the goal, or (2) misgauge how well you are doing at meeting the goal. The best antidote to these problems is to write down your goal and your behavior in meeting it. If you have written down your goal along with everything you have done to fulfill it, you will have an unambiguous record of your progress.

Record-keeping is illuminating in many ways. People often find that simply recording everything they eat and drink in a given day gives them pause—without such a record, they often lose track of what they put into themselves. Usually people find this means that they have eaten, smoked, or drunk more than they realized, but sometimes it also brings positive surprises. Martha Sanchez-Craig described an experiment in which subjects were assigned either an abstinence or a controlled-drinking goal. One client who had been assigned an abstinence goal reviewed his drinking self-monitoring records for the week and found he had had eleven drinks. Reminded that his goal was abstinence, he excitedly burst out, "Isn't that beautiful. Over the whole week I drank less than I used to drink in a single day!"[7]

What was most important in this record-keeping, besides simply showing this man he could drink dramatically less than he used to, was what he learned about the situations in which he drank. He reported that this part of the exercise was most valuable to him, because it gave him a real "understanding of what is behind my drinking."

EXERCISE

If you have severe addictive episodes that you find intolerable, record their times, dates, and circumstances. This information will help you both to analyze the circumstances that lead to these incidents and to evaluate your success at reducing them.

Giving and Receiving Feedback

Family and friends are often the best sources of feedback on how you are doing in your change efforts. You need to solicit their opinions and to be aware of their reactions. Alternatively, you may be reading this book to deal more effectively with other people who are fighting addictive behaviors. In this case, your question may be, "What is the best way to influence other people beneficially?" In the first place, how do you help people realize they need to change? In the second, how do you offer feedback about how well they are doing to make sure they continue?

The answers to these questions are complicated. You need to be sensitive to other people to discover the best way to communicate with them. There are general rules, however:

- You can't succeed at helping people if you're not genuinely interested in their progress.
- Feedback has to respect who the other person is—diatribes and assaults on people's integrity will produce more negative effects than positive.
- Feedback that is low-key and steady, more often positive than negative, and directed at specific behaviors rather than at the person's basic self-worth has a better chance of getting through.

▸ People more readily accept feedback when they ask for it or see it as a legitimate concern of the other person.

▸ People must have a course of action to take in response to the feedback, or else they will reject it.

▸ If you want to get the most from feedback that others give you, you must be open to hearing information about yourself without thinking primarily how to defend your position.

Concretely, in the area of addiction (such as responding to someone who is trying to moderate his or her drinking or eating), recommendations for providing feedback and support include:

▸ Be clear about your view of the need for the person to eat or drink less.

▸ Show your support and desire for the person to improve and be healthier.

▸ Offer practical assistance while avoiding placing yourself in the position of constantly monitoring the person's behavior.

▸ Remind the person of why he or she selected a goal and help maintain the motivation to change.

▸ Respond positively as the person maintains changes in eating or drinking behavior.

▸ Acknowledge the person's new status as a moderate drinker or eater, such as by giving him or her free rein in a mildly challenging situation (like a party), then respecting his ability to make his own choices.

Receiving active, no-nonsense feedback from people you care about is among the best ways to get you to change any troubling behavior. An organization, group, or family that emphasizes caring and honest communication will reduce addiction from every possible angle. Such communication should emphasize positive responses, but include direct, unemotional criticisms or complaints when problems arise in such areas as work performance or communication. If you have people you can count on for such caring feedback, you are more likely to nip problems in the bud before they lead either to addiction in the first place or to relapses.

CASE

What do you do if your spouse or coworker drinks too much? A man asked one of us this question. But he already had as much knowledge about the answer as practically anyone in America. This man had himself stopped smoking when his wife asked him to quit after they got married. In fact, she stopped having sex with him until he quit. I informed this man that alcoholics and crack addicts find it harder to give up cigarettes than to quit drinking or using drugs. Therefore, his wife had helped him by providing the motivation to quit the worst addiction.

Is the answer to this question, then, to threaten addicted spouses until they change their drinking (or smoking, or eating) behavior? Not entirely. Creating strong incentives in the form of penalties or disapproval is part of the picture. Another part for this man was his wife's clear signal to him that she was concerned for him and their future children, and that this was *why* she was urging him to stop and withholding physical affection in the meantime.

Clearly, their relationship supported the wife's request, her encouragements, and her sanctions. This man was willing to respond to his wife's wishes rather than to fight them, and he did want sex with her (conditions that do not always hold true). The wife's successful efforts can be generalized to the following suggestions for changing a family member's behavior:

1. *Strong family relationships facilitate behavior change.* They make people care enough to change the addict's behavior and the addict care enough to strive to change.

2. *Telling the person directly to change is important.* Back up a complaint with more than incessant whining. Disapproval of the addiction and appropriate actions are also necessary.

3. *Negative pressures don't work by themselves.* You must combine them with positive incentives, support, and a sense that you want the person to change for his or her own good as well as your own.

4. *Getting the person into a program (Weight Watchers, Smokenders, Alcoholics Anonymous) is one way to go, but this is no more successful than efforts that take place entirely within the family.* Even when the

person enters a formal program, family pressures and support are the main guarantees of success in the program and afterward.

5. *The same principles apply to coworkers and employees.*

Summary: The Need for Feedback and How to Get and Give It

You should also be able to ask people close to you how well you are doing in your change program, assuming you feel that they care for and want the best for you. Therapy can be a good place to ask a neutral observer to review your progress with you. Whether in therapy or out, you need objective signposts, including your own record-keeping, to measure progress.

When offering feedback yourself, focus on behaviors that affect you directly. Voice your concerns or complaints in a caring but unemotional way. That is, your efforts should be geared toward reaching the other person, not toward letting off steam. Occasionally, these well-meaning efforts will fall short, in which case you may need to take a stronger position, up to and including breaking off the relationship. This is necessary both to make your feelings clear and to protect yourself. Not that it is your job to punish the person; rather, the loss of the relationship becomes an unavoidable (and, you might hope, informative) consequence of the person's actions.

Keeping Yourself on Track

Despite the popularity of imposed treatments, or "interventions," change efforts aren't nearly so hard to begin as they are to continue. Most people have already made many resolutions to change before they call enough attention to themselves to become the object of an intervention. Before going into the specifics of maintaining change efforts, however, we want to record here the Golden Rule of Behavior Change:

Golden Rule of Behavior Change

> It is easier to swim with the current than against it. You will succeed better when your rewards and goals for change are part of the core of your daily life.

When you have to remind yourself of why you are doing something and what to do, you will do it less well and have a greater chance of failing or quitting. On the other hand, you will succeed at change if the rewards for the new behaviors are built into the structure of your life, are consistent with other things that are important to you, and are supported by those near and dear to you and by your social and work groups.

EXAMPLES

One woman found that she ate a sweet with a co-worker every time the coffee wagon came around to her floor. The woman gained weight steadily over her five years on this job, although she still weighed less than her friend. Finally, the friend went to an experimental dietary program being run at a local hospital. It emphasized protein and complex carbohydrates (pasta and potatoes were permitted without butter or cream), and regular exercise to fill time usually filled with aimless eating.

The first time the co-worker excused herself to go for a walk, this woman inquired about the program. Delighted, the co-worker asked her if she wanted to join also. "No, I don't," she replied, "but I want to walk with you every day and I'd appreciate it if you told me what you learned about food and diet while we're at it." In fact, she valued the co-worker's company as the best thing about coffee breaks; only now she had to do something healthy to get the value of the co-worker's company. "I can't believe my luck," she thought. "I've got a voluntary personal trainer and dietary consultant where I used to have a boon eating companion."

Rewarding Your Efforts

Any plan for change is a long-range one. That is, achieving your ultimate goals remains far in the future. This is most obvious in the case of a weight-loss program. You can eat correctly for days, weeks, and months—and still be very far from the weight you desire. What, then, will keep you going until you get there? For after the Golden Rule there is a second rule of behavior change: people won't do something for nothing. If the addiction serves some purpose and provides any rewards on its own, what rewards will the new behaviors substitute for the addictive rewards?

There are several.

- *Virtue is its own reward.* You will feel better because you know you are doing the right thing. And you can help this feeling along by constantly reminding yourself of your virtuousness.
- *Note and celebrate your small gains.* Every morning, when you wake up, think of how you breathe easier since you quit smoking. Reflect on your good night's sleep now that you have cut back on caffeine. Programs like Weight Watchers use the scale to detect even small weekly weight loss.
- *Rely on group support and approval.* When you lose any weight, everyone in the Weight Watchers group cheers your progress. Or family or friends can serve this role by noting how well you are doing at a change effort. "How long has it been since you've quit smoking? That's marvelous."
- *Envision the new you that lies at the end of the path of behavior change,* the thin, or drug-free, or sober person. You're getting closer to being that person all the time.
- *Develop new rewards to replace the addiction.* That is, seek a pleasurable substitute when previously you may have taken a break by smoking, drinking coffee or an alcoholic beverage, or eating a sweet bun.
- *Attach rewards to carrying through your change plan,* so that doing the right thing brings you something you like. For example, whenever you take your morning walk, buy yourself a flower or some other nonaddictive reward that you might previously have passed by. These sustaining rewards should be real and easy to obtain, so that you *want* to continue getting them.

EXERCISE

List three realistic rewards you can provide yourself that you would like to have but that you rarely get, the way you live your life currently. How can these be built into your day to replace the addictive behavior or to reward your virtuous activities?

The Rewards of Living

Rewards work best when you don't need to go looking for them. Your change effort will be that much easier to the extent that the life you ordinarily live reinforces the behaviors you want. This is why a change of setting—or of social group—may facilitate quitting drugs, drinking less, eating better, having sounder relationships, or implementing any policy of change you like. One man said, "It was easy for me to quit smoking when I got promoted from working on the floor of the factory to working in the office. Everyone down on the floor smoked. Everyone 'inside' didn't. I almost felt quitting was a requirement for the promotion."

Replacement Activities: Exercising

You can find new rewards in your new life. If you are losing weight or quitting smoking or undertaking practically any other behavior change, exercising will support your effort to eliminate the addiction. Exercise accomplishes this because it (1) is healthy, makes you feel good, and raises your self-esteem; (2) gives you a new interest and skill; (3) makes you more attractive; (4) uses up time and energy in a constructive way (as long as it does not become an obsessive focus—or addiction—in your life).

Whenever possible, you should build such exercise or other replacement activities into your ordinary routines. The first step toward a vigorous life is to find the exercise opportunities that are all around you. For example, you can exercise by parking your car farther from work, by climbing stairs instead of using the elevator, by developing the habit of walking during your lunch break. One woman even developed a program of exercise built around cleaning her house! Unfortunately, some naturally occurring changes in our lives work in the opposite direction: one study found that when secretaries switch to computers they may gain weight because of the loss of physical activity associated with typing and filing.

Planning for "High-Risk" Situations

Alternative activities are especially crucial for your weakest moments, those times when the misery of your condition is most likely to overcome you. You need to put in place contingency plans for the "high-risk" situations where you have always gone wrong in the past.

EXAMPLE

On a weekend night when you have no plans, you typically become intensely frustrated with your lack of social success and your overweight. It is on these nights that, as you become miserable, you binge-eat. Instead, plan to go to the gym on these nights. If you don't feel like going out, learn to switch on an exercise video—or read a book you've stashed away for just this occasion—as soon as you feel the urge to eat the foods that are worst for you to assuage your depression. Get into the experience of being by yourself, and try to enjoy it.

Dealing with Failure

Rewards for success are great, but everyone must deal with failure. And failure is harder to handle than success. In fact, the evidence is not that addicts have less success than nonaddicts, but that they overreact more to failure. For example, after slipping and having a drink or smoke or failing to adhere to a diet, a person may conclude, "Well, I've failed at my goal again, so I might as well give it up entirely."

Instead, you need a plan for reinstituting your goals even at the moments you do worst at achieving them. To accomplish this, you have to recognize and plan for the possibility of failure. You have to believe in your goals sufficiently so that you will continue to shoot for them even when you aren't perfect. If you fail enough, you may need to conceive different goals or a different way of achieving them. But goals that work more often than not should not be jettisoned just because you sometimes fall short of them.

How Your Goals Fit into Your Life

The Ladder of Life

Goals are achieved by making small incremental steps toward final goals. This is as true of career and family goals—which take decades to develop fully—as it is of quitting addictions. Addicts have less experience at and less tolerance for sustained efforts that take long periods to accomplish. Whether you have an addiction or not, you need to visualize your entire life in terms of the goals you are pursuing and the steps that are necessary to get there. Envision something you want to accomplish. Then imagine plateaus—mini-goals that occur on the way to your ultimate destination.

In the following chart, we describe three sets of progressive goals separately, as individual ladders: one for a man who has been unable to establish a permanent relationship with a woman, one for a woman who wants to become a licensed psychotherapist, and one for a man who wants to restore positive relationships with his children and ex-wife after an unpleasant divorce. Think of the individual rungs you need to climb to move you toward your ultimate goals.

Goal Ladders		
Establish Relationship	*Become a Psychotherapist*	*Heal Family After Divorce*
Create stable relationship	Start own therapy practice	Positive family celebrations
Begin sexual involvements	Get therapy license	Parents speak about children's needs
Begin dating	Get job at therapy center	Parents avoid criticizing one another
Ask women out	Complete graduate therapy program	Parents speak to children about family
Meet women	Gain admission to graduate program	Create satisfactory custody arrangements
Socialize with friends	Free up time to attend school	Restore friendly or civil relations with ex-wife

The Life-Goals Grid

Psychologists W. Miles Cox and Eric Klinger have developed a model of goal-setting and achievement in working with alcoholics. Their approach, like the Life Process Program, focuses not on drinking but on the alcoholic's life context and the fulfillment of goals in family, work, and leisure life. Cox and Klinger liken the set of goals the alcoholic or other individual may pursue to a grid. Each column in the grid represents a separate goal—a promotion at work, dealing positively with family matters, buying a house, resolving a legal problem, completing a hobby, etc. These goals are parallel to and concurrent with the goal of eliminating the addiction. Arranged under the goals are the steps needed to reach the goal.[8]

The chart below presents an example of a grid for a man who wants to reduce his drinking and smoking, improve his family and work life, and develop some positive activities. Obviously, the steps can be more detailed—how will this man do his work better? Your grid may have as many rows and columns as you wish.

Different life goals often reinforce one another. The task is to associate the achievement of one goal with another: for example, having a stable social life will usually enhance your career goals. In particular, to the extent that you can realize that quitting the addiction is a part of gaining what you want in other areas, these other goals will support and reward your behavior change. For instance, ceasing to smoke or drink can help your marriage and job, your health and financial goals. This is the Life Process Program feedback loop. Once you are on it, you can progress with growing momentum. The man whose case is represented by the grid should be able to cut back eating and drinking by devoting more positive attention to work, family, and other activities. These steps will increase his positive feelings about his life and lower his anxiety level, which in turn should make it easier for him to stop his excessive consumption.

A Life-Goals Grid

GOALS				
Family	*Work*	*Addiction(s)*	*Project(s)*	*Activities*
Enjoy home life	Get promotion	Stop excessive drinking and eating	Complete patio	Jog regularly
Spend time with kids	Impress boss	Come home right after work	Spend more time at home	Jog mornings, weekends
Come home on time	Master job requirements	Limit work breaks	Take masonry course	Stop excessive eating
Think about family life	Concentrate on work	Lower anxieties at work and home	Ask brother-in-law for help	Spend more time at home

CASE

A man finds he needs to stop on his way home for several drinks after a tough day at work. Often, he has had several drinks at lunch with his friends. Finally, he usually has a drink or two in his easy chair before he goes to bed. At his wife's insistence, one day he counts his drinks and finds he has had ten! He is truly frightened, because he hasn't realized how much alcohol he has been consuming, and because he doesn't see a way out of the life-style he has created around drinking throughout the day. Finally, he realizes he is alienating his wife and preteen daughter and son, with whom he hardly exchanges a pleasant word before they go to bed.

The easiest drinking to eliminate is that before getting home. He knows that his groggy and irritable state when he arrives home hurts family interactions. Instead of stopping at the bar, one day he comes home directly and asks his son and daughter if they'd like to toss a ball around. Stunned, the children agree. After dinner, the man goes over the day's homework assignments with each child. Missed homework assignments are a constant irritant in the family. The man realizes that one of things he is drinking to avoid is his frustration that his children's grades aren't as good as he thinks they should be. This night he has one drink before turning in, and he is relieved to count a total of five drinks for the day.

Thus he begins a plan of drinking less and concentrating on his children more. He knows he should have been doing this all along, and he is now finally taking steps to relieve his guilt and resentment over not being a more active father. His wife also appreciates the effort he is making, and they spend more time talking to each other. With his home life no longer such a negative experience, he finds that he has almost no urge to drink at night. Next he starts to wonder what he can do to cut down his urge to drink at work.

Contradictory Goals

Of course, some of your activities and goals may be in part contradictory. Life isn't perfect, you know. To get a task done, you may need to concentrate purely on the job at hand. This may leave little attention for thinking about new behaviors, like cutting back your coffee drinking. First, you may see that ultimately the new behavior will assist you at what you're trying to accomplish. In other words, there may be no conflict. At the other extreme are conflicts you will have to resolve before you can accomplish what you want.

CASE

Gail was an investment banker who was required to produce complex reports during intense bouts of work. Although she had done her job well for years and had been praised and promoted, she always retained doubts and insecurities about her ability to perform up to standard.

Gail smoked. The few times she had tried to cut back as part of a smoking-cessation program, she was convinced that her concentration was suffering and that she couldn't do her required work. She quickly returned to her nicotine fix to focus her attention.

Gail had to find a way to eliminate her work anxieties before she could quit smoking. Her first step was to quit smoking during a vacation (she already smoked less around her family at home). Her second was to explain her situation to her boss and to ask him if he could shift some of her work to a colleague for the next month. (As it turned out, her boss told her she was as productive during her first smoke-free month at work as she had been during her last month as a smoker.)

Finally, Gail implemented a plan for whenever she felt her concentration slipping: she breathed deeply, put on a pair of sneakers she kept under her desk, and walked rapidly around the courtyard outside her office building. The hot Indian summer the first fall she quit made this dash a humid one. Fortunately, letting her boss know what she was doing made Gail less self-conscious when she returned, perspiring, from these quick walks.

The Integrated Life

A perfectly integrated life would be one in which people's lives provided all the necessary rewards and signposts for doing the right thing. Addiction of all sorts would be eliminated in this life-style. The bad news is that nobody attains such a perfectly integrated life. The good news is that people get close enough so that they no longer have to feel as though they are walking on eggs, making lists of what they can and cannot do and how well they have done during the past day, week, or month. It's a good thing this is the case, because if people were expected to make such lists forever, only one in a hundred people would ever permanently quit smoking, instead of the one in two who have actually licked the habit!

People get beyond the "list" stage to a place where the rewards of the new life-style are so well entrenched as to make relapse a virtual impossibility. There are certainly cases of people who have quit smoking or drinking for years, even decades, who suddenly return to their addictions. But these are rare. In other words, the best guarantee that you will eliminate an addiction is living a nonaddicted life-style for a number of years. Then, even in the few cases where relapse does occur, your ability to resume your positive life-style is that much better established and easier to accomplish.

The point is that you can let go of your addicted self-image. You can have enough practice and put enough life structures into place to make sure that relapse is unlikely, as unlikely as it is for a previously unaddicted person to develop your old addiction. This point is reached when you gain so much from the person you have become—enough success at your life goals, enough acceptance and praise from others, enough confidence in yourself—that to take the steps back toward addiction would be more difficult than to go forward without it.

CHAPTER 14

CHANGING THE BEHAVIOR

•

THAT OBSCURE OBJECT OF DESIRE

YOU MAY EXPERIENCE life changes that enable you to quit addictions, but you can also adopt techniques for changing the addictive behavior directly. At some point, you must *cut back* or *quit* your consumption or your involvement in an activity. Then you must *maintain* your moderation or else *avoid* the activity, and *recover* quickly if you should slip back briefly to excess. Though the disease approach emphasizes that you must quit, it offers little in the way of specific techniques for doing so, aside from telling you to rely on group support. As for recovering from a relapse and resuming your progress, the disease model actually places obstacles in your path by magnifying the relapse.

In recent years, cognitive-behavioral therapists have developed more constructive approaches to habit change. Interestingly, these professionals have begun looking to self-quitters to find out which techniques work best. That is, researchers have begun asking people who quit smoking or drugs, or quit or cut back their drinking, or lost weight on their own, what methods they have used: how they began to change their habits, how they maintain their progress, and how they overcome cravings and relapses. Sometimes these methods resemble ones that cognitive-behavioral therapists have recommended. But often the methods used are highly personal and less elaborate than those a therapist would give you. We will describe for you some cognitive, behavioral, and situational techniques for changing habits.

A 1990 Gallup Poll asked people what health behaviors they had changed and how they did so. The table below shows the methods people used to lose weight (note that people could—and did—give more than one response):

The Most Popular Ways to Lose Weight[1]

Just cut out snacks and desserts	42%
Just eat less of everything	37%
Start to exercise more	32%
Cut down on fatty foods	32%
Stop eating at night	29%
Eat more fruits and vegetables	20%
Start counting calories	19%
Eat less red meat	17%
Use low-calorie foods and drinks	12%
Follow a diet plan from a doctor	11%
Eat more filling, low-calorie foods	10%
Join a weight-loss group	9%
Use a special diet food (e.g., protein powder)	3%
Follow a diet book	1%

As you can see, people *least often* use the methods you read most about or see advertised most frequently on television—diet books, powder diets, and weight-loss groups. In general, the methods people use most frequently to lose weight are the same ones that diets and exercise programs recommend. But people adopt these methods in their own idiosyncratic ways.

This same situation prevails in the case of smoking. We once reviewed with a leading behaviorist (Tim Baker, of the University of Wisconsin) some surprising results he had obtained from a clinical trial of a smoking-cessation program. It seemed that the control group (the comparison group that met with therapists but received no treatment) initially outperformed the treatment group in quitting smoking. Dr. Baker gave an example of why he thought this had happened:

> In the control group, when a person describes a problem, the therapist must sit neutrally. So a man might come in with a story like this (the man had already stopped smoking and was trying to maintain his abstinence): "I'm having lunch this week with my ex-mother-in-law. I'm really worried about the meeting. First of all, this woman makes me tense. Secondly, she smokes the same brand of cigarettes I used to smoke. I think my chances of relapsing are high."

> In this case, the therapist might just nod and say something neutral like "That does seem bad," but offer no concrete suggestions. As a result, the ex-smoker, considering he was supposed to be learning how to stay off cigarettes, will often make up his own therapy. With nothing forthcoming from the therapist, he'll start rehearsing or planning his own techniques for making sure the lunch doesn't turn into a disaster that drives him back to cigarettes.[2]

In chapter 4, we saw that a 1990 study published in the *Journal of the American Medical Association* found that those who quit smoking on their own were *twice* as likely to stay away from tobacco as those treated in smoking-cessation programs.[3] Baker's overachieving "placebo" group is, in fact, typical.

The difficulty of *teaching* people effective addiction-quitting techniques has been demonstrated by the history of research on smoking-cessation programs. That is, beginning in the 1970s, a group of techniques showed promise in helping people quit cigarettes. Encouraged, behaviorists bundled together these techniques—like exercise, group support, negative imaging of smoking, and techniques for coping with the urge to smoke—figuring that if *one* such method was successful then all of them combined would multiply success rates. But this has never happened, and smoking-cessation treatment never exceeds the early success rates reported by these programs, while often showing far inferior results.

What all of this shows is that *which* techniques or *how many* techniques the individual relies on doesn't matter. The question is: do the techniques—individually or together—work for that individual? How do we know whether they will or not? The answer is that a person often can figure out the techniques that will work best for him or her. Furthermore, when you select your own techniques, you are enhancing your *self-efficacy*—that is, the sense that you determine the outcomes in your life, and thus that you can attain the goals you desire. Self-efficacy is perhaps the crucial ingredient in cure.

The Life Process Program does not dictate any specific techniques for quitting an addiction or for living a nonaddicted life. Instead, we encourage you to discover and develop whatever techniques make the most sense from among your own array of options. This self-discovery and self-management is the essential procedure that underlies the success of any specific technique. Nonetheless, learning about the techniques others have used may help speed your own selection and adoption of change methods. This chapter will give you a chance to review the techniques adopted by both cognitive-behavioral therapists and self-curers.

Breaking the Addictive Cycle

The *sine qua non* of addiction is the addictive cycle, in which a person turns a casual exposure to an activity or substance into an all-out binge. According to the disease theory, this cycle is unavoidable once the individual makes the first move and has a sip or taste of the forbidden substance or any exposure to the addictive experience (like gambling, or a sexual encounter). Actually, however—as we will demonstrate throughout this chapter—cognitive, behavioral, and situational techniques can break the cycle. Instead of launching into the downward spiral every time you drink, or eat a rich food, or have a date with an eligible mate, or make the first bet, or buy the first blouse, you can learn how to short-circuit the process and exit the spiral.

Obviously, if you master such techniques on an ongoing basis, you become an actual moderate or controlled drinker, or eater, or lover, or shopper. Short of achieving the goal of transforming an addictive involvement into a normal, healthy one—and even then—you must sometimes practice damage control. That is, you need to learn how to avoid converting one slip into an all-out disaster. Thus, any or all of the techniques in this chapter can be applied to one or more of the following goals:

- dealing with your urges so you can avoid giving in to them at all (abstinence);
- structuring and regulating your reactions to an activity (moderation);
- avoiding allowing an indulgence to get out of hand entirely (damage control—preventing relapse)

The realism and flexibility of the Life Process Program are its greatest advantage over the disease ideology. Instead of burdening you with an irrelevant sense of guilt for not achieving perfection—or for sometimes not even wanting to—the Life Process Program recognizes the reality of slips and occasional backsliding. And instead of lecturing you on your powerlessness in the face of temptations and slips, it provides practical tools for negotiating the ups and downs of recovery.

The Stages of Quitting

Quitting an addiction is a long process, involving different phases. What may work best at one stage need not be most effective at another. Psychologists Carlo DiClemente and James Prochaska have identified five stages of change in quitting an addiction (in this case, smoking). The stages are:

1. *Precontemplation.* The person hasn't even identified the behavior as a problem.

2. *Contemplation.* The person has become at least ambivalent, saying things like: "I sometimes wonder if I drink too much," or "I may be repeating myself in the relationships I form with men," or "I wonder if I have the strength to lose weight [or give up smoking]."

3. *Commitment and action.* The turning point at which the person decides to change or quit the behavior. Key statements at this point are: "I've decided I've got to change. I just can't go on like this anymore!" These sentiments are accompanied by an effort to change.

4. *Maintenance.* This is the effort required to maintain the change: to keep off drugs, cigarettes, or alcohol; to drink, eat, or shop moderately; to avoid addictive relationships or gambling.

5. *Relapse.* Of course, people often fail at or give up on their change effort. Relapse is so common that it needs to be considered as an aspect of change. The question is how people respond to relapse, whether they renew their commitment to change, and how they go about getting back on track.[4]

Techniques That Quitters Use

We can identify three types of strategies or techniques for changing addictive habits:

▸ *cognitive* (such as thinking about consequences, counting to ten before acting);

▸ *behavioral* (such as setting aside a small amount to consume, having only as much as a controlled-using companion);

▸ *social/situational* (such as avoiding high-risk places, associating with people whom you want to impress).

Different people may use different combinations of techniques. Some techniques are remarkably idiosyncratic: a man looked at a picture he carried around of a pair of cancerous lungs each time he wanted a smoke; a woman taped a picture of her overweight self in a bathing suit on the refrigerator; a man always thought about an ex-wife who sneered, "He'll never quit gambling," whenever he had the urge.

The particular items in this list are not especially important. Psychologist Saul Shiffman asked subjects who had quit smoking to describe the techniques they used, which he classified as either behavioral or cognitive.

Techniques for Avoiding Smoking[5]

Behavioral	*Cognitive*
1. Eating or drinking something	1. Thinking about positive health consequences of quitting
2. Physical activity, exercise	2. Thinking about negative health consequences of smoking
3. Relaxation	3. Thinking about other negative consequences (e.g., how kids will react)
4. Distracting activity	4. Willpower (no specific coping thoughts)
5. Escaping the situation	5. Self-punitive thoughts ("I'm such a weakling")
6. Delaying action	6. Delay ("I'll hold off")
7. Other behavioral coping	7. Distracting thoughts
	8. Other cognitive coping

Shiffman found that any cognitive coping technique a person selected was as good as any other for the purpose of quitting smoking. *The one exception was self-punitive thoughts (such as motivating yourself by putting yourself down: "I've never been any good at quitting"). This approach is totally ineffective.*

Drinking was a somewhat different matter. For the purpose of abstaining from alcohol, the effectiveness of the techniques used varied more. Self-punitive thoughts (like telling yourself how bad you were if you had a first drink) were ineffective, just as they were with smoking. In addition, exercise worked *against* avoiding alcohol. Relaxation techniques and practicing drink-refusal techniques worked quite well. Following are the successful behavioral and coping techniques for avoiding drinking that Shiffman and his colleagues identified:

Techniques for Avoiding Drinking[6]

Men	*Women*
relaxation	techniques for refusing drinks
delay	willpower
seeking social support	reviewing negative health consequences of drinking
willpower	
self-reevaluation	
thinking of something else to do	

Willpower was the only technique that was helpful for both men and women in avoiding drinking. Since willpower is a no-no for disease-theory advocates, it is worth describing an account of willpower by an abstaining alcoholic. This description is from a series of interviews conducted by a Kentucky physician, Arnold Ludwig, with alcoholics who quit drinking on their own:

> I just say I'm not going to do it. . . . I think it is just willpower. It's having reached a logical conclusion about given circumstances . . . and saying, "Is it in your best interest to drink or not? No, don't drink!"[7]

DiClemente and Prochaska combined their research on stages of quitting addictions with coping mechanisms, or self-motivators, people use for these various stages. These techniques are outlined on the next page.

Among these strategies, the researchers found dramatic relief and social liberation *least* effective. But they point out that different strategies can be helpful at different stages. For example, consciousness-raising is an essential step for someone who has not been thinking about quitting at all (*precontemplation stage*). For someone who has been thinking about it (*contemplation*), self-liberation is a key turning point in making the decision to quit (*commitment*). Counterconditioning comes into play as a reinforcement strategy for someone who is trying to keep up the change (*maintenance*).

You can mull over the strategies in this chapter, try out different techniques, borrow when necessary, or invent your own; but always remember that *there never has been and never will be a single set pattern that can free us all from any addiction.*

***Coping Mechanisms in Quitting Addictions*[8]**

Cognitive Techniques

- *consciousness-raising* ("I recall information people have given me on the benefits of quitting smoking");
- *self-liberation* ("I tell myself I am able to quit smoking if I want to");
- *self-re-evaluation* ("My dependency on cigarettes makes me feel disappointed in myself");
- *environmental re-evaluation* ("I stop to think that smoking is polluting the environment");
- *dramatic relief* ("Warning about health hazards of smoking move me emotionally").

Behavioral Techniques

- *counterconditioning* ("I do something else instead of smoking when I need to relax or deal with tension");
- *stimulus control* ("I remove things from my home that remind me of smoking");
- *reinforcement management* ("I am rewarded by others if I don't smoke").

Situational Techniques

- *social liberation* ("I find society changing in ways that make it easier for the nonsmoker");
- *helping relationships* ("I have someone who listens when I need to talk about my smoking").

Picking Your Technique(s)

The lists of techniques we have reviewed that people *actually* use are superior to disease therapies for combating addiction. The disease method consists primarily of dire warnings not to do something at all costs. The lists above instead describe what works for people—that is, how people persuade or remind themselves that the addiction is less important than other things, which the addiction jeopardizes.

The drawback to these lists is that they provide so many options. The research of Shiffman and his colleagues showed that different behavioral and cognitive techniques work for avoiding smoking and for avoiding drinking. Different techniques work for men and women. In addition, the researchers found that different techniques work better for different types of temptation—that is, stress at work or school as opposed to being offered a substance at a party. Different techniques also work better or worse depending on how strong a temptation the person faces, how long he or she has had a drinking problem or has been smoking, how old the person is, or other personal characteristics (like religious orientation). As Prochaska and DiClemente show, which technique works best also depends on the stage the person has reached in the process of quitting.[9]

Clearly, trying to figure out which of all these techniques is going to work best for you would be a staggering task! You could never be sure whether you had everything covered. Suppose you're a young woman who had a moderately severe drinking problem for only a few years. You need techniques for both smoking and drinking; you need techniques for handling both stress and availability of the substance; you need techniques to use shortly after quitting and for a longer period down the line. The better approach is to build techniques from your *own* experience, to try techniques on and to see how they work by trial and error, and to assemble techniques that you believe in and that you *own*.

EXERCISE

Think of times when you have kept an activity under control and when you have binged. What was the difference between the two situations: Was it the people you were with? Was it the setting you were in? Was it your mood? How did you approach the situation? Following are some examples of answers you may come up with:

Loss-of-Control (or Control) Situations

Mood: Tense, happy, excited, depressed, bored, unguarded

Setting: Work, home, client's house, club, party

Companions: Ex-mate, old friend, relatives

Circumstances: Celebration, business meeting, family get-together, confrontation with mate

Strategies used for control: Set aside a small amount to consume, thought about consequences of actions, counted to ten before having any, didn't go to a place where you had binged in the past, stayed with people before whom you didn't want to look bad, found an alternative activity

Now, based on what you find has worked for you in the past in avoiding relapse, maintaining abstinence, or whatever your goal is, describe an ideally positive situation and then a perfectly horrid and high-risk one. Which components of each situation are most/least under your control? What situations should (can) you avoid? What things should make you cautious (a particular setting or mood, for example)? What things can you do to minimize the risk you face?

What techniques have you used with the most success, either in general or for the particular situation you will be facing? What techniques do you think would be useful (relaxation, refusal skills, alternative activities) that you need to develop or practice more? (Return to consider the techniques you have available or need to learn after you have completed reading the rest of this chapter.)

Mind over Matter: Cognitive Techniques

To help you consider the range of strategies with which you can attack addictive behavior, we will review the three principal kinds of techniques, beginning with cognitive. By understanding each type of technique, you will be better able not only to choose methods that work for you, but also to compose your own.

Cognitive techniques are ways of thinking about the object of your addiction or the activity to make you less likely to indulge or to splurge.

Associating Negative Thoughts with the Addiction

Psychologists have had some success with aversive conditioning—the coupling of unpleasant sensations with the object of addiction. For example, giving someone a mild shock or a chemical agent that makes him throw up as he drinks—so that vomiting and drinking become inextricably associated in his mind.

These methods have developed unsavory reputations, however. Aversive conditioning has been ridiculed by portrayals like that of the boy in the film *Clockwork Orange* who is shocked out of his violent behavior and then is victimized himself. However, using the mind to associate negative images with a behavior (called *covert sensitization*) has proved to be just as effective as actually receiving shocks and other aversive stimuli. For example, the image and smells of nausea can be paired with the alcoholic's drinking to cause involuntary gagging.[10]

Even the use of sensory conditioning (instead of chemicals) may be too unpleasant for most people to try. But other unpleasant imagery besides vomiting can be brought to bear. Having such negative images in your own mind not only makes them more portable, but also brings them under your control. They thus become tools you can apply whenever needed. For example, smokers can imagine licking a dirty ashtray, or visualize pictures they have seen of clouded lungs of smokers or tracheotomies that people have undergone for throat cancer.

Here is where you can let your imagination run wild. What is the worst fear or experience with the addiction you have had? Is it seeing yourself rummaging through an ashtray to reclaim a cigarette butt, grabbing food off your child's plate when you were hungry, puking in front of someone you were in love with? Are you afraid of suffering a heart attack or lung cancer, or do you have an image of yourself looking ridiculous when intoxicated or appearing obese in a bathing suit in front of people you want to impress? Do you fear being caught in a particularly humiliating sexual liaison, or losing your house and family because of overwhelming shopping bills or gambling debts?

Instead of pushing this image out of your memory (which is often hard to do anyhow), make it an active and regular part of your thinking process. Practice it, both in general and as an adjunct to countering the urge to smoke, drink, use drugs, eat too much of the wrong foods, or whatever. One alcoholic, whenever he felt like a drink, would

> think back to the worst time, such as waking up in jail and the blackouts and the worrying about whether I'd hit somebody with my car and the time that the fellow brought me home, where my wife and two boys saw me.[11]

You should be able to recapture this image at a *moment's* notice.

Guided Imagery and Visualization

Guided imagery is a therapeutic technique akin to free association that is popular in Europe. The individual fantasizes freely about a situation until reaching an irresolvable impasse, at which point the therapist intervenes and leads the person to a safe resolution.[12] Visualization is familiar to Americans through sports psychology. Here an athlete envisions a successful performance—swinging through and hitting a ball, winning a difficult competition, completing a perfect dive or skating figure.

With addictive behavior, you can envision going through a tense or difficult situation without smoking, drinking, going shopping, taking a Valium, or overeating. Imagine yourself at a full buffet table selecting a small piece of food from every other plate, filling your plate once, and then talking with people, instead of stuffing yourself. The story of the smoker anticipating a difficult meal with his ex-mother-in-law is another example of rehearsing alternative scenarios rather than relying on the addiction. He could imagine himself smiling calmly at his mother-in-law's probing questions, waiting until she was finished, politely asking her whether she wanted another cup of coffee, and then showing her the latest pictures of her grandchildren.

Overcoming addiction is a matter not just of ceasing to do something, but of reorienting your life to follow a new path. However, some of the rewards you will get from this reorientation are far in the future. Eating moderately for a few weeks will only help you lose a few pounds, and you still won't fit into an old pair of jeans or be able to roller-skate gracefully. Here is where you can fruitfully give in to your image of the person you will someday be if you keep on your current course. Give yourself *now* the rewards you are seeking from changing your behavior by imagining them—the ability to breathe freely, or to go through a day without thinking constantly about when you're going to catch a smoke.

There Must Be a Better Way—Rehearse Your Reasons for Quitting

You have already identified the situations and feelings that are most likely to lead to excessive or addictive behaviors: boredom, loneliness, depression, anxiety, failure, stress, being attacked by other people. You probably associate these events with negative thoughts—"Life isn't worth living"; "Nobody cares about me"; "It doesn't matter what I do now anyhow"; "I need something to make me feel better"—that precede the addictive behavior. Psychologists in the addiction field such as Martha Sanchez-Craig use *cognitive-restructuring* techniques to eliminate self-defeating thoughts in these situations and to develop alternative, constructive thoughts—or self-talk—to use instead.[13]

These reminders can be used at two stages in the process of change. First, you can say them to yourself when you are solidifying your value judgments—that is, when you are moving from being "on the fence" or "thinking about" changing your habits to a firm determination to change. Second, you can use them again at moments of behavioral choice—that is, when you are actually out there facing the temptation to smoke, drink, use a drug, shop, or gamble. Simply have ready the reasons you have for not overindulging. These consist of internal pep talks: "I quit using drugs because I was constantly worried about being caught," or "I've invested so much in my change; I can't give it up now in this one moment." Remind yourself of the disappointment you will feel the next day, along with hangovers, guilt, and all the other negative feelings that come from resorting to the addiction.

At the same time, focus on the positive experiences you have had as a result of not indulging: "Since I stopped smoking, I can take a hike without huffing and puffing," or "My house and clothes and hair smell so much better"; "Since I've given up coffee, I never find myself yawning during the day"; "I feel so much better about myself since I stopped going to singles bars." Most important of all, concentrate on your ability to overcome unpleasant, threatening, or challenging situations or feelings: "I've had these feelings before and gotten over them"; "This situation isn't as bad as it looks—it never is"; "The way to overcome this upset is to get on track and try to solve the problem." These statements evoke your self-efficacy: "I know I can deal with life without the assistance of the addiction."

Managing Cravings

As we shall see in the section below on relapse prevention, cravings for the addiction are not really the major reason people relapse. Nonetheless, some addicts do give in when they feel cravings induced by a familiar setting, or mood, or seeing the drug again. Strong physical cravings may be associated with drug addictions, particularly cigarette, cocaine, and heroin addictions. Patrick Biernacki explains how heroin addicts who remain off drugs cope with these sensations:

> Managing cravings and not submitting to them is accomplished by people experiencing them by placing the thoughts in a negative context, then intentionally thinking of things not related to drugs, and then doing non-drug-related things. What people think about, and do, instead of fulfilling cravings for drugs are intimately associated with the [new] social worlds they are participating in and their related identities and perspectives.[14]

In other words, for Biernacki, former addicts combat a craving for the drug by re-emphasizing internally how they have quit the addiction and become a new person, with a better life, who would not choose to return to the old, addicted life-style. Note how the Life Process Program reassures you that this transition is possible. When you are encouraged to believe you *are* the person living your current life, rather than the lifelong addict the disease theory says you are, you can more easily manage your cravings.

Idle Hands: Behaviors/Activities

Behavioral techniques are activities or actions you use to stave off, replace, or limit your addictive behavior.

Exercising and Other Alternatives

A primary example of an activity people substitute for the addiction is physical exercise. Any activity that occupies your time and takes your mind off your preoccupation with the addiction can be used in the same way. However, besides simply filling time, a behavioral alternative to the addiction must be worthwhile and constructive in itself and must not be carried out in an addictive way. After all, chewing gum is one alternative to smoking, smoking is one alternative to eating, gambling is one alternative to drinking, and so on. If the activity with which you replace the addiction is negative in its own right, you may gain very little from the exchange.

Escape

Another behavioral response is immediately to exit a dangerous situation—one where something is being served that you can't resist, or when you feel yourself about to slip. Clearly, being prepared to get out of a place that isn't good for you is a helpful response to have in your repertoire. However, this response has its drawbacks. There are some situations that you cannot exit, or that are not good for you to leave—for example, a job that would be too costly to quit, or complicated relationships with close relatives—and you must be able to cope with these as well. Thus, you must have techniques in place that you can carry within you to fight off relapse.

Limiting Your Behavior

One way to control addiction is to place restrictions on your consumption or involvement in an addictive activity. In the previous chapter, we discussed controlled drinking; the simplest version of behavioral control of alcoholism is to limit your number of drinks. Though abstinence is a viable alternative for many individuals with drinking problems, it is not with eating, shopping, or love relationships.

In place of ruling eating completely off limits, people can count calories or strictly delineate the foods they will eat at a meal. A typical diet, like that of Weight Watchers, involves measuring and setting out all the food to be eaten at a given sitting.

One woman who has vastly overspent has devised a number of ways to control her impulse shopping. In the first place, she uses only one credit card or carries only one or two blank checks. When she goes to the store, she has a shopping list from which she will not deviate. Even with something she has planned to buy, she relies on a mental checklist before making the purchase: "Do I really need it?" "Will I be happy about this purchase tomorrow?" "Is this something I'm sure I will use more than once or twice in the next several months?"[15]

If you have had difficulties as a result of going overboard in love affairs, then you can limit the amount of contact you have with a person with whom you are beginning a relationship. It may be a delicate task to explain to prospective partners that you enjoy their company but have other activities and relationships you care about, or that you simply want to spend time alone. However, making this clear from the outset conveys to the other person that you value a diversified life and have other important relationships. And taking this approach will make you more appealing to the best kinds of people—those with healthy lives themselves.

Situational Controls

Situational techniques are those that involve actively modifying your environment, such as structuring or controlling your surroundings to limit the addiction. For example, in the case above, the woman who had only one credit card or who carried only a couple of blank checks was using environmental (as well as behavioral) controls. Other obvious examples of environmental controls are to avoid high-risk situations. That is, simply stay away from bars, or department-store sales, or gambling casinos, or parties.

Out of Sight, Out of Mind

With food and other addictions, it is possible to structure your "local" environment. That is, keep high-calorie foods out of the house. Alternatively, you can make it hard to see or reach a fattening food, and you can place fruit in a prominent place in the kitchen. One woman who loved peanut butter but who was eating it compulsively kept it in the trunk of her car, so that it wasn't easily available but she could get it when she needed to use it for her kids' sandwiches. Wrapping portions of necessary but potentially dangerous foods into appropriate serving sizes is another way to make sure you don't splurge. One woman wrapped slices of bread individually and kept them in the freezer so she could pull out one slice at a time to toast and eat.

Groups and Getting Help from Others

The people and places you associate with influence your behavior. Joining a group is the most popular—although not necessarily the most successful—way of combating addiction. For example, the Anonymous groups (Alcoholics, Gamblers, Overeaters, etc.) offer people the chance to spend time with other people doing something other than drinking, gambling, eating, or whatever. The Life Process Program emphasizes seeking out people and groups that will offer you support in eliminating your addiction, but without keeping the addiction at the center of your life. In other words, if you join Alcoholics or Gamblers or Overeaters Anonymous, your life continues to revolve around addiction. Alternatively, you can find groups of people who don't drink or take drugs or smoke but, rather, are engaged in more constructive pursuits. (Joining a group as a way of quitting an addiction, and groups as a part of your world, are dealt with in chapter 16.)

Controlling Your World

Behavioral techniques alert people to the effects of cues and situations, and rewards and punishments, on their behavior. But some people take this message one step further. That is, instead of eliminating a particular cue—like keeping candy out of sight in the house—or rewarding themselves with a movie when they eat right during the day, they start to look at their whole world as a behavioral environment. Behavioral techniques, thus writ large, become situational ones. You can design the path of least resistance, and put rewards in place, for doing the "right" thing. You can get your whole family involved. This is one way to combat the "disease" of the dysfunctional family, or the family that incites and rewards self-defeating or hurtful behaviors of all kinds.

EXAMPLE

Psychologist Alan Marlatt described a woman who attended an eating clinic called Sea Pines (at Hilton Head beach). The woman was deeply impressed by a behavioral lecture given by the director of the clinic, Peter Miller: "it was like a light bulb flashing on inside my head." Most participants in such clinics lose weight *during* their stays, but put it back on when they return home. This woman instead saw how she could use behavioral principles employed at the clinic to structure her family's life, and not just with eating. For example, she made it easier for her family to eat well by having the right foods around; she planned out her week in advance to recognize when she would be in danger of overeating (such as at business lunches) and came instead prepared with her own lunches; she let the kids have rewards (like watching special TV programs) after their schoolwork was done. The secret was, she found, "to alter the [general] principles I learned to fit the situation at hand."[16]

Managing Relapse

Mark Twain said, "Quitting smoking is easy; I've done it hundreds of times!" For about 80 percent of smokers and those with other addictions, the first attempt to quit is not the last. Rather, quitting is a "two steps forward, one step back" process. Since relapse is a common experience on the road to a stable nonaddict identity, it is important to understand and deal with relapse sensibly and realistically. This is where the Life Process Program diverges most dramatically from disease treatment. Instead of preaching that relapse is a toboggan ride to doom, it shows how you can work around episodes of relapse and even reinterpret them as beneficial experiences that strengthen your commitment to quit.

What causes relapse? The leading experts in relapse prevention are psychologists Alan Marlatt and Judith Gordon (the former is director of the Addictive Behaviors Research Laboratory at the University of Washington). According to their interviews with ex-addicts, relapse is not generally triggered by physical cravings, even in the case of substance addictions such as to drugs, alcohol, and cigarettes. Addicts of all types relapse in response to stress and to feelings of anxiety, fear, anger, frustration, or depression, when they seek the solace or comfort of the addiction. Social pressures and interpersonal conflicts are other major causes of relapse.[17]

Marlatt and Gordon have pioneered a relapse-prevention strategy consisting of the following steps (you will see that these involve cognitive, behavioral, and situational techniques):

1. *Stop, look, and listen.* You must stop the rush of events or behavior and pay attention to your situation. If possible, retreat to a quiet place to contemplate what you are doing.

2. *Keep calm.* It doesn't pay to become guilty or to chastise yourself, since these reactions only prompt more addictive behavior. Nor will panic help you get back on track.

3. *Renew your commitment.* Instead of giving up on your plan to stay nonaddicted, now is the time to reassert your desire and your commitment to be free of the addiction. Remind yourself of your success up to this point.

4. *Make an immediate plan.* You had a plan for licking your addiction from which you temporarily departed. Start right now to map out how you will proceed from here on with your plan.

5. *Ask or look for help.* Look for support from whomever you count on. Now is the time to turn to friends and helpers. In doing so, you will let them know that you are serious and that you don't want to let them down.

6. *Review the relapse situation.* After your slip, instead of punishing yourself, analyze the elements in the situation that created your slip. There is much to learn in this, and to avoid in the future.[18]

If these techniques don't prevent you from relapsing altogether, that does not mean you must give up on the techniques, and it certainly does not mean you are addicted for life. Attitudes like "I've failed once, so I'm bound to fail again" or "This only shows that I really am addicted, so why fight it?" are self-fulfilling prophecies; they bring about the very outcome they predict. If you interpret one slip as meaning that you have totally lost control, then you will likely lose control. If you believe that one shopping spree or one fattening snack or one use of a drug invalidates the weeks or months you spent not doing these things, then you lose the sense of self-efficacy you demonstrated by your period of moderation or abstinence.

If, on the other hand, you understand that addiction and recovery are not all-or-none, black-or-white things, then you can interpret a relapse as just one moment in a seesaw process. Occasionally, even after the balance of forces in your life has shifted slightly in favor of recovery, it shifts *back* temporarily to favoring addiction. As more weight is piled on the recovery side, however, the balance becomes stable, and relapse is a very unlikely event. For example, there *are* occasional cases when people become smokers again after years of abstinence. But this is not a simple case of relapse. It is a statement that the person no longer has the desire to live a smoke-free life.

Nonetheless, for some time the key to long-term progress may lie in how you handle relapses. Marlatt's fundamental principle is to regard a lapse as a temporary detour on your journey to freedom. Moreover, it is an *opportunity* for learning. In order to re-establish control, your focus should be on what you might have done differently rather than what you did wrong. In other words, you should seek to avoid repeating your mistakes. For example, someone who took a drug when he visited an old girlfriend may realize that he is especially susceptible and insecure at such a moment. Either he will need to avoid these meetings, or he should go to them only when he is confident he has a plan for handling them without drugs.

Instead of dwelling on the negative implications of a slip, you can gain confidence from having abstained before the slip and from having regained mastery afterward. Having tried to quit in the first place is a harbinger of future success, and you should view a series of such attempts as a series of successful experiences. Moreover, each relapse can help you make your next attempt more successful. DiClemente and Prochaska tell those who relapse to think of themselves as "quitters in the making." Marlatt and others often rely on images and analogies in treatment, likening quitting an addiction to a long journey.

We like to visualize the relapse process as a train ride, a ride during which the passenger can get off at any stop.

CASE

A former alcoholic (he had been drinking constantly and was near suicide) had been almost totally abstinent for close to two years. Very occasionally, he would have a glass of wine with his family, which seemingly was no problem for him. However, he had had two or three troubling and explosive relapses. During the first relapse, he had driven drunk and lost his license for six months, multiplying his difficulties and those of his family. During less severe relapses, he had gone drinking with friends, once calling his wife to pick him up, a second time staying out all night without calling home (he slept in a friend's truck).

The man's relapses invariably involved going to a local bar where a group of heavy-drinking friends hung out and where he drank beer all evening. His first, more severe relapse had occurred when he had been cheated by a customer and he drove himself to the bar. The second and third resulted when he met a friend on the street who invited him to the bar.

This man's relapses, and alternatives, could be represented by merging, parallel train routes with the stops designated on the opposite page.

In treatment, the man considered how at each stop he had and has a chance to switch trains. For example, in lieu of getting enraged, he practiced superior coping techniques. Because he liked several of his old drinking buddies, he wanted to be able to talk to them (and, in any case, he didn't want to have to walk the neighborhood he and they frequented with his head down). Therefore, he developed the options of inviting the friend for a cup of coffee or just shooting the breeze in the street.

Treatment for this man had focused primarily on enhancing his communication and help-seeking skills. But he had already shown strong self-sufficiency in devising alternatives to abandoning his sobriety. He had succeeded sometimes in going to the bar and avoiding drinking, which required his telling the bartender when he arrived that he would drink only ginger ale. He had also shown he could call his wife and/or avoid driving after getting drunk. Most important of all, even after his worst relapse episode, he hadn't given up the ghost and resumed his alcoholic drinking. In fact, therapy may have benefited him most simply by laying out his options and letting him know he could choose—and already had chosen—alternatives to abusive drinking and self-defeating drunken behavior.

EXERCISE

Map out a "train route" you have traveled down in your addiction, and propose a set of alternatives for each stop along the way.

Every former and current addict has been down one of these tracks. What is most important to realize is that, contrary to what the disease-oriented travel guide tells us, we all know that this trip is far from inevitable, no matter how far down the track we have already gone.

Limiting Relapse: Which Stop to Get Off At?

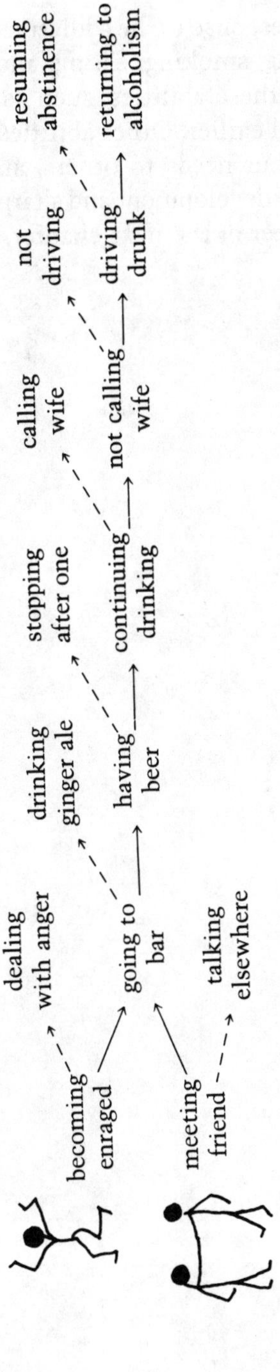

Looking Ahead

Controlling your response to the addictive object or activity—like gambling, sex, drinking, smoking, eating, and shopping—requires certain abilities. Some of these abilities, such as those involved in planning, have been outlined earlier. Other abilities, such as coping with stress, communicating your needs to others, and dealing with your family and job, require the development and sharpening of certain skills. These skills are the subject of the next chapter.

CHAPTER 15

▼▼▼▼▼▼▼

LIFE
SKILLS
•
IF YOU
DON'T
HAVE THEM,
GET THEM¹

I N CHAPTER 14, we saw how the Life Process Program deals directly with overcoming the addictive behavior. But this is a smaller focus within the larger picture. Quitting addictions requires that you deal with *life* more effectively, with less reliance on artificial but self-defeating props—like Valium, cigarettes, shopping, and smothering love relationships. There is no shortcut to more effective coping. To take effective control of your life, you need to be able to:

▶ identify negative feelings so you can alleviate or cope with them, and so that you can deal directly with the problems that cause them;

▶ reflect on a problem, so that you don't react instinctively or negatively, but think through a constructive, purposeful response;

▶ "cool out," to relieve tensions and relax without creating more problems for yourself;

▶ deal effectively with other people, so that you can respond appropriately to the needs of others and have your own needs met;

▶ earn a living, hold a job, accomplish work and other life goals;

▶ feel at ease with yourself and your ability to handle your world.

The table below provides a list of specific life skills. Many of these skill areas are outlined in a book by Peter Monti and his colleagues, *Treating Alcohol Dependence*, a manual for alcoholism counselors.

Necessary Life Skills

- Problem-solving
- Communication
- Relaxation
- Being alone
- Intimate relationships
- Job skills
- Refusal skills
- Breaking the flow
- Self-efficacy

This chapter will not by itself remedy any deficiencies you have in these areas; that will depend on the effort you put into improving your skills. To facilitate that effort, this chapter *will:*

▸ identify and illustrate relevant skills;

▸ describe the kinds of exercises and experiences that will enhance your coping skills;

▸ describe programs and resources to which you can turn for skill enhancement and learning.

Problem-solving Skills

Addicts—and the addict in all of us—dream of a nirvana where problems and cares are eliminated. But life is filled with changing circumstances and difficulties with which we must cope. Most people face daily responsibilities like dealing with children, balancing job and family obligations, and commuting to work. In addition, every human being at some point faces traumas like the death of a parent, losing a job, divorce, or having a best friend move far away. Addicts frequently cite such difficulties as the reason they are distressed and became addicted. But in many cases these explanations don't hold water, because most people in situations that are as bad or worse—including returning from a Vietnam War zone, growing up in an abusive or addicted family, having a chronic illness—don't become addicts. Rather, the lesson to learn is what abilities enable most people to avoid resorting to such drastic remedies.

Time-out: Halting the Cascade to Addiction

Addictive behaviors are automatic responses, ones you produce without thought in certain situations. Their immediacy and uncontrolled nature are the mark of addiction. You need techniques to stop this flow of thoughts and events that end up with a bout of something that you don't want to do. You can begin to cope only when you give yourself the space to think, plan, and react sensibly. Developing an array of functional coping techniques, on which you can confidently rely at trying moments, is the key to avoiding addiction.

Certain events or situations lead you to think, and then to act, in self-defeating ways:[2]

event/situation/stimulus ⟶ thought pattern ⟶ feelings/actions

You have learned to identify high-risk situations, feelings, and thought patterns. You must be able to go from the step of recognizing a compulsive or destructive thought pattern ("I'm weak," "I can't handle this," "I've already taken one bite/drink/smoke, I might as well give in totally," "I'm depressed," "I'm tense") to short-circuiting it. Reprogramming yourself to change such a pattern involves the following steps:

1. *Recognize the pattern.* Identify the high-risk situation and the high-risk thought pattern you are embarked on. ("I'm feeling depressed about my weight; I'm lonely. If I have something to eat, I'll feel better. But then I'll be gaining more weight, and I'll never get my life where I want it to be.")

2. *Replace negative thoughts with positive ones.* Use self-enhancing thoughts, the opposite of the ones you have been thinking. ("I feel so good every time I exercise and don't eat too much. And I did that nearly every day last week. I see I can behave this way whenever I want to.")

3. *Don't panic.* This is not the worst situation you have faced. Practice relaxation techniques, reframing your thinking. ("I'm not really hungry. This is an emotional reaction, not genuine hunger. I am going to read that book I got from the library now.") *Pause for a count of ten before you take any action.* If you still aren't prepared to make sensible decisions, count to ten once again. If you are feeling uninhibited, shout "STOP" as loudly as you can.

4. *Return to (2) and rehearse your positive thoughts.* When you are at a point where you feel you are capable of doing your best thinking, create a plan to carry on. ("I forgot about food when I got absorbed in my book. Then I took a walk. Tomorrow night will be good: I'm going to the movies with a friend. I must tell her that I'm trying to lose weight when she calls, and that we should walk to the movies and not go for ice cream afterward.")

How to Stop Beating Up on Yourself

Spending a lot of time critiquing your behavior has the unfortunate side consequence of making you realize just how many ways you can go wrong. And we all have gone wrong many times. Replaying exactly how wrong you have gone is called "beating yourself up," and it is useless. ("I should never have eaten *two* pieces of that cake. I didn't even enjoy it. I have no self-control.")

You need to defuse these feelings and then redirect your desire for change into formulating a plan of action. You can make plans only when you are feeling efficacious and good about yourself. (The next evening, facing the same events that led to overeating, make plans at the *beginning* of the evening. "I always get hungry at around ten o'clock. I need to buy some cottage cheese and fruit for a snack to be ready. I have my book ready, and I also have to keep in mind how *good* I feel when I go out for a walk.")

All human beings beat themselves up to some extent. It is a universal experience. But decreasing or short-circuiting the experience is both possible and necessary. Of course, you want to do better in various areas of your life. You will improve primarily by executing *proactive,* or previously designed, plans. Make yourself this deal: You will avoid thinking about the incident for a whole day. Promise that the *next* day you will think out how you want to behave differently the next time, and try the new behavior sequence out the very next time the situation arises.

Problem-solving Strategies

The alternative to reacting to every upset as a challenge to your emotional stability, and then seeking solace in your addiction, is to develop a calm, realistic approach to dealing with problems.[3] The following table presents a flow diagram for problem-solving. It specifies that you:

- recognize when you are troubled or feeling bad;
- identify the source of your bad feelings or problem;
- review your possible strategies for addressing the problem and select the best one;
- check to see how well the strategy is working, including asking others how you are doing;
- explore alternative solutions to see if you can handle the problem even better.

Underlying this problem-solving approach is a faith on your part that you can solve your problems. What you may have to overcome is a tendency to throw your hands in the air and say, "It doesn't matter what I do; I can't ever succeed." More than any specific techniques, belief in the process and persistence are at the heart of successful problem-solving.

Problem-Solving Techniques

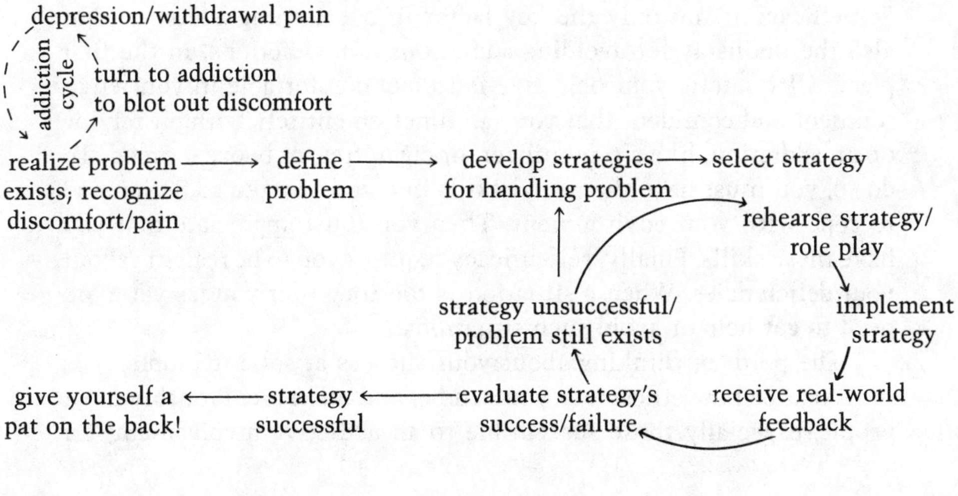

Of course, everyone uses problem-solving skills all the time without realizing it. You should realize how you go about solving the many daily problems you face in life, many of which you don't consider problems because you deal with them so matter-of-factly.

EXERCISE

Think about how you drive to a place where you have never been before. You might first look at a large map, to find out the general vicinity of your destination. You then examine the large arteries that approach this location. Then you work out the local roads that will take you to these highways, and from these highways to your destination. You might also call someone who knows the route for help with directions.

Consider a problem you want to solve or goal you want to achieve. Just as you map out a driving route, think of a general strategy for attacking this problem or goal. Then break it down into small, manageable steps. You may also ask others who have had a similar problem or who are simply good problem-solvers for advice.

Self-Efficacy

The primary goal of the Life Process Program is to enhance your faith that you can manage your life. Self-efficacy is the belief that you can deal with the situations you face and attain the goals you seek.[4] Self-efficacy is not only the key factor in overcoming addiction, but also the mainstay for avoiding addictions, all addictions, in the first place. Ultimately, your objective is to feel comfortable in your environment and confident that you can function entirely without relying on an addiction, like a tranquilizer, or cigarettes, or booze, or food. To do so, you must have the actual skills in place to avoid addiction and to cope with your environment. Then you must appreciate that you have these skills. Finally, self-efficacy requires you to be realistic about your deficiencies. When a situation is too tough for you (as yet), you need to get help or avoid such situations.

The point of thinking about your success at solving problems is to recognize how efficacious you can be, and often are. Probably most people, especially those susceptible to an addictive involvement, err in the direction of underestimating how competent they are. When you are aware that you have faced a difficult situation or solved a problem, be sure to congratulate yourself appropriately for a job well done! Acknowledging your success will improve your accuracy in figuring out what you can and can't accomplish, so that you neither under- nor overestimate your competence. The accumulation of this kind of success should give you a general feeling of confidence in facing the world.

On the other hand, the greatest danger from prolonged addiction is demoralization, or the loss of confidence that you can ever change. Often, having some small success—any success—at self-regulation can inspire a sense of self-efficacy and further change. One man, for example, sprained his ankle. After having it treated, he was given a course of therapy for regaining the original strength in his foot. He followed the plan assiduously. When his therapy was done, he asked himself how come he could never apply the same persistence to getting the rest of his body in shape, and he promptly began an exercise program. Or consider the alcoholic who used the following logic to decide he could quit drinking: "It's just the whole idea that, damn, if I can lick cigarettes I know I can lick liquor."[5]

Relax

The greatest danger of relapse comes when you experience some unpleasant emotional state, like stress and resulting feelings of anxiety or depression.[6] Being able to dispel negative emotional states ("dysphoria") is thus very important for avoiding your addiction.

Why Are You Tense, Angry, or Depressed?

Obviously, it pays to minimize anxiety and depression in the first place, to alleviate the emotional pressures that cause addiction. Much of this book's focus on accomplishment and coping in life is applicable to reducing these negative emotional states. If you are selecting good relationships and situations and succeeding better at work and love, your emotional state will improve and you will be less susceptible to addiction.

Sometimes very immediate circumstances—such as a period when work is demanding or unsatisfying—will make you depressed or anxious. Sometimes simply working hard and staying up late will upset your mood in ways that are hard to recognize. When you feel bad or tired, it pays to accept that there is a reason you feel this way. Such acceptance first enables you to try to figure out what's bothering you. It then gives you "permission" to feel bad. You need to understand that people do feel bad and that you're not terribly disadvantaged or different from others because you have some bad periods.

Drugs—including tranquilizers, sleeping pills, diet pills, cigarettes, and coffee—can make you depressed and anxious. People who quit drinking or taking drugs may start drinking more coffee or smoking more or using tranquilizers or sleeping pills. Although doing so may compensate in some ways for the forbidden substance, it also inevitably makes you tense or depressed. Selecting substitutes for a discontinued addiction requires planning and common sense.

Relaxation Responses

People often use cigarettes, alcohol, food, drugs, and so on to relax—even though, after a point, these addictions create increasing levels of tension. Relaxing without artificial aids is a key to nonaddictive living. You need to call on relaxation techniques as you encounter those pivotal times when you turn to your addiction.

There are many methods of relaxing yourself.[7] Some of these methods are well known, like transcendental meditation. TM is trademarked and taught in formal courses. At the opposite extreme, you might take a nap or a walk for relaxation. The methods you use to deal with an addiction can include many ways of releasing tension, such as exercise, yoga, reading, and, yes, pleasurable activities like having sex or a glass of wine. You may also rely on specific relaxation techniques for times when your tension or bad mood seems likely to overcome you and drive you to one or another extreme of unhealthiness.

One such method is PMR (Progressive Muscle Relaxation). This involves tensing and then relaxing individual areas of your body. PMR entails the following steps:

1. Select a quiet place without distractions.
2. To a count of ten, tense each muscle group in turn (hands, arms, shoulders, neck, face, chest, abdomen, buttocks, thighs, calves, feet), then relax that muscle group for ten seconds.
3. Concentrate on the muscles you are relaxing, and nothing else.
4. Repeat the series of muscle tensing and relaxing.

You will get better at doing these exercises the more you practice them. Select progressively more tense situations in which to practice the technique. Start while lying on your couch at home, then select a quiet moment sitting at your desk (perhaps at lunch, if you don't want to interrupt your work). Then begin to incorporate your "relaxation response" during activities—doing housework or errands, or while you are exercising. After a time, you will be able to relax yourself in this way during the most active, and tense, moments in your life, without those around you even being aware.

The quickest relaxation technique is deep breathing. Practice deep-breathing techniques so that you can implement them rapidly at tense moments. Lean back, close your eyes, picture a pleasant scene (like a lake or a meadow) in as much detail as possible, and take as much air comfortably into your lungs as you can. Release it slowly. Repeat, inhaling and exhaling slowly, for five minutes at a time.

The chart on the following page describes a five-phase program for gradually developing relaxation techniques to use in real-life settings, from a quiet, controlled environment to the most stressful, addiction-provoking situations. As an intermediate stage that prepares you for actually confronting tense events, you can imagine the events in detail while relaxing. Start with fifteen seconds of stressful image, then increase the time, accompanying each period of stress with your relaxation exercise. Finally, put yourself in a real-life situation that is mildly stressful and call on yourself to relax. Progress to more and more challenging situations as you succeed in relaxing until you can handle even the scenes and situations that used to drive you to your addiction.

The aim of these exercises is to develop techniques that enable you to relax at will. In the area of relaxation, like everything else, you can buy into any level of involvement. Any technique or image you

Relaxation Techniques

	Phase 1	*Phase 2*	*Phase 3*	*Phase 4*	*Phase 5*
techniques	Relaxation techniques: deep breathing, Progressive Muscle Relaxation, detailed positive images	Relaxation techniques: relaxed state	Relaxation techniques: relaxed state	Detailed negative images of addictive, stressful moment/relaxation techniques: relaxed state	Relaxation techniques: relaxed state
setting	controlled environment/reclining	controlled environment/nonreclining	real-life environment/activity	controlled, quiet environment	progressive trials in real-life, stressful, addictive settings

can rely on to relax you that isn't physically harmful is something you can use. And these techniques and images are just as good as the most expensive tapes of waves breaking and TM courses.

Dealing with People

Second to dysphoria as a cause of addictive relapse are people problems. This includes both pressures from others to act in a certain way, and tensions like anger or loneliness brought about by unsatisfactory interpersonal dealings.[8] Drinking, smoking, eating, drug use, and so forth are ways people deal with their feelings toward others. For example, some respond to rejection by drinking, or use alcohol to smooth social interactions or to allow them to blurt out resentments they can't express when they are sober.

The best way to practice your social skills is to interact with people. Social skills can be taught through group exercises in communication, feedback, assertiveness, and so on. Trained leaders model or describe the preferred techniques, and group members discuss them. Participants then practice them in role-playing exercises. Many programs teach such skills, including courses in assertiveness training and group leadership skills. Alternatively, life is a constant laboratory for experiencing and practicing your interactions with others.

Managing Anger

Anger and interpersonal conflict are the primary interpersonal prods to addiction. The worst relapse suffered by the alcoholic in the last chapter was as a result of anger at a client. Beyond addictive relapse, if you are unable to recognize or manage anger, you can poison your relationships and isolate yourself. There are two directions in which you can err in managing anger: reacting passively and bottling up your feelings, or lashing out aggressively. Either of these responses damages your ability to control your feelings or to deal with the people or situations that triggered your response, thus making it difficult to resolve the current problem and setting the stage for future trouble. You need to develop a constructive, assertive style of managing your anger.[9] The diagram on the following page portrays aggressive, assertive (preferred), and passive reactions to anger.

First, recognize your personal signs of anger:

Managing Anger

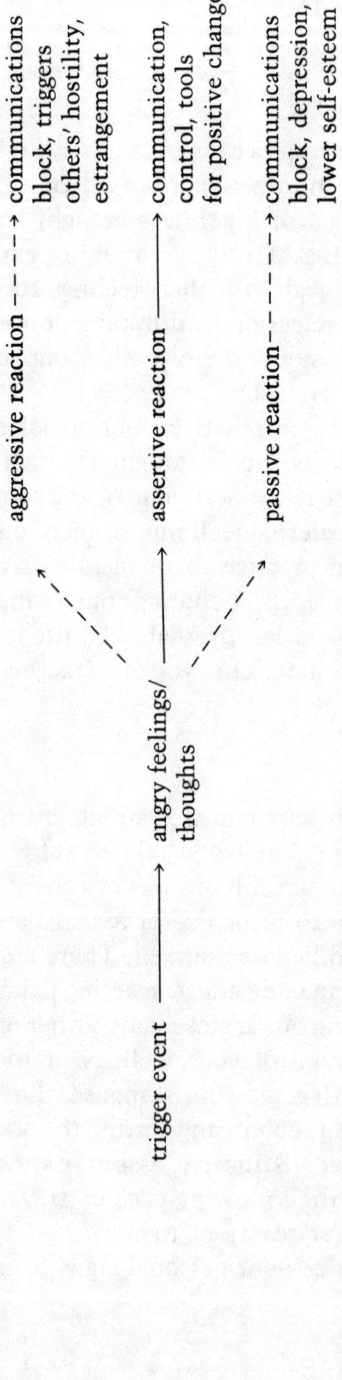

- feelings of:
  tension
  frustration
  hurt
  helplessness

- physical tension such as:
  headaches
  sweating
  muscle spasms
  rapid heartbeat/difficulty breathing

Identify situations or people that trigger angry feelings and thoughts:

- your father hollering at your mother;
- a co-worker who tries to score points off you in meetings that include your boss;
- your children not doing their homework;
- your wife's messy closet.

Develop skills that help you slow down your angry reaction, calm yourself, and take control of the situation:

- Count to ten before acting or saying anything.
- Employ relaxation techniques.
- Tell yourself to "slow down," "chill out," or some reminder that pulls you up short.
- Leave the room while you compose yourself.

Think about what you can do in this situation to resolve the problem and become less upset:

- Clearly tell the person involved that you are unhappy and the reasons you feel this way.
- Determine whether the person really is saying what you think you hear—for example, by repeating to him what you are hearing him say.
- Determine whether he has understood what you said.

- Try to reach an agreement with the other person that one or the other or both of you will change your behavior.
- Lower your expectations for the interaction.
- Relax.
- Leave the situation with dignity and resolve it later if possible. Meanwhile, don't beat yourself up or dwell on negative thoughts about the person with whom you fought.

Interpersonal conflict is tough; if you resolve the situation, you deserve a pat on the back. If you are unable to resolve it satisfactorily, try to tolerate human frailty and relax. Remember that conflict is part of life and problem interactions will occur, but that you can endure and overcome them. As you practice anger management, however, your skills will improve to the point where you can manage situations you might never have dealt with successfully in the past.

Communications Skills

If you cannot communicate your needs in a way that makes it likely they can be fulfilled, you may turn instead to addictions for sustenance. Isolation and continual discontent in interpersonal relationships are strong precursors to addiction and to relapse.

A sample of necessary communications skills includes:

- listening;
- receiving feedback/criticism;
- giving feedback/criticism;
- helping;
- expressing personal needs.

In addition, some special areas of interpersonal dealings and communications worth noting are:

- expressing yourself in a group;
- dealing with strangers;
- resisting social pressure.

Listening and helping. You often want to get your opinion across to others, to change how they think, or feel, or treat you. *Empathic* communication techniques are those which allow you to understand and respect the person with whom you want to communicate.[10] To influence or help people, keep in mind the following steps:

1. *Put yourself in the other person's shoes.* Try to grasp his or her perspective. More important, *accept and sympathize* with this perspective. Although trying to score points against others may be effective in debating, it doesn't work in maintaining relationships. The operative word is "nonjudgmental." Refrain from expressing your value judgments and, if possible, avoid forming such judgments.

2. *Ask questions.* Surprisingly, questioning people respectfully is the most effective change technique. Ask them to explain their problems to you, and to tell you how they have attempted to remedy them. Respect the efforts they have already undertaken.

People rarely respond when you simply direct them to do something for themselves. Unasked-for advice is the easiest thing in the world to reject. If, instead, you consider the problem *with* the person, you help to clarify the nature of the problem and to open up new options for coping with it.

3. *Listen.* Listening is a skill. It requires empathy, effort, and practice. You can't listen when you are trying primarily to make your own points. The best exercise for sharpening your listening skills is to repeat the other person's point to see if the person agrees that you have understood it. If not, try again.

Any working arrangement should not be concluded until the involved parties have reiterated their understanding of what took place and of the decisions that were made. This first makes clear to everyone that they have all understood one another. It also clarifies the actions everyone is to take once the meeting or interaction is over.

EXERCISE

The next time someone describes a problem, make every effort to be helpful. Concentrate your full attention, using the techniques described above. *Don't give advice, but only ask questions. Listen.* If the person asks for your opinion, state your views succinctly.

After a time, ask the person if the conversation has been helpful up to that point. If the person says no, ask why you haven't been helpful and how you could be more so. If the person says yes, ask what has been most helpful. Keep in mind that some people complain but aren't really seeking help. Even so, you should be able to help them sharpen their focus and reframe a problem through a careful interaction.

Expressing your needs, criticizing another person. There isn't a big difference between helping people and offering them criticism, and many of the same ideas apply.[11] However, you usually criticize others not because you disinterestedly want them to improve, but because they are bothering you. You need them to change to make your life better. Criticizing others is a special challenge to your self-restraint and ability to couch things in a positive way. Just as when you are trying to help someone, you need to avoid bombarding the person with a communication he or she will instantaneously reject. Hollering may make you feel good, but in most cases it will only lead to more frustration and more reason to holler. Screaming may occasionally be useful for letting people know they are way out of bounds—for example, if they are belittling or degrading you. For anything more complicated, however, you need more finesse.

A typical situation of this kind occurs when someone you deal with regularly is doing something that annoys you or makes you unhappy, so that you resent the person and periodically strike out in retaliation. For example, alcoholics often find they cannot express their resentments against their wives unless they are drunk. Instead of resorting to an addiction, you want to change this interaction, especially the way the other person is treating you. Consider the following techniques:

1. *Be clear about the source of your discontent.* Make sure that this person is really making you unhappy. Ask yourself whether you are merely taking advantage of an easy target—perhaps someone who is lower on the totem pole than yourself.

2. *Start on a positive note.* Begin the interaction by finding some point of agreement or something you admire or think the person is doing right. This will put both of you in a better frame of mind for the discussion.

3. *Make factual comments.* Express yourself directly but moderately. Don't berate or belittle the person. Instead, identify specifically what you think the person is doing wrong or what you don't like.

4. *Make clear when you are expressing your personal feelings.* Say that you don't like something because it bothers you, not because it is wrong or because the other person is bad or stupid.

5. Unless the person is attacking you, *offer suggestions rather than direct challenges.* Ask if there is another way the person could do something—"Have you considered . . . ?"—or describe options—"Someone I knew once tried this, and it really worked well."

6. *Ask if the person understands what you are upset about.* Before the discussion is over, make sure you both agree on how the two of you will act differently in the future.

And, remember, maintain a calm, firm voice throughout.

Special Situations

(1) *Expressing yourself in a group.* In A.A., people alternate between passive listening and rote testimonies. The opposite is active, involved, creative participation. Many people find such participation, particularly when it involves going against the group, to be very anxiety-producing.

Consider a situation in which you have a strong point of view, but others in the group are more verbal, and you are afraid they will reject your comments. In fact, when you do speak briefly, your comment gets little reaction or even a negative one. You begin to think that perhaps your point isn't that valuable. Nearly everyone finds it unnerving to present new ideas to a group, especially when it means breaking the flow of the group interaction. But some people find it particularly difficult to participate in group conversations. By being aware of group dynamics, however, you can get a handle on the group situation and your role in it:

▸ Those who talk the most do not necessarily have the best contributions to make. Conversely, the fact that you haven't said much, or the group hasn't listened to you when you did talk, does not mean your contributions aren't valuable. Your ideas may be valuable, but you may not have conveyed them so that others in the group have grasped them.

▸ Talk to group members individually outside the group. This will allow you to check whether your ideas are as good as you think and to gather support before you try to speak up at a meeting. You might tell someone who thinks your idea is good that you had a hard time bringing it up at the last meeting, and ask for assistance. You may be surprised to learn that others in the group are struggling with similar problems.

(2) *Dealing with strangers and rejection.* You come to a party where you know no one, and no one is introduced to you. How will you proceed to make contacts and enjoy yourself, rather than become a wallflower and consume party intoxicants?

A party is an opportunity to find out about other people's lives, and also to create individual relationships. Think of it not as a group interaction, but a series of one-on-one encounters. First you need to relax; approach the party as an entertainment made up for your enjoyment. Rather than looking for Prince or Princess Charming, think of it as a play that you may or may not like.

Sizing up strangers and demonstrating that they will enjoy talking to you can be daunting, but take the chance to approach a likely-looking person and strike up a conversation. Some people may reject you initially or soon after you approach. You must understand that this has little to do with who you are and much to do with the situation or their own personalities. Instead of allowing your self-esteem to dip, praise yourself for the effort you made. After all, if everyone rejected all strangers, no one would ever meet anybody new! You can only feel sorry for those who aren't able to put themselves out to meet you. Of course, you will still feel bad momentarily if you are ignored or rejected, because that's a normal human response. But don't let such feelings, temporary as they often are, propel you to the false comfort of the addiction.

(3) *Resisting social pressure.* People often turn—or return—to an addiction because of social pressure. For example, someone offers you a drink, or drug, or cigarette, or dessert. Or a person asks you to come to the racetrack or to a singles' bar or to a group or setting where you

have always had bad experiences in the past. You need to know how to say no effectively.

- *Be prepared.* Recognize that people will importune you and resolve that you will refuse.
- *Say no decisively.* Don't invite reinvitations because you sound uncertain or willing to be persuaded.
- *Look the person in the eye when you refuse.* Don't feel self-conscious, as though you are somehow failing the person. It will help you to reject the offer if you realize that the person isn't thinking of your best interests in the first place.
- *Don't make excuses.* Excuses can be argued with, and you have already said no. You can, however, suggest an alternative activity to this person to show that you like him or her and do want to spend time together under the right circumstances.
- *Make clear that you won't tolerate continued importunings,* and tell the person to stop asking you. Then change the subject. If the person can't deal with this, you must get away from him or her.

Finding Love

Much of addiction—and of life—revolves around the effort to satisfy unmet needs for intimacy and love. In books, therapy, and groups, people try to resolve the riddles of love. It is safe to say that, more often than not, they do not find what they are looking for, totally or even in part. The point of this chapter is that the same skills that will help you deal with other areas of life offer the best chances for satisfaction in love. These include:

- being able to deal comfortably with other people;
- expressing your needs in a positive way, thereby enhancing the likelihood that others will respond to your requests;
- finding groups of people to associate with who engage in wholesome and constructive activities;
- dealing with life problems and achieving life goals.

These aren't the only answers. They are the ones you can most readily and directly work on, however. The best practice for love relationships comes from forming relationships of all kinds. The best way to be open to love is to have warm and supportive contacts with people, so that you aren't desperate in your search for intimacy. If there is one exercise you can engage in to find people whom you will enjoy being with and who offer the potential for love, it is to get out in the world—for example, by finding groups of people who are engaged in activities you can genuinely respect and enjoy.

The Family Situation

A lot of addiction is associated with family behavior—with frustration and tension at home, with familiar interaction patterns that set off unwanted behaviors, with useless, repetitive mutual criticisms. There are few homes where there is not some room for improvement in any or all of these areas. *A fundamental assumption of the family approach is that everyone is involved in the problem;* it is not a "disease" that one person has. There is more than enough blame to go around, but blame is beside the point; corrective action as a family or unit is called for.

Before returning to family-therapy issues, however, let us review your obligations to yourself, to the world, to the members of your family, and to an addicted spouse or child:

- Fundamentally, you can't help another person by violating your own safety and happiness, the safety of other family members, and your own moral standards.

- You need to protect yourself. A relationship that is destroying you *must* be changed or terminated.

- You cannot sustain a relationship that requires you to lie to others, to treat people badly, or to violate other moral precepts. You'll always lose out because your other relationships will suffer and because you will reaffirm your identity as a victim.

- You are obligated to protect helpless family members, especially children. Think, as a negative role model, of a woman like Hedda Nussbaum, who placated her lover, Joel Steinberg, to the point of allowing him to kill their adopted daughter.

Behaving Yourself

Whether you are in therapy on your own or with other family members because of difficulties with a spouse or child (including their addictions), you are looking to map out a course of action for yourself. Family therapy provides an explanation of how family members set one another off or support one another's improper behavior. But this is not an excuse for you to continue the addictive behavior, even in the absence of change by others. Your greatest control is over yourself. And since you are a part of the whole system, your positive changes will improve the whole family.

EXAMPLE

A family is mired in constant mutual criticism and recrimination. When one member tries to act positively, he or she is quickly brought up short by criticism from another family member. Nonetheless, whenever one family member acts politely and helpfully for as long as a day, the whole atmosphere in the family improves preceptibly. At the same time, it *is* difficult to sustain the positive behavior when others in the family don't commit themselves to change.

What Do You Get from the Addiction?

If your behavior sustains an addiction in another person, *you* get rewards from the addiction as well. Your spouse's addiction makes you feel needed. For example, it gives you a sense of power or of being useful. Your spouse's addiction may *prove* to you how virtuous you are. An addiction can provide you, as the nonaddicted spouse, with specific benefits. You may feel your partner is open or warm, or sexually available, only when he or she is intoxicated. Or else your partner's weakness or problems may make you feel more secure—their obesity, for example, means they cannot have other lovers.

EXERCISE

Although you resent your spouse's addiction, think of what benefits you have gotten from it, at least in the past. Have you ever welcomed your spouse's addicted behavior, even pressured him or her to eat or drink more, because you anticipated some benefit? Examine any desires you have to see your spouse act excessively or out of control.

Because both people in the relationship depend on artificial but essential rewards, *both* are addicted. In the epitome of this kind of relationship, a violent couple, the dominant individual *and* the submissive one, are addicted to the rewards of the abusive relationship.

Planning Together

A family planning effort should involve everyone affected by a decision, but particularly the married couple.[12] What all parties agree must change should be specified beforehand (e.g., no violence, minimizing shouting, insisting on courtesy), so that everyone knows what to shoot for. Much of the work involved in such family efforts is in translating mutual complaints into negotiated tradeoffs.

EXERCISE

List the two or three things your family can change that will make your household a more pleasant place. Under each item, list the two or three things each of you can do to foster this change.

Let's Make a Deal (Behavioral Contracting)

When you and your partner (not only mates or spouses, but parent and child) point out specific behaviors that each doesn't like, draw a link between the two irritants. For example, a woman goes on an eating binge whenever her husband criticizes her. The deal is that he refrains from criticism while she refrains from indulging in ice cream and cake. Really, the aim is to understand the linkage between your behavior and your partner's so that both parties will change. For example, if a child resents parental restrictions and responds by returning home late and drunk, parents and child need to work out a mutually agreed upon contract to which all can adhere.

CASE

A man liked to drink after work; his wife was a teetotaler. As soon as the man poured a drink at home, his wife deserted him for the evening. Out of resentment, and because he no longer had anything else to amuse himself with, the man drank more than ever.

The contract between this couple was that (a) the wife would accept moderate drinking and not criticize it or indicate by her gestures that she thought drinking was wrong; (b) the husband would drink no more than fifteen drinks a week, as many as four drinks only one night in the week, and not drink at all one night.

Such deals represent compromises. You give up certain things, like behaviors you habitually resort to, in return for changes in the behavior of another family member. You need to respond to the person in a new way that reduces or minimizes the other party's unwanted behavior. When a husband returns home late and drunk, a wife may need to find the strength to lock him out. If he beats her, she needs to withdraw from the relationship, to prove that she will not accept this behavior. Some behaviors are, of course, intolerable, and you must insist on their absolute elimination.

You also need to withdraw from the cycle of addiction when you are excusing or compensating for a child's or mate's misbehavior. To clean up after someone, to make amends for a spouse or child (called "enabling"), is to make it easier for the person to continue in an addiction or other irresponsible conduct. Excusing family violence may be a way of trying to ease the situation, but it makes it more likely that the person will attack a spouse or child again. You are also conveying tacit approval of the person's behavior when you shield him or her from its consequences. It is often very painful to break out of this pattern by allowing the person to deal with a problem of his or her own creation. But the alternative is to deal with more and worse examples of the problem down the road.

Make Your Household a Pleasant Place

Nearly every home could use a more positive interpersonal climate—the result of more positive comments, interactions, and activities. Think about the ratio of negative to positive comments in your home—how many criticisms and reminders versus how many words of praise and fun. A few words subtracted from one side and added to the other each hour can substantially improve the tone of your household interactions and the feelings of family members. A negative climate at home, on the other hand, creates a sense of estrangement and detachment that may make *all* family members more prone to addiction.

It also pays to plan for positive, non-job-related household interactions involving as many members, in different combinations, as possible. Planning for a babysitter and a night out with your spouse, setting aside specific evenings for sex, taking each child out once a month for a special event, organizing family outings other than those initiated by invitations from others—all count toward this goal. It seems strange that people grow to accept ways of talking and interacting with those they are closest to that they would never accept from strangers. But this is an almost inevitable consequence of familiarity and inertia. Anything that breaks up this acceptance, such as interacting with people outside the family unit, will help to highlight how far you may have slipped from the worthwhile goal of family activity.

EXERCISE

Catalogue your caring behaviors toward other family members. How many things have you done that you consider demonstrate the love you feel for your family? Increase this number. The flip side of the exercise is to "catch your spouse (or child) doing something nice." Make a big deal when you notice this. It will be more likely to occur again.

Work

Anything that takes up eight or more hours a day will have a major impact on your life. And that is only if you are lucky enough to have a job, or an involving job. It is an indisputable fact that people with a reliable way of making a living and good job skills are less likely to have addictions of most kinds. Unemployed people are more likely to be addicted to alcohol, drugs, and cigarettes (although perhaps not to coffee); they are even more likely to be addicted to overeating, gambling, and shopping, though without a job they can less readily afford these addictions; they are more likely to have violent and destructive family and love relationships.

Having touted the value of work, however, we must also warn that people we see in therapy regularly describe job problems as major difficulties in life. Dealing with business organizations, work demands, and unpleasant co-workers takes a steady toll on people.

CASE

A woman found that she was constantly upset at work. She thought of herself as a competent worker, and she had had good success at her jobs. More than this, she valued being friendly with others. Perhaps because she was single, she looked for more emotional satisfaction at work than her co-workers did. In any case, she found that she seemed to annoy people with her openness and her intense style of interacting, and she found that she was often the butt of group jokes.

In therapy, the woman learned she needed to put up more barriers at work. Whether it was the group atmosphere or her own problem, she needed to think through how she was coming across to others, instead of of venting her first impulse. Though she felt it was unfortunate to limit her contacts with other people like this, she soon saw the value of this approach. Indeed, people seemed to find it easier to relax around her when she held herself more aloof. At the same time, she worked on building the other areas of her life outside of work so that she would be less emotionally dependent on her job and work organization for emotional sustenance.

Work offers important satisfactions. It does not replace the rest of your life, however. Work relationships are just that; they depend for their existence on your job and work environment. You can't ask more of co-workers than is appropriate without getting yourself in trouble. Sometimes a work relationship will elevate itself beyond the workplace. Given how rare this is, however, you need to be prepared to deal with people at work as co-workers, not as parents, lovers, or children.

Looking Ahead

The skills that are necessary to change addictive habits and live a productive life must be integrated into your whole life-style, particularly the groups with which you live and work. Otherwise, they remain group exercises and remembered skills, rather than resources for living. The Life Process approach emphasizes personal development through work, family, maturity, friendships, community, and childrearing as the primary means for changing addictions. Part III raises our sights to this larger perspective and addresses these contexts for change.

PART III

CHANGING COMMUNITIES, CHANGING LIVES

CHAPTER 16

INTEGRATING CHANGE INTO YOUR LIFE

GROUPS AND YOUR SOCIAL WORLD

THE LIFE PROCESS PROGRAM is geared toward improving the way you function within your real environment, especially your social environment—the people with whom you deal in your home, workplace, and community. Shaping your group experiences is a primary focus of this approach, one that can support or undermine any individual skills you develop. This, more than anything else, keeps addiction out of your life. When you change the groups to which you belong, you become, in a sense, a different person. Healthy behavior becomes the status quo, the addiction an aberration that now is unthinkable.

One way of modifying your environment is to leave behind defeatist relationships and select new groups to join. However, people are not so infinitely flexible that they can throw over every group to which they belong. You don't want to get a divorce in order to quit smoking or lose weight; you don't want to change jobs every time something about your life bothers you. How do you find new satisfactions within your current groups, or modify these groups to fit your needs, or join additional groups, or find new, helpful friends to supplement your existing social network?

The key to these changes is the values they serve. The Life Process Program is a value-oriented approach. It recognizes that one of the ways your group memberships affect you is by the values they communicate. If your work organization denies you and others respect, then you and your co-workers will constantly be fighting to overcome this essential deficiency in your lives. And no amount of therapy can change this. Furthermore, if you are concerned solely with your personal satisfaction or your possessions, you can never find enough rewards in living to overcome addiction. Community participation is not a luxury; it is vital to your health as well as to the survival of our society.

Reorganizing your life to eliminate addiction by means of the Life Process Program involves the following conditions:

- Your daily life and social environment provide the rewards you need to live without your addiction.
- Your work, social, and family groups support the behaviors you want to adopt.
- You will change groups, find new friends, join with other people as needed to assist you in making the changes you want.
- The groups in which you participate express positive values beyond those of simply eliminating the addiction.
- You are part of and contribute to your community.

Community Reinforcement Approach

One therapy that focuses on the addict's social environment is the Community Reinforcement Approach (CRA), devised by George Hunt and Nathan Azrin. This approach highlights the principles of arranging your social world to discontinue addictions or to support new behaviors. CRA has consistently shown the best results of any treatment for alcoholism. It achieves these results by ensuring that the alcoholic's social world reinforces sobriety and provides rewards for a constructive social and work life. CRA addresses every aspect of the alcoholic's life—including married life, job-seeking and work life, and leisure time.

For many socially isolated alcoholics, this therapy requires that the individual be *assigned* social connections, like a buddy system and a Job Club. Marriage partners (or buddies) are taught to reinforce sobriety. For example, wives are instructed to lock their spouses out when they return home drunk. But they are also taught to act positively when their husbands remain sober. This approach, called *reciprocity marriage counseling,* aims to make wives and husbands one another's best supporters in sobriety. Marriage partners are also encouraged to create a daily ritual to make sure their spouses take their Antabuse.[1]

The Job Club is a peer and counseling organization for helping alcoholics assess their work skills so that they can find and keep a suitable job. Aspects of jobs that have caused them to drink in the past (like stress or time away from home) are taken into account in the job-selection process. Alcoholics are also taught drink-refusal skills and a time-out procedure for waiting out weak moments and temptations and urges to drink. Social and recreational activities are designed for clients to fill leisure time without drinking.

CRA lays out exactly how a spouse should make sure the alcoholic takes Antabuse. It provides a detailed plan for seeking jobs, being interviewed, and keeping one's name on file with a potential employer. These prescriptions may be too arduous to be worthwhile for most people other than severe alcoholics with little life structure. Nonetheless, this approach makes clear that, when family, work, and leisure life all point you in the same direction, more often than not you will succeed. The Community Reinforcement Approach also makes clear how important it is to have a family, a social group, and a job in order to function successfully.

The Community Reinforcement Approach

- Reciprocity marriage counseling
- Creating a buddy system
- Training partners to administer disulfiram (Antabuse)
- Job Club
- Leisure-activity planning
- Time-out and drink-refusal skills
- Social-skills training
- Creating a community

The woman who attended the Sea Pines weight-loss clinic (in chapter 14) took away a message very similar to CRA's. You will remember that this woman discussed the behavioral message she heard at Sea Pines with her family, structured her life to support good eating and weight loss, and generalized the behavioral approach to reinforce her children's completion of their homework and other positive behaviors.

What you can learn from these environmental approaches is a set of general, but crucially important, guidelines:

- The behavior your various social groups reinforce is the behavior you will find it easiest to practice.
- You can analyze, choose, and influence the groups you participate in to make sure they support the behaviors you want.
- A well-integrated and full life, including family, job, community, friends, and leisure activities, is the best therapy.

Finally, you will have a better chance of quitting an addiction, or of losing weight, if your spouse and family and friends

- understand and endorse your goals;
- actively support you;
- understand the mechanics of your program (like avoiding sweets or giving yourself small portions);
- don't practice the addiction themselves.

The Work Organization

Outside of the family, the organization most people spend the most time in is their work (many spend *more* time there than at home). You don't have to work in a smelting or a chemical plant or in a mine in order for work to hurt your health—*all* work organizations affect people's feelings and behaviors.

Until the 1980s, unrestricted smoking was a fact of life in most organizations. In the eighties, however, smoking and other employee behaviors and organizational factors—such as drinking, overeating, stress, and so on—were addressed by many organizations. You yourself probably became more aware of your health behavior and that of your co-workers. For example, did co-workers smoke around you and encourage you to smoke? Did fellow workers drink too much or use drugs at company functions or outside of work?

Almost every organization has put in place a policy on smoking, identifying areas where people can smoke and banning smoking elsewhere, removing cigarette vending machines, and supporting smokers' efforts to quit. Nonetheless, in some workplaces you still may be affected by secondary smoke. This often occurs because the modern office building recirculates air between offices, and you inhale pollutants of all kinds. In this case, always remember that you are allowed to ask your company to measure the quality of its ambient air. And you may not be forced to breathe other people's smoke at meetings or in your office.

The Alcohol and Drug Scare at Work

Today, most offices are also preoccupied with alcohol and drugs. Businesses are frequently informed in advertisements that "nearly every work place suffers from drug and alcohol abuse—if you don't know about your addicted and alcoholic employees, then you are burying your head in the sand." Ads like these are meant to worry employers about their liability and safety and to prompt them to purchase an Employee Assistance Plan, or EAP. A *New York Times* feature on EAPs reported that 80 percent of Fortune 1,000 executives and public officials believed that substance abuse is a "significant or very significant problem in their organizations." However, the article also reported the following results of a survey of human-resources executives on the impact of the EAPs they had established:

> The overwhelming majority saw few results from these programs. In the survey, 87 percent reported little or no change in absenteeism since the programs began and 90 percent saw little or no change in productivity ratings.[2]

Why are EAPs so ineffectual? In the first place, the hysteria about drug and alcohol abuse is unwarranted for most workplaces, particularly with professional and white-collar employees. Not many—if any—of your co-workers in such organizations are likely to be abusing drugs and alcohol. In the second place, as we have seen, the treatments to which most employees who abuse substances are referred or are coerced into attending don't work. In particular, most EAP drug-and-alcohol programs are dominated by recovering alcoholics who project their world views and problems onto everyone, rather than determining what might help the individual employee. Most employees do much better to stay at work and receive some counseling about the range of problems they have—financial, marital, interpersonal, work-related—than to be shipped out to a chemical-dependence clinic that is totally unconnected with the rest of their lives.

Harnessing the Work Group for Support

When the whole group is pointed toward healthful behavior, you will find it easier to be healthy, too. For example, your co-workers may throw frequent office parties when someone changes jobs, has a birthday, gets married, and so on. When your group can agree that they shouldn't forget healthy eating habits at these parties—that fruits and juice can replace doughnuts and soda—you may set a healthy tone for the workplace. Selections available in vending machines and company lunchrooms send the same messages, and you should feel free to inquire about or influence these company and vendor policies.

There are other ways to harness the benefits of the group for healthy behavior. Kelly Brownell of the University of Pennsylvania has instituted competitions in which various work groups compete against one another to lose weight. The progress of the competing groups is monitored and displayed, encouraging everyone to watch his or her eating and to exercise.[3] Other companies provide rewards for employees who lose weight or quit smoking. Of course, there can be a fine line between group support for behavior change and group coercion. People should be recruited gently, and it is against the law to demand that people lose weight simply to hold a job.

How to Approach a Coworker's or Employee's Substance Abuse

If you want an employee to drink less or quit drinking or smoking, you:

- Establish the proper rules and evidence for your request (you can't make a request that exceeds established company or union rules, for instance);
- Communicate your reasons clearly, and in terms of behavior (e.g.,

"Your smoking pollutes the air in the office," "You are late too often or not performing adequately");

▸ Apply sufficient sanctions ("This must stop or I'll have to let you go");

▸ Combine your request or demand with supportive efforts ("We'll pay for you to attend a program you think will help you," or "Let me know when you feel I am creating pressures at work that you think make you need to smoke," or drink, or whatever);

▸ Create a supportive company environment by making sure that other people aren't smoking or engaging in excessive or unhealthy behavior, and that the organization is addressing problems that encourage addictions, such as stress and negative working conditions.

Real Problems at Work

Addictive problems are part of larger problems in people's lives. Many people experience their most severe problems at work. These problems most often result from the climate of the organization—tension, overwork, inadequate recognition, management or interpersonal styles that are irrational or unsupportive. When individuals abuse drugs or alcohol, their behavior is often linked to stress, malaise, alienation, and insecurity they feel at work.

Americans are uneasy and unfamiliar with facing these problems in groups like the work setting. That is why we so readily fob them off on EAP professionals who are far less familiar with the personalities and the problems of our co-workers than we are. And, of course, if the problems you face result from management practices and are organization-wide, then winnowing out individual sufferers for treatment will not have much of an impact.

How do you deal with personal problems in organizations? You might ask yourself:

▸ Is there someone at your organization you can talk to when you have a problem? This can be a friend or a boss. But an organization should have someone formally assigned to handle employees' personal problems. Such individuals can be company employees or outside counselors. Their job is not necessarily to resolve all problems. They may assist people in finding whatever help is needed—family counseling, legal assistance, and so on.

▸ Is it anyone's job at your organization to think about improving organizational functioning? Many problems extend beyond single individuals. If regular bottlenecks appear, or if many people are upset about similar things, the organization needs ways to identify and address these problems. The person responsible can be the human-resources person or another professional who devotes at least some time to organizational problems.

▸ Can your organization confront a given individual's problems or handle interpersonal problems within the work setting? T-groups (sensitivity groups) and meetings where people gathered ouside the office to speak frankly about one another were once all the rage. Their fascination has faded, primarily because being sensitive to co-workers outside the workplace doesn't necessarily translate into useful results when people return to work.

But sometimes individuals in the organization do go beyond the pale, or things obviously are not working correctly, so that people feel troubled and demand a change.

CASE

One high-powered advertising firm had an extremely intense president. During project meetings, the man frequently became enraged at employees, and meetings often ended in tears and bad feelings. In addition, the president had begun to prolong his lunches by sitting at the bar. People noticed that his worst outbursts were in the afternoons after he had been drinking.

Finally, finding the repeated outbursts increasingly unpleasant and detrimental to business, a group of executives and co-owners of the company confronted the president. They had prearranged for him to enter an inpatient alcohol clinic, and they made it clear that he had better undergo the treatment if he wanted to continue at his post.

The company executives were a sophisticated, tolerant group of people. They did not believe that the president had a disease of alcoholism that needed to be cured. Indeed, no one complained when he occasionally had wine at company celebrations after his treatment. They understood that he had an underlying problem, one of impatience and of dissatisfaction with his own role in the company, that led to his outbursts.

But to have the president seek treatment for his personal problems and his screaming jags would be difficult. Sending him to an alcoholism center was simpler, since the company's group insurance paid for alcohol treatment and the man's drinking was part of his problem. Yet in treatment he never addressed his communication style, his manner of criticizing people, or his discontent with his own job. But he heeded his colleagues' message that he needed to change and used the treatment break to reconsider his approach to work, to colleagues, and to lunchtime drinking.

People in this company, like people everywhere, are uncomfortable confronting others—particularly executives and superiors—about their bad behavior. Indeed, the organization in this case was unusually committed to group morale and to trying to address the bad feelings the president was creating. Organizations don't generally give employees permission to discuss these things and rarely have ways to resolve such problems. Instead, they look for professional assistance, usually in the form of EAP substance-abuse programs. However, what if a boss doesn't drink, but belittles or bullies employees when cold sober—the typical situation? Such behavior is hard for the average employee to confront, at least without endangering his or her job.

Organizations need to address communications, group problem-solving, and individual interactions at a group level. Rather than bicker about such things at general meetings, the best approach is to institute a training seminar involving at least managerial staff. Such seminars address many of the same skills we have outlined in this book for addiction treatment. Although professional people usually do not have the same degree of skill deficiencies as most alcoholics and drug addicts (who are disproportionately of low socioeconomic status), nearly everyone can benefit from sharpening his or her group and personal skills. In addition to instituting such training, the organization must indicate that it supports improved communications and problem-solving. In this way, it can avoid relying on individual therapy or addiction treatment for problems that are caused or exacerbated by the organization's overall climate.

Group Support

Twelve-Step and Other Support Groups

This book has found much to criticize in A.A. and other twelve-step groups. Let's use the deficiencies of these groups as a starting point for describing what to look for in a support group. Support groups *can* be valuable. Social support is a major dimension of healthy human functioning, not only for avoiding addictions, but for maintaining all aspects of human well-being. The flaws of A.A. and other twelve-step groups that we have outlined are:

- They are religious and dogmatic, they promote a point of view, and they demand strict adherence to group policy, allowing members no personal choices or individual variations.
- They undermine individual confidence and strength by insisting on members' weakness and predicting the worst outcomes for those who violate group policies or who leave the group.
- They will not permit people to evolve out of the addict identity—you are an alcoholic, an addict, a compulsive shopper, or whatever forever.
- They are completely focused on alcohol (or eating or shopping) and on the *group itself,* ignoring the quality of members' lives and their functioning outside the group.

CASE

A number of friends (some of whom belonged to A.A. themselves) advised Tracy to go to A.A. because she had gotten sloppy drunk a couple of times. At A.A., Tracy learned and accepted that she had a disease. After a few months, she concluded that she had been wrong in thinking she could ever control her drinking.

Even after she accepted the A.A. dogma, Tracy still wasn't entirely comfortable with A.A. What bothered her most was that the group instructed people not to get angry, because anger drove so many to drink. In fact, Tracy sometimes became angry during A.A. meetings and stood up and spoke her mind about policies she objected to. The leadership always quickly put a lid on these discussions. After the meeting, other members would come up to her and tell her, "Way to go! I'm bothered by the same things."

After almost a year of A.A., Tracy went on a drinking binge. She drank more than she ever had before attending A.A. Her behavior frightened her, and she checked herself into a hospital treatment program, returning to A.A when she got out. But, still feeling discontented, she had more than one serious drinking binge.

Increasingly frustrated, Tracy left A.A. One reason she felt she had to leave was that she decided she could drink normally. But her old friends who remained in A.A. viewed her as deluded. Saying she was in denial, they told one another at meetings that "Tracy is drinking," as though she were standing on a street corner with a paper bag. Actually, Tracy would occasionally drink from a can of beer at a party, put it down, and forget where she had left it. After several years of indoctrination at A.A., it is remarkable that she was able to return to moderation so unself-consciously.

A.A.'s primary advantage (and disadvantage) is that it is everywhere. No alternative group has recruited as many members, nor should one, because only a religious-dogmatic group puts so much energy into proselytizing, converting people to its point of view, and creating lifelong devotees. Nearly all twelve-step groups, not only those devoted to alcohol or drugs but groups that have formed around compulsive shopping and gambling and sexual addiction, are just as dogmatic and closed-minded as the original A.A. model. On the other hand, A.A. chapters vary, some to the point where the group barely resembles the parent organization. We sometimes correspond with out-of-the-way A.A. chapters in which, aside from the proscription of drinking, everything else A.A. supposedly swears by (such as the disease model) is called into question.

Because of a growing awareness that A.A. doesn't meet all people's needs—and because mandatory assignment to A.A. may violate people's civil and constitutional rights—alternatives to A.A. have begun appearing throughout the United States. S.O.S. (Secular Organizations for Sobriety) has rapidly grown as a support group for recovering alcoholics who reject A.A.'s focus on a "higher power." Many courts now offer drunk drivers a choice of S.O.S. or A.A. In most respects other than its nonreligious character, however, S.O.S. is quite similar to the A.A. program. Rational Recovery (R.R.), on the other hand, rejects the twelve-step philosophy almost entirely. R.R. is based on Albert Ellis's rational-emotive therapy, which confronts people with the irrationality of self-defeating thinking. The group claims that problem drinkers do not have a disease and recognizes that people can outgrow their alcoholism—in fact, it encourages people to wean themselves from the group. R.R. challenges the notion of "powerlessness" in favor of the belief that alcohol-dependent individuals can get control of their behavior by changing the way they think about their drinking.

The drawback is that R.R. shares Americans' abstinence fixation. It doesn't accommodate alcoholics trying to moderate their drinking (although they may obviously do so after they leave the group). Methods of Moderation (M.O.M.), a recovery group founded by atheists, is the only American support group that accepts and encourages the goal of moderation. A British group that aims for moderation, Drink Watchers, has not found fertile roots in the United States. In any case, *you* have the right to question any dogma about treatment, and to seek or create support for your view of the best way to proceed.

Some support groups for drug addicts, such as Narcotics Anonymous, have taken over A.A.'s philosophy—and problems. The worst case of a self-help group that lost its way was Synanon, a program for heroin addicts in California organized by an ex–A.A. member, Chuck Dederich. Although for a time Dederich became Hollywood's fair-haired boy and Synanon its favorite charity, eventually the cultlike nature of the organization was revealed. Dederich, who had hired a goon squad to intimidate members who wanted to quit, pleaded guilty to a conspiracy to kill dissident former members and opponents. Though twelve-step groups today reject any comparison with Synanon, it was once widely accepted as a guiding light in the field, and many of its peculiarities were held up as helpful group principles.

Clearly, Synanon is at the extreme end of the spectrum of "self-help" groups that insist on lifelong membership. Synanon was an example of a "therapeutic community" (TC)—a nonmedical residential program. Phoenix House, which began in New York City and spread nationwide, is the most successful TC chain. At Phoenix House and other TCs, the emphasis is on teaching inner-city addicts prosocial values and life skills. These programs deny that addicts have lifelong diseases, and instead view addictions as self-destructive and stupid habits that can be replaced. Therapeutic communities have succeeded at giving many addicts a new start in life by creating for them (in programs that last from eighteen months to two years) the kind of constructive natural environment the addicts have not previously experienced. Nonetheless, for reasons we discuss in chapter 18, TCs have not really made a dent in the nation's drug problems.

Other support groups do not have the same flaws as disease and twelve-step groups like Alcoholics Anonymous. For example, several support groups of ex–mental patients (such as the National Alliance of Psychiatric Survivors) have been formed to help people resist and overcome disease diagnoses and medical pressures to take drugs or to remain institutionalized. These groups want to help people *escape* labels and dogmas, not to trap people with them.

People may form their own self-help groups. The most effective groups are not prepackaged ones that people simply join to follow rules set up by others. To find a constructive support group for addictions or any other purpose, you should seek groups that meet these criteria:

- They welcome individual diversity and support the personal goals of members.
- They accept member input on goals, approaches, and rules.
- They *empower* people by enhancing their confidence in themselves and their ability to grapple with problems or accomplish their personal goals.
- They encourage and reward improved functioning *outside* the group, with emphasis on relationships and activities that aren't tied to the group.
- They accept and *welcome* that members will eventually outgrow the group by becoming fully independent or forming associations outside the group.

EXAMPLE

One woman had tried to write for years, but had never completed a story that she was satisfied with or felt comfortable showing to other people. Finally, a friend told her about a writers' group to which the friend belonged. Members met once a month to talk about their writing projects, pass around or read aloud excerpts from their writing, and comment on one another's work. Members also discussed practical questions, like submitting their work to publishers and magazines, and contractual issues.

The woman enjoyed the group from the start. She found that, even though group members worked in a variety of styles and media, people participated eagerly in critiquing one another's work, but in helpful, open ways. She felt her writing improve, and she also learned more about the ropes of submitting articles for publication. Finally, a little more than a year after joining the group, she had an article accepted by a national magazine. She was fêted by the group for her triumph.

Everything in this story applies to groups of former addicts as well. A positive support group encourages you to suceed in dealing with the key matters in your life, not because this proves that the group is right, but because other group members with similar concerns have accepted you and wish you to succeed at your chosen path, even should it differ from theirs. However, the only way you can be sure a self-help group expresses your personal views is by playing a role in organizing it. But whether you join an existing group or start one on your own or with friends, a successful self-help support group will offer you:

- strength and independence;
- success in all areas of functioning;
- openness toward new experiences, other people, and even other groups.

The *sine qua non* of the healthy group experience is that it not become an ultimate preoccupation in itself, but that it lead you to reimmerse yourself in life outside the group with renewed vigor, health, and success.

Nontherapy Groups

People find support through many groups, not only those organized specifically to help their members. People join community, church, and social-service groups, the Sierra Club, YMCA volleyball teams, and other groups in order to associate with positive, like-minded people. In the case of addictions, it is possible to find people who don't smoke, take drugs, or drink without joining Smokenders, Narcotics Anonymous, or A.A. On the other hand, you really need to evaluate the healthfulness of your current leisure groups—such as the Elks, the bowling club, or other male-bonding groups—if people in these groups routinely smoke, overeat, and drink too much.

Individual Therapy

If you turn to a therapist for addiction treatment, you should begin by checking his or her training and reputation. Then ask the therapist for an assessment of your problem and for a treatment plan. A treatment plan outlines:

- the *goals* of the therapy;
- the *methods* used to achieve the goals;
- a *timetable* for completing the course of therapy.

The plan for addiction-as-a-disease treatment is:

- *goal:* abstinence;
- *methods:* soul-searching and following the twelve steps;
- *timetable:* for inpatient treatment, twenty-eight days (or whatever the limit for insurance payment for a hospital stay); for twelve-step groups, the rest of your life.

The poverty of disease treatments is revealed by a therapist's inability to point to concrete results of therapy, concrete ways to achieve them, and a specific timetable for achieving them.

CASE

A couple entered therapy for the husband's alcohol dependence, although the husband had almost completely eliminated his drinking binges. The treatment center followed the disease model. From the start, the couple didn't see eye to eye with the therapist. "I just don't want to go through life focused on my alcoholism," said the husband. "I want to progress beyond this point."

The couple also had a difficult time pinning the therapist down about goals and a timetable. They even produced their own set of goals.

When the therapist failed to address these, they became disillusioned. In place of the first therapist, they located a therapist who explored the problems—an inability to deal with feelings and to negotiate angry and tense situations—that underlay the husband's occasional binges.

Criteria for accepting a therapist or style of therapy are that:

- you are comfortable with the therapy; it is consistent with your values; its philosophy and goals make sense and seem valuable to you;
- you develop specific measuring points against which you check the progress in therapy;
- the therapy can adapt to and evolve with your changing needs and perspectives.

Changing Groups/Seeking Love

As youngsters grow up, they frequently identify the kind of people they want to be by associating with people whose behavior they want to emulate. For example, an adolescent who wants to be more intellectual or artistic will seek people with these attributes as friends. This is also often true for young people who adopt a gay life-style, or those who become drug users or school dropouts.

Beyond our teens and early twenties, we become less malleable and less anxious to alter our lives like this. It is difficult for people to move, change jobs, or get divorced as a way to facilitate most behavior changes. Perhaps if we have been associating with a heavy-drinking or gambling or shopping crowd, or belong to a drug-using group, we will be willing to undergo such major social disruptions as late as our thirties or beyond. But this prospect becomes more unpalatable and unworkable the more addictions we want to quit.

Nonetheless, we can still make use of changes in personal and group associations to change ourselves. For example, if you want to exercise more in your free time, you may look for neighbors who ride their bikes or jog on weekends to become friendly with. When you quit smoking, you may goad your lunchmates into quitting, too, or else you may find a new group of people to sit with at lunch. Other group changes do not occur because of the urge to quit an addiction, but nonetheless facilitate the process. For example, many people do change jobs in middle age. One consideration when you do so may be how the new work arrangement will support health behaviors you want to adopt. At the same time, you can work to structure the job to support personal changes, so that you get off on the right foot at the new job.

CASE

A man who interviewed for a job as an accountant noticed that none of the people he interviewed with had an ashtray, so he never lit up a cigarette. When he returned home from the interview, he thought what a good opportunity this was to quit smoking. Later he reported that he rarely felt an urge to smoke at his new job, because that environment was never associated in his mind with cigarettes and smoking.

Another change people may make, willingly or unwillingly, is in their marriage partners. Given the instability of marriage and the tendency for many people today to remain single into their thirties and beyond, one of the addictive habits people most commonly seek to change is unhealthy and self-destructive love affairs. This is the ultimate in seeking healthy social associations—in no other case is the issue of whom you want to spend your time with so clearly the focus as when you choose a mate. At the very least, you will want to know whether that person overdoes behaviors that you are concerned to control—you don't want to become involved with someone who drinks or eats or shops or watches television too much when you are trying to do less of these things.

People who have had a number of relationships and have matured are less likely to evaluate relationships purely in romantic terms. The issue becomes not "Who will drive me wild?" but "Who is a good mate?" At this stage of their lives, people usually have become more interested in what kind of partners they like being with. This requires asking yourself what qualities you want in a person with whom you choose to be involved, and how you determine if a person has them. When people end up with abusive spouses, on the other hand, they seem not to be good at evaluating such questions. For example, they may have observed their lovers abusing others. But they were unconcerned about this at the time, for they thought their love was special. Perhaps, secretly, they even welcomed the abuse of others, as a sign that their partners loved only them.

CASE

In his novel, *People Like Us,* Dominick Dunne tells of the murder of his daugher, Dominique Dunne, by her boyfriend John Sweeney, and of Sweeney's trial. In an earlier magazine article, the elder Dunne described how, prior to the murder, Sweeney assaulted a male acquaintance of his daughter's when Dominique spoke with the man. This behavior was an example of Sweeney's violence and selfishness (Dunne also discovered that Sweeney had beaten other women with whom he was involved) which should have been a sign to Dominique Dunne of the quality of person with whom she was involved, and of what he might do to her.

Dominique Dunne should not be blamed for her own murder. But if we are to control our lives and not simply accept abuse as some accidental fate that befalls us, we need to look at potential mates in terms of how they treat others. When someone is incapable of forming trusting relationships with anyone else and even abuses or mistreats others, that person is not a good bet for you, either.

A good mate is a good person, someone you can respect and whose behavior and qualities you admire. The questions to ask about a lover are thus:

- Is this a good person?
- Does he or she have a positive impact on the world?
- Does he or she display traits I admire, enjoy, and would want to emulate?
- Does he or she have good relationships and treat other people well?
- Is this person in control of himself or herself?
- Does he or she get real rewards in life?
- Is he or she addicted to love or other fantasies?

In other words, the best way to guarantee love and worthwhile relationships is to think about whether the person you are attracted to is worthwhile. At the same time, this will help you concentrate on whether your own behavior is worthwhile, and, if not, what you are doing to improve it.

Addiction as Selfishness, Social Values as the Cure[4]

Addiction represents a preoccupation with oneself and one's own needs. The best antidote for it, then, would seem to be one that brings a person into contact with others in constructive, mutual ways. Yet in our society the most commonly chosen therapeutic response to addiction is private treatment, where the entire focus of the interaction is the person's own problems. The contradiction, the futility, in this was painfully evident in a conversation one of us had with the publisher of a recovery magazine, himself a recovering alcoholic. We asked whether they ever featured articles on the environment or the dangers of nuclear holocaust. He looked at us uncomprehendingly. "We can't afford to worry about those things," he said. "All of our energy is taken up with our recoveries."

Our analysis of addiction gives us a whole other line of attack. People get stuck in addictions not because they have too little time or concern for themselves; rather, they have too little time for others and for the outside world. This discrepancy is getting worse as Americans turn more and more inward—as indicated by their inventing new diseases to suffer from and new treatments to exorcise them. For example, Hedda Nussbaum, while being brutalized by Joel Steinberg, was constantly in therapy. Yet she had no time for the problems of the children ostensibly in her care, whom Steinberg was also brutalizing, and whom she was neglecting. What she and Steinberg shared was an exclusive preoccupation with themselves—with their own feelings and needs—that precluded any concern for the needs of those children.[5]

The answer to addiction is not to spend more time looking for new treatments, but to spend more time attending to other people and situations besides your own. People with spouses and children, who are involved with their families and co-workers and communities, are less likely to become addicted and more likely to get over addiction. If you are addicted, you need to design ways to:

- focus less on yourself;
- learn and practice prosocial behavior;
- develop real concerns in life—political, environmental, community, helping others.

Therapy usually involves professionals in listening to people recite their complaints and difficulties and then suggesting means of improvement. An alternative would be to assign the "patient" community-oriented work: to help others, to assist with beneficial projects, to read the newspaper and report on local and global issues. Instead of reciting a litany of personal problems, parents could be asked to work on improving their interactions with their children. All of these things focus people outside themselves—a principle that should set the tone for your self-help efforts.

Take, as an example of antisocial values, an addiction to gambling. Habitual gamblers spend their time in nonproductive activity away from their families, communities, and work, whether in glitzy hotels or rundown dives. They squander family resources shooting to gain something for nothing. Gambling is a bald example of addiction as a value, and not a chemical, disorder. Yet alcoholism-as-disease proponents try to sell people on using hospital beds for these gamblers. Even when it does not take such a preposterous form, disease-model therapy for problems like gambling concentrates on why the gambler is ailing instead of making clear that the gambler's behavior is antisocial and unacceptable.

Let's Play Therapist

Instead of an inspiring example of how someone quit an addiction, we will conclude with a case of a person who has not yet been able to quit. This vignette brings together the change techniques presented in these last three chapters—changes in the habit itself, in one's personal skills and capacities, and in one's environment and values—together with the assessment and goal-setting techniques presented in the previous four chapters. Here is a person who *wants* to quit an addiction (in this case smoking), who is in an environment where the habit is very much disapproved of, but who still has not given it up. *Why* hasn't she done so? Using the Life Process Program, can we analyze her situation and make recommendations that will help her quit? And, in doing so, can we learn more about quitting our own addictions?

Lorraine is a systems analyst who holds a high staff position in a major insurance company. She began smoking as a graduate student in computer science. Lorraine had progressed nicely in her career. Having waited until her thirties to get married, she now had two children. Her marriage ended in divorce, however, and Lorraine found herself a single parent. Although her husband made a good salary, Lorraine had asked for little in the divorce and took less child support than her attorney thought she was entitled to. But Lorraine was used to fending for herself and didn't want to rely on a man she no longer loved.

Lorraine continued to smoke (she was now over forty) even though she had been able to quit for several months at a time. Recently, she had taken a good management position in a prominent insurance company. She found that she was the only person at her professional level out of forty people in her department who smoked, and she was restricted to smoking in her office, while she worked. When her company brought in a Smokenders program for its remaining employees who smoked (about fifteen lower-ranking people in Lorraine's department), Lorraine felt obliged to attend.

Once again she quit, but this time her abstinence lasted only a few days. She found it relatively easy to give up cigarettes over the weekend, at home, where her children had already begun bothering her to quit. But at work, Lorraine found that she became intensely anxious when she faced a new systems problem without a cigarette. Quickly, she lit up a cigarette, which she was convinced cleared her mind and focused her attention. Faced with what she felt was a choice between being unable to do her job and continuing to smoke, she chose the latter.

The function cigarettes served for Lorraine was a conscious one, was steeped in her view of herself, and was part of her work and family life. Her position in life, her personal and professional associations, and her values clearly would lead her to quit. Yet she felt she couldn't, because smoking was integral to her work style, and she feared her competence would disappear along with her smoking habit. How might she proceed in order to quit? (Keep in mind that she has stopped briefly in the past and that she has recently gone through a Smokenders program without success.) Let's list the areas of change Lorraine might need to accomplish in order to quit for good:

1. *Personal changes.* Lorraine might try to lick the insecurity that fueled her addiction. But after more than a dozen successful years in the work world, is this a real possibility for her? Lorraine realized that other people had insecurities, too, but that she gave in to insecurity

more readily than others. Could she learn to stop coddling herself and readily venting her anxieties, anxieties she admitted everyone had?

2. *Life changes.* Lorraine fiercely guarded her independence and asked for little support from her ex-husband. As a result, she considered herself the only bulwark between her children and the poorhouse (as well as the principal provider for their future college expenses). But was Lorraine taking an undue burden on herself? Should she let her husband contribute more—should she demand that he do so? Would knowing there was more of a cushion behind her reduce the tension she felt about doing her job perfectly?

3. *Work changes.* Could Lorraine's boss say to her: "Lorraine, obviously, by investing in this course for you we would like to have you quit smoking. I understand that this may make concentrating difficult for a certain period. Please be aware that I understand this; we hired you because we know what good work you do, and we know that you will pick up that level of performance as soon as you are able"? This speech would address the fear Lorraine said underlay her smoking; perhaps its message would allow her to relax, maybe to take a walk, whenever she felt her mind wandering at work and panic setting in. The question is, did her boss and her organization accept Lorraine's controlled anxiety as an indicator that Lorraine *was* performing at a peak level?

It might easily turn out that nobody noticed any decrement in Lorraine's work during her peak withdrawal periods—especially considering the better health, sleep, and energy levels Lorraine would experience without smoking. Many of those who quit smoking in the Marsh study of British ex-smokers we cited made similar discoveries when they quit—that their smoking was actually *hurting* their overall performance. An important part of the Smokenders class Lorraine attended was to warn participants about the withdrawal they would experience. (This was a way for the group to justify its own role in helping people overcome the withdrawal distress.) But such an emphasis was not what Lorraine needed—it only added to her fear that she would fall apart at work if she stopped smoking.

4. *Values changes.* It seems obvious that Lorraine was worried about the wrong things. For example, of how much use to her children would she be if she became ill with emphysema or lung cancer? They would certainly prefer a healthy mother even if this meant having a little less financial security and fewer video games and clothes. If Lorraine could

see the important things clearly—the way it is so easy for those of us reading this book to see them—then she might reorient her values and change her behavior quite readily.

What strategy do you imagine would work best for Lorraine? Of course, Lorraine must select the strategy, not we. People can make clear how much Lorraine's smoking bothers them, and how they want to support her efforts at change, but they need to let Lorraine decide what the best way for her is. For example, Lorraine might consider it unprofessional to ask her boss to reassure her about her productivity. But she might *promise* herself that, the next time she saw a relatively easy work week coming, she would use that "breather" to stop smoking and to endure the decrement in performance she anticipated, so that she might emerge from that period with a solid week of abstinence under her belt.

As Lorraine's case shows, it may not be easy to dislodge an addiction that continues to serve a function for a person. What one must do is to explore the psychological and life terrain that supports the addiction and ferret out its root causes. This is more than a matter of tricks, groups, and techniques. Of course, quitting an addiction involves scary choices and sacrifices—like risking the competence at work and the independence from her ex-husband that Lorraine prized. But going at life without the safety net of the addiction often shows people that they are capable of living without such crutches, that their worst fears are not as bad as they suspected and may be altogether groundless.

Summary: The Life Process Program and Prosocial Values

One thing that cannot be denied is that Lorraine is doing the wrong thing, as an example for her children, for her own health, for the people in the offices next to her into whose rooms her smoke leaks. The Life Process Program explores with addicted people what their behavior reveals about their core values. It gives people an opportunity to own the values that underlie their behavior, so that they may change those values or uncover other, more positive values that the addictive behavior has obscured. Finally, it helps them structure alternative prosocial ways to spend their time, ways that are good for them, for the people they are involved with, and for society.

Rather than reinforce people's irresponsibility, addiction treatment does better when it expects that people will meet their social and legal obligations. For example, chapter 18 reviews the strong evidence that arresting abusive husbands works better than having police or social workers reason with warring spouses. The real issue is to refocus people's attention from their deficiencies and misfortunes to their responsibilities to others. Where necessary, the Life Process Program works with people to remove obstacles that prevent them from contributing to their own and others' lives.

The Fundamental Principle of Addiction

Addiction is quite literally not a deficiency of intake, it is a deficiency of output.

The fact that the Life Process Program is value-oriented does not mean that it is merely punitive. Recognizing that many environmental influences can lead you to get mired in a repetitive pattern of bad choices, it helps you sort out the value issues involved, actively break the negative behavior pattern, and find rewards from more constructive behavior.

Overall, then, the Life Process Program incorporates social values in the following ways:

- It makes clear the difference between appropriate and inappropriate behavior, disapproves and punishes misbehavior, and suggests positive alternatives.

- It assists those who make a good-faith effort to practice more constructive behaviors.

- It looks—both from the individual's and from society's standpoint—at how to support prosocial behavior, to make doing the right thing the most rewarding route to take.

Writing about *Mental Health in America*, psychologist Joseph Veroff and his colleagues at the University of Michigan have observed a peculiarity in the way Americans try to heal their psyches:

> Psychotherapy . . . is the only form of psychic healing that attempts to cure people by detaching them from society and relationships. All other forms [of human psychic healing] . . . bring the community into the healing process, indeed use the interdependence of patient and others as the central mechanism in the healing process.[6]

In this book, we try to reverse this American anomaly. As difficult as it may be, it is our only chance to right ourselves as individuals and as a society. Similarly, making our children more integrated members of our communities gives them their best chance of contentment and success, as well as of avoiding addiction and self-destructive involvements.

CHAPTER 17

KIDS HAVE TO BE MADE INTO ADDICTS

•

YOU CAN PREVENT ADDICTION[1]

It is possible to introduce the concepts of recovery to the very young. Imagine whole classrooms full of children to whom recovery and the 12 Steps are familiar, comfortable, *normal* tools for everyday living. Imagine the possibilities.

J. S. Rudolph, editor, *Sober Times*[2]

Alcohol/drug addiction is not necessarily a permanent condition, but one which, in fact, can be remedied. The best possible outcome would be for the student to elect to drop this handicap. . . . The student may have a vested interest in not being identified as handicapped. . . . We are concerned about the permanence of that particular label.

Lake Washington School Board
(Kirkland, Washington)[3]

With this statement, the Lake Washington School Board proclaims . . . that drug addiction is, in essence, a self-inflicted condition that can be controlled by a form of will power ("electing to drop the handicap"), not an involuntary illness or disease.

Industry spokesperson's response to
Lake Washington School Board[4]

There is an ongoing debate as to whether alcohol and drug addiction are diseases. Although I feel no compulsion to choose sides, I do know that I have never known an addicted child or adult who did not use drugs or alcohol to

> compensate for or hide from other deep-seated emotional problems. People use mind-altering substances to create a state of happiness or comfort that they think cannot be achieved any other way.
>
> —E. Kent Hayes, codirector, National Menninger Youth Advocacy Program[5]

ADDICTION IN THE YOUNG is an explosive issue, one that threatens to tear apart society as well as individual families. We are afraid that many teenagers are genetically programmed to become alcoholics, that school children are being addicted to increasingly potent street drugs, that satanic groups are inducing innocent kids to worship the devil, and on and on. These nightmares frighten conscientious parents into believing that they cannot ensure their children will grow up physically and morally intact. And then there are the discouraging reports that a child's weight is determined at birth, however good the child's eating habits. We have never felt more out of control of raising our children.

This chapter is about how we have the responsibility, and the power, to prevent addiction in our children. It is true that parents cannot control everything that influences a child's behavior. Nonetheless, we present the common-sense and well-founded notion that parents can reduce the risk that a child will form destructive habits. The Life Process Program for children is very similar to that for adults—except here we have the opportunity to prevent rather than cure. And prevention is vastly preferable: it is easier, less costly, and more reliable. The values, skills, and myriad connections to life that help people overcome addiction are the same ones that enable children to avoid addiction in the first place. Only there is less stress and a better chance of success before the fact.

This chapter is for parents, but also for those who are concerned that they are predetermined (whether by genes or by role models) to repeat an addicted parent's misery. Much of the chapter is about raising a nonaddicted child. At the same time, we will show how young people from *unfavorable* family environments, with family histories of alcoholism and abusive behavior, decisively reject these destructive precedents and achieve a normal, self-regulated life. Just as people outgrow their own addictions, children outgrow their parents' bad examples.

Adolescent alcohol and drug abuse is most parents' most pressing concern. But let us counter the hysteria surrounding these behaviors by beginning with a part of every family's life: eating. This normal, everyday behavior offers the best way into considering the Life Process Program, because it most easily illustrates how parents teach, directly or by example, either healthful or addictive habits. In instilling healthy eating habits, something nearly every human being is concerned about, we discover Life Process principles that serve equally well when it comes to alcohol and drug abuse and all other self-destructive behavior.

Teaching a Child Healthy Eating Habits

Chapter 5 presented evidence that people can determine their own weight, no matter what genes they inherit. Addiction to food (including bulimia and anorexia) is no more permanent or incurable than other addictions, and people's weight often varies a great deal throughout their lives. One can change one's "natural" weight—provided that the change is consistent with one's overall way of life. The worst eating problems are the result of unrealistic goals for thinness, combined with a life-style of overeating, poor nutrition, and minimal physical exertion.

The keys to consistent and healthy weight control for anyone lie in integrating eating habits into a healthy life-style. You will succeed at weight control if you:

- structure eating around regular mealtimes and treat food and its surrounding rituals with respect;
- eat slowly enough to appreciate your food;
- approach food as one of life's ordinary pleasures rather than as an emotional release;
- recognize healthy foods and their importance in a proper life-style;
- associate with people (of whatever age) who eat sensibly and value fitness.

Several manuals translate these principles into detailed guidelines for starting infants and children out with a balanced diet and good eating habits.[6] Here are some highlights:

1. *Involve the whole family in healthful eating and exercise habits.* Rarely does one family member, young or old, practice good eating habits in isolation. Imagine the difference it makes for a child to grow

up in a family that hikes and bicycles as opposed to one that watches television and eats snack foods as its primary recreation. If the whole family eats well, exercises regularly, and keeps trim, you are less likely to need to deal with childhood obesity; and if you do, you will be able to deal with it more readily.

2. *Be aware of food values.* You need to know relative food values and nutritional cooking practices so that this information becomes second nature to children.

3. *Use food for nourishment, not for reward and punishment.* Let children enjoy food straightforwardly, for what it is. Don't demand that children eat as a sign that they appreciate your cooking, and don't use food to reward children for obedience or good behavior. Creating such associations may suggest to children that they can use eating throughout their lives as a way of gaining an emotional lift.

4. *Don't force food on children, but make clear that nutritional foods are essential.* Children should not feel they have to eat when they are not hungry, just to satisfy others' demands. On the other hand, you don't do your children a favor when you permit them to skip their vegetables and then give them ice cream. Remember this line: "If you're hungry, eat your dinner before you have dessert."

5. *Encourage children to recognize and ask for only the food they want.* Children need to learn to connect how much and what kinds of food they need or want to eat and what they ask for. Though children shouldn't necessarily be forced to clean their plates, they should learn to ask for appropriate amounts, or to underorder and then ask for more if necessary.

6. *Realize that children will be drawn to high-calorie foods.* A child who is forbidden candy or other sweets is more likely to crave them and to eat junk food on the sly. It is better to allow children to have desserts and sweet snacks as occasional treats, while presenting a model of normal eating centered on healthy meals.

7. *Intervene gently in regulating the overweight child's diet.* You can combat childhood obesity within the family framework. Monitor overweight children's eating to determine what modifications may make a real difference in their calorie intake; at the same time, encourage them to get out of the house and exercise. But beware of restricting their diet so heavily that you encourage a perpetual sense of deprivation

or a need for constant eating restrictions. The result can be that the child will alternate between these states, a possible precursor of the binge-starvation cycle of bulimia. The goal is to strengthen, not override, the child's self-regulation. Keep in mind that children sometimes move unpredictably between overweight (or underweight) and normal weight as their bodies develop.

8. *Make clear your respect for your child regardless of his or her weight.* Weight problems are easier to deal with when they are not bound up with children's sense of self-worth. Although a child may be mocked by others for being overweight, parents must not convey the message that weight problems are signs of inadequacy and failure. Obviously, encouraging children to lose weight while still indicating to them that you care for them and think they are worthwhile is a difficult task. But both you and the child need to keep perspective: a life is a long time to come to grips with any problem, and a secure sense of personal worth is the best tool for losing weight, gaining healthy eating habits, and tackling all the issues a lifetime will present.

9. *Promote basic values of health, responsibility, and self-control.* The Life Process approach is based on the idea that no behavior occurs in a vacuum. You need to encourage fundamental values in children that will affect all areas of their lives, including their eating habits. In order to resist pressures to eat unhealthily or hurt themselves in many ways, children need to value health. They need to understand that they are responsible for their own actions. And they need to value self-control that includes, but extends beyond, how they eat.

These rules make the most sense when they are applied within a stable family environment. Rules for promoting healthy eating in children imply that food is available and family meals are well organized, and that children are provided with lunches or instructions for buying meals at school. Our recommendations work best where parents are actively engaged in the household, family members communicate, and money, health, and emotional problems do not overwhelm the family.

What About the Dysfunctional Family?

Not every household meets these criteria. In fact, quite a few do not. These are broken homes or the underclass or families in which parents are alcoholic, are mentally ill, or have some other severe problem. These are the families that have appeared front and center in the media and recovery books under the rubric of "dysfunctional" homes. Indeed, some homes are so clearly disrupted that it seems remarkable that children emerge from them without obvious addictions or emotional problems. But there are two things we need to remember—the majority of children of alcoholics do not become alcoholics, just as the majority of children of abusive parents do not abuse their own children.

At the same time, nearly every family has some flaw or foible that can, in some sense, be called dysfunctional. This unsurprising fact has become a pretext for labeling nearly every family as diseased. As noted in chapter 2, estimates of the number of "children of trauma" have risen as high as 96 percent of the population. It seems as though everyone envies children with alcoholic parents, and people want to claim they, too, are laboring under the weight of their parents' dysfunctions!

Of course, if it is true that everyone comes from a dysfunctional family, then the alcoholic home doesn't seem like such an abnormality. Rather, family problems look to be a basic part of the human condition. And, in many ways, this is true. Every family struggles with similar issues: balky children who don't volunteer for chores or do their homework thoroughly or willingly, parents who frequently criticize or snap at each other, adults who sense the disapproval of their parents or who constantly relive childhood conflicts with their now middle-aged siblings. No one escapes these things entirely. (This is why television series like *The Simpsons* and *Roseanne,* along with those about "good" families like *The Cosby Show,* appeal to so many viewers.) None of our problems as individuals or families is unique.

For example, a lot of families encounter divorce. Though divorce is never a happy situation, it certainly doesn't make a family dysfunctional. What prevents this outcome is that the parents—or one parent—maintain a firm family structure for the children. There may even be some advantages in asking children to help out a single parent and younger siblings. After all, many of the children whom today we protect from any kind of responsibility for themselves or others do not end up the strong human beings we would wish. Plenty of children become more "dysfunctional" than their parents despite having many more resources—including more attention from parents—than their parents ever had.

What about the claims we reviewed in chapter 2 that alcoholism is predestined in the genes, including premature claims that a gene for alcoholism has been discovered?[7] What if, as some researchers have claimed, a particular gene were present in about 70 precent of the worst alcoholics (about 5 percent of the population), but also in 25 percent of the population as a whole? This would mean that fewer than one in five of those with this gene would be likely to become alcoholic. Would it be best, then, to tell children with this gene that they should never drink? For many children, convincing them that they could not help drinking excessively would simply make this outcome more likely to occur. Thus, from what we know of alcoholism, *we would cause more children to become alcoholics by recommending lifetime abstinence than we would rescue from alcoholism with such a warning.*[8]

What would be the best policy for people with this hypothetical gene? We would tell them:

- Be careful to regulate your drinking and be aware of when you are drinking so much that you are getting into trouble.
- Learn the life skills (like communication and self-regard) that make it unnecessary to rely on drinking and that provide gratifications superior to those of excessive drinking or addiction.
- Keep enough in control of your life and develop the structures—like family, work, and recreation—that will make you unlikely to give yourself over to an addiction.

In short, we would tell these "genetically marked" children exactly what we should recommend to everyone as the best policy for avoiding addiction.

Expecting the Best or the Worst: Which Is the Best Way to Forestall a Drinking Problem?

In the era of "children of alcoholics" and "alcoholic genes," people believe the unbelievable—that, if they have a relative who drank too much, their children are likely to do the same, *even when they don't know the relative.* As if going to bars, getting drunk, and neglecting one's family were written in the genes! As preposterous as it sounds, this scenario has been made to seem plausible to a majority of Americans through a constant campaign of misinformation.

Of course, it doesn't pay to paper over a parent's emotional or other problems, either. Ignoring such problems makes it harder for a child to recognize and come to terms with them, as well as to avoid similar problems. Nonetheless, striving to maintain a stable home—even when you or your spouse is impaired in some way—will give your children the best chance to flourish. At the other extreme, accounting for your child's misbehavior as being the inevitable result of your own—or, worse, some distant relative's—problems is the worst way of all to go.

CASE

Selma married a man from a different ethnic background who had different drinking habits from what she was used to. On many weekends, her husband disappeared for a night of drinking. Selma was unsettled by this, but she got used to having her husband stagger home in the middle of the night, struggle out of his clothes, and sleep until noon the next day. She simply took the children to the library on Saturday morning or to church on Sunday.

The kids joked about the whole scene, referring to it among themselves as "Dad's getting down." When the children became teenagers, they experimented with drugs. It never occurred to Selma to relate this to her husband's behavior. When the kids went to college, her husband quit going out on weekends and often drank at home before going to bed.

Without the genetic connection's being conceived, the family progressed into the next generation without incident. All the children were sober individuals who married moderate drinkers; their father reduced his drinking substantially as he got older; and Selma looked at her brood with contentment and satisfaction. Once someone mentioned to Selma, now a grandmother, that she could still join an Al-Anon chapter. "Whatever for?" she asked with astonishment. The alcoholic inheritance had been stamped out of her family.

Obviously, Selma's life was not without problems. On the other hand, would it have been better to identify her husband as an alcoholic or her family as dysfunctional? Should she have given her husband an ultimatum or gotten a divorce? Perhaps many would answer yes. But from Selma's standpoint, she did the right thing, and now, with her children and grandchildren around her and her husband a more relaxed senior citizen, her life seems an enviable one.

CASE

Margaret, a medical social worker, has been divorced from an alcoholic husband for several years. Speaking of her teenage son, she says:

> I've been very concerned about Tim. Since he's been old enough to understand, I've been teaching him about alcoholism, about the genetics of it. I told him he's taking a terrible chance if he drinks. He may drink at first with his friends and think he's fine, and then it may hit him all of a sudden later. I'm trying to teach him that drinking is not going to be a social pleasure for him. I worry that he may think that, because he gets away with it for a few years, it won't happen to him. I tell him it could happen to him at any time.

Tim has continued to drink with his friends—with no guidance, except for his mother's ominous prediction, as to the meaning and possible consequences of his drinking.

Teaching Your Children: *Not* to Drink or *How* to Drink?

Tim's mother should have been more concerned to teach Tim healthy attitudes and sensible guidelines about drinking—guidelines that any parent would do well to practice. It is generally better to teach children *how* to drink than *not* to drink, as long as the teaching parent drinks comfortably himself or herself. Like food, alcohol can be a guilty pleasure, a desperate consolation, a solitary emotional release that reeks with the temptation to excess. Or it can be a shared pleasure, indulged during family and social rituals and restrained by those rituals and the values they represent. If your children do not have the benefit of a clearly positive model at home, you can still try to balance the negative media images of drinking they see with positive ones. Don't let your adolescent children's ideas about drinking be shaped by horror stories of alcoholism.

There is another world out there of moderate and healthy drinking that *everyone* benefits from knowing about. You cannot do better than to approach alcohol just as healthy-drinking individuals, families, and cultures do:

- Don't make a big fuss about drinking. Instead, expose children gradually to alcohol in a family setting in which moderate drinking is a way to enjoy being together and to celebrate special occasions.
- Assume people will behave themselves when they drink, and refuse to associate with those who *don't* act in this way.
- Don't excuse alcoholism as an uncontrollable disease—it gives the problem drinker too easy an "out."

Obviously, training children to drink moderately makes more sense for people for whom moderate drinking comes naturally. In other words, we are preaching primarily to the people who already know what to do. Today, however, in a world where school districts can withhold Grimm story books that describe Little Red Riding Hood taking her grandmother some wine, we want to reassure moderate drinkers that the age-old bromides they learned from their grandmothers (like putting Amaretto on a teething baby's gums) or their grandfathers (who told them a glass of wine completes a good meal) or their fathers (a beer on a hot day with friends is one of the great pleasures in life) are still sound and are worth passing on.[9]

How Young People Grow Away From Parental Alcoholism

Not all parents start with a knowledge of how to transmit healthy attitudes about drinking. What if a parent has a drinking problem? Recall that most alcoholics—*especially in stable families*—do not transmit alcoholism to their children. Indeed, a bad parental example can actually make a young person *less* likely to abuse alcohol: many young people are able to look critically at their parents' excesses and choose a different path for themselves.[10] As moving as many found Louie Anderson's book, *Dear Dad: Letter from an Adult Child,*[11] and as difficult as Anderson's road to adulthood was, most people struggle in less dramatic ways to achieve wholeness despite the presence of alcoholism in their families. Many do not think of themselves as "adult children," but simply as adults.

CASE

Paul grew up with an alcoholic father until he went to college. Paul's father, whose outlook was formed in the era of Hemingway and Fitzgerald, of W. C. Fields and Dean Martin, delighted in anecdotes that treated drinking as naughty, titillating, a kind of forbidden fruit with mysterious powers of good and evil. The father's drinking, which also expressed deep disappointment and anguish over how his life had turned out, was accompanied by considerable cruelty toward his family. In response, Paul swore as a child that he would never touch a drop of alcohol in his life.

Paul attended a special academic high school that kept him and his classmates on a demanding schedule that left them little time to socialize. He did not, in fact, drink until he was twenty-one and nearly out of college. This is the point where some children of alcoholics go straight from abstinence to excess, since the all-or-none model of drinking they have learned does not give them any middle ground to explore.

Paul, however, had been exposed to a different style of drinking. Invited out to dinners with his older sister and her husband, he met graduate students and young professionals who drank beer, wine, and liqueurs in a context of good conversation and enjoyment of the company of others. At first, he declined to join in the drinking. Still, he could not help noticing that this was a far cry from his father's nursing a bottle of vodka all day long. In fact, no one he knew *except* his father drank inappropriately! Finally, when he saw his own friends and peers drinking in the same moderate way as his sister's friends, he began to do the same.

At a party not long after he graduated from college, Paul was embarrassed when someone ribbed him for being mildly intoxicated. Drinking was still new to him, and he was uncomfortable about "looking drunk." Not then or in the two decades since has Paul felt any impulse to drink compulsively. Although he retains a prudent wariness of the effects of alcohol (for example, he rarely drinks alone and avoids drinking when he is angry), he could not be a compulsive drinker and still be the person he is—or associate with the people he esteems.

How Parents Can Help—and How Children Do It on Their Own

In retrospect, two factors worked in Paul's favor. First, he came from an intact family that worked around his father's drinking to maintain an orderly life-style. His mother was a sober, hardworking woman, and his father had a job, ate his meals at home, and participated in family rituals. The household was able to support Paul's educational needs. Second, Paul made his own moves in life, going through a normal maturation that took him away from the peculiarities of his family.

Anthropologist Linda Bennett and her colleagues investigated what prevents children of alcoholics from becoming alcoholics themselves.[12] These researchers found that family social rituals protect children from following the alcoholic parent's example. Those couples that are most deliberate in choosing and preserving elements of a family heritage are the *most protected* from passing alcoholism along. Bennett's research identifies the following methods for breaking the cross-generational transmission of alcoholism:

- *First,* the parental family should preserve its rituals (such as family dinners and holiday celebrations) in spite of the parent's alcoholism. Simply keeping to a consistent family dinnertime can insulate a child from the most destructive consequences of parental alcoholism.

- *Second,* the child should separate from the family sufficiently to form positive relationships elsewhere. This disengagement exposes the child to nonalcoholic models and increases the likelihood of finding nonalcoholic living partners.

- *Third,* the child should choose a spouse who brings nonalcoholic family rituals to their marriage. The opportunity to participate in one's in-laws' family life provides an added buffer against alcoholic drinking.

- *Fourth,* the second-generation couple should deliberately create its own family heritage, in part by separating to some degree from the alcoholic family.

This research directly addresses the primary issue—how *not* to transmit alcoholism—as opposed to our strange preoccupation with marking people, incorrectly, with the inevitable inheritance of alcoholism. Children can bypass family troubles and establish new lifestyles for themselves, whatever disadvantages they have endured. In order for children of alcoholic parents to succeed in drinking normally, they must:

- outgrow social and personal problems their parents had (for example, by leaving a ghetto environment or succeeding economically where their parents had not);
- observe positive models of behavior among their peers and in the community;
- develop the emotional strength to evaluate their childhood experiences critically;
- establish a personal identity distinct from their parents';
- make a conscious decision to separate themselves from their parents' example.

These Life Process principles take us far away from the hubbub about "the gene for alcoholism"—and give much more reason for optimism and hope.

Making Peace with a Parent's Alcoholism

Some spokespeople in the alcoholism field recommend that children be taught to distinguish between the parent as a person and the parent's "disease," so that they can blame the parent's hurtful behavior on the latter. This idea is misguided as a technique for children and for "adult children" who are coming to terms with painful childhood memories. It simply isn't helpful to begin a habit of dissociation from personal responsibility that may make it harder to assume responsiblity for one's own life later on. Whether you are explaining difficult things to a child or struggling to master your own experience, we think you will find the following guidelines more empowering:

▸ Alcohol (or any other addiction) doesn't make people destructive or cruel. Instead it allows people to express cruelty and destructiveness that they feel.

▸ Seeing people as they really are doesn't mean having to hate them. You can feel compassion for their suffering, understand the limited options that led them to make their choices, and still acknowledge their responsibility for their actions.

▸ People are not to blame for their past victimization. But this does not excuse their continued misbehavior.

▸ Accepting the good and the bad, the lovable and the inexcusable, about people equips you to deal with people and to know whom to trust.

Phyllis Hobe, in her book *Lovebound,* observed that the children of alcoholics she met would be better off learning improved coping skills (along the lines described in chapter 15) than undergoing the ritualistic self-labeling that Al-Anon encourages.[13] If you want to participate in a group, make sure it is one that will help you with problem-solving and support you in your efforts to change, not one that focuses on long-ago conflicts and insists that you fit yourself into a preset mold.

What Happens When Kids Take Drugs

The fears parents have about teenage drug and alcohol abuse are like *Invasion of the Body Snatchers:* an alien, mysterious force—in this case, drugs—appears and takes over your child's body, so that this once-normal youth no longer makes emotional contact with you. The result of this vision of drugs and drug effects is the war on drugs. There are two wars on drugs, actually. One is the war on the streets between gun-toting gang members and the police, or between U.S. and Latin American military forces and international drug cartels (or, more usually, poor farmers). The other is the war parents feel they are conducting for the minds and souls of their children, usually with the help of self-assured experts who claim either to prevent drug use or to perform magical treatments that will bring your child back into the fold.

If this is how you see the problem, you will probably welcome drug programs that try to scare children by saying the most frightening things possible about drugs and drug use—like showing people trapped in bottles or dying in car accidents or their brains frying or parents weeping at children's gravesides (all of these advertisements have been presented by private treatment centers with active marketing campaigns, like Fair Oaks, or by the government-supported Partnership for a Drug Free America). If you discover your child is using drugs, you are likely to be frightened and to react impulsively. You may well turn to an expensive, high-powered program, one that practices "tough love" or that attacks the medical disease of "chemical dependence."

The fallacy of the belief that drugs *determine* a person's behavior and that ceasing to use drugs will remedy what ails a person is evident in all the findings about adolescent drug abuse reviewed in chapter 3. *Most* children who use drugs do so casually and ultimately reject drug experimentation, simply because they grow up and have better ways to spend time, and because they have more to lose than to gain from drug use. People who have the worst substance-abuse problems, on the other hand, are those who cannot gain a foothold in life. They more often come from deprived environments or from seriously disrupted homes, or have severe personal or emotional problems. Drugs do not make people indolent, antisocial, or delinquent. Rather, people choose to use drugs because drugs allow them to feel and act in ways they need or want to.

What, then, are the solutions for preventing and treating adolescent substance abuse?

Prevention

A recent summary of evaluations of adolescent substance-abuse prevention programs revealed a remarkable finding—nineteen out of twenty-two programs did not reduce substance use. Indeed, many of these prevention programs led to *increased* substance use by young people![14]

How could such a result occur? Other analyses have examined *which* programs produce the best (or worst) results, and for which groups of young people. By far the worst programs are the ones that, paradoxically, are most popular and oft-used—so-called information campaigns.[15] These programs rely on ex-addicts and alcoholics or other spokespeople to relate negative information about alcohol and drugs to children, often in a very forceful or frightening manner. The epitome of such a speaker is David Toma, who holds forth for five hours at a time, alternately screaming at audiences and telling gory war stories about drug and alcohol abusers killing themselves, one another, or their children.

Toma charges $5,000–$10,000 a speech, and he is in great demand. Why? Because his message apparently reassures communities and parents that they are doing something—even though he disparages parents' efforts and emphasizes how singular and irreplaceable is his role. At the end of one of Toma's sessions, several children typically come forth—as at a revival meeting—to confess their drug use and to seek help. Toma speaks to them after his lectures and then leaves town. What happens to these youngsters—usually the highest-risk kids in the school or community? The evidence we have suggests they rebound more virulently into drug use. Indeed, a made-for-television movie that trumpeted Toma's career and success at reaching young people unselfconsciously revealed that one such unfortunate kid committed suicide after Toma departed!

In comparison studies, other methods have had far more success than information or scare programs.[16] One alternative tries to raise children's self-esteem. However, the impact of these programs is often hard to measure—perhaps because the esteem-building activities or groups seem so artificial. A school self-esteem program often seems paltry when children are bombarded with esteem-destroying experiences, like those regularly encountered in the ghetto.

One type of prevention program that has shown some success with inner-city adolescents offers alternative activities for deprived children—such as the Conservation Corps, or Head Start for younger children. However, here again the problem is the duration of the change. As time passes, children become more and more similar to their cohorts who didn't undergo the program.

Among the programs that have shown good success are those that teach children refusal skills (skills outlined in chapter 15). These programs have worked in teaching kids (primarily middle-class students) to avoid smoking. However, the Rand Corporation recently evaluated a program that produced good success for both suburban and inner-city schools in preventing children from beginning to smoke cigarettes *and* marijuana. The bad news for the program was that it did not affect kids' drinking. Also, those children who *already* smoked continued to smoke, and actually smoked *more* following the program. Finally, although the program had initial success in preventing kids from smoking or using marijuana, the evaluation is still unable to say how permanent this effect will be.[17]

We see that the questions involved in evaluating a prevention program are:

- Does the program produce a positive change?
- For which children does it produce such change? Does this include high-risk children and those who in fact already use or abuse a substance?
- How enduring is the change?

The program evaluated by the Rand Corporation had another interesting component. Having first been presented with reasons *why* people use cigarettes or marijuana (cigarette ads, for example), children then discussed both the appeal of the drug and the reasons for *not* using it. The reasons the kids came up with tended to be couched in terms relevant to young people—cigarettes make you smell bad and less attractive to other girls and boys. What this component adds to the skills training is an emphasis on addressing children's motivations *on their own terms* and on arming children with ways to counteract the arguments that many do find compelling as reasons to begin drug habits, legal or otherwise.

A program conducted by Alan Marlatt and his colleagues at the University of Washington is one of the very few to show success with young people who already have problems. The subjects were college students who had displayed drinking problems. Three groups of students (randomly chosen) were offered a simple assessment session, an informational package, or a skills-training program. After one year, students in the skills program showed the greatest decrease in drinking. The informational package included material on the effects of alcohol, alcoholism, alcohol and the family, and even responsible decision-making in drinking. The skills program was more experiential and practical; it included training in recognizing blood alcohol levels, relaxation techniques, nutrition and exercise, drink-refusal skills, and relapse prevention.

In addition, the skills program contained a session in a mock bar in which student drinkers were given nonalcoholic drinks that they believed contained alcohol. The students became more giddy as they drank until, at the end of the session, they were told they hadn't been drinking alcohol at all. Heavy-drinking students often believe that alcohol makes them more lively and attractive to others. Through this exercise, they now could directly experience that these effects were not the results of drinking, but of their own capacities. They saw that *they,* and not the alcohol, controlled their consciousness.[18]

The few successes in prevention programs, along with the many failures, tell us the following:

1. *Telling kids bad things about drugs and lecturing them not to drink, use drugs, or smoke is ineffective and often counterproductive.* This approach is least useful for the high-risk children who already may be using these substances. Furthermore, the scare approach is disrespectful to children; it lets them know that people don't consider them capable of making their own decisions. Yet these programs are the most common, and preferred, programs in American schools.

2. *Talking to children in their own terms and allowing them to think through the reasons for taking or not taking drugs gives them more power to choose.*

3. *Offering children constructive alternatives makes the most sense and has been shown to help the highest-risk and most disadvantaged children.* Unfortunately, these programs are usually temporary or stopgap, and their effects fade along with memories of the program.

4. *Skills training, which has shown good results in therapy, also has worked well in prevention programs for young people, even those who have abused substances.*

Treatment

The fastest-growing portion of the addiction treatment system has been among young people. In the 1980s, the number of adolescents hospitalized in private mental hospitals—most often for substance abuse—increased by 450 percent (according to a 1990 NBC Nightly News segment with Robert Bazell). Often forced into these expensive inpatient programs, they are all stamped with the same label—"chemically dependent"—and undergo the "treatment" of filling out twelve-step "*mea-culpa*" sheets describing their misdeeds and attending groups. They learn nothing about the coping skills that could possibly keep them out of trouble in the future.

This expensive system is a national disgrace. It is completely ineffective and worse—rife with fraud, mismanagement, overcharges, and child neglect and abuse. The centers that promulgate this approach are often money-making factories that minimize expenses by turning over the treatment of children to recovering addicts or relying on A.A. and group sessions with other inmates. Adolescents thus often spend much of their therapy time with older recovering people, who usually have had worse problems than the teens. These addicts or alcoholics then serve as models and teach children the same tired and dangerous ideas *they* have learned about addiction. In peer-group programs, where kids are coerced into endorsing the approved antidrug ideas of the treatment center, what children learn primarily is how to go along with the group. It is for this reason that relapse is so high—when children return to their communities, they simply fall under the sway of the peers who got them involved with drugs in the first place!

It may sometimes be necessary to separate adolescents from unhealthy—or dangerous—home environments, and some children need to be guarded lest they hurt themselves. But offering this protection is far from bringing about the changes people need in their lives. Treatment and prevention efforts can have little effect unless they address the whole context of a young person's life—the child's family and peer-group environments and the values and skills these environments promote. If treatment is to be beneficial, it must deal with the young person's self-esteem, coping and decision-making skills, relationships with family and friends, and opportunities and motivation for constructive activity.

More to the point, treatment rarely is needed if these fundamental issues have been addressed throughout a young person's upbringing. Coping with adolescent drug abuse after the fact is not the place you want to be. Whatever you do at this stage is likely to be difficult, disruptive, and expensive. But if that is the reality you face, adopt as best you can a calm, problem-solving outlook. Look for help you need, but abide by your instincts when you feel that what you are being told violates your values or isn't helpful. Examine the guidelines presented in the previous chapters on adult addiction for help in keeping your bearings. Here again, the Life Process Program points the way out of troubled waters.

Don't confuse rule-breaking with addiction. Try not to overreact; be aware where your child's conduct falls on the continuum of teenage behaviors. There are normal expressions of adolescent experimentation and adventurousness (things you might have done yourself) that sometimes run afoul of some authority. There is peer-influenced risk-taking that is unhealthy and dangerous, but that most teens undergo during adolescence without lasting ill effects. And there is seriously self-destructive or antisocial behavior. Such behavior can demand disciplinary action; psychological, skills-oriented, and family counseling; or, as a last resort, the removal of adolescents from their current environments. Labeling all teenage involvement with drugs or alcohol "chemical dependency" or "addictive disease" is no help in any of these cases.

When peer-group rituals go too far, it may be difficult to draw the line between normal growing pains and the influence of a pathological environment. A newspaper article titled "The Big 'D' for Denial: Are You Denying Your Child's Problem?" describes a game played by upper-middle-class teenagers called "Century Club":

> To become "Century Club" members, players must drink a shot of beer a minute for a hundred minutes. Peer pressure, combined with the normal devil-may-care attitude of the age group, creates a deadly mix.

This author concludes that "thousands of youngsters, just like yours, have become alcoholics long before they've reached the legal drinking age."[19] Closer to the mark is this comment by Dr. Morris Chafetz, founding director of the National Institute on Alcohol Abuse and Alcoholism:

> Another way American teenagers have been victimized is by recent changes in the definition of a drinking problem. Teens' risky experiments with alcohol, once thought of as a normal part of adolescence, are now called problem drinking.[20]

The great bulk of teenage drinkers, even at the behavioral extreme represented by the "Century Club" (assuming the account is true), will not end up addicted. Still, the fact that the children of well-to-do families assert themselves in such an ugly and dangerous way raises troubling questions about the values—or absence of values—in their social milieu. It is a real concern for the individual, the family, the community, and society. It is not helpful, however, to define and deal with this problem as alcoholism or prealcoholic behavior.

What if your child experiments with drugs? One of the differences between adolescents and their parents that fuels overtreatment of teens is adults' interpretation of drug use as inherently pathological. Whereas adolescents and college students at one time used drugs discreetly and then outgrew drug use on their own, adolescents today are frequently caught by parents and "sentenced" to treatment. But as we saw in chapter 3, a study by psychologists at the University of California found that youths who used drugs moderately had better-integrated personalities than either heavy users or abstainers. Shirley Feldman, deputy director of Stanford University's Center for Study of Family, Children and Youth, commented on this study:

> There's a whole big world out there and, psychologically speaking, experimentation is healthy in most youths. . . . This may be hard for some people to take, but the real issue is knowing when to put on the brakes.[21]

Don't accept treatment uncritically. Treatment for drug use not only is no panacea; it can attack the psyche of the intended beneficiary and can have the opposite of the planned effect. Two psychologists who have investigated adolescent drug use for many years warn that

> treatment programs are purposefully blurring the distinction between use and abuse . . . and preying on the national drug hysteria to scare parents into putting their teenager in treatment with as little provocation as having a beer or smoking a joint. . . . Aside from the adverse effects on the family relationships and long-term consequences of mislabeling the teenager, placing normal youngsters in drug treatment will place them square in the middle of a group of drug-abusing youths. As a result, if they did not enter treatment as abusers, they may well exit it as abusers. . . .[22]

All too often a child is harassed into accepting whatever identity the treatment program thrusts upon him or her. If you come under pressure to ship your child off to a treatment center for "chemical dependency" because of some behavioral infraction, don't ignore your own good sense and your understanding of what is best for your child. If you believe that your child is being mislabeled and railroaded, trust your instincts and resist. Even if your child is seriously misbehaving, you have a better chance to act effectively if you can keep this difficult period in perspective. The way you respond now is likely to influence your life and your child's for a long time. Whatever you choose to do for your child, do not become locked into the idea—or allow your child to become convinced—that he or she has a lifelong disease.

Acknowledge and explore the reasons your child uses drugs or alcohol. Telling a child to "just say no" does not address the reasons why the child has said "yes" in the first place. What does he or she get out of it? What does it mean in his or her social context? What adjustments in his or her life would it take to make drug abuse unnecessary or unpalatable? In other words, don't be afraid to get *inside* the youthful perspective in which drugs are not a "no-no," but a "maybe" or even a "yes-yes." If you just talk like former drug czar William Bennett and say all illicit drug use is evil, you'll be talking past your child, who has already heard and rejected those pronouncements. Instead, control your anxieties enough to understand what is going on with your child. The more seriously you take your child's concerns, the more seriously your child is likely to take your concerns.

Help create alternatives that satisfy the needs the child has tried to satisfy with drugs or alcohol. What motives are driving the drug use: the need to belong, to escape, to prove oneself, to feel grown-up? How closely is the drug use tied to the child's peer-group involvements? Is there a way of relating differently to these same peers, or is it desirable (and possible) for the child to find a different peer group? Would the child benefit most from independent activities and involvements that you can encourage or support? How are you contributing to the problems the child is trying to remedy through drug use? But remember, whatever changes you decide are needed, you can't just prescribe these remedies because *you* think they should be satisfying enough to replace drugs. You have to work from the child's subjective experience with drugs—where they fit in the fabric of the child's life.

Reassert standards of responsible behavior. Understandable as the child's drug use may be, it undoubtedly threatens the fulfillment of positive goals. You need to make this clear, together with the all-important principle that your child must accept the basic obligations that all people have to one another and to society. On the one hand, you still need to empathize with and support, not reject and disown, a child who uses drugs. On the other, the child cannot ignore your standards with respect to school, family, the community, and the law. To allow your child to ignore these standards for the reason that he or she takes drugs is to give up the standards and to support the child's decision to rely on drugs.

Promote and nurture positive values. When an adolescent develops a serious drug or alcohol problem, some difficult questions present themselves: Has the child had a chance to form a secure sense of value, to understand that there are things more important than television, the latest fashions, and mindless conformity—things such as achievement and contributing to other people's lives? Does the child have a predictable household routine and a quiet place to study? Does the family encourage and reward learning and achievement? Is there sufficient disapproval at home of antisocial acting out, but not harsh repression that stifles creativity or normal high spirits? Is the child taught integrity in dealings with people outside the household? Does he or she gain self-respect from doing things well, and do you recognize and reward these accomplishments? Do family members share their thoughts and feelings and express affection and praise for one another?

Unless you and your child address these questions, any treatment the child receives will be an empty exercise. If, on the other hand, these questions are addressed throughout the child's early upbringing, addiction treatment is very unlikely to be an issue. For this reason, the discussion of treatment ultimately leads to a discussion of values—the core of the Life Process Program.

Your Job Is to Create a Valuable Person

It should be welcome news that drugs are not so powerful and the world not so arbitrary as we might fear. Yet for some parents this message is unsettling. The drug-as-bogey myth serves the same purpose as the alcoholism-gene myth, in that it enables parents troubled by their children's misbehavior (or guilty about their own conduct) to blame problems on external forces. If the source of the behavior lies in genetic programming, or in the power of a drug, or in a malign peer group, then it isn't your fault. Yes, it *is* comforting to know that you aren't completely responsible for your children's actions in an environment full of all kinds of influences and pressures. But we—and our children—need to believe that we can govern our own lives. This confidence is the opposite of addiction.

We give our children the best chance of avoiding addiction and living a constructive, fulfilling life by transmitting positive values (those described in chapter 11) and life skills. The issue is not whether children will, at some time or another, drink too much or try an illicit drug; it is whether *their lives are about something more than that.* Neither adults nor adolescents will be corrupted by drugs if they have a structure of values, attitudes, beliefs, and activities incompatible with frequent or excessive intoxication. Values become real for children when parents live them rather than preach them, and when they are conveyed in an atmosphere of mutual respect. Specifically, children can withstand the pressures toward drug abuse and other antisocial and self-destructive misbehavior when they believe—and feel—the following:

- You are responsible to yourself and to others for making your way in life and for controlling your behavior.
- Your own feelings, rights, and well-being are important, and so are those of others.
- Commitments to others are to be honored.
- Mutual relationships are the cornerstone of a meaningful and valuable life.
- Fun, adventure, creativity, and surprise are part of a full life.
- Thinking about yourself, your relationships, and your behavior will make you a better person.
- You need a serious purpose or purposes in life.
- With all its risks and dangers, the world is a manageable place in which you can succeed and be happy if you apply yourself in pursuit of your goals.

▸ Exercising your problem-solving skills in challenging situations (including making mistakes) is an essential part of learning and growing.

▸ When things get tough, there are people you can turn to for help.

▸ Knowing how to do something well is among life's most gratifying experiences, and nothing else can replace it.

▸ Productive activity is satisfying in itself, brings admiration from others, and enables you to achieve key rewards and goals in life.

▸ Physical health is an essential foundation for well-being and contentment.

These items, which for the most part could have come from a nineteenth-century schoolbook, constitute the moral atmosphere of a family unlikely to be threatened by drug or alcohol abuse. If you value yourself, the things you make or do, and your relationships with and responsibilities toward others, you will not become seriously addicted in the long run. This is because these values and abilities directly contradict the experience of addiction. Keep in mind that addiction is an experience of fear, passivity, irresponsibility, the perception that the world is irrational and out of control, an exclusive focus on your own needs, preoccupation with negative emotions, lack of self-confidence and coping skills, and avoidance of challenges by accepting the easiest, most predictable solution for life—a drug or another repetitive habit.

CHAPTER 18

WHERE THE SOLUTIONS REALLY LIE

•

RE-ESTABLISHING COMMUNAL TIES

ALTHOUGH the Life Process Program is oriented primarily toward self-help and effective therapy, we cannot change America's addiction problems without addressing our social and physical environment. Even the best addiction treatment will not significantly affect America's overall levels of addiction. Treatment is simply too expensive, too inexact, and too belated for therapy to do anything but apply first aid. The only way we can really do something about addiction is to create a world worth living in.

In place of our current failed public policies toward drug and alcohol abuse, this chapter outlines what we need to do to control addiction, to address our social problems more effectively, to preserve the freedom that has made our society exceptional, and to deal compassionately with substance abusers and addicts who are willing to participate in their cures. What we must *stop* includes:

- punishing casual drug users while absolving chronic drug abusers of responsibility for their crimes because they are "addicted";
- accepting intoxication or addiction as an excuse for failing to meet normal obligations to others, and especially for crimes of violence;
- imposing on children and adults the appealing but self-serving morality tales of addiction served up by the worst addicts and criminals;
- aggressively recruiting people into costly, ineffective modes of treat-

ment while suppressing less costly, less invasive modes that have been shown to work better;

- violating people's autonomy over their bodies through random or universal drug testing;

- mandatory sentencing of people to treatment or to A.A. and similar organizations that are thinly veiled religious cults;

- viewing addiction as an individual pathology while ignoring the social problems that generate addiction;

- the decimation of the poorest communities and the isolation of nearly all communities.

These policies only reinforce the addictive mind-set. Instead, we must transform a society that rewards addictiveness into one that gives us stronger reasons *not* to be addicted than to be addicted. Ultimately, this is something we can do *only* as a society. We're all in it together.

The Law

Our statutory and judicial responses to drug use, alcoholism, and crimes committed by drug users and drunkards are based on fear and misinformation. The case against drugs is not as dire as it is incessantly portrayed to be by public officials, treatment personnel, and the media. No drug is inevitably addictive or regularly produces "loss of control." We must recognize that, as a matter of course, people regulate their behavior when drugs are available, even when they take drugs, and even when they become intoxicated!

Today, on the basis of our mistaken ideas about drug addiction, we punish controlled users, yet we excuse addicts and alcoholics who commit crimes against life and property. If an athlete said he smoked marijuana happily in the privacy of his home without bothering anyone, he would be kicked out of professional sports. On the other hand, if he beats his wife and plays lackadaisically but explains it is because of his drinking or drug use (like Darryl Strawberry), he is congratulated for his bravery. This reversal of reasonable, civilized standards is rationalized by the disease model of alcoholism and drug addiction.

Darryl Strawberry has over the years abused his wife, fathered illegitimate children, fought with teammates, and complained that he wasn't appreciated (Strawberry demanded that his salary be raised from $1.8 million to $3 million after batting .225 in 1989). After Strawberry was treated for alcoholism at the Smithers Center in New York, the City and County of Los Angeles declined to prosecute him for assaulting his wife with a gun. According to a Los Angeles prosecutor, Strawberry's "problems with alcohol in our judgment lie at the root of the family problems that resulted in his arrest." For his part, Strawberry declared, "I'm a sick person getting well." Teammates who had fought with Strawberry for years, treatment professionals, and sports columnists were almost universal in their praise for Strawberry when he entered treatment instead of standing trial.[1]

We have already seen that societies that declare certain behavior off limits and refuse to accept intoxication as an excuse have fewer of these behaviors. Remember the remarkable finding in chapter 2: of 17,515 arrests recorded in New York's Chinatown between 1933 and 1949, there were no reports of public drunkenness or drunken disorderliness! In the United States today, by explaining to people that intoxication and addiction are permissible reasons for misconduct, we simply guarantee that more such incidents will occur. And, of course, because ordinary criminals *do* frequently drink and use drugs, they will have readily available these excuses for their crimes. Drinking and drug taking are cited increasingly as reasons why people steal, kill, and commit all sorts of crimes.

In the case of drug users, we frequently explain behavior that we say we want to control—like child abuse—by claiming that people who, say, smoke crack can't be expected to control themselves. Drug users often tell us (not only in court, but in TV features on drugs, such as those shown by PBS) that their cocaine use is the reason they commit crimes against others, including their family members. If only we took crack, we hear, then we, too, would steal, abuse our children, and perhaps prostitute them as well to get money for drugs. Yet data presented in chapter 3 show that most cocaine users—including crack users—don't become compulsive users or commit crimes.

In fact, middle-class crack addicts who quit the drug usually give as their reason for quitting that if they maintained their habits they might be led to behave in more antisocial ways, like stealing. In other words, they *refuse* to commit crimes to continue their addictions, just as most smokers would quit smoking if they had to prostitute themselves to continue their habits. Yet addicts who have violated all their civilized obligations are presented as typical drug users, thus becoming a strange kind of role model. In other words, we assume that drug users who *don't* commit crimes are just like addicts who do. We reason that these law-abiding users are actually in the greatest danger, since they *haven't* yet become criminals and addicts, and thus they most need to be discovered and stopped.

Alcoholism and drug addiction are not the only addictive diseases used to defend people for their misconduct and crimes. Baseball player Wade Boggs explained a long-standing extramarital affair as symptomatic of his "sexual addiction." More frightening is the profusion of defenses used for abusing and killing family members. Women who have killed their loved ones have successfully used PMS and postpartum depression as their defenses. Increasingly, women (like Francine Hughes in *The Burning Bed*) use the battered-woman syndrome to explain why they kill abusive husbands instead of leaving them. In domestic disputes, we are often faced with "dueling diseases": whereas Charlotte Fedders explained in her book, *Shattered Dreams* (written with Laura Elliott), that she couldn't leave her husband because she suffered from the battered-woman syndrome, he defended himself successfully for battering her on the grounds of his depression. Rather than helping people overcome or avoid violence, these disease defenses merely abet and excuse family assaults.

The legal ramifications of our addiction mythology have become unworkable and out of control. We need major revisions of our attitudes and laws governing drugs and other addictions:

1. *Drug use in which the only crime is taking the drug should be legalized.*

Drug use doesn't cause crimes, and people shouldn't be punished for simply using drugs. Drug use, intoxication, and addiction should not be punishable in themselves. Our courts are overloaded to the point of paralysis with trivial cases of drug possession and minor drug selling, because we insist that drug use *per se* be made into a crime. As a result, our legal system has become almost incapable of dealing with people who commit crimes against property and people, including homicide, whether or not these criminals are under the influence of drugs and alcohol.

Many fear that legalizing drugs will increase addiction and drug-associated crime, as though the only thing keeping most ordinary citizens from becoming drug addicts were laws against drug use. But most people have internal brakes or stabilizers built into the very logic of their lives that limit any involvement they have with drugs. Indeed,

Americans have sharply curtailed the most potent drug addiction of all—smoking—even though it is legal. They have done so primarily in response to growing public disapproval of smoking. We have reviewed the evidence showing that crack and cocaine are no more addictive than other drugs such as alcohol, and less so than cigarettes. The crucial issue for minimizing drug use under a policy of legalization is that we as a society not endorse intoxication the way we have endorsed gambling.

As for the fear of violence caused by the chemical effects of crack, Ira Glasser, executive director of the American Civil Liberties Union, reported the following:

> A recent study of crack and homicide in New York showed that three-quarters of "drug-related" homicides were caused by territorial disputes and other incidents related to the criminal trafficking system. Only 7.5 percent of the homicides were related to the effects of the drug itself, and two-thirds of those involved alcohol, not crack.[2]

Two researchers who conducted a study of crack-using women in inner-city Oakland and San Francisco concluded, "The relative incidence of problem users of crack is no different from other drugs." They noted as well that "no pharmacologically caused link between crack and violence has been established," and that the violence occurring in connection with the illegal distribution and sale of crack "is not, as a rule, perpetrated by people who are high on crack."[3]

Claiming that drugs make people criminals hurts us all. The uncontrolled behavior of some drug users (and, more often, drug merchants) has been used as a pretext for abridging the liberties of everyone. Indiscriminate search-and-seizure laws have met with public approval because Americans have been convinced that their well-being is imminently threatened by neighbors using drugs. But expensive government raids on garden stores and people who buy equipment to grow marijuana plants in their basements are not likely to have a major impact on America's addiction problems. They do signify a growing government and public indifference to personal rights.[4]

If we de-demonize drug use, we can undercut the violent illicit drug market and redirect resources to essential community-development programs. We will also be able to *liberalize the medical use of currently illegal drugs.* One television news magazine described the case of a Vietnam veteran whose farm was raided and who was ruined financially because he tried to raise marijuana to treat his own glaucoma. Surely, this is the *reductio ad absurdum* of American moralism about drugs. Likewise, experiments show that nonaddict hospital patients do not enjoy narcotic drugs and that, when allowed to regulate their own analgesia, they rapidly cut back on intravenous narcotics, using *less* of the drug than physicians prescribe.[5] Opiates should be freely available to surgical patients and those with intractable pain, and people should be allowed to regulate their own intravenous flow of narcotics in hospitals.

Similarly, a more low-key attitude toward currently illegal drugs would allow us to proceed with another sensible public-health measure: namely, the distribution of clean needles to drug users who otherwise would risk contracting AIDS from shared needles. A policy of not exempting drug users from accountability for their actions does *not* mean exposing them unnecessarily to a plague whose spread must be checked for the sake of everyone's well-being. If we understand the Life Process view that drug use is a coping mechanism that people learn and can unlearn, we can work with addicts to help them unlearn it. Meanwhile, moralistic attitudes toward drugs and addiction must not interfere with appropriate public-health responses to real disease.

2. *All crimes against people, property, and society should be prosecuted without regard to criminals' prior substance use.*

Addiction and intoxication should not be entered as defenses or as extenuating circumstances to soften the crime or its penalities. Indeed, the only way intoxication should be considered is as an aggravating factor, so that people should be punished more severely for crimes like reckless driving or assault committed when under the influence of drugs or alcohol.

3. *Random drug testing is illegal and should be terminated everywhere in America.*

Drug testing without reasonable cause is an unconstitutional assault on traditional American values of personal privacy. Testing people for drug use that can't be observed directly disregards public behavior in favor of private biochemistry. It is as if we don't care how people perform at their jobs and as citizens; we just want to know what they are doing with their bodies on their own time.

We intrude more and more into people's personal behavior as Americans seemingly become oblivious to their birthrights. A former secretary of the Department of Health and Human Services explained the need for coerced drug testing in terms chillingly reminiscent of McCarthyism: " 'Absence of Evidence' in an employee does not mean 'Evidence of Absence.' "[6] In other words, not displaying illegal or irresponsible behavior does not protect you from an assumption of guilt. Justice Thurgood Marshall wrote in his dissent from a U.S. Supreme Court decision allowing random drug testing of railroad workers, "History teaches that grave threats to liberty often come in times of urgency, when constitutional rights seem too extravagant to endure."[7]

Today, rather than resist pressures to submit to drug testing, organizations proudly announce their intention to conduct urine tests on their own members as *proof* that they have nothing to hide. As an example, consider the program at Johns Hopkins Hospital:

> Mandatory random drug and alcohol testing is to be carried out among 1,500 staff physicians here at Johns Hopkins Hospital, one of the leading medical research institutes in the United States. The testing was decided on unanimously by the medical board and the board of trustees because the hospital wants to demonstrate its concern about providing a drug-free environment for staff and patients. . . . The plan for random drug testing has met *no* opposition from staff doctors or medical students.[8]

Drug testing is random in more ways than one. People who are regularly prescribed tranquilizers (like Betty Ford) or amphetamines (like Kitty Dukakis) or antidepressants (like those being treated for depression, obsessive-compulsive disorder, obesity, etc.) will not be penalized for positive drug tests. The sensible addicts, then, will be sure to bring a doctor's note.

4. *Work-performance standards and other standards of conduct in American society (for example, in schools) need to be reaffirmed.*

We already have ample laws defining and disallowing misconduct, and employers should have ways to make sure people do their jobs other than by examining their urine. Every large-scale effort to test workers finds imperceptible amounts of drug use (even these few positives are often discounted as testing errors), and the programs are massively expensive.[9]

If the only guarantee against intoxication on the part of bus drivers and pilots is constant drug testing, then we will surely miss the majority of drunken transportation workers. It is simply impossible to test all pilots and drivers whenever they get in a vehicle. (Incidentally, although intoxicated airline pilots have become a major issue, the FAA has never traced a commercial passenger airline crash or fatality to a drunken pilot.[10]) Could urine testing have been employed to prevent the most famous driver accused of drunkenness—Exxon *Valdez* Captain Joseph Hazelwood—from grounding his ship? (It is important to note, however, that a jury refused to convict Hazelwood of reckless endangerment, because all witnesses testified that Hazelwood was not drunk on board the *Valdez*.)

The best way to prevent drunkenness on the job by boat and airline pilots and others in sensitive positions (like workers in nuclear plants) is to alert everyone, those in sensitive positions and those in contact with them, that intoxication on the job is intolerable and must be reported. It violates the individual's obligations to the community and to public safety—a violation that rightly arouses the outrage of others. But violation of the public trust seems to be tolerated even by those charged with protecting our safety, like urban police departments.

CASE

The New York Times ran as a front-page story the case of Robert Biangazzo, a former New York cop who sold his gun and badge to get cocaine. The story was presented to prove "that even blatant drug addiction can flourish undetected . . . [and to show] the difficulty of weaning anyone, police officer or not, off drugs."[11]

Biangazzo was on antidrug duty. During his training and service, he consistently used angel dust, marijuana, and cocaine and drank excessively, often with fellow trainees or officers. Biangazzo spent tremendous amounts of money, not only on drugs, but on automobiles and accessories like gold jewelry for his girlfriend. He robbed crack dealers, and eventually traded his gun and badge for drugs. Biangazzo's drug use was finally discovered, and he was sent to treatment, after which he was dismissed from the force.

The point of the newspaper story was the old saw that drugs can bring anyone down, even a cop. It is actually a tale about a deeply disturbed young man whose entire life had been pervaded by drug use and deception, who shirked the duties of a police officer—committing more crimes as a cop than he solved or prevented—and whose behavior was not only ignored but supported by fellow officers. He wasn't in a culture of denial but, rather, one of criminal corruption and moral degradation.

The article argues for the old standbys: random drug testing and treatment. In fact, drug testing had already been introduced into the New York Police Department when Biangazzo served between 1984 and 1986. Hence, the article argues for better and more random testing. As for treatment, in the three years since he left the force, Biangazzo has alternated between treatment and addiction. He was interviewed at an addiction treatment center "where he is undergoing his eighth attempted cure in half a dozen different places."[12]

Likewise, dismissing employees (from factory workers to baseball players) who are apprehended for incidental drug use, while retaining addicts who are impaired in their job performance, is the opposite of a social policy that encourages responsibility and productivity. If your mailman is an alcoholic or a drug abuser who doesn't always show up for work and doesn't cover his route in time to complete his deliveries, you are told when you complain: "We can't fire anybody if alcohol or drugs are involved." Increasingly, this is becoming a refrain of American labor.

5. *Replace coerced treatment with an awareness of the penalties for not fulfilling one's social responsibilities.*

As we have made clear throughout this book, there is no justification for forcing people into treatment, particularly when they haven't committed a crime. Such coercion is often rationalized by the handy assertion that a person is "in denial." It may be enforced by emotionally brutal "interventions" based on the premise "that anyone—especially a recovering alcoholic—has the right to invade another's privacy, as long as he's trying to help."[13] As reported in an article entitled "Drunk Until Proven Sober," a city employee in Vancouver, Washington, was falsely branded an alcoholic, forced into treatment, and eventually fired after having offended her superiors by testifying in support of a co-worker's claim of sexual harassment.[14]

Even if coercion were acceptable on moral and constitutional grounds, the popular treatments to which people are committed are simply too ineffective to justify it. In fact, evidence on the impact of remanding drunk drivers into treatment is that people are less likely to be rearrested if they undergo ordinary judicial sanctions instead![15] In a thoroughgoing matched comparison of eight counties in California, drunk-driving offenders whose licenses were suspended or revoked had fewer crashes over the next four years than those who were "rehabilitated."[16] In other words, penalizing people for breaking laws, while letting them know we expect them to change, is not only the appropriate legal procedure but the most effective way of discouraging drunken misbehavior. Family-violence studies reveal similar results. At one time, police were encouraged to negotiate with an abusive spouse and to encourage the family to work things out on their own. Comparison studies revealed, however, that arresting the abuser was the most effective means of preventing future family violence.[17]

In a staggering lapse of constitutional scruple, courts are routinely mandating first-time drunk drivers to attend Alcoholics Anonymous meetings.[18] The rationales offered by this practice—that drunk drivers usually are alcoholics or problem drinkers and that A.A. is an effective "treatment"—do not hold water. In any case, forcing people into twelve-step organizations is a form of spiritual coercion. Even where the group refrains from the typical A.A. emphasis on God, *forcing people into conversion experiences where they must adopt a new self-concept—that of addict—is illegal and immoral.* It cannot be supported constitutionally. But informing people of right and wrong and of what the society, community, family—or you personally—will tolerate is not only correct, but necessary.

6. *Offer people treatment, not as an alternative to punishment, but as help for those who are seeking to set their lives straight.*

Today, not only are people often forced into treatment, but they are allowed to escape punishment if they accept treatment. The temptation to enter treatment whether or not one thinks one is addicted—or cares to do anything about it—is overwhelming. Of course, people should be allowed to seek whatever treatment they feel will help them. In particular, therapies like those outlined in chapter 15 offer people ways of dealing with their problems other than through violence and addiction. These treatments, which assist people in finding more constructive and satisfactory alternatives in life, should be widely available on a voluntary basis.

Although this approach may sound too simple and straightforward to be true, the criminal-justice system has begun to recognize its validity. A Maryland judge ruled in 1989 that an atheist could not be made to attend A.A., because A.A. attempts to alter people's beliefs about themselves and about spiritual matters (like the existence of a "higher power"). Moreover, the judge wrote, court-mandated A.A. attendance burdens a voluntary fellowship with unwilling participants. The defendant's attorney, Ellen Luff, concluded:

> Those making drug policy must be wary of trampling on the First Amendment in their zeal to help or cure drug and alcohol abusers. . . . Attempting to precipitate a conversion experience [means] the First Amendment has been violated.[19]

As an example of how the courts can handle reasonable, voluntary treatment options, the judge in this case outlined a policy to be followed henceforth in place of coerced A.A. attendance:

> After a defendant is found guilty of a crime involving drugs or alcohol, if probation is to be granted, the defendant will be given several weeks to devise his or her probation program. After the program is reviewed by the probation department, the court will then sentence the defendant to comply with the terms of probation the defendant has designed. If the defendant does not comply with the agreed upon terms, then he or she will be incarcerated.[20]

Here, just because people have misbehaved or committed a crime, they are not treated like incompetent infants or imbeciles who have no hope of rectifying their misconduct. Instead, the burden is placed on them to do so.

Government Policy

U.S. government policy for combating drug use by its citizens is to encourage drug testing, coerce people into treatment, arrest drug users, and expand police (and military) powers. Increasingly, our foreign policy—including invading foreign countries or supporting military operations by local forces against farmers and leftist political groups—is determined by our perceptions of how well other nations are responding to our drug problems. All of these policies are said to be required because Americans are being assailed with drugs, internally and from overseas. If drugs are killers, and people—especially children—can't be expected to resist their impact, then clearly this policy is necessary.

On the other hand, as we noted in chapters 3 and 17, drug use by adolescents and college students has declined steadily since the early eighties, and the two drugs against which we have failed to make headway with young people—alcohol and tobacco—are legal and are produced and sold domestically. But once we as a society decide that an experience is uncontrollable, that we have no chance to resist its appeal, the horse is already out of the barn. We can try more and more tactics to save people from their own actions, but these efforts are doomed to fail. Instead, we are infantilizing Americans by convincing them they cannot resist or control drug or alcohol use, that they need to be protected from their own urges, and that they may be forced into treatment for their own good.

Once again, our policy is based on a misunderstanding of the nature and sources of addiction. People do not become addicted to drugs accidentally, or because they are unwittingly exposed to a drug, thinking it is a pleasurable intoxicant or a medical analgesic, only to discover that it has suddenly taken control of their lives. The small number of people who become addicted systematically pursue the feelings associated with intoxication (such as a sense of power or comfort) because they can't get these feelings in any other way. These unfulfilled needs that lead people to compulsive and self-destructive acts are best remedied in the following ways:

1. *Instead of overseas interdiction efforts, Americans must address the domestic conditions that spawn drug and other addictions.*

Our idea seems to be that America's interests and needs should dictate the flow of world events—including whether people should live or die—when it comes to keeping drugs out of the United States. Of course, we are only fooling ourselves with such misguided efforts, wasting vital resources and diverting attention from the conditions we must address at home in order to redirect our society. Our primary need as a nation is to integrate a growing minority underclass into the mainstream values and economy of our country. To do this, we must develop (a) educational programs that teach children skills with which to participate in the economy and cope with life, (b) adequate housing in which people can live reasonably secure lives, (c) communities that are safe enough to make normal human life possible, (d) health and nutritional care that protects those most vulnerable, particularly the young, (e) a comprehensive policy toward contraception, abortion, and prenatal care that makes sure children are born into families that want them, safeguards prenatal health, and gives the newborns some reasonable hope of succeeding in the world.

2. *America can succeed at its social goals only by maintaining a viable economy.*

Successive administrations proudly announce renewed campaigns to reach Mars and build space stations, along with devoting money to Star Wars and continued massive military-hardware development programs. Meanwhile, we *expand* rather than limit Social Security benefits and other entitlement programs. One thinks of an improvident friend or relative who—after buying an expensive new car and taking a Caribbean vacation—borrows money to pay his credit-card bills. America is awash in uncontrollable debt, and we seemingly lack the national and individual will even to *consider* making the sacrifices necessary to reduce it. We need to change our sense of entitlement (middle- and upper-class Americans as well as the underprivileged) when it begins to endanger our economy.

Curtailing our out-of-control entitlement programs is not a popular idea to those who work in human services, or to most Americans. But, by the end of the century, we will have fewer employed Americans supporting an ever-expanding pyramid of retired citizens. At the same time, we continue to spread our net to encompass pension, insurance, and disability payments for new diseases—for example, Social Security has now ruled alcoholics to be disabled and to require government subsidies when they can't work because of their drinking. Health-care expenses generally in the United States are the greatest per capita of any nation in the world—and they are expanding more rapidly than those of any other advanced country. Meanwhile, the *fastest-growing part of the private health-care system* is hospital treatment for emotional problems, primarily substance abuse. In 1990, *The Wall Street Journal* revealed that, "for companies of more than 5,000 employees, psychiatric and 'substance abuse' [health-care] benefits rose 47% last year."[21]

We must cut these costs by *making rational allocations of—that is, humanely rationing—health care* so that our health-care expenditures will do the most good. We simply cannot spend the massive sums required to save incredibly premature infants who will never lead normal lives, to maintain artificially the lives of people who are on the verge of death and will never regain their functioning, to pursue every care option all the time. In most cases, the benefits we think we gain from unrestricted access to health care are illusory and even counterproductive. And as health care swamps the rest of the economy, we will cease to be able to provide needed care—even reasonable and cost-effective kinds—for more and more Americans. This need for cost-effective health care applies especially to addiction treatment.[22]

3. *Replace medical models of alcoholism/addiction treatment with community-, skills-, and values-oriented counseling.*

Hospital treatment for alcoholism and addiction was originally connected to the detoxification of extremely alcoholic and addicted individuals. This treatment has no impact on the addiction problem, even for the advanced addicts and alcoholics to whom it was originally applied. It is the most expensive treatment, yet it addresses none of the community, environmental, and personal issues crucial to reversing addiction. It is even *less* appropriate for the mainstream of middle-class patients who now enter addiction treatment. It is least effective of all, and most counterproductive, for the growing youth population in mental and chemical-dependence hospitals.

In a 1990 report that (like many before it) questions the effectiveness of America's allocation of resources to combat alcoholism, the Institute of Medicine of the prestigious National Academy of Sciences has called for *Broadening the Base of Treatment for Alcohol Problems.* The report "recommends that the full range of alternative treatment settings and modalities be established in each community. . . ." Such a comprehensive treatment system would not be biased in favor of the most profitable forms of treatment (i.e., private hospital programs). Instead, it would finance treatment as long (and only as long) as needed "in the lowest cost social model or medical model setting of appropriate quality to which the individual is matched." Finally, the report recognizes, "a community component of treatment is an essential part of the treatment system."[23]

The Institute of Medicine's prescription is closely connected to what this book has been about. The Life Process Program emphasizes that treatments that work are directed toward improving the ways people manage their lives and cope within their immediate environments. Such treatment nurtures the skills people need to function effectively. It appeals to basic values in people's lives and asks what values people need to develop or express in order to participate in society. Most of all, it relies on a community to instill values, to restrain misbehavior, and to help people cope. There is a limit to how well any treatment can hope to succeed if it does not rely on a community, or if there is no community to rely on.

Community-oriented Treatment for Individuals

What are the implications for individual treatment of a view of addiction that emphasizes the importance of the community? Addiction treatments that rely on communities oriented toward functional coping have had good success. For example, evaluations have given positive evidence of the success of therapeutic communities (TCs), which we described in chapter 16.[24] TCs have ambitious goals for their clients. These communities seek an end point to treatment at which a person is expected to have become an "ex-addict." In this type of program, a successful outcome requires people to become fully functioning members of their home communities.

Creating therapeutic communities to combat addiction raises a troubling question, however. Why are there so many people who need years of reconditioning therapy to learn how to live and participate in society? Is there any way to influence this process fundamentally, at an earlier point in people's lives? At best, a therapeutic community is a special environment structured to have some of the beneficial characteristics of a natural environment. Resorting to this elaborately contrived mode of treatment constitutes an admission that we're not doing many simpler, more obvious things to help people in their "real" lives.

Based on demonstrated efficacy,[25] the Community Reinforcement Approach (CRA)—described in chapter 16—should be adopted as the most effective currently available treatment for alcoholism. Instead of placing a person in an artificial treatment environment, CRA treats the person in the community, and community resources are mobilized to support the person's recovery. This approach most closely resembles natural recovery that occurs outside treatment altogether. Since CRA doesn't require brick-and-mortar structures and teams of medical personnel, it is the most cost-effective treatment on record for alcoholism.

Community-based treatments (such as those recommended by the Institute of Medicine) are almost invisible in the United States. Between 1966 and 1975, however, Iowa had in place a low-cost treatment system steeped in completely natural community settings. Starting with Cedar Rapids, forty-three Iowa communities formed citizens' groups, raised funds locally, and hired community alcohol coordinators to organize individual treatment efforts. The citizens who undertook these spontaneous initiatives saw that neither prison nor the state mental hospital served the needs of alcoholics, and they wanted to develop a flexible, humane approach that directly answered those needs.

Local efforts were supported by the University of Iowa, which trained the community coordinators, monitored results, and gave helpful feedback. Coordinators were chosen "mainly for their common sense and their empathy for alcoholics" and were encouraged to deal with each case on an individualized basis. The director of alcohol studies at the University of Iowa, Harold Mulford, described the work of one of the coordinators:

> Bob explains to alcoholics that no one can give them, or sell them, a solution for their problem. They must get it the old-fashioned way—work for it. Any benefit they get from others' efforts to help them is in proportion to the effort they themselves put into the process. To encourage widespread responsibility, Bob does nothing for the alcoholic that the alcoholic can assume responsibility for, and he does nothing for the alcoholic that someone else in the community will take responsibility for.
>
> The coordinator is an outreacher, a motivator, an advisor, a consultant, a friend, a confidant, and a follow-upper. . . . Serving as a catalyst for the natural rehabilitation forces, he helps alcoholics restore and strengthen social relationships—through job, family, Alcoholics Anonymous, church and social activities. He also helps them use appropriate community services and resources to resolve whatever medical, legal, financial, religious, or other problems they might have.[26]

In 1975, however, large-scale federal and state funds for treatment became available through the National Institute on Alcohol Abuse and

Alcoholism (the creation of the NIAAA, paradoxically, was spearheaded by alcoholic Iowa Senator Harold Hughes, who then went on to make a fortune in the private alcoholism-treatment business[27]). The community centers were placed under the State Alcoholism Authority, which imposed the orthodox medical model of treatment. As Mulford tells it:

> The citizens' efforts, being built from the bottom up, were reprogrammed with directives from the top down. The centers' operations were soon standardized, professionalized, and thoroughly bureaucratized. . . . The new state authority designed its own monitoring system—not for research, but to police the centers' conformity to the state's directives.[28]

Despite all the lip service paid to volunteerism in America, a grassroots initiative—one for which people willingly appropriated local funds because they could see what was going on and feel they were part of it—was suppressed by the momentum of American bureaucracy. The dissolution of the Iowa community system was begun under a Republican (Nixon-Ford) administration. Jimmy Carter, a man who extolled community values, did nothing to reverse it, nor did Ronald Reagan, a philosopher of self-help and independence from the federal government.

In President Bush's fiscal-1991 budget earmarking about $10.5 billion for drug abuse, roughly $3.5 billion was targeted for drug treatment/prevention programs. Another billion dollars or more was directed to alcoholism treatment. George Bush was not about to dismantle our massive treatment bureaucracy, despite his espousal of "a thousand points of light" and community service, and these funds were to be channeled into the standard list of medically oriented, status-quo treatments.

Government expenditures under Bush have been roughly equally matched by private treatment expenditures, putting America's 1991 figure for treatment of alcohol and drug abuse at around $10 billion. Meanwhile, the Democrats, represented by Senator Joseph Biden, have had only one suggestion for enhancing our war on drugs: don't spend less on interdiction and police efforts, but increase overall expenditure for our drug problems to $15 billion—the greatest increase to be in treatment and for researching the medical cure for addiction (Biden sees putting about $1 billion alone into researching the biological sources of addiction).

Looking at the results of the medicalization of the Iowa community program can give us a feeling for where we have been going nationally—and where we are headed even more rapidly today. In the two years after the 1975 statewide program was introduced in Iowa, the number of centers increased, paperwork vastly multiplied, accreditation requirements were instituted, and hospital treatment became the principal means for addressing alcoholism. The recovery rate for alcoholics, so far as it could be measured, was about the same as before. But only half as many clients were being served, at twice the cost!

Meanwhile, one rural county decided that it would be less costly to continue to fund their own center than to meet the requirements for state and federal funds. They managed to keep their independent center going by convincing the state that the center was not an alcoholism *treatment* facility, requiring state accreditation and licensing, but "was simply employing a coordinator to help the community deal with troubled drinkers." According to Mulford, this one surviving center

> has annually been serving about 250 individuals . . . on an annual budget of less than $45,000. That would treat only three or four cases in a nearby hospital-based center, and only one or two in one of the more expensive clinics.[29]

These astonishing figures have major implications for national treatment policy. The billions of dollars Americans now spend annually to treat a relatively small number of alcoholics would fund tens of thousands of community coordinators around the country. If each of these served 250 persons (in the nonintensive way described by Mulford), there would be more than enough community-based programs to serve every American who had a drinking problem.

Not only that, but the active presence of these coordinators in our neighborhoods, involving many more people in alcohol rehabilitation as part of the fabric of community life, would undoubtedly raise awareness of alcohol problems and enhance the natural social processes that restrain excessive drinking. As Mulford concludes:

> All of us, including problem drinkers, share responsibility for the alcohol problem. . . . Each of us is responsible for re-

> straining his or her own drinking behavior and everyone else's. Alcohol excess is a people problem, not a technological problem. . . .
>
> The alcoholism-disease way of thinking leads us to disown our responsibilities to keep each other reasonably sober as a part of the process of keeping each other human. Instead, it encourages us to relinquish our authority for informally constraining each other's drinking behavior to designated "experts" who are all too eager to assume the task.[30]

Robin Room, director of the Berkeley Alcohol Research Group, who studied community responses to drinking problems around the world, reports having been "struck with how much more responsibility . . . [developing nations] gave to family and friends in dealing with alcohol problems, and how ready . . . [technological societies] were to cede responsibility for these human problems to official agencies or to professionals.[31] Yet drinking problems as we know them are unknown in most preindustrial societies, except those that have been conquered by outside powers. The more we defer to experts and their technological magic, the more we lose the really effective informal and formal mechanisms by which societies control alcohol abuse.

Those who wish to contribute to the solution of our drug and alcohol problems might well start by asking some hard questions of government officials at the local, state, and federal levels:

- How is the taxpayers' money being spent on treatment?
- What kind of accountability is there?
- What evidence is there of cure rates and of the costs and benefits?

We need to know why cost-effective programs like Iowa's are regularly supplanted by hospital boondoggles supported by government and insurance funding. Why aren't real community-based programs being implemented nationwide? For example, most communities subsidize private treatment centers by forcing drunk drivers into these programs. Yet few such referrals qualify as alcoholics, whereas time and again research shows that simple skills-training and decision-making sessions are vastly more effective for the generally younger drivers in these programs.[32]

Saving the Community

One reason we don't invest in more effective, less expensive, community programs is that very often we don't have much of a community to invest in. Thus, we need first to address the absence of community in order to remedy the problems we seek to address. Imagine an inner-city crack addict (say, in Washington, D.C.) who is rounded up and sent to a twenty-eight-day hospital program. The bed he occupies represents an investment of $100,000–$250,000 annually. When he leaves the hospital, he returns to a dilapidated building, no job, a disintegrated family and community structure, and a life built around using drugs with friends. In this example, we see how useless are Biden's and others' calls for enhanced treatment opportunities and for a biomedical cure for addiction. None of these will even begin to address this man's ruined life.

Any investment in community resources is better than any investment in hospital-oriented medical treatment for addiction. A community resource is an investment that transcends any individual treatment episode and that enhances the infrastructure of the community. Examples are community centers, day-care centers, athletic leagues, job-training programs, drop-in centers for the elderly, street-front legal programs or programs that offer financial, job, or any other practical advice, and enhanced educational attention for children. These programs, however distant they seem from the addiction problem, actually offer better chances for people in a community to avoid or overcome addiction and alcoholism than intensive addiction treatment that is limited in duration and isolated from the ongoing flow of people's lives.

Community malaise and disintegration are apparent not only in America's inner cities, however. Middle-class and suburban Americans are less involved with their communities and the people around them than ever before. Increasingly, the models of living that we follow are the condo communities of transient young professionals, retirement communities where older people with resources pay to have their free time and activities organized for them, and suburban enclaves with gates and guarded entrances where people never drop in on one another and would never think of sharing or seeking help for personal problems from friends and neighbors.

It is this environment that has fostered the remarkable American craze for twelve-step support groups. For, if you have a problem, the belief is that you must seek understanding from someone with whom all you have in common is that problem. Your friends, relatives, or neighbors cannot help you in this regard. As we have seen, this approach is wrong on the face of it—you are *less likely to develop an addictive problem* when you are part of a wholesome, fully realized community. Of course, joining a twelve-step program leaves you less time and energy for community involvements that are not focused exclusively on your particular addiction.

Regaining Our Moral Bearings: Liberty and Responsibility

What Are Our Values?

Our approach throughout this book has emphasized social values. We must turn to the community as a source of standards and sanctions for regulating behavior. Thus, we must not apologize for asking people to behave well or for teaching and expecting children to contribute to the well-being of others. Citizenship, involving community projects, should be taught as a practicum in schools—including park clean-ups, car washes to raise money for community needs, or helping the elderly. And when adolescents misbehave en masse, as they have done at concerts around the country, adults, rather than apologize for children who destroy community property, must forcefully assert how they expect people to behave.

Criminal behavior is demoralizing America. This is true first of all about street crime, which is tearing the heart out of our inner cities and making community and street life unbearable in many places. At the same time, Americans sense that those in positions of advantage and power—like former Speaker of the House Jim Wright and financiers (like Michael Milken), or those in HUD or on New York City local school boards who seem to have looted government programs for their personal advantage—steal and cheat as a matter of course. Honest Americans now feel that they are a shrinking and beleaguered minority.

Leveraged buy-outs, insider trading, profiteering by businesspeople and politicians, and opportunistic litigation symbolize an America in which personal advantage is the highest goal. Americans seemingly are being taught to take any edge they can get, no matter what the impact on other human beings, even friends, co-workers, and fellow citizens. This preoccupation with personal enrichment and material possessions reflects a nationwide lack of social responsibility and scruples. Surveys conducted by the University of Michigan and UCLA found that contemporary high-school seniors and college freshmen were substantially more interested in leisure time, organizational power, and consumer goods than they had been in the mid-seventies. Meanwhile, "fewer think it important to help others, correct social and economic inequities, or develop a meaningful philosophy of life."[33]

Commitment to the Larger Community

Without any sense of commitment to the larger society, to public service, and to community, we can't possibly fight the environmental, social, economic, health—and addiction—issues that confront us. For example, American corporations must show a willingness to locate in cities that cannot survive without renewed economic activity. To restore meaning to our individual lives, all of us must make a shared commitment to our public needs. This commitment encompasses community planning and beautification, environmental concerns such as water supply and trash disposal, community-coordinated police patrols, and relationships and mutual responsibilities among citizens. We must address the fears that enervate and demoralize us—fears of violent crime, of children's being kidnapped or abused, of economic collapse or environmental catastrophe. How real, how exaggerated are these fears? To the extent that they are real, what can we do about them?

We need to affirm values that support our community and nation. These include values toward public service, strict enforcement of laws and regulations, and creating an ethos of hard work toward long-term goals that fosters economic growth. Not only does attacking community issues and problems oppose addiction at its roots, but the very process of doing so brings people together in purposeful relationships. Our society will work when we take responsibility for our actions, hold others responsbible for theirs, strive to better our schools and communities, and believe in ourselves and our neighbors. In any case, this is the only kind of world we can really live in.

Freedom and Responsibility

We have said a great deal about the way our society conceives of and deals with substance use and abuse and addictive behavior. We have seen that these commonly held views and practices do not work very well, at least for individual treatment. Now we go further to ask what kind of moral atmosphere they are creating.

Our answer is a troubling one. The way the United States typically reacts to the challenges posed by drugs and other potentially addictive involvements itself promotes addiction. That is because anything that assaults people's dignity, weakens their sense of self-efficacy, and compromises their ability to trust and work cooperatively with one another makes the resort to addiction more likely. In place of the dehumanizing premises of the War on Drugs, let us work to restore two fundamental principles—liberty and responsibility—to the forefront of our national consciousness. Embedded in our traditions and affirmed by our Constitution is the conviction that personal freedom is of inherent value. At the same time, people who claim the right to be free must be responsible for the way they exercise their freedom. If this expectation of responsibility permeates people's dealings with one another, it will be self-fulfilling: most people will live up to it.

Endorsing Moderation and Self-Control

At the local as well as the national level, we must encourage moderation, self-regulation, and integration of the individual into community life. One of the best resources we have for keeping addictions under control is a tradition of moderation and self-control that one generation passes on to the next in many cultures. Most people learn to regulate their behavior reasonably well in most areas of life. We need to generalize from these examples of successful mastery and take them—not their opposite—as models for the young.

The use of alcohol is the best example of how moderation can be taught, since alcohol has been used constructively for so many centuries. Those ethnic groups and nations that are best equipped to deal with alcohol, and that have the lowest rates of alcoholism, are those that have made alcohol a part of normal community life. An example of a positive initiative in this direction is the chain of "family taverns" started by Mike and Brian McMenamin in Oregon. Although the idea of including children in a drinking establishment may seem strange to many Americans, the McMenamin brothers say they are "just following our age group. We like to get together with friends, drink beer and bring the family."[34]

The taverns, some of which include movie theaters, eating places, shopping areas, and hotel rooms, are designed as real community centers where drinking takes on the positive emotional tone of the surrounding activities and relationships. "The key is a sense of community, the coming together of family and friends at a central gathering place."[35] A novel idea? It is as old as the Colonial American inn, from a period when drinking problems were uncommon even though per-capita alcohol consumption was high. Not only drinking but eating, exercising, shopping, intimate relationships—all of these have a more benign character amid a network of people who care about one another and share other interests and fulfillments.

Moderation comes naturally when the social context checks the impulse to excess and keeps things in balance. When, instead, those who should know better choose to endorse values of fear and helplessness, we are allowing our worst values to drive out the best.

Self-Efficacy and Empowerment

People—parents and community members—have the power to teach and model values of moderation and self-control. Indeed, there is no substitute for assuming this role within your family and community. If you fail to take responsibility for transmitting values and promoting healthy development, your children are that much less likely to acquire these values and skills. And the fear with which people have been impressed by disease myths and drug-scare campaigns is the biggest impediment to this sense of personal power.

Contrary to the cliché that the disease model marks a scientific and humanitarian advance over old-fashioned moralism about addiction, the disease model of addiction is both punitive and disempowering. In its place, we can do no better for our physical and emotional well-being than to construct a social and values-oriented model—one that has as its centerpiece the active, alert, self-directed human being, exercising freedom and taking responsibility for his or her actions and for humankind.

CHAPTER 19

A ROAD MAP

WHERE WE'VE BEEN AND WHERE YOU NEED TO GO

This chapter provides a summary of the Life Process Program.

The Life Process Program as a Nondisease Approach to Addiction

1. *The Life Process Program is a nondisease approach to addiction.* Addiction is a way of coping with life, of gaining a desired *experience.* You can be addicted to any powerful involvement that gives you experiences such as comfort, power, belonging, or relaxation. Few people reach the point of total dependence on any addictive experience. But if you rely on an addictive activity as a major source of feelings you need, you lose more productive ways to achieve these feelings, thereby creating a growing dependence. *It is the familiarity and reliability of the experience in providing desired feelings that you depend on in an addiction.*

2. *Disease treatments simply don't work.* Although disease advocates claim both that their age-old bromides are nonpareil successes and that biological discoveries are constantly revealing new truths about addiction, neither of these sources provides anything of value for combating addictions. Understanding addiction as a disease serves primarily to convince you that you have little chance of reversing your inherited weaknesses. Embracing the disease philosophy offers you

only one method for fending off perpetual temptations to relapse—to hold on to the therapy or group for dear life.

3. *The processes that work in solving addiction have been identified.* The Life Process Program takes its methodology from two key sources: evaluations of therapies shown to be effective (such as the Community Reinforcement Approach) and a detailed analysis of how the majority of people overcome addiction—on their own.

4. *The key to fighting addiction is to enhance your natural life experiences.* The disease approach views addiction as a self-contained phenomenon, a "primary disease"; the Life Process Program sees it primarily as a result of your interactions with the world. The best starting place for overcoming an addiction is to recognize and expand your existing strengths. But you must also analyze your involvements—the work, play, home, and other environments that make up your life. You must make these more comfortable, more gratifying, more supportive of your not returning to an addiction.

5. *Addiction does not have to be a lifelong label.* There are few people who have no chance of escaping addiction. *More people outgrow addiction over the course of their lives than fail to do so.* Youth is a special advantage in eventually outgrowing addiction, but it is far from essential.

Assumptions About Addicts and Addiction

1. *The Life Process Program believes that addiction is a changeable state of being and not a person's identity or a biological imperative.* As a result, your addiction—and you—can change with time and experience.

2. *Unlike conventional treatment, our approach explores the unique experience of each individual.*

3. *The Life Process Program accepts that people are informed observers of their own conditions.* In fact, it assumes that you, the addict, must apply the primary desire and wherewithal to change.

4. *Because addiction grows out of the search for meaning, reassurance, and feeling, you can overcome addiction only by enhancing your ability to deal with and gain satisfaction from your environment.*

5. *The crucial difference between the Life Process Program and the disease approach is the issue of self-efficacy versus powerlessness.* The Life Process Program is aimed at enhancing your feelings of power—your belief that you can make the things you want come true. This sense of efficacy affects more than your addictive behavior itself. The Life Process Program seeks to make you more efficacious in life as a whole, so that you can approach living confidently, including personal, professional, and spiritual issues.

The Key Steps in Overcoming Addiction

1. *You need to want to change.* The ingredient most crucial to changing is motivation—the desire to change. No science of addiction can bypass this old chestnut. That is why having tried to quit smoking and then relapsing can mean that you are more likely to succeed at a subsequent try. The repeated efforts show that you want to quit and are going to keep at it until you get it right.

2. *Rely on what is important to you beyond the addiction.* The main sources of the motivation to quit an addiction are the things you hold important in your life. Work, family, pride, religion, health—any and all values that contradict the urge to be addicted are assets to rely on. If you don't have such values—or enough of them—then you need to get them.

3. *Improve your skills and your confidence.* Learning to do things well, to deal better with problem areas, and to see yourself as a competent person are crucial links in overcoming addiction. Knowing you can accomplish what you set out to do and having faith that you can attack your problems will outweigh your urge for your addiction.

4. *Invest in the key building blocks of your life—friends, family, job, career, hobbies, healthful activities.* Having the ingredients of a successful life in place is the best antidote to addiction. These things

give you the reasons not to be addicted, the motivation to cease addiction, and the strength to quit and stay unhooked.

5. *The strongest answer to addiction is the community.* Belonging to a supportive social group—one with prosocial values that don't support addictive excesses—makes it unlikely you will be addicted. Social support is also useful for overcoming addiction, provided the support focuses on something more than the addiction. Real community reinforces the entire fabric of your life, whereas support predicated on sharing an addiction holds the danger of becoming a preoccupation not unlike the addiction itself. Strengthening communities, therefore, is the single most important thing society can do to encourage health and reduce addiction.

We repeat here a capsule summary of the Life Process Program that was first presented in chapter 8.

The Life Process Program Summarized

Nondisease Approach

—addiction to an experience

—failure of disease treatment

—emphasis on natural processes

- builds on individual strength
- focuses on social environment

—treatment is finite

Different Assumptions from Disease Approach

—person as evolving being

—individualized treatment

—client-centered

—coping prevents addiction

—goal: personal efficacy

Elements

—motivation

—values

—skills

—life involvements: family, work

—community

APPENDIX

WHAT THE *JAMA* STUDY ON GENES AND ALCOHOLISM TELLS US

THE CLAIM OF THE DISCOVERY of a gene for alcoholism is part of a burst of scientific and popular optimism about how well we understand and can help people with emotional problems through biomedical means. Would that we could "cure" these problems so simply, but the reality is otherwise. As a result, major claims about discoveries of the genes responsible for emotional-behavioral disorders appear frequently, and then fade away with little fanfare as they are disproved. In 1987, a *New York Times* headline announced, "Defective Gene Tied to Form of Manic-depressive Illness."[1] In 1988, the *Times* headline was "Schizophrenia Study Finds Strong Signs of Hereditary Cause."[2] In 1990, it was "Scientists See a Link Between Alcoholism and a Specific Gene."[3] Each of these stories announced that a study had produced the first concrete evidence linking the malady in question to a particular gene.

Both the schizophrenia and manic-depressive discoveries have been explicitly refuted by additional research and further analysis of the original findings.[4] As a result, in 1989, the *Times* published a story entitled "Scientists Now Doubt They Found Faulty Gene Linked to Mental Illness."[5] This story received less attention than the announcements of positive findings, however, appearing not on the front page but deep within the paper. The article revealed that new findings had reversed an earlier finding that a defective gene was associated with manic-depressive disorder. The article furthermore noted that "the new findings underscore the difficulty of assigning specific causes to such a complex and variable illness," and that such problems also plague efforts to identify the genetic role in schizophrenia. One of the authors of the original study linking a gene to manic-depressive disorder announced, "We are back to square one." However, readers probably will not balance the new, disconfirming evidence on genes and manic-depressive disorder or schizophrenia against the earlier, front-page proclamations of scientific breakthroughs.

The study reported in the *Times* linking alcoholism to a specific gene was published in the *Journal of the American Medical Association* on April 18, 1990, by a research team led by Kenneth Blum and Ernest Noble.[6] The lead article in *JAMA*, it was accompanied by press releases, a news conference in Los Angeles, and video interviews with the study's authors transmitted via satellite by the AMA to all television stations in the country. The alcoholism-gene study examined material from the brains of dead alcoholics and comparison subjects. The study included a total of seventy cadavers, thirty-five designated as alcoholic and thirty-five control cases. The genetic marker was found in the brains of 69 percent of alcoholics in the study (although, for some reason, this was reported as 77 percent in the study's abstract and all newspaper accounts), but only 20 percent of the nonalcoholics.

From the start, questions were raised about the study and its findings, often by leading proponents of genetic explanations of alcoholism. These issues included:

1. *Why did such a high percentage of alcoholics have this particular gene variant?* Is the gene discovered by these researchers the only one to influence alcoholism? If it is not, then the fact that nearly 70 percent of alcoholics in the study had this genetic material seems remarkable, even to disease-theory adherents. One such adherent (Dr. Daniel Flavin, scientific director of the National Council on Alcoholism and Drug Dependence) remarked: "It's very surprising that in a disease like alcoholism, where the speculation is that this is probably influenced by many genes, that there is such a strong association. I don't know quite what to make of it at this point."[7]

2. *Was this positive finding an accident?* Blum and Noble examined a large number of possible abnormalities in the brains of their alcoholics. Besides the nine genetic probes they performed and evaluated for the *JAMA* study, the team had investigated chemical differences in this particular set of brains for seven years and had come up negative on many other measures. This examination of a multiplicity of rela-

tionships risks becoming a fishing expedition that turns up a spurious positive result. For this reason, researchers who were questioned about the *JAMA* study cautioned that additional research must be designed to examine the relationship between the identified gene and alcoholism. Many expressed some skepticism: Donald Goodwin, the psychiatrist whose research first pointed to the inheritance of alcoholism, noted that "the history of this kind of work so far has been a failure to replicate."[8]

Moreover, this was not an orthodox gene-mapping study. Enoch Gordis, director of the NIAAA (who strongly adheres to disease and genetic views of alcoholism), noted in an editorial in the issue of *JAMA* in which the gene study appeared that it was possible "the differences between the groups were caused by characteristics of the groups that were unrelated to alcoholism. This type of comparison . . . cannot substitute for . . . complex family studies."[9] The standard practice in gene-mapping research is to identify genes in a range of living, related persons. This "family-tree" approach can then trace whether or not various relatives with a specific genetic marker develop a given disease. A trained genetic researcher, Paul Billings (at the time director of the Clinic for Inherited Disease at New England Deaconess Hospital), commented about the Blum-Noble study, "If this type of genetic analysis was carried out for a disease or a behavior less attractive than alcoholism, it would never get published. It tells you nothing of significance."[10]

3. *What does this gene have to do with alcoholism?* Indeed, the odd thing about this and some other recent genetic discoveries is how little they say specifically about alcoholism or drug addiction. The gene Blum and Noble identified is a dopamine-receptor gene. Some claim that dopamine, a chemical produced in the body, stimulates the pleasure centers of the brain. According to Dr. Noble, then, this gene isn't really about alcohol and compulsive drinking: "The good Lord did not make an alcoholic gene, but one that seems to be involved in pleasure-seeking behaviors."[11]

All of these points are moot because, eight months after the original study appeared, another study of the so-called "alcoholism gene" was published in the *Journal of the American Medical Association* (the same journal that published the original study). This study found that the gene was no more common in a population of alcoholics than in a normal population, or in alcoholic members of two families relative to nonalcoholic members. On the basis of their own and other available research on the gene, the researchers—from the genetics section of the National Institute on Alcohol Abuse and Alcoholism—declared that "Population and pedigree studies reveal a lack of association between the dopamine D_2 receptor gene and alcoholism."[12] We ask readers, especially those who heard of the original study, whether they learned about the study disproving this link. Do you think that most educated people in America continue to believe that the alcoholism gene has been identified?

Even if Blum and Noble's results had held up, what might the genetic source for "pleasure-seeking behavior" look like? If all pleasurable behavior is motivated by genes, then do all of us who crave pleasure intensely have "addict brains"? Or only those who cannot control these cravings? There are two areas of behavior more pleasurable for most people than any other—sex and eating. Are those who are willing to sacrifice nearly everything for sex and for illicit affairs, or who eat chocolates or other foods compulsively, the people who get the most pleasure from these acts? Are rapists, philanderers, and binge eaters genetically different from other people? If we examine baseball star Wade Boggs's genes, will we discover why he kept a secret mistress for years?

Indeed, combining claims of genetic determination of behavior with new discoveries that just about everything—sex, drugs, alcohol, eating, shopping, smoking, working—can be addictive leaves us with some very nonscientific-seeming theories. No matter how much alcoholism you find in people with the "pleasure-seeking gene," you can always say *this* isn't the only addiction they might have. Rather, you need to examine *every possible kind of pleasure-seeking behavior in which people engage* in order to test whether this gene is at work.

At the same time, if all of us with excesses in one area or another share some gene that drives our search for pleasure, then is the addictive gene really an abnormality? Or is it a mark of the human condition? How much will it help us to decide that all our excesses are due to our biological makeup? Will we then take drugs to stop smoking, or have brain operations to reduce our sex drives? This book takes quite a different approach to dealing with addiction, one that focuses on those sources of addictive behavior—the really significant ones, as we show—that remain within our own control.

NOTES

Introduction

1. J. Gurin, "Remaking Our Lives," *American Health,* March 1990, pp. 50–52.

2. Ibid., pp. 50–51.

3. Ibid., p. 52.

4. J. Gurin, "Eating Goes Back to Basics," *American Health,* March 1990, pp. 96–101.

Chapter 1
Why It Doesn't Make Sense to Call Addiction a "Disease"

1. This article—S. Peele, "Second Thoughts About a Gene for Alcoholism," *The Atlantic,* August 1990, pp. 52–58—is summarized in the appendix.

2. D. Cahalan and R. Room, *Problem Drinking Among American Men* (New Brunswick, N.J.: Rutgers Center of Alcohol Studies, 1974); B. A. Christiansen and M. S. Goldman, "Alcohol-related Expectancies Versus Demographic/Background Variables in the Prediction of Adolescent Drinking," *Journal of Consulting and Clinical Psychology* 51 (1983): 249–57.

3. S. A. Brown, M. S. Goldman, and B. A. Christiansen, "Do Alcohol Expectancies Mediate Drinking Patterns of Adults?" *Journal of Consulting and Clinical Psychology* 53 (1985): 512–19; G. A. Marlatt, "Alcohol, the Magic Elixir: Stress, Expectancy, and the Transformation of Emotional States," in E. Gottheil, K. A. Druley, S. Pashko, and S. Weinstein, eds., *Stress and Addiction* (New York: Brunner/Mazel, 1987), pp. 302–22.

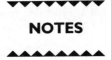

4. S. Schachter, "Pharmacological and Psychological Determinants of Smoking," *Annals of Internal Medicine* 88 (1978): 104–14.

5. G. Bigelow, I. A. Liebson, and R. Griffiths, "Alcoholic Drinking: Suppression by a Brief Time-out Procedure," *Behavior Research and Therapy* 12 (1974): 107–115.

6. K. M. Fillmore, "Relationships Between Specific Drinking Problems in Early Adulthood and Middle Age: An Exploratory 20-Year Follow-up Study," *Journal of Studies on Alcohol* 36 (1975): 882–907.

7. J. P. Pierce, M. C. Fiore, T. E. Novotny, E. J. Hatziandreu, and R. M. Davis, "Trends in Cigarette Smoking in the United States: Educational Differences Are Increasing," *Journal of the American Medical Association* 261 (1989): 56–60; U.S. Department of Health, Education, and Welfare, *The Smoking Digest: Progress Report and a Nation Kicking the Habit* (Washington, D.C.: U.S. Department of Health, Education, and Welfare, 1977).

8. W. R. Miller and R. K. Hester, "The Effectiveness of Alcoholism Treatment: What Research Reveals," in W. R. Miller and N. K. Heather, eds., *Treating Addictive Behaviors: Processes of Change* (New York: Plenum, 1986), pp. 121–74.

9. J. M. Brandsma, M. C. Maultsby, and R. J. Welsh, *The Outpatient Treatment of Alcoholism: A Review and Comparative Study* (Baltimore, Md.: University Park Press, 1980); K. S. Ditman, G. G. Crawford, E. W. Forgy, H. Moskowitz, and C. MacAndrew, "A Controlled Experiment on the Use of Court Probation for Drunk Arrests," *American Journal of Psychiatry* 124 (1967): 160–63; P. M. Salzberg and C. L. Klingberg, "The Effectiveness of Deferred Prosecution for Driving While Intoxicated," *Journal of Studies on Alcohol* 44 (1983): 299–306.

10. G. E. Vaillant, *The Natural History of Alcoholism: Causes, Patterns, and Paths to Recovery* (Cambridge, Mass.: Harvard University Press, 1983).

11. E. Gordis, "Accessible and Affordable Health Care for Alcoholism and Related Problems: Strategies for Cost Containment," *Journal of Studies on Alcohol* 48 (1987): 582.

12. Vaillant, *Natural History of Alcoholism*, p. 284.

13. Ibid., p. 316.

14. Ibid., p. 293.

15. Miller and Hester, "Effectiveness of Alcoholism Treatment," p. 136.

16. S. Peele, *Diseasing of America: Addiction Treatment Out of Control* (Lexington, Mass.: Lexington, 1989), pp. 194–95.

17. D. R. Rudy, *Becoming Alcoholic: Alcoholics Anonymous and the Reality of Alcoholism* (Carbondale, Ill.: Southern Illinois University Press, 1986), p. 38.

18. Ibid., p. 89.

19. J. Durso, "Gooden Is Focus of Concern," *New York Times*, June 26, 1987, pp. B11–B12.

20. Richard Weedman, quoted in M. Worden, "Adolescent Treatment on the Hot Seat," *U.S. Journal of Drug and Alcohol Dependence,* June 1985, p. 14.

21. G. B. Melton and H. A. Davidson, "Child Protection and Society: When Should the State Intervene?" *American Psychologist* 42 (1987): 174.

22. R. Regan, "In Short/Football," *New York Times Book Review,* October 7, 1990, p. 18.

23. R. L. Bangert-Drowns, "The Effects of School-based Substance Abuse Education—A Meta-Analysis," *Journal of Drug Education* 18 (1988): 243–64; M. D. Newcomb and P. M. Bentler, "Substance Use and Abuse Among Children and Teenagers," *American Psychologist* 44 (1989): 242–48; N. S. Tobler, "Meta-Analysis of 143 Adolescent Drug Prevention Programs: Quantitative Outcome Results of Program Participants Compared to a Control or Comparison Group," *Journal of Drug Issues* 16 (1986): 537–67.

24. This organization has been known as the National Council on Alcoholism (NCA) for most of its life. The NCA began as the National Committee for Education on Alcoholism in 1944, but changed its name in the early 1950s. The NCA's primary focus has always been alcoholism. However, in 1990, in order to gain greater credibility in the addiction field, the NCA renamed itself the National Council on Alcoholism and Drug Dependence (NCADD). See B. H. Johnson, "The Alcoholism Movement in America: A Study in Cultural Innovation," doctoral dissertation, University of Illinois at Urbana-Champaign, 1973; M. E. Lender and J. K. Martin, *Drinking in America: A History* (New York: Free Press, 1982).

25. Miller and Hester, "Effectiveness of Alcoholism Treatment," p. 122.

26. Gordis, "Accessible and Affordable Health Care," p. 582.

27. "Inpatient Psych Rates Zoom," *Health Care Competition Week,* July 24, 1989, p. 2.

28. "Gooden Tells of Cocaine Use," *New York Times,* June 26, 1987, p. D17.

29. Durso, "Gooden," pp. B11–B12.

30. Lender and Martin, *Drinking in America.*

31. E. Goodman, "Do Our Drug Treatment Programs Label Patients as Losers?" *Boston Globe* syndicated column, September 19, 1990.

Chapter 2
Are People Born Alcoholics?

1. D. Shepherd and R. F. Slatzer, *Bing Crosby: The Hollow Man* (New York: St. Martin's Press, 1981), p. 113.

2. Ibid., pp. 197–98.

3. L. Leamer, *King of the Night: The Life of Johnny Carson* (New York: William Morrow, 1989).

4. M. Clinch, *Robert Redford* (London: New English Library, 1989).

5. G. E. Vaillant, *The Natural History of Alcoholism: Causes, Patterns, and Paths to Recovery* (Cambridge, Mass.: Harvard University Press, 1983), p. 187.

6. Ibid., pp. 284–89.

7. D. Cahalan and R. Room, *Problem Drinking Among American Men* (New Brunswick, N.J.: Rutgers Center of Alcohol Studies, 1974); K. M. Fillmore, "Women's Drinking Across the Adult Life Course as Compared to Men's: A Longitudinal and Cohort Analysis," *British Journal of Addiction* 82 (1987): 80–111.

8. Vaillant, *Natural History of Alcoholism*, p. 61.

9. Ibid., p. 27.

10. Cahalan and Room, *Problem Drinking;* R. Caetano, "Drinking Patterns and Alcohol Problems in a National Sample of U.S. Hispanics," in *Alcohol Use Among U.S. Ethnic Minorities* (Rockville, Md.: National Institute on Alcohol Abuse and Alcoholism, 1989), pp. 147–62; D. Herd, "The Epidemiology of Drinking Patterns and Alcohol-related Problems Among U.S. Blacks," in *Alcohol Use Among U.S. Ethnic Minorities*, pp. 3–50.

11. Cahalan and Room, *Problem Drinking;* D. J. Armor, J. M. Polich, and H. B. Stambul, *Alcoholism and Treatment* (New York: Wiley, 1978).

12. Vaillant, *Natural History of Alcoholism*, p. 226.

13. C. McCabe, *The Good Man's Weakness* (San Francisco: Chronicle Books, 1974), pp. 31–32.

14. M. L. Barnett, "Alcoholism in the Cantonese of New York City: An Anthropological Study," in O. Diethelm, ed., *Etiology of Chronic Alcoholism* (Springfield, Ill.: Charles C Thomas, 1955), pp. 179–227.

15. B. Glassner and B. Berg, "How Jews Avoid Alcohol Problems," *American Sociological Review* 45 (1980): 647–64.

16. B. Glassner and B. Berg, "Social Locations and Interpretations: How Jews Define Alcoholism," *Journal of Studies on Alcohol* 45 (1984): 16–25.

17. M. Mann, *Marty Mann Answers Your Questions About Drinking and Alcoholism*, rev. ed. (New York: Holt, Rinehart and Winston, 1981).

18. G. D. Talbott, in D. Wholey, ed., *The Courage to Change* (Boston: Houghton Mifflin, 1984), p. 19.

19. T. Reich, "Biological Marker Studies in Alcoholism," *New England Journal of Medicine* 318 (1988): 180.

20. Fillmore, *Women's Drinking;* L. N. Robins, J. E. Helzer, T. R. Przybeck, and D. A. Regier, "Alcohol Disorders in the Community: A Report from the Epidemiologic Catchment Area," in R. M. Rose and J. Barrett, eds., *Alcoholism: Origins and Outcomes* (New York: Raven Press, 1988), pp. 15–29; L. Öjesjö, "Risks for Alcoholism by Age and Class Among Males: The Lundby Community Cohort,

Sweden," in D. W. Goodwin, K. T. Van Dusen, and S. A. Mednick, eds., *Longitudinal Research in Alcoholism* (Boston: Kluwer-Nijhoff, 1984), pp. 9–25.

21. B. W. Lex, "Alcohol Problems in Special Populations," in J. H. Mendelson and N. K. Mello, eds., *The Diagnosis and Treatment of Alcoholism*, 2nd ed. (New York: McGraw-Hill, 1985), pp. 96–97.

22. Cahalan and Room, *Problem Drinking;* M. E. Hilton, "Drinking Patterns and Drinking Problems in 1984: Results from a General Population Survey," *Alcoholism: Clinical and Experimental Research* 11 (1987): 167–75.

23. K. M. Fillmore, "Prevalence, Incidence, and Chronicity of Drinking Patterns and Problems Among Men as a Function of Age: A Longitudinal and Cohort Analysis," *British Journal of Addiction* 82 (1987): 77; K. M. Fillmore and L. Midanik, "Chronicity of Drinking Problems Among Men: A Longitudinal Study," *Journal of Studies on Alcohol* 45 (1984): 228–36.

24. L. D. Johnston, P. M. O'Malley, and J. G. Bachman, *Illicit Drug Use, Smoking, and Drinking by America's High School Students, College Students, and Young Adults: 1975–1987* (Rockville, Md.: National Institute on Drug Abuse, 1988).

25. S. Peele, *Diseasing of America: Addiction Treatment Out of Control* (Lexington, Mass.: Lexington, 1989).

26. Cahalan and Room, *Problem Drinking.*

27. K. M. Fillmore, "Relationships Between Specific Drinking Problems in Early Adulthood and Middle Age: An Exploratory 20-Year Follow-up Study," *Journal of Studies on Alcohol* 36 (1975): 882–907.

28. L. D. Johnston, P. M. O'Malley, and J. G. Bachman, *Illicit Drug Use, Smoking, and Drinking by America's High School Students, College Students, and Young Adults: 1975–1988* (Rockville, Md.: National Institute on Drug Abuse, 1989).

29. M. M. Gross, "Psychobiological Contributions to the Alcohol Dependence Syndrome: A Selective Review of Recent Research," in G. Edwards, M. M. Gross, M. Keller, J. Moser, and R. Room, eds., *Alcohol-related Disabilities*, WHO Offset Publication No. 32 (Geneva: World Health Organization, 1977), p. 121.

30. Reich, "Biological Marker Studies."

31. B. Mishara and R. Kastenbaum, *Alcohol and Old Age* (New York: Grune and Stratton, 1980).

32. G. M. Barnes, "Alcohol Abuse Among Older Persons," *Journal of American Geriatrics Society* 22 (1969): 244–50; D. Cahalan, I. H. Cisin, and H. M. Crossley, *American Drinking Practices* (New Brunswick, N.J.: Rutgers Center of Alcohol Studies, 1969); E. L. Gomberg, *Drinking and Problem Drinking Among the Elderly* (Ann Arbor: Institute of Gerontology, University of Michigan, 1980).

33. "Lee Marvin Hangs Up His Guns," *Globe*, August 13, 1985, pp. 2–3.

34. R. Stall, "Respondent-independent Reasons for Change and Stability in Alcohol Consumption as a Concomitant of the Aging Process," in C.R. Janes, R. Stall, and

S. M. Gifford, eds., *Anthropology and Epidemiology: Interdisciplinary Approaches to the Study of Health and Disease* (Boston: D. Reidel, 1986), p. 293.

35. Authors' oral interview with Diana Preice, August 9, 1989.

36 M. Bragg, *Richard Burton: A Life* (New York: Warner, 1988).

37. J. Pereira,"As Addiction Crisis Mounts, Experts Delve into the Root Causes," *Wall Street Journal*, August 1, 1989, pp. Al, A6.

38. S. Peele, "The Implications and Limitations of Genetic Models of Alcoholism and Other Addictions," *Journal of Studies on Alcohol* 47 (1986): 63–73; S. Peele, "Second Thoughts About a Gene for Alcoholism," *The Atlantic*, August 1990, pp. 52–58.

39. C. R. Cloninger, M. Bohman, and S. Sigvardsson, "Inheritance of Alcohol Abuse," *Archives of General Psychiatry* 38 (1981): 861–68.

40. "New Insights into Alcoholism," *Time*, April 25, 1983, pp. 64, 69.

41. D. Lester, "Genetic Theory: An Assessment of the Heritability of Alcoholism," in C. D. Chaudron and D. A. Wilkinson, eds., *Theories on Alcoholism* (Toronto: Addiction Research Foundation, 1988), p. 17.

42. D. W. Goodwin, F. Schulsinger, L. Hermansen, S. B. Guze, and G. Winokur, "Alcohol Problems in Adoptees Raised Apart from Alcoholic Biological Parents," *Archives of General Psychiatry* 28 (1973): 238–43.

43. D. W. Goodwin, F. Schulsinger, J. Knop, S. Mednick, and S. B. Guze, "Alcoholism and Depression in Adopted-out Daughters of Alcoholics," *Archives of General Psychiatry* 34 (1977): 751–55.

44. R. M. Murray, C. A. Clifford, and H. M. D. Gurling, "Twin and Adoption Studies: How Good Is the Evidence for a Genetic Role?" in M. Galanter, ed., *Recent Developments in Alcoholism* (New York: Plenum, 1983), pp. 25–48.

45. M. A. Schuckit, N. Butters, L. Lyn, and M. Irwin, "Neuropsychologic Deficits and the Risk for Alcoholism," *Neuropsychopharmacology* 1 (1987): 45–53.

46. M. A. Schuckit and E. O. Gold, "A Simultaneous Evaluation of Multiple Markers of Ethanol/Placebo Challenges in Sons of Alcoholics and Controls," *Archives of General Psychiatry* 45 (1988): 211–16.

47. C. R. Cloninger, "Neurogenetic Adaptive Mechanisms in Alcoholism," *Science* 236 (1987): 410–16.

48. C. R. Cloninger, S. Sigvardsson, and M. Bohman, "Childhood Personality Predicts Alcohol Abuse in Young Adults," *Alcoholism* 12 (1988): 494–505.

49. H. Hoffman, R. G. Loper, and M. L. Kammeier, "Identifying Future Alcoholics with MMPI Alcoholism Scores," *Quarterly Journal of Studies on Alcohol* 35 (1974): 490–98; M. C. Jones, "Personality Correlates and Antecedents of Drinking Patterns in Adult Males," *Journal of Consulting and Clinical Psychology* 32 (1968): 2–12; R. G. Loper, M. L. Kammeier, and H. Hoffman, "MMPI Characteristics of College Freshman Males Who Later Become Alcoholics," *Journal of Abnormal Psychology*

82 (1973): 159–62; C. MacAndrew, "Toward the Psychometric Detection of Substance Misuse in Young Men," *Journal of Studies on Alcohol* 47 (1986): 161–66.

50. C. MacAndrew, "What that MAC Scale Tells Us About Men Alcoholics," *Journal of Studies on Alcohol* 42 (1981): 617; C. MacAndrew, "Similarities in the Self-Depictions of Female Alcoholics and Psychiatric Outpatients," *Journal of Studies on Alcohol* 47 (1986): 478–84.

51. Vaillant, *Natural History of Alcoholism,* p. 106.

52. T. K. Greenfield, J. Guydish, and M. T. Temple, "Reasons Students Give for Limiting Drinking: A Factor Analysis with Implications for Research and Practice," *Journal of Studies on Alcohol* 50 (1989): 108–15.

53. E. Harburg, D. R. Davis, and R. Caplan, "Parent and Offspring Alcohol Use: Imitative and Aversive Transmission," *Journal of Studies on Alcohol* 43 (1982): 497.

54. Ibid., p. 498.

55. E. Harburg, W. DiFranceisco, W. D. Webster, L. Gleiberman, and A. Schork, "Familial Transmission of Alcohol Use: II. Imitation of and Aversion to Parent Drinking (1960) by Adult Offspring (1977): Tecumseh, Michigan," *Journal of Studies on Alcohol* 51 (1990): 245–56.

56. G. Elal-Lawrence, P. D. Slade, and M. E. Dewey, "Predictors of Outcome Type in Treated Problem Drinkers," *Journal of Studies on Alcohol* 47 (1986): 41–47; M. Sanchez-Craig, D. A. Wilkinson, and K. Walker, "Theories and Methods for Secondary Prevention of Alcohol Problems: A Cognitively Based Approach," in W. M. Cox., ed., *Treatment and Prevention of Alcohol Problems: A Resource Manual* (New York: Academic Press, 1987).

57. G. M. Barnes and M. Windle, "Family Factors in Adolescent Alcohol and Drug Abuse," *Pediatrician* 14 (1987): 13–18.

58. P. Hobe, *Lovebound: Recovering from an Alcoholic Family* (New York: New American Library, 1990).

59. D. Sifford, "A Psychiatrist Discusses Creative Writers and Alcohol," *Philadelphia Inquirer,* January 2, 1989, p. 5-C.

60. H. Gravitz and J. Bowden, *Recovery: A Guide for Adult Children of Alcoholics* (New York: Simon & Schuster, 1987), preface.

61. R. J. Ackerman, *Perfect Daughters: Adult Daughters of Alcoholics* (Deerfield Beach, Fla.: Health Communications, 1989); C. Black, *It Will Never Happen to Me* (Denver: Medical Administration Co., 1981); J. Woititz, *Adult Children of Alcoholics* (Deerfield Beach, Fla.: Health Communications, 1983).

62. E. E. Werner, "Resilient Offspring of Alcoholics: A Longitudinal Study from Birth to Age 18," *Journal of Studies on Alcohol* 47 (1986): 34–40.

63. J. G. Woititz, "A Study of Self-Esteem in Children of Alcoholics," doctoral dissertation, Rutgers University, 1976, pp. 53–55.

Chapter 3
Which Is the Most Addictive Drug of All?

1. S. Cohen, "Reinforcement and Rapid Delivery Systems: Understanding Adverse Consequences of Cocaine," in N. J. Kozel and E. H. Adams, eds., *Cocaine Use in America: Epidemiologic and Clinical Perspectives* (Rockville, Md.: National Institute on Drug Abuse, 1985), p. 151.

2. G. Kolata, "Experts Finding New Hope on Treating Crack Addicts," *New York Times*, August 24, 1989, p. A1.

3. Ibid., p. B7.

4. National Institute on Drug Abuse, *National Household Survey on Drug Abuse: 1988 Population Estimates* (Rockville, Md.: National Institute on Drug Abuse, 1989).

5. G. M. Barnes and M. Windle, "Family Factors in Adolescent Alcohol and Drug Abuse," *Pediatrician* 14 (1987): 13–18; R. Jessor and S. L. Jessor, *Problem Behavior and Psychosocial Development: A Longitudinal Study of Youth* (New York: Academic Press, 1977); D. B. Kandel, "Marijuana Users in Young Adulthood," *Archives of General Psychiatry* 41 (1984): 200–209.

6. P. G. Erickson and B. K. Alexander, "Cocaine and Addictive Liability," *Social Pharmacology* 3 (1989): 249.

7. P. G. Erickson, E. M. Adlaf, G. F. Murray, and R. G. Smart, *The Steel Drug: Cocaine in Perspective* (Lexington, Mass.: Lexington, 1987), p. 109.

8. K. Abdul-Jabbar and P. Knobler, *Giant Steps* (New York: Bantam, 1985).

9. S. Peele, "Addiction as a Cultural Concept," *Annals of the New York Academy of Sciences* 602 (1990): 205–20.

10. D. F. Musto, *The American Disease: Origins of Narcotic Control* (New York: Oxford University Press, 1987).

11. J. A. O'Donnell, H. L. Voss, R. R. Clayton, G. T. Slatin, and R. G. W. Room, *Young Men and Drugs: A Nationwide Survey* (Rockville, Md.: National Institute on Drug Abuse, 1976).

12. L. N. Robins, J. E. Helzer, M. Hesselbrock, and E. Wish, "Vietnam Veterans Three Years After Vietnam: How Our Study Changed Our View of Heroin," in L. Brill and C. Winick, eds., *The Yearbook of Substance Use and Abuse*, vol. 2 (New York: Human Sciences Press, 1980), pp. 213–30.

13. Dr. Mitchell Max, interviewed on National Public Radio's *Morning Edition*, May 4, 1989; cf. J. Porter and H. Jick, "Addiction Rare in Patients Treated With Narcotics," *New England Journal of Medicine* 302 (1980): 123.

14. Max interview.

15. B. K. Alexander, S. Peele, P. F. Hadaway, S. J. Morse, A. Brodsky, and B. L. Beyerstein, "Adult, Infant, and Animal Addiction," in S. Peele, *The Meaning of*

Addiction: Compulsive Experience and Its Interpretation (Lexington, Mass.: Lexington, 1985), pp. 73–96.

16. R. K. Siegel, *Intoxication* (New York: Dutton, 1989).

17. P. Biernacki, *Pathways from Heroin Addiction: Recovery Without Treatment* (Philadelphia: Temple University Press, 1986), p. 7.

18. D. Waldorf, "Natural Recovery from Opiate Addiction: Some Social-Psychological Processes of Untreated Recovery," *Journal of Drug Issues* 13 (1983): 255–56.

19. Biernacki, *Pathways,* p. 53.

20. Ibid., p. 51.

21. Waldorf, "Natural Recovery," p. 269.

22. Biernacki, *Pathways,* p. 177.

23. L. M. Silverstein, J. Edelwich, D. Flanagan, and A. Brodsky, *High on Life: A Story of Addiction and Recovery* (Middletown, Conn.: Jerry Edelwich, New England Association of Reality Therapy, 1981), pp. 148–49.

24. Ibid., p. 166.

25. Erickson et al., *Steel Drug,* p. 137.

26. Ibid., p. 129.

27. H. J. Shaffer and S. B. Jones, *Quitting Cocaine: The Struggle Against Impulse* (Lexington, Mass.: Lexington Books, 1989).

28. R. K. Siegel, "Changing Patterns of Cocaine Use: Longitudinal Observations, Consequences, and Treatment," in J. Grabowski, ed., *Cocaine: Pharmacology, Effects, and Treatment of Abuse* (Rockville, Md.: National Institute on Drug Abuse, 1984), pp. 92–110.

29. Erickson et al., *Steel Drug,* p. 54.

30. Ibid., p. 126.

31. Ibid., p. 127.

32. Ibid.

33. Are all the efforts we have been making to fight drugs justified by about a quarter of a million daily cocaine users? In order to create more alarming figures to justify his demands for greater expenditures for drug treatment and biological cures for addiction, Senator Joseph Biden released a Senate Judiciary Committee report in May 1990 claiming there were over two million cocaine addicts in the country. Biden counted *weekly* cocaine users in the NIDA survey as addicts. Thus, even those, like Biden, seeking to alarm us with evidence of massive drug addiction tell us that most addicts seem content to use the drug about once a week—a far different image from the zonked-out crack head that television portrays as the typical cocaine user. Cf. J. Sullum, "The One-Percent Solution," *Reason,* August-September 1990, p. 17.

34. L. D. Johnston, P. M. O'Malley, and J. G. Bachman, *Illicit Drug Use, Smoking, and Drinking by America's High School Students, College Students, and Young Adults: 1975–1989* (Rockville, Md.:National Institute on Drug Abuse, 1990).

35. J. L. Falk, "Drug Dependence: Myth or Motive?" *Pharmacology, Biochemistry and Behavior* 19 (1983): 388.

36. C. Reinarman, D. Waldorf, and S. Murphy, "The Call of the Pipe: Freebasing and Crack Use as Norm-bound Episodic Compulsion," in C. Reinarman et al., *Cocaine Changes* (Philadelphia: Temple University Press, in press).

37. Erickson et al., *Steel Drug*, p. 128.

38. B. Ford and C. Chase, *The Times of My Life* (New York: Ballantine, 1979).

39. R. R. Clayton, "Cocaine Use in the United States: In a Blizzard or Just Being Snowed?" in Kozel and Adams, eds., *Cocaine Use in America*, pp. 8–34.

40. Jessor and Jessor, *Problem Behavior.*

41. D. B. Kandel and V. H. Raveis, "Cessation of Illegal Drug Use in Young Adulthood," *Archives of General Psychiatry* 46 (1989): 115.

42. M. D. Newcomb and P. M. Bentler, "Substance Use and Abuse Among Children and Teenagers," *American Psychologist* 44 (1989): 246.

43. J. Shedler and J. Block, "Adolescent Drug Use and Psychological Health," *American Psychologist* 45 (1990): 626.

44. Ibid.

45. National Institute on Drug Abuse, *National Household Survey.*

46. Ibid.

47. P. Kerr, "Rich vs. Poor: Drug Patterns Are Diverging," *New York Times*, August 30, 1987, pp. 1, 28.

48. Ibid., p. 1.

49. S. Blakeslee, "8-Year Study Finds 2 Sides to Teen-Age Drug Use," *New York Times*, July 21, 1988, pp. A1, A23.

50. Robins et al., "Vietnam Veterans."

51. Kolata, "Experts Finding New Hope," pp. A1, B7.

52. Dr. Ansley Hamid, quoted in G. Kolata, "Temperance: An Old Cycle Repeats Itself," *New York Times*, January 1, 1991, pp. 35, 40.

53. Robins et al., "Vietnam Veterans," p. 229.

Chapter 4
Smoking: The Toughest Habit to Lick?

1. L. T. Kozlowski, D. A. Wilkinson, W. Skinner, C. Kent, T. Franklin, and M. Pope, "Comparing Tobacco Cigarette Dependence with Other Drug Dependencies:

Greater or Equal 'Difficulty Quitting' and 'Urges to Use,' but Less 'Pleasure' From Cigarettes," *Journal of the American Medical Association* 261 (1989): 898–901.

2. J. P. Pierce, M. C. Fiore, T. E. Novotny, E. J. Hatziandreu, and R. M. Davis, "Trends in Cigarette Smoking in the United States: Educational Differences Are Increasing," *Journal of the American Medical Association* 261 (1989): 56–60; U.S. Department of Health, Education, and Welfare, *The Smoking Digest: Progress Report and a Nation Kicking the Habit* (Washington, D.C.: U.S. Department of Health, Education, and Welfare, 1977).

3. J. R. Hughes, S. W. Gust, R. M. Keenan, J. W. Fenwick, and M. L. Healey, "Nicotine vs Placebo Gum in General Medical Practice," *Journal of the American Medical Association* 261 (1989): 1300–1305.

4. M. Waldholz, "Study Questions Nicotine Gum's Ability to Help Smokers Quit Over Long Term," *Wall Street Journal*, March 3, 1989, p. B2.

5. S. Schachter, "Recidivism and Self-Cure of Smoking and Obesity," *American Psychologist* 37 (1982): 436–44.

6. S. Cohen, E. Lichtenstein, J. O. Prochaska, J. S. Rossi, E. R. Gritz, C. R. Carr, et al., "Debunking Myths About Self-Quitting: Evidence From 10 Prospective Studies of Persons Who Attempt to Quit Smoking by Themselves," *American Psychologist* 44 (1989): 1355–65.

7. M. C. Fiore, T. E. Novotny, J. P. Pierce, G. A. Giovino, E. J. Hatziandreu, P. A. Newcomb, T. S. Surawicz, and R. M. Davis, "Methods Used to Quit Smoking in the United States: Do Cessation Programs Help?" *Journal of the American Medical Association* 263 (1990): 2760–65 (emphasis added).

8. W. Gerin, "(No) Accounting for Results," *Psychology Today*, August 1982, p. 32.

9. E. Hecht, "A Retrospective Study of Successful Quitters," paper presented at the Annual Meeting of the American Psychological Association, Toronto, Canada, August 1978.

10. R. Baker, "Secrets of the Svelte," *New York Times*, May 6, 1989, p. 27.

11. R. D. Caplan, S. Cobb, and J. R. P. French, Jr., "Relationships of Cessation of Smoking with Job Stress, Personality, and Social Support," *Journal of Applied Psychology* 60 (1975): 211–19.

12. A. Marsh, "Smoking: Habit or Choice?" *Population Trends* 37 (1984): 20.

13. Pierce et al., "Trends in Cigarette Smoking."

14. L. D. Johnston, P. M. O'Malley, and J. G. Bachman, *Illicit Drug Use, Smoking, and Drinking by America's High School Students, College Students, and Young Adults: 1975–1989* (Rockville, Md.: National Institute on Drug Abuse, 1990).

15. K. E. Warner, "Till Death Do Us Part: America's Turbulent Love Affair with the Cigarette," in *1990 Medical and Health Annual* (Chicago: Encyclopedia Britannica, 1990), pp. 60–79.

16. J. Istvan and J. D. Matarazzo, "Tobacco, Alcohol, and Caffeine Use: A Review of Their Interrelationships," *Psychological Bulletin* 95 (1984): 301–26.

17. M. K. Bradstock, J. S. Marks, M. R. Forman, E. M. Gentry, G. C. Hogelin, N. J. Binkin, and F. L. Trowbridge, "Drinking-Driving and Health Lifestyle in the United States: Behavioral Risk Factors Surveys," *Journal of Studies on Alcohol* 48 (1987): 147–52.

18. R. R. Clayton, "Cocaine Use in the United States: In a Blizzard or Just Being Snowed?" in N. J. Kozel and E. H. Adams, eds., *Cocaine Use in America: Epidemiologic and Clinical Perspectives* (Rockville, Md.: National Institute on Drug Abuse, 1985), pp. 8–34.

19. P. D. Nesbitt, "Chronic Smoking and Emotionality," *Journal of Applied Social Psychology* 2 (1972): 187–96.

20. Marsh, "Habit or Choice?" pp. 19–20.

21. Johnston et al., *Illicit Drug Use.*

22. Marsh, "Habit or Choice?" p. 15.

23. Ibid., pp. 17–18.

24. G. A. Marlatt, S. Curry, and J. R. Gordon, "A Longitudinal Analysis of Unaided Smoking Cessation," *Journal of Consulting and Clinical Psychology* 56 (1988): 715–20.

25. T. H. Brandon, D. C. Zelman, and T. B. Baker, "Delaying Smoking Relapse with Extended Treatment," in T. B. Baker and D. S. Cannon, eds., *Assessment and Treatment of Addictive Disorders* (New York: Praeger, 1988), pp. 151–79; S. T. Tiffany and T. B. Baker, "The Role of Aversion and Counseling Strategies in Treatments for Cigarette Smoking," in Baker and Cannon, eds., *Assessment and Treatment,* pp. 238–89.

26. Marsh, "Habit or Choice?" p. 20.

27. F. A. Oski, "Now an Ex-Smoker," *New York Times,* January 12, 1984, p. A32.

28. Baker, "Secrets of the Svelte," p. 27.

Chapter 5
Obesity: Are People Biologically Programmed to Be Fat?

1. T. Hall, "And Now, the Last Word on Dieting: Don't Bother," *New York Times,* January 3, 1990, pp. C1, C6.

2. Linda Dulan, quoted in H.-J. Klatt, "Disease Label Often Inaccurate, Dangerous," *Journal* (Addiction Research Foundation), January 1, 1989, p. 11.

3. J. K. Phelps and A. E. Nourse, *The Hidden Addiction: And How To Get Free* (Boston: Little, Brown, 1986).

4. C. Bouchard, A. Tremblay, J. P. Després, A. Nadeau, P. J. Lupien, G. Thériault, J. Dussault, S. Moorjani, S. Pinault, and G. Fournier, "The Response to Long-Term

Overfeeding in Identical Twins," *New England Journal of Medicine* 322 (1990): 1477–82.

5. Ibid.; G. Kolata, "Where Fat Is Problem, Heredity Is the Answer, Studies Find," *New York Times*, May 24, 1990, p. B9.

6. R. E. Nisbett, "Hunger, Obesity, and the Ventromedial Hypothalamus," *Psychological Review* 79 (1972): 433–53.

7. W. Bennett and J. Gurin, *The Dieter's Dilemma: Eating Less and Weighing More* (New York: Basic Books, 1982).

8. J. Polivy and C. P. Herman, *Breaking the Diet Habit: The Natural Weight Alternative* (New York: Basic Books, 1983).

9. Bennett and Gurin, *Dieter's Dilemma,*, p. 282.

10. Ibid., pp. 281–82.

11. Ibid.

12. S. L. Gortmaker, W. H. Dietz, Jr., A. M. Sobol, and C. A. Wehler, "Increasing Pediatric Obesity in the United States," *American Journal of Diseases of Children* 141 (1987): 535.

13. W. H. Dietz, Jr., and S. L. Gortmaker, "Do We Fatten Our Children at the Television Set? Obesity and Television Viewing in Children and Adolescents," *Pediatrics* 75 (1985): 807–12.

14. Bennett and Gurin, *Dieter's Dilemma*, pp. 279–80.

15. M. Clark and C. Leslie, "Why Kids Get Fat: A New Study Shows Obesity Is in the Genes," *Newsweek*, February 3, 1986, p. 61.

16. A. J. Stunkard, J. R. Harris, N. L. Pederson, and G. E. McClearn, "The Body-Mass Index of Twins Who Have Been Reared Apart," *New England Journal of Medicine* 322 (1990): 1483–87.

17. Kolata, "Where Fat Is Problem," p. B9.

18. P. B. Goldblatt, M. E. Moore, and A. J. Stunkard, "Social Factors in Obesity," *Journal of the American Medical Association* 192 (1965): 1039–44.

19. F. E. M. Braddon, B. Rodgers, M. E. J. Wadsworth, and J. M. C. Davies, "Onset of Obesity in a 36 Year Birth Cohort Study," *British Medical Journal* 293 (1986): 299–303; A. J. Stunkard, E. d'Aquili, S. Fox, and R. D. L. Filion, "Influence of Social Class on Obesity and Thinness in Children," *Journal of the American Medical Association* 221 (1972): 579–84.

20. S. M. Garn, "Continuities and Changes in Fatness from Infancy Through Adulthood," *Current Problems in Pediatrics* 15, no. 2 (1985): 1–47; T. B. Van Itallie, "Health Implications of Overweight and Obesity in the United States," *Annals of Internal Medicine* 103 (1985): 983–88.

21. Garn, "Continuities and Changes," p. 22.

22. S. M. Garn, personal communication, April 24, 1984.

23. Garn, "Continuities and Changes"; Gortmaker et al., "Increasing Pediatric Obesity."

24. Garn, "Continuities and Changes," p. 21.

25. Ibid., p. 41.

26. S. Schachter, "Recidivism and Self-Cure of Smoking and Obesity," *American Psychologist* 37 (1982): 436–44.

27. R. W. Jeffery, A. R. Folsom, R. V. Luepker, D. R. Jacobs, R. F. Gillum, H. L. Taylor, and H. Blackburn, "Prevalence of Overweight and Weight Loss Behavior in a Metropolitan Adult Population: The Minnesota Heart Survey Experience," *American Journal of Public Health* 74 (1984): 349–52.

28. A. J. Hartz, "Natural History of Obesity in 6,946 Women Between 50 and 59 Years of Age," *American Journal of Public Health* 70 (1980): 385–88.

29. R. R. Wing and R. W. Jeffery, "Outpatient Treatments of Obesity: A Comparison of Methodology and Clinical Results," *International Journal of Obesity* 3 (1979): 261–79.

30. S. Abraham and C. Johnson, "Prevalence of Severe Obesity in Adults in the United States," *American Clinical Nutrition* 33 (1980): 364–69.

31. Polivy and Herman, *Breaking the Diet Habit*, pp. 195–96 (emphasis added).

32. Garn, "Continuities and Changes," p. 29.

33. Ibid., pp. 17–21; S. M. Garn, M. La Velle, and J. J. Pilkington, "Obesity and Living Together," *Marriage and Family Review* 7 (1984): 33–47.

34. S. M. Garn, S. M. Bailey, and I. T. T. Higgins, "Effects of Socioeconomic Status, Family Line, and Living Together on Fatness and Obesity," in R. M. Lauer and R. B. Shekelle, eds., *Childhood Prevention of Atherosclerosis and Hypertension* (New York: Raven Press, 1980), p. 203.

35. Garn, "Continuities and Changes," p. 24.

36. E. Z. Woody and P. R. Costanzo, "The Socialization of Obesity-prone Behavior," in S. S. Brehm, S. M. Kassin, and F. X. Gibbons, *Developmental Social Psychology: Theory and Research* (New York: Oxford University Press, 1981), pp. 211–34.

37. Ibid.

38. K. J. Hart and T. H. Ollendick, "Prevalence of Bulimia in Working and University Women," *American Journal of Psychiatry* 142 (1985): 851–54.

39. *Philadelphia Inquirer*, n.d., p. 1-D.

40. Bennett and Gurin, *Dieter's Dilemma*, p. 278.

41. T. A. Wadden, J. A. Sternberg, K. A. Letizia, A. J. Stunkard, and G. D. Foster, "Treatment of Obesity By Very Low Calorie Diet, Behavior Therapy, and Their Combination: The Five-Year Perspective," *International Journal of Obesity* 13, suppl. 2 (1989): 39–46.

42. M. B. Harris and J. T. Snow, "Factors Associated with Maintenance of Weight Loss," paper presented at the Annual Meeting of the American Psychological Association, Toronto, Canada, August 1984.

Chapter 6
Addictions to Gambling, Shopping, and Exercise: How We Evade Moral Responsibility

1. M. Dowd, "Addiction Chic: Are We Hooked on Being Hooked?" *Mademoiselle,* October 1989, p. 251.

2. Linda Grey, quoted in ibid., p. 251.

3. S. Peele with A. Brodsky, *Love and Addiction* (New York: New American Library, 1976).

4. D. J. Weisz and R. F. Thompson, "Endogenous Opioids: Brain Behavior Relations," in P. K. Levison, D. R. Gerstein, and D. R. Maloff, eds., *Commonalities in Substance Abuse and Habitual Behavior* (Lexington, Mass.: Lexington Books, 1983), p. 314.

5. R. Restak, "The Brain Makes Its Own Tranquilizers!" *Saturday Review,* March 5, 1977, pp. 7–11.

6. A. W. Schaef, "We're a Nation of Addicts," *New Age Journal,* March/April 1987, p. 43.

7. T. E. Dielman, "Gambling: A Social Problem," *Journal of Social Issues* 35 (1979): 36–42.

8. S. Blume, "Gambling: Disease or 'Excuse'? High Rollers Suffer from an Illness," *U.S. Journal of Drug and Alcohol Dependence,* August 1989, p. 15.

9. *Star Ledger,* December 5, 1987, p. 20.

10. J. Rosecrance, "Controlled Gambling: A Promising Future," in H. J. Shaffer, S. A. Stein, B. Gambino, and T. N. Cummings, eds., *Compulsive Gambling: Theory, Research, and Practice* (Lexington, Mass.: Lexington Books, 1989), pp. 147–60.

11. Blume, "Gambling," p. 15.

12. Arnold Wexler, quoted in R. E. Vatz and L. S. Weinberg, "Gambling: Disease or 'Excuse'? Betting on a Behavioral Approach," *U.S. Journal of Drug and Alcohol Dependence,* August 1989, p. 15.

13. R. Wright, "Up to Speed," *New Republic,* July 31, 1989, p. 42.

14. C. Welles, "America's Gambling Fever: Everybody Wants a Piece of the Action—but Is It Good for Us?" *Business Week,* April 24, 1989, pp. 112–20.

15. J. Barron, "Has the Growth of Legal Gambling Made Society the Loser in the Long Run?" *New York Times,* May 31, 1989, p. A18.

16. Ibid.

17. H. R. Kaplan, "State Lotteries: Should Government Be a Player?" in Shaffer et al., *Compulsive Gambling*, pp. 187–203.

18. Ibid.; P. Passell, "Lotto Is Financed by the Poor and Won by the States," *New York Times*, May 21, 1989, p. E6.

19. Welles, "America's Gambling Fever."

20. Larry Charles, quoted in ibid., p. 118.

21. D. F. Jacobs, "Gambling Behaviors of High School Students: Implications for Government-supported Gambling," National Policy Symposium on Lotteries and Gambling, Vancouver, British Columbia, 1988; D. F. Jacobs, "Illegal and Undocumented: A Review of Teenage Gambling and the Plight of Children of Problem Gamblers in America," in Shaffer et al., eds., *Compulsive Gambling*, pp. 249–92.

22. H. Lesieur and R. Klein, "Pathological Gambling Among High School Students," *Addictive Behaviors* 12 (1987): 129–35.

23. K. Thomas, "Out of Control," *Boston Tab*, August 8, 1989, p. 12.

24. Luther R. Gatling, quoted in J. Mundis, "A Way Back from Deep Debt," *New York Times Magazine*, January 5, 1986, p. 23.

25. Ibid., p. 25.

26. Nancy Dombrowski, quoted in ibid., p. 24.

27. "Shopping Addiction: Abused Substance Is Money," *New York Times*, June 16, 1986, p. C11.

28. J. Damon, *Shopaholics: Serious Help for Addicted Spenders* (Los Angeles: Price Stern Sloan, 1988).

29. *Sally Jessy Raphael: "Spendaholics,"* transcript, June 8, 1989 (New York: Multimedia Entertainment, 1989), p. 8.

30. Ibid., p. 5.

31. Ibid., p. 8.

32. Ibid., p. 11.

33. Ibid., p. 14.

34. Ibid., p. 7.

35. Robert G. McMurray, quoted in R. J. Trotter, "Rethinking the High in Runner's High," *Psychology Today*, May 1984, p. 8.

36. A. Yates, K. Leehey, and C. M. Shisslak, "Running: An Analogue of Anorexia?" *New England Journal of Medicine* 308 (1983): 253.

37. Ibid., p. 255.

38. Ibid., p. 253.

39. S. B. Jones and D. C. Jones, "Serious Jogging and Family Life: Marathon and Submarathon Running," paper presented at the annual meeting of the American Sociological Association, Chicago, September 5–9, 1977.

40. W. P. Morgan, "Negative Addiction in Runners," *The Physician and Sportsmedicine* 7 (1979): 61.

41. Ibid., p. 63.

42. Yates et al., "Running," p. 254.

43. Morgan, "Negative Addiction," p. 67.

Chapter 7
Love, Sex, and Codependence: Overcoming Trauma

1. R. E. Vatz and L. S. Weinberg, "Gambling: Disease or 'Excuse'? Betting on a Behavioral Approach," *U.S. Journal of Drug and Alcohol Dependence*, August 1989, p. 15.

2. Edward Armstrong, quoted in "U.S. Group Helps Sex-Addict Christians Cope with Urges," *Toronto Star*, February 16, 1989, p. L4.

3. M. Beattie, *Codependent No More: How to Stop Controlling Others and Start Caring for Yourself* (New York: Harper/Hazelden, 1987), p. 27.

4. Ibid., p. 31.

5. Ibid., p. 46.

6. Ibid., p. 111.

7. Ibid., p. 34.

8. J. R. Cruse, *Painful Affairs: Looking for Love Through Addiction and Codependency* (Deerfield Beach, Fla.: Health Communications, 1989).

9. D. Tennov, *Love and Limerence* (Briarcliff Manor, N.Y.: Stein & Day, 1979); M. R. Liebowitz, *The Chemistry of Love* (Boston: Little, Brown, 1983).

10. W. Kaminer, "Chances Are You're Codependent Too," *New York Times Book Review*, February 11, 1990, pp. 1, 26–27; E. Rapping, "Hooked on a Feeling," *The Nation*, March 5, 1990, pp. 316–19; C. Tavris, "Do Codependency Theories Explain Women's Unhappiness—or Exploit Their Insecurities?" *Vogue*, December 1989, pp. 220, 224–26.

11. Tavris, "Do Codependency Theories," p. 226.

12. E. Schappell, "In Rehab with the Love Junkies," *Mademoiselle*, October 1989, p. 253.

13. S. Peele with A. Brodsky, *Love and Addiction* (New York: New American Library, 1976), pp. 119–48.

14. See L. Williams, "New Rallying Cry: Parents Unite," *New York Times*, May 25, 1989, pp. C1, C10.

15. For insight into the sources of romantic insecurity in a person's background and early life history, as well as self-help strategies for overcoming this insecurity,

see C. G. Hindy, J. C. Schwarz, and A. Brodsky, *If This Is Love, Why Do I Feel So Insecure?* (New York: Fawcett, 1990).

16. B. English, "In the Best Interests of the Child?" *Boston Globe Magazine,* July 16, 1989, pp. 18, 48.

17. J. Kaufman and E. Zigler, "Do Abused Children Become Abusive Parents?" *American Journal of Orthopsychiatry* 57 (1987): 191.

18. D. Goleman, "New Studies Finding Many Myths About Mourning," *New York Times,* August 8, 1989, pp. C1, C6.

19. Jack Mearns, quoted in S. Campbell, "Scholar Delves into Aftermath of Relationships," Hartford *Courant,* August 1, 1989, p. B1. Cf. J. Mearns, "Coping with a Breakup: Negative Mood-Regulation Expectancies and Depression Following the End of a Romantic Relationship," *Journal of Personality and Social Psychology,* in press.

20. P. Hobe, *Lovebound: Recovering from an Alcoholic Family* (New York: New American Library, 1990), p. 10.

21. Ibid., p. 10.

22. Ibid., pp. 3–4.

Chapter 8
The Life Process Program

1. Our Life Process Program is based on discussions and interviews with hundreds of ex-addicts, on studies of therapy effectiveness, on our life experiences and treatment experiences with addicts, and on our own previous work on addiction as represented by *Love and Addiction* (New American Library, 1976), *How Much Is Too Much* (Spectrum, 1981), *The Meaning of Addiction* (Lexington Books, 1985), *Visions of Addiction* (Lexington Books, 1987: chapter 10, "A Moral Vision of Addiction"), and *Diseasing of America* (Lexington Books, 1989). We first presented a self-cure model of addictions in "Out of the Habit Trap," *American Health,* September-October 1983.

We also refer in this book to other work on natural remission in addiction presented (for cocaine) by Patricia Erickson and her colleagues in *The Steel Drug* (Lexington Books, 1987), Howard Shaffer and Stephanie Jones in *Quitting Cocaine* (Lexington Books, 1989), and Ronald Siegel in "Changing Patterns of Cocaine Use" (National Institute on Drug Abuse, 1984); (for crack) by Craig Reinarman and his colleagues in *Cocaine Changes* (Temple University Press, in press); (for heroin) by Patrick Biernacki in *Pathways from Heroin Addiction* (Temple University Press, 1986) and Dan Waldorf in "Natural Recovery from Opiate Addiction," *Journal of Drug Issues* (1983); (for alcohol) by Arnold Ludwig in "Cognitive Processes Associated with 'Spontaneous' Recovery from Alcoholism," *Journal of Studies on Alcohol* (1985), Ron Stall, "Respondent-independent Reasons for Change and Stability in Alcohol Consumption as a Concomitant of the Aging Process," (D. Reidel, 1986), Barry Tuchfeld, "Spontaneous Remission in Alcoholics," *Journal of Studies on Alcohol* (1981), and George Vaillant, *The Natural History of Alcoholism* (Harvard

University Press, 1983); (for cigarettes) by Alan Marsh in "Smoking: Habit or Choice?" *Population Trends* (1984), Alan Marlatt and his colleagues in "A Longitudinal Analysis of Unaided Smoking Cessation," *Journal of Consulting and Clinical Psychology* (1988), Carlo DiClemente and James Prochaska in "Processes and Stages of Self-Change" (Academic Press, 1985), and Saul Shiffman in "Coping with Temptations to Smoke" (Academic Press, 1985); (for several addictions) by James Prochaska and Carlo DiClemente in "Common Processes of Self-Change in Smoking, Weight Control, and Psychological Distress" (Academic Press, 1985), and Stanley Schachter in "Recidivism and Self-Cure of Smoking and Obesity," *American Psychologist* (1982).

Some of our specific treatment methods are adapted from Peter Monti and his colleagues' manual for *Treating Alcohol Dependence* (Guilford, 1989). We also wish to point out the important work of such other researchers as Harold Mulford in "Rethinking the Alcohol Problem: A Natural Processes Model," *Journal of Drug Issues* (1984); Jim Orford in *Excessive Appetites* (Wiley, 1985: chapters 13 and 14, "Decisions and Self Control" and "Giving Up Excess as Moral Reform") and Nathan Azrin, who developed the Community Reinforcement Approach (CRA). Rudolph Moos and his colleagues at Stanford have pioneered in measuring environmental factors in alcoholism and its remission in "Assessing Life Stressors and Social Resources," *Journal of Substance Abuse* (1989). Richard Longabaugh and his colleagues have also developed and evaluated an "Environmental Treatment of Alcohol Abusers" (paper available from Butler Hospital, Providence, R.I.). Alan Marlatt and Judith Gordon's *Relapse Prevention* (Guilford, 1985) has been a major contribution to treatment of addictions of all kinds.

Azrin (with Robert Sisson) describes his Community Reinforcement Approach in chapter 16 of Reid Hester and William Miller's *Handbook of Alcoholism Treatment Approaches* (Pergamon Press, 1989). This volume contains other important contributions on alcoholism treatment, including Miller's "Increasing Motivation for Change" (chapter 4) and Helen Annis and Christine Davis's "Relapse Prevention" (chapter 11). Annis and Martin Graham have also created the "Situational Confidence Questionnaire" (Addiction Research Foundation, Toronto, 1988) to measure self-efficacy in coping with life situations. Another important compendium of approaches to alcoholism treatment is W. Miles Cox's *Treatment and Prevention of Alcohol Problems* (Academic Press, 1987), which includes the work of Martha Sanchez-Craig and her colleagues, "Theory and Methods for Secondary Prevention of Alcohol Problems." Saul Shiffman and Thomas Wills's volume *Coping and Substance Use* (Academic Press, 1985) includes such important analyses of stages and techniques of self-initiated change as Shiffman's "Coping with Temptations to Smoke" (chapter 9) and Prochaska and DiClemente's "Processes and Stages of Self-Change" (chapter 13) and "Common Processes of Self-Change in Smoking, Weight Control, and Psychological Distress" (chapter 14).

Other important sources take the form of practical self-help manuals providing detailed guidance for the lay reader who is concerned to master a particular addiction. They include, in the area of obesity, Kelly Brownell's *LEARN Program for Weight Control* (The LEARN Education Center, Dallas, 1990), and, for smoking, the Clear Horizons program (Fox Chase Cancer Center, Philadelphia, 1989). Common-sense approaches to reducing excessive drinking can be found in William Miller and Ricardo Muñoz's *How to Control Your Drinking* (rev. ed., University of New Mexico Press, 1982) and Roger Vogler and Wayne Bartz's *The Better Way to Drink: Moderation and Control of Problem Drinking* (New Harbinger, 1985).

Finally, we are encouraged to see the enlightened research and clinical perspectives represented by the works listed here make their way into public-policy recommendations in a report of a committee of the Institute of Medicine (National Academy of Sciences) entitled *Broadening the Base of Treatment for Alcohol Problems* (National Academy Press, 1990).

Chapter 9
Quitting as Life Process: The Case of Paula

1. All quotations in this chapter are from authors' interview with "Paula." Person and place names and other identifying details have been changed.

Chapter 10
Are You an Addict? Assessing Addiction in the Life Process Program

1. W. R. Miller, "Increasing Motivation for Change," in R. K. Hester and W. R. Miller, eds., *Handbook of Alcoholism Treatment Approaches: Effective Alternatives* (New York: Pergamon, 1989), pp. 67–80.

2. G. E. Vaillant, *The Natural History of Alcoholism: Causes, Patterns, and Paths to Recovery* (Cambridge, Mass.: Harvard University Press, 1983), pp. 296–97.

3. E. Harburg, R. Gunn, L. Gleiberman, P. Roeper, W. DiFranceisco, and R. Caplan, "Using the Short Michigan Alcoholism Screening Test to Study Social Drinkers: Tecumseh, Michigan," *Journal of Studies on Alcohol* 49 (1988): 522–31.

4. R. Room, "The U.S. General Population's Experiences of Responding to Alcohol Problems," *British Journal of Addiction* 84 (1989): 1291–1304.

Chapter 11
Assessing Your Values: Knowing What Is Important to You

1. G. A. Marlatt, S. Curry, and J. R. Gordon, "A Longitudinal Analysis of Unaided Smoking Cessation," *Journal of Consulting and Clinical Psychology* 56 (1988): 715–720.

2. A. Ellis and R. A. Harper, *A New Guide to Rational Living* (N. Hollywood, Calif.: Wilshire, 1975).

3. B. S. Tuchfeld, "Spontaneous Remission in Alcoholics," *Journal of Studies on Alcohol* 42 (1981): 632.

4. S. Peele, "Out of the Habit Trap," *American Health*, September-October 1983, pp. 42–47.

5. G. Edwards, J. Orford, S. Egert, S. Guthrie, A. Hawker, C. Hensman, M. Mitcheson, E. Oppenheimer, and C. Taylor, "Alcoholism: A Controlled Trial of 'Treatment' and 'Advice,'" *Journal of Studies on Alcohol* 38 (1977): 1004–31.

6. H. Kristenson, *Studies on Alcohol Related Disabilities in a Medical Intervention*, 2nd ed. (Malmö, Sweden: University of Lund, 1983). Patients were screened according to elevated liver enzyme (GGTP), and half were given feedback based on this measure. Five years later, these patients, compared with those not given this feedback, showed lower rates of disease, hospitalization, death, and sick days and other work absences.

7. Tuchfeld, "Spontaneous Remission," p. 633.

8. National Public Radio (WGBH-FM, Boston), *Thinking About Drinking*, October 4, 1987.

9. P. Biernacki, *Pathways from Heroin Addiction: Recovery Without Treatment* (Philadelphia: Temple University Press, 1986), p. 159.

Chapter 12
Assessing Your Resources: What Do You Have That You Can Count On?

1. L. C. Sobell, M. B. Sobell, and T. Toneatto, "Recovery from Alcohol Problems Without Treatment," in N. Heather, W. R. Miller, and J. Greeley, eds., *Self-Control and Addictive Behaviors* (New York: Pergamon, in press).

2. J. Hollobon, "Solo Recovery Surprise: Problem Drinkers Confound Experts," *Journal* (Addiction Research Foundation), October 1, 1990, p. 4.

3. J. Mervis, "NIMH Data Points Way to Effective Treatment," *American Psychological Association Monitor*, July 1986, pp. 1, 13. One popular version of this cognitive therapy, written by a physician who felt antidepressant drug treatment was ineffective, is D. D. Burns, *Feeling Good: The New Mood Therapy* (New York: New American Library, 1981).

4. In his recent book, *Darkness Visible: A Memoir of Madness* (New York: Random House, 1990), novelist William Styron reacts with ambivalence to medical approaches to depression. "I shall never learn what 'caused' my depression," he avers, "as no one will ever learn about their own. To be able to do so will likely forever prove to be an impossibility, so complex are the intermingled factors of abnormal chemistry, behavior and genetics." Styron strongly criticizes both drug treatment and psychotherapy as useless. In fact, he says, "I think that the combination of a couple of drugs really augmented my despair. I believe their promiscuous use is very dangerous." Instead, Styron found "the real healers were seclusion and time," and he welcomed hospital treatment primarily because it gave him the space to recover on his own.

5. D. Goleman, "Men at 65: New Findings on Well-Being," *New York Times*, January 16, 1990, pp. C1, C12.

6. Ibid.

7. Stephen Pittel of the Wright Institute in Berkeley, California, uses a similar resource-assessment approach in counseling drug addicts.

Chapter 13
I'm Not the Person I Want to Be: How People Carry Out Plans to Change

1. J. Rosecrance, "Controlled Gambling: A Promising Future," in H. J. Shaffer, S. A. Stein, B. Gambino, and T. N. Cummings, eds., *Compulsive Gambling: Theory, Research, and Practice* (Lexington, Mass.: Lexington Books, 1989), pp. 150–51.

2. M. Sanchez-Craig, D. A. Wilkinson, and K. Walker, "Theory and Methods for Secondary Prevention of Alcohol Problems: A Cognitively Based Approach," in W. M. Cox, ed., *Treatment and Prevention of Alcohol Problems: A Resource Manual* (Orlando, Fla.: Academic Press, 1987), pp. 287–331.

3. Ibid.

4. J. M. Polich, D. J. Armor, and H. B. Braiker, *The Course of Alcoholism: Four Years After Treatment* (New York: Wiley, 1981).

5. Sanchez-Craig et al., "Theory and Methods," p. 310.

6. W. R. Miller and R. F. Muñoz, *How to Control Your Drinking,* rev. ed. (Albuquerque: University of New Mexico Press, 1982); R. Vogler and W. Bartz, *The Better Way to Drink: Moderation and Control of Problem Drinking* (Oakland, Calif.: New Harbinger, 1985).

7. Sanchez-Craig et al., "Theory and Methods," p. 309.

8. W. M. Cox and E. Klinger, "Incentive Motivation, Affective Change, and Alcohol Use: A Model," in W. M. Cox, ed., *Why People Drink: Parameters of Alcohol as a Reinforcer* (New York: Gardner, 1990), pp. 291–314.

Chapter 14
Changing the Behavior: That Obscure Object of Desire

1. J. Gurin, "Eating Goes Back to Basics," *American Health,* March 1990, pp. 96–101.

2. T. B. Baker, discussion at Third Annual Indiana University Conference for Research on Clinical Problems, May 29, 1987.

3. M. C. Fiore, T. E. Novotny, J. P. Pierce, G. A. Giovino, E. J. Hatziandreu, P. A. Newcomb, T. S. Surawicz, and R. M. Davis, "Methods Used to Quit Smoking in the United States: Do Cessation Programs Help?" *Journal of the American Medical Association* 263 (1990): 2760–65.

4. C. C. DiClemente and J. O. Prochaska, "Processes and Stages of Self-Change: Coping and Competence in Smoking Behavior Change," in S. Shiffman and T. A.

Wills, eds., *Coping and Substance Use* (Orlando, Fla.: Academic Press, 1985), pp. 319–43.

5. Adapted from S. Shiffman, "Coping with Temptations to Smoke," in Shiffman and Wills, eds., pp. 223–42.

6. Adapted from L. W. Neidigh, E. L. Gesten, and S. Shiffman, "Coping with the Temptation to Drink," *Addictive Behaviors* 13 (1988): 1–9.

7. A. M. Ludwig, "Cognitive Processes Associated with 'Spontaneous' Recovery from Alcoholism," *Journal of Studies on Alcohol* 46 (1985): 55.

8. Adapted from DiClemente and Prochaska, "Processes and Stages."

9. Ibid.; J. O. Prochaska and C. C. DiClemente, "Common Processes of Self-Change in Smoking, Weight Control, and Psychological Distress," in Shiffman and Wills, eds., *Coping and Substance Use,* pp. 345–63.

10. W. R. Miller and R. K. Hester, "The Effectiveness of Alcoholism Treatment: What Research Reveals," in W. R. Miller and N. K. Heather, eds., *Treating Addictive Behaviors: Processes of Change* (New York: Plenum, 1986), pp. 121–74.

11. Ludwig, "Cognitive Processes," p. 56.

12. E. Klinger, "Imagery and Logotherapeutic Techniques in Psychotherapy: Clinical Experiences and Promise for Application to Alcohol Problems," in W. M. Cox, ed., *Treatment and Prevention of Alcohol Problems: A Resource Manual* (Orlando, Fla.: Academic Press, 1987), pp. 139–56.

13. M. Sanchez-Craig, D. A. Wilkinson, and K. Walker, "Theory and Methods for Secondary Prevention of Alcohol Problems: A Cognitively Based Approach," in Cox, ed., *Treatment and Prevention,* pp. 287–331.

14. P. Biernacki, *Pathways from Heroin Addiction: Recovery Without Treatment* (Philadelphia: Temple University Press, 1986), p. 130.

15. Based on a case presented on *Morning Edition,* National Public Radio (WBUR-FM, Boston), December 7, 1989.

16. G. A. Marlatt, "Cognitive Assessment and Intervention Procedures for Relapse Prevention," in G. A. Marlatt and J. R. Gordon, eds., *Relapse Prevention: Maintenance Strategies in the Treatment of Addictive Behaviors* (New York: Guilford, 1985), pp. 209–10.

17. G. A. Marlatt, "Relapse Prevention: Theoretical Rationale and Overview of the Model," in Marlatt and Gordon, eds., *Relapse Prevention,* p. 39.

18. G. A. Marlatt, "Cognitive Assessment and Intervention Procedures for Relapse Prevention," in Marlatt and Gordon, eds., *Relapse Prevention,* table 4-2.

Chapter 15
Life Skills: If You Don't Have Them, Get Them

1. A number of books outline the techniques reviewed in this chapter, primarily for use with alcoholics, such as Reid Hester and William Miller, *Handbook of*

Alcoholism Treatment Approaches: Effective Alternatives (New York: Pergamon Press, 1989) and W. Miles Cox, *Treatment and Prevention of Alcohol Problems: A Resource Manual* (Orlando, Fla.: Academic Press, 1987). We are particularly indebted to Peter Monti, David Abrams, Ronald Kadden, and Ned Cooney, *Treating Alcohol Dependence: Treatment Manual for Practitioners* (New York: Guilford, 1989), for material on which the charts and skills sessions in this chapter are based. This book is now being used as the "gold standard" for skills training for alcoholics in research sponsored by the National Institute on Alcohol Abuse and Alcoholism.

2. A. Ellis and R. A. Harper, *A New Guide to Rational Living* (N. Hollywood, Calif.: Wilshire, 1975); Monti et al., *Treating Alcohol Dependence.*

3. Monti et al., *Treating Alcohol Dependence,* pp. 83–87; T. J. D'Zurilla and M. R. Goldfried, "Problem Solving and Behavior Modification," *Journal of Abnormal Psychology* 78 (1971): 107–26.

4. A. Bandura, "Self-Efficacy Mechanisms in Human Agency," *American Psychologist* 37 (1982): 122–47; H. M. Annis and C. S. Davis, "Self-Efficacy and the Prevention of Alcoholic Relapse," in T. B. Baker and D. S. Cannon, eds., *Assessment and Treatment of Addictive Disorders* (New York: Praeger, 1988), pp. 88–112.

5. B. S. Tuchfeld, "Spontaneous Remission in Alcoholics," *Journal of Studies on Alcohol* 42 (1981): 634.

6. G. A. Marlatt, "Relapse Prevention: Theoretical Rationale and Overview of the Model," in G. A. Marlatt and J. R. Gordon, eds., *Relapse Prevention: Maintenance Strategies in the Treatment of Addictive Behaviors* (New York: Guilford, 1985), p. 39.

7. Monti et al., *Treating Alcohol Dependence,* pp. 89–103; T. Stockwell and C. Town, "Anxiety and Stress Management," in Hester and Miller, eds., *Handbook,* pp. 222–30.

8. G. A. Marlatt, "Relapse Prevention."

9. E. Harburg, E. H. Blakelock, and P. Roeper, "Resentful and Reflective Coping with Arbitrary Authority and Blood Pressure: Detroit," *Psychosomatic Medicine* 41 (1979): 189–202, developed the Harburg Anger Expression scale, showing that either bottling up anger or expressing extreme hostility were psychologically problematic and led to somatic symptoms, such as higher blood pressure, and even higher death rates. See also Monti et al., *Treating Alcohol Dependence,* pp. 103–8, from which some of the following guidelines are adapted.

10. C. R. Rogers, "The Characteristics of a Helping Relationship," *Personnel and Guidance Journal,* September 1958, pp. 6–16. This article is a classic that—along with the Anderson article in the next note—is one to which we have long been indebted. Both are used as Harvard Business School cases and are collected in many volumes of organizational behavior.

11. J. Anderson, "Giving and Receiving Feedback," Procter & Gamble Internal Company Document; E. F. Chaney, "Social Skills Training," in Hester and Miller, eds., *Handbook,* pp. 206–21; Monti et al., *Treating Alcohol Dependence,* pp. 55–60.

12. T. J. O'Farrell, "Marital and Family Therapy for Alcohol Problems," in Cox, ed., *Treatment and Prevention*, pp. 205–34.

Chapter 16
Integrating Change into Your Life: Groups and Your Social World

1. The Community Reinforcement Approach (CRA) was developed for treating severely alcoholic patients after they left the hospital. Its success now permits it to be conducted on an outpatient basis. Azrin now recommends that CRA be conducted with Antabuse (disulfiram), a drug that makes the alcoholic ill if he or she drinks alcohol. Outside of the CRA approach, Antabuse therapy has not proved effective, because alcoholics often stop taking the drug. Without Antabuse, CRA has been shown to be highly effective. In the first test of the CRA package where Antabuse was not administered, Hunt and Azrin found that "CRA-treated patients were drinking on 14% of days compared with 79% drinking days in the hospital-treated control group. Unemployed days were 12 times higher in the traditional treatment group, and institutionalized days were 15 times higher relative to those in CRA."

By building into the alcoholic's social network a check for making sure the alcoholic continues taking Antabuse, CRA has shown even higher rates of abstinence. Working and noninstitutionalized days have also heavily favored CRA versus standard-treatment control groups. However, no trial of CRA using Antabuse has ever been as effective as this first trial in terms of the monumental differential in working days and days not institutionalized for CRA-treated versus standard alcoholism patients. Few if any people reading this book are likely to be candidates for Antabuse, particularly as a lifelong prescription. But the principles of CRA are exceedingly valuable for any addiction at any level of severity. A reference for CRA is R. W. Sisson and N. H. Azrin, "The Community Reinforcement Approach," in R. K. Hester and W. R. Miller, eds., *Handbook of Alcoholism Treatment Approaches: Effective Alternatives* (New York: Pergamon, 1989), pp. 242–58.

2. M. Freudenheim, "Business and Health: Acknowledging Substance Abuse," *New York Times*, December 13, 1988, p. D2.

3. S. Peele, "Does Your Office Have Bad Habits?" *American Health*, September 1985, pp. 39–43.

4. A values approach to the causes of and cures for addiction is outlined in S. Peele, "A Moral Vision of Addiction: How People's Values Determine Whether They Become and Remain Addicts," in S. Peele, ed., *Visions of Addiction: Major Contemporary Perspectives on Addiction and Alcoholism* (Lexington, Mass.: Lexington Books, 1987), pp. 201–33; S. Peele, "A Values Approach to Addiction: Drug Policy That Is Moral Rather than Moralistic," *Journal of Drug Issues* 20 (1990): 639–46.

5. Nussbaum's self-centeredness is a focus of the major book on this tragedy: J. Johnson, *What Lisa Knew: The Truth and Lies of the Steinberg Case* (New York:

Putnam, 1990). See R. Coles, "The Death of a Child," *New York Times Book Review,* April 8, 1990, pp. 1, 30–31.

6. J. Veroff, R. A. Kulka, and E. Douvan, *Mental Health in America: Patterns of Help-Seeking From 1957 to 1976* (New York: Basic Books, 1981), quoted in H. Kushner, *Who Needs God* (New York: Summit Books, 1989), p. 93.

Chapter 17
Kids Have to Be Made into Addicts: *You* Can Prevent Addiction

1. Stanton Peele has writen extensively about the hysteria over adolescent substance abuse and about more effective ways to deal with the problem: see *Don't Panic: A Parent's Guide to Understanding and Preventing Alcohol and Drug Abuse* (Minneapolis: CompCare, 1983); "The 'Cure' for Adolescent Drug Abuse: Worse Than the Problem?" *Journal of Counseling and Development* 65 (1986): 23–24; "Running Scared: We're Too Frightened to Deal with the Real Issues in Adolescent Substance Abuse," *Health Education Research* 2 (1987): 423–32; "What Can We Expect from Treatment for Adolescent Drug and Alcohol Abuse?" *Pediatrician* 14 (1987): 62–69.

2. J. S. Rudolph, book review, *Center City Review* (Hazelden Educational Materials), Winter 1990, p. 4.

3. M. Worden, "Chemical Dependency 'Self-inflicted': School Argues," *U.S. Journal of Drug and Alcohol Dependence,* August 1985, p. 4; see also "Addiction a 'Handicap': Civil Rights of Drug Using Teen Upheld in Oregon," *U.S. Journal of Drug and Alcohol Dependence,* July 1985, pp. 1, 26.

4. Worden, "Chemical Dependency," p. 4.

5. E. K. Hayes, *Why Good Parents Have Bad Kids* (New York: Doubleday, 1989), p. 191.

6. One book on which our recommendations are based is E. Satter, *Child of Mine: Feeding with Love and Good Sense* (Palo Alto, Calif.: Bell, 1986). Few weight-control books published since the 1980s have escaped set-point theory (see chapter 5). Fortunately, even some books that accept this inaccurate and pessimistic notion can still contain useful information and advice.

L. H. Epstein, A. Valoski, R. R. Wing, and J. McCurley, "Ten-Year Follow-up of Behavioral, Family-Based Treatment for Obese Children," *Journal of the American Medical Association* 264 (1990): 2519–23, found stable long-term weight loss in children resulting from an eating-behavior program aimed at the entire family.

7. K. Blum, E. P. Noble, P. J. Sheridan, A. Montgomery, T. Ritchie, P. Jagadeeswaran, H. Nogami, A. H. Briggs, and J. B. Cohn, "Allelic Association of Human Dopamine D_2 Receptor Gene in Alcoholism," *Journal of the American Medical Association* 263 (1990): 2055–60.

8. For an interpretation of the "alcoholism-gene" finding, see the appendix to this book. Cf. S. Peele, "Second Thoughts About a Gene for Alcoholism," *The Atlantic,* August 1990, pp. 52–58.

9. We forgive you for thinking that we made up the story about Little Red Riding Hood. See R. Cohen, "With Boycott and Ads, a Battle Over Selling," *New York Times,* April 23, 1990, p. C18:

> In Empire, Calif., some 400 copies of "Little Red Riding Hood" are locked away in a storage room of the public school district because the classic Grimm's fairy tale recounts that the little girl took a bottle of wine to her grandmother. "That passage condones the use of alcohol," said Lynn McPeak, the district's interim curriculum director.

What might Ms. McPeak make out of the following passage in *The First Book of Jewish Holidays,* written for very young children by Robert Garvey and Sam Weiss (New York: KTAV Publishing House, 1954)?

> **Passover:** Passover is a happy time. We are happy to be free. On the first and second nights we have a Seder. My whole family is there, singing and having a good time. Everybody drinks four glasses of wine. . . .
>
> **Shabbat:** Shabbat comes once a week. . . . It is a day of rest. It starts on Friday evening, when mother lights the candles. Then daddy comes home and says the kiddush over the wine and challah.
>
> Next morning we all go to the synagogue. Back home again, we have a nice dinner and sing songs and take it easy. In the evening, when the three stars are out, daddy says the habdolah. I hold the candle, smell the spices and sip a little wine from the kiddush cup.

10. E. Harburg, D. R. Davis, and R. Caplan, "Parent and Offspring Alcohol Use: Imitative and Aversive Transmission," *Journal of Studies on Alcohol* 43 (1982): 497–516.

11. L. Anderson, *Dear Dad: Letters from an Adult Child* (New York: Viking, 1989).

12. L. A. Bennett, S. J. Wolin, D. Reiss, and M. A. Teitelbaum, "Couples at Risk for Transmission of Alcoholism: Protective Influences," *Family Process* 26 (1987): 111–29.

13. P. Hobe, *Lovebound: Recovering from an Alcoholic Family* (New York: New American Library, 1990).

14. R. L. Bangert-Drowns, "The Effects of School-based Substance Abuse Education—A Meta-Analysis," *Journal of Drug Education* 18 (1988): 243–64.

15. N. S. Tobler, "Meta-Analysis of 143 Adolescent Drug Prevention Programs: Quantitative Outcome Results of Program Participants Compared to a Control or Comparison Group," *Journal of Drug Issues* 16 (1986): 537–67.

16. M. D. Newcomb and P. M. Bentler, "Substance Use and Abuse Among Children and Teenagers," *American Psychologist* 44 (1989): 242–48.

17. P. L. Ellickson and R. M. Bell, "Drug Prevention in Junior High: A Multi-Site Longitudinal Test," *Science* 247 (1990): 1299–1305.

18. J. S. Baer, D. R. Kivlahan, K. Fromme, and G. A. Marlatt, "Secondary Prevention of Alcohol Abuse with College Student Populations," in G. Howard, ed., *Issues in*

Alcohol Use and Misuse by Young Adults (Notre Dame, Ind.: Notre Dame University, in press).

19. L. Carton, "The Big 'D' for Denial: Are You Denying Your Child's Problem?" *Boston Tab*, February 6, 1990, p. 14.

20. M. E. Chafetz, "Alcohol and Innocent Victims," *Wall Street Journal*, March 5, 1990, p. A14.

21. "Drug Study Cites Behavior Traits: Youths Who Limited Use Are Seen as Best Adjusted in Comparison of Groups," *New York Times*, May 9, 1990, p. A24.

22. Newcomb and Bentler, "Substance Use," pp. 246–47.

Chapter 18
Where the Solutions Really Lie: Re-establishing Communal Ties

1. "Strawberry Not Charged," *New York Times*, March 10, 1990, p. 46; J. Durso, "Ring of Support Awaits Strawberry," *New York Times*, February 25, 1990, pp. C1, C4. For a rare nonexculpatory view of the Strawberry affair, see I. Berkow, "Strawberry's Demons, and Rum," *New York Times*, February 5, 1990, p. C6.

2. I. Glasser, "We Can Control Drugs, but We Can't Ban Them" (letter), *New York Times*, November 20, 1989, p. A22.

3. S. Murphy and M. Rosenbaum, "Myths About Crack" (letter), *New York Times*, February 8, 1990, p. A28.

4. A persuasive summary of both principled and pragmatic arguments for drug decriminalization can be found in E. A. Nadelmann, "Drug Prohibition in the United States: Costs, Consequences, and Alternatives," *Science* 245 (1989): 939–47.

5. E. Rosenthal, "Powerful New Weapons Change Treatment of Pain," *New York Times*, February 13, 1990, pp. C1, C12.

6. Otis Bowen, quoted in Stan T. Plona, MetPath, Inc., solicitation letter, July 1989.

7. S. Mydans, "Powerful Arms of Drug War Arousing Concern for Rights," *New York Times*, October 16, 1989, p. B10. Cf. D. J. Greenblatt and R. I. Shader, "Say 'No' to Drug Testing," *Journal of Clinical Psychopharmacology* 10 (1990): 157–59.

8. "Research Centre Will Drug-test Staff," *Journal* (Addiction Research Foundation of Ontario), April 1, 1990, p. 2.

9. C. Culhane, "Drug Testing Too Costly, Invasive—Study," *U.S. Journal of Drug and Alcohol Dependence*, August 1986, p. 1; C. Mohr, "Drug Test Policy Caught in Snags," *New York Times*, December 18, 1988, p. 41; Greenblatt and Shader, "Say 'No' to Drug Testing."

10. E. Weiner, "Jury Weighs Drunken Flying Charge," *New York Times*, August 17, 1990, p. A14.

11. R. Blumenthal, "He Wore a Badge, Then He Sold It for Crack," *New York Times*, May 8, 1990, p. A1.

12. Ibid., p. B10.

13. J. Davidson, "Drunk Until Proven Sober," *Special Report on Health*, May-July 1990, p. 47.

14. Ibid., pp. 42–48.

15. K. S. Ditman, G. G. Crawford, E. W. Forgy, H. Moskowitz, and C. MacAndrew, "A Controlled Experiment on the Use of Court Probation for Drunk Arrests," *American Journal of Psychiatry* 124 (1967): 160–63; P. M. Salzberg and C. L. Klingberg, "The Effectiveness of Deferred Prosecution for Driving While Intoxicated," *Journal of Studies on Alcohol* 44 (1983): 299–306.

16. M. W. Perrine and D. D. Sadler, "Alcohol Treatment Program Versus License Suspension for Drunken Drivers: The Four-Year Traffic Safety Impact," in P. C. Noordzij and R. Roszbach, eds., *Alcohol, Drugs and Traffic Safety* (New York: Elsevier Science Publishers, 1987), pp. 555–59.

17. A. Shupe, W. A. Stacey, and L. R. Hazlewood, *Violent Men, Violent Couples* (Lexington, Mass.: Lexington Books, 1987).

18. J. Hight, "Mandatory AA Stirs Up Controversy," *Boston Herald*, June 8, 1990, p. 47, 49.

19. E. Luff, "The First Amendment and Drug/Alcohol Treatment Programs: To What Extent May Coerced Treatment Programs Attempt to Alter Beliefs Relating to Ultimate Concerns and Self Concept?" in A. S. Trebach and K. B. Zeese, eds., *Drug Policy 1989–1990: A Reformer's Catalog* (Washington, D.C.: Drug Policy Foundation, 1989), p. 263.

20. Ibid., p. 262. For complete text, see Queen Anne's County (Maryland) Criminal Case No. 3588, decided March 16, 1989.

21. T. W. Ferguson, "Any Wonder Medical Premiums Are Rising Like Crazy?" *Wall Street Journal*, May 22, 1990, p. A21.

22. S. Peele, "Research Issues in Assessing Addiction Treatment Efficacy: How Cost Effective Are Alcoholics Anonymous and Private Treatment Centers?" *Drug and Alcohol Dependence* 25 (1990): 179–82.

23. Institute of Medicine, Division of Mental Health and Behavioral Medicine, *Broadening the Base of Treatment for Alcohol Problems* (Washington, D.C.: National Academy Press, 1990). (Quotations are from the press release accompanying the volume.)

24. G. De Leon, "The Therapeutic Community: Status and Evaluation," *International Journal of Addictions* 20 (1985): 823–44; C. Winick, "An Empirical Assessment of Therapeutic Communities in New York City," in L. Brill and C. Winick, eds., *The Yearbook of Substance Use and Abuse*, vol. 2 (New York: Human Sciences Press, 1980), 251–93; R. L. Hubbard, M. E. Marsden, J. V. Rachal, H. J. Harwood, E. R. Cavanaugh, and H. M. Ginzburg, *Drug Abuse Treatment: A National Study of Effectiveness* (Chapel Hill: University of North Carolina Press, 1989).

25. W. R. Miller and R. K. Hester, "The Effectiveness of Alcoholism Treatment: What Research Reveals," in W. R. Miller and N. K. Heather, *Treating Addictive Behaviors: Processes of Change* (New York: Plenum, 1986), pp. 121–74; R. W. Sisson and N. H. Azrin, "The Community Reinforcement Approach," in R. K. Hester and W. R. Miller, eds., *Handbook of Alcoholism Treatment Approaches: Effective Alternatives* (New York: Pergamon, 1989), pp. 242–58.

26. H. Mulford, "Enhancing the Natural Control of Drinking Behavior: Catching Up with Common Sense," *Contemporary Drug Problems*, Fall 1988, pp. 324–25.

27. L. Collins, "The Hughes for All Seasons Has a New Life," Des Moines *Register*, March 6, 1988, pp. 1A, 9A.

28. Mulford, "Enhancing the Natural Control," p. 323.

29. Ibid., p. 332.

30. Ibid., p. 333.

31. R. Room, "Closing Statement," *Evaluating Recovery Outcomes*, conference proceedings (San Diego: Program on Alcohol Issues, University Extension, University of California, San Diego, 1988), p. 43.

32. R. A. Brown, "Conventional Education and Controlled Drinking Education Courses with Convicted Drunken Drivers," *Behavior Therapy* 11 (1980): 632–42; K. M. Fillmore and D. Kelso, "Coercion into Alcoholism Treatment: Meanings of the Disease Concept of Alcoholism," *Journal of Drug Issues* 17 (1987): 301–19; E. Vingilis, "Drinking Drivers and Alcoholics: Are They From the Same Population?" in R. G. Smart, F. B. Glaser, Y. Israel, H. Kalant, R. E. Popham, and W. Schmidt, eds., *Research Advances in Alcohol and Drug Problems*, vol. 7 (New York: Plenum, 1983), pp. 299–342.

33. "The '80s Materialism Marks American Youth," *Wall Street Journal*, May 16, 1990, p. B1.

34. S. G. Hauser, "Family Fun at the Tavern," *Wall Street Journal*, May 17, 1989, p. A16.

35. Ibid.

Appendix: What the *JAMA* Study on Genes and Alcoholism Tells Us

1. H. M. Schmeck, Jr., "Defective Gene Tied to Form of Manic-depressive Illness," *New York Times*, February 26, 1987, pp. 1, B7.

2. H. M. Schmeck, Jr., "Schizophrenia Study Finds Strong Signs of Hereditary Cause," *New York Times*, November 10, 1988, pp. 1, B22.

3. L. K. Altman, "Scientists See a Link Between Alcoholism and a Specific Gene," *New York Times*, April 18, 1990, pp. A1, A18.

4. W. F. Byerley, "Genetic Linkage Revisited," *Nature* 340 (1989): 340–41; M. Robertson, "False Start on Manic Depression," *Nature* 342 (1989): 222.

5. H. M. Schmeck, Jr., "Scientists Now Doubt They Found Faulty Gene Linked to Mental Illness," *New York Times*, November 7, 1989, p. C3.

6. K. Blum, E. P. Noble, P. J. Sheridan, A. Montgomery, T. Ritchie, P. Jagadeeswaran, H. Nogami, A. H. Briggs, and J. B. Cohn, "Allelic Association of Human Dopamine D_2 Receptor Gene in Alcoholism," *Journal of the American Medical Association* 263 (1990): 2055–60.

7. Daniel Flavin, quoted in R. A. Knox, "Scientists Link Alcoholism to Gene Defect," *Boston Globe*, April 18, 1990.

8. Donald Goodwin, quoted in ibid.

9. E. Gordis, B. Tabakoff, D. Goldman, and K. Berg, "Finding the Gene(s) for Alcoholism," *Journal of the American Medical Association* 263 (1990): 2095.

10. Paul Billings, quoted in R. Bazell, "The Drink Link," *The New Republic*, May 7, 1990, p. 13.

11. Altman, "Scientists See a Link," p. A18.

12. A. M. Bolos, M. Dean, S. Lucas-Derse, M. Ramsburg, G. L. Brown, and D. Goldman, "Population and Pedigree Studies Reveal a Lack of Association Between the Dopamine D_2 Receptor Gene and Alcoholism," *Journal of the American Medical Association* 264 (1990): 3156–60.

INDEX

ABOUT THE AUTHORS

STANTON PEELE, Ph.D., is a social psychologist, health-care researcher, and therapist. He has been a leading figure in the addiction field since his pioneering work, *Love and Addiction,* was published in 1975. His most recent book, *Diseasing of America: Addiction Treatment Out of Control,* was published in 1989. In the same year, Dr. Peele received the Mark Keller Award for the best article published in the *Journal of Studies on Alcohol* during the years 1987–88. His current research concerns the cost-effectiveness of competing medical therapies.

ARCHIE BRODSKY is Senior Research Associate at the Program in Psychiatry and the Law, Massachusetts Mental Health Center, Harvard Medical School. A professional writer and health-care activist, he is co-author of *Love and Addiction* and numerous other books in psychology, medicine, and human services. Known for his advocacy of midwifery and women's rights in childbirth, he is also active in the National Writers Union.

MARY ARNOLD, M.B.A., was a marketing manager for fifteen years in Fortune 500 companies. She is a community and environmental activist and the mother of three children.